Please remember that this is a library book,
and that it belongs only temporarily to each
person who uses it. Be considerate. Do
not write in this, or any, library book.

EDUCATIONAL IMPLICATIONS OF PIAGET'S THEORY

Educational Implications of Piaget's Theory

Edited by

IRENE J. ATHEY, *The University of Rochester*

DUANE O. RUBADEAU, *Algoma College, Ontario*

GINN–BLAISDELL *A Xerox Company*

WALTHAM, MASSACHUSETTS • TORONTO • LONDON

CONSULTING EDITOR · William J. Meyer, *Syracuse University*

Preface

This book is intended to provide students of education and psychology with an interesting and useful collection of writings on the educational implications of Jean Piaget's theory. Professor Piaget, of the University of Geneva, is undoubtedly one of the most prolific authors and theorists of this century. His main efforts have centered around the development and refinement of his theory of cognitive development, leaving the task of application of his findings to others.

The readings in this volume represent a significant sample of the research dedicated to the application of Piagetian theory to the educational setting, but are by no means intended to be all-inclusive in scope.

The papers are divided into six sections. *Section I* explores the general implications of Piaget's theory for the educational setting. *Section II* examines the implications of Piaget's theory for early childhood education. *Section III* lists studies involving Piaget-oriented programs for educationally handicapped children. *Section IV* includes investigations concerned with communication in language and art. *Section V* represents a sampling of articles on the implications of Piaget's theory for instruction in science and mathematics. Finally, *Section VI* includes articles describing attempts at test development based on the Piagetian conceptual framework.

Many of the papers included in this book were edited or abridged to some degree. In all abridgments, the deleted materials involved redundancies with other papers in this book. A complete listing of references cited in each article will be found at the end of the book.

We are most grateful to the many authors and publishers who granted permission to reprint the articles included in this collection. We also express our sincere appreciation to Dr. William J. Meyer, of Syracuse University, Consulting Editor for Ginn–Blaisdell, for his assistance and suggestions on the manuscript; to Miss Theresa Wilson, for her outstanding work in typing the manuscript; and to Misses Norie Washington, Donna Barr, Candy Taft, Jill Sawyer, and Linda Macior, for their diligent efforts in reading and proofreading the manuscript.

I. J. A.

D. O. R.

Contents

III   The Educationally Handicapped

IV Communication in Language and Art

V Science and Mathematics

VI Test Development

From Theory to Classroom   328

   Anne M. Bussis, *Educational Testing Service*

Concept Assessment Kit–Conservation   344

   Marcel L. Goldschmid, *McGill University*
   Peter M. Bentler, *University of California at Los Angeles*

Introduction

Educational principles have their roots in the wisdom of the ages. The history of western culture shows that the beginnings of modern educational thought may be found in many ideas of the ancient Greeks. From that time on, the ideas of many great thinkers representing several different disciplines have been woven into the fabric of current educational philosophy and practice.

On reading Piaget, one is immediately conscious of this rich background of tradition. Of course, men who make significant contributions to science or the humanities frequently owe much to the work of their predecessors. Piaget is no different in this respect. He is remarkable rather in that his thinking is derived from so many disciplines, and that he is able to integrate his ideas from such varied sources as philosophy, biology, logic, and mathematics to create a theory of human cognition. In philosophy, Piaget falls in the rationalist tradition headed by Plato, and his epistemology bears clear marks of the influence of Kant's doctrine of mental categories. His concept of the active, growing organism continuously molding its psychological world and changing itself in the process seems to be akin to Bergson's notion of perpetual change. Psychologically, Piaget is perhaps closest to the Gestalt school of thought. The Gestalt notions of psychological field and differentiation, for example, are clearly applicable to his system. Piaget himself has acknowledged this affiliation, but has also pointed to several important differences. However, it is Piaget's biological training which permeates his whole theory, in the sense that cognitive functioning is seen as a special case of biological functioning, and its operations analogous to those of bodily processes. His dictum that thought is action internalized was also expressed by Rignano in *The Psychology of Reasoning* (1923).

Piaget has thus drawn upon many disciplines for the content of his thought and has woven these disparate ideas into a comprehensive theory which he has then applied to different areas of inquiry such as perception, moral judgment, mathematical and logical thinking, etc. Through his endeavors in these areas, Piaget has contributed enormously, albeit indirectly, to contemporary thinking about educational philosophy and practice. The extent of this contribution will emerge in the discussion of certain issues which are currently the focus of attention among psychologists and educators.

No attempt at a comprehensive review of Piaget's theory of genetic epistemology will be made in this chapter. The reader who is unfamiliar with this theory will find a general description of the developmental stages in the early articles of this book, and a more detailed account in Flavell's (1963) *The Developmental Psychology of Jean Piaget*. Rather than a repetition of these aspects of the theory, the major principles which have direct bearing on education will be extracted and their educational implications reviewed briefly. More complete discussions of these implications will be found in the articles which follow.

Psychological Principles

The principles enumerated below do not provide a comprehensive account of Piaget's theory, but they do constitute major and important aspects of it.

1. *The organism actively molds the world of the intellect.* While intellectual growth is depicted in Piaget's theory as a process of slow inward evolutionary unfolding, it is not to be construed as primarily a passive process. On the contrary, intellectual functioning is viewed as a particular manifestation of biological functioning; the intellect goes to work on the raw data of experience in much the same way as the digestive system goes to work on the intake of food. Hence thinking is an organized activity, which is manifested in certain characteristic ways of interaction with the environment. It is this continuous activity which brings about the growth of intelligence in accordance with a predetermined biological pattern, with the organism continuously participating in its own growth.

For Piaget then *thought is action internalized.* The very young child's intellectual functioning consists of sensory and motor adaptations to environmental events. It is, in fact, a process of assimilating experience through his mouth, eyes, ears, and skin surfaces. Erikson (1959) has called this the period of taking-in, of the "incorporative mode." For Piaget it represents the ascendance of *assimilation* over accommodation, the latter being the process by which the organism changes in order to absorb new experiences. The child's later abilities to represent events symbolically through the processes of memory, imagination, and conceptualization are grounded in these early sensory, perceptual, and motor experiences.

2. *Learning takes place through adaptation of existing cognitive structures.* Intellectual growth occurs in response to three variables: maturation of the nervous system, experiences with physical reality, and interaction with the social milieu. Assuming the first of these, transactions with the physical and social environment will be assimilated insofar as they can be fitted into the existing cognitive organization. In this process, however, the organization is changed, and thus becomes capable of a new level of assimilation at the next encounter. The tension created by the imbalance between assimilation

and accommodation provides the motivating force for intellectual growth and expansion resulting in the attainment of new levels of equilibrium or understanding. The need to explore and learn initiates within the organism and becomes self-perpetuating, like R. W. White's (1959) drive for *competence.*

3. *Intellectual development is continuous but results in qualitative differences.* Aristotelian logic set down the various operations which govern formally correct reasoning, without claiming that these were the operations actually followed in the processes of deductive and inductive inference. According to Piaget, these operations (such as identity, negation, implication etc.) are the ones that characterize adult thought. Operational thought, in exploring the possible as opposed to the real, performs a number of logical maneuvers such as combination, reversal, disjunction, etc., on the propositional content, and in addition can reason about its own processes. By contrast, the preoperational thought of the child is tied to the world of physical objects, governed by perception rather than reason, and is unable to comprehend such concepts as conservation or reversibility, transitivity, and classification.

The butterfly does not resemble the caterpillar from which it evolved, although its development from one to the other may be traced at every step. Adult logical thinking is qualitatively different from the sensorimotor adaptations of the infant, or the preoperational and concrete operational thought of older children, but it is founded on these earlier stages, and depends for the elaborateness of its functioning on the richness of experience at each stage along the route.

4. *Development is uneven both across and between stages.* Piaget uses the terms *horizontal and vertical décalages* to conceptualize two observed phenomena of cognitive development. The first refers to the fact that, even when a level of thought is attained, it need not be uniformly applied in all areas. Hence a child may attain the concept of conservation but ordinarily this will be related to the conservation of mass before it is applied to weight or volume. Vertical décalage refers to the fact that a problem with similar content is approached at different stages with a completely different level of functioning. In the social–emotional realm, Erikson has drawn attention to the different levels of approach at different ages to lifelong problems such as maintaining a balance between trust and mistrust, or establishing one's autonomy with respect to others. The difference in these levels is undoubtedly related to the development of cognitive functioning.

Educational Implications

The educational implications which appear to follow from the above principles drawn from Piaget's theory are set forth in this section. Again, they are not intended to be exhaustive, but simply the most important and far-reaching.

1. *Discovery learning, especially in the early years, is indicated.*   Piaget's theory is not only compatible with, but seems to demand some form of activity curriculum, or what Isaacs refers to as "living learning." The processes of finding out, testing, and manipulating, which together constitute the process of discovery learning, are "inherently educative, or, if one prefers, generative of the true inward learning that turns into development or growth" (Isaacs, 1965). This is the *only* way the young child can learn; and while the adult may use symbolic and verbal manipulations to organize his information for the solution of problems, there are many occasions when he too can learn more effectively through appropriate activity; e.g., one may "know" the geographical character of a terrain either by studying a contour map or by walking over the area. Piaget would advocate more of the latter kind of activity in areas of learning in which the adult has not been "socialized," i.e. has not gone through the requisite stages.

The child's natural tendency to explore and manipulate the environment to his own ends must be sustained and encouraged by the school. For many a child of school-entering age, the self-motivating force which up to that time has informed his waking life, gives way to learning motivated by extrinsic factors such as the desire to please authority figures, fear of failure, or material rewards. Learning which takes place under these conditions is usually superficial, meaningless and unrelated, and very often forgotten. It tends to reinforce the artificial boundary between school learning, and learning outside school, which is decried by critics who call for a more "relevant" system of education at all levels.

Piaget's theoretical system takes into account the dependence of thought processes on the growth of language, but his experimental work has shown the extent to which these functions do not overlap. Very young children and older children in some areas may understand more than they can verbalize. Conversely, children at all levels may have a verbal facility which belies their lack of understanding of what the words convey. The teacher who has studied Piaget's stages of cognitive development is likely to be more sensitive to the disparity between language and thought, relative to the child's particular level of cognition.

Hence the teacher's role is not the passive and uninspiring one of simply allowing the child to develop at his own rate, nor even that of providing intellectual nourishment which the child may sample cafeteria-style. Rather it is that of participant in a mutual learning situation, stimulating, encouraging, and leading the child on to new levels of understanding.

2. *Individual differences should be encouraged and developed.*   In learning situations of the type described, children will respond differently and, in view

of their existing cognitive organization which has grown out of past experiences, will learn different things from the same experience. This fact should be a source of gratification rather than dismay to the teacher. Yet traditional schooling is based largely on the opposite assumption that *most* children are capable of learning a prescribed body of content that *all* children need to know. Hence a teacher who attempts to provide for individual differences in interest and aptitude among children may experience conflict in trying to live up to expectations to cover the prescribed curriculum. Though most curriculum writers see their units as "guides" which do not absolve the teacher from the responsibility of adapting and elaborating on these materials to meet the special needs of particular groups, or individuals, the lamentable fact is that the lockstep horizontal organization on an age–grade basis, with its accompanying curricula, has led to a suppression, rather than a fostering of "individual differences." Goodlad[1] maintains that there is no area of psychology in which the gap between knowledge and practice is greater than in the area of individual differences. Even in kindergartens and nursery schools where the pressure on the teacher is not so great, one frequently finds the entire group of children engaged in the same activity at almost any hour of the day. So-called innovative practices which are currently attracting national attention (nongraded organization, pupil-team learning, programmed instruction, and so on) are long overdue attempts to provide for individual differences in *achievement*, albeit for the most part within the existing organizational framework of the school.

A stage theory that shows not only the orderly sequential development of thought processes but also the approximate ages at which the successive stages emerge, might appear almost antithetical to the concept of individual differences. Yet Piaget's theory places firmly on the shoulders of the teacher the responsibility for knowing the experiential background which has brought each child to the particular level of functioning he has reached, and the areas in which he has lagged or forged ahead. At the same time, the theory enables her to compare each aspect of the child's thinking against the general developmental schedule. She knows that the preoperational child is capable of a large range of logical activities such as comparing, ordering, discriminating, cause-and-effect reasoning, and others;[2] but knowing the processes of his thinking, she is also aware of the limitations of his thought and can plan appropriate activities which will broaden and deepen his understanding so that the transition to the next stage is more fully

• • • • • • • •

[1]"Learning about Individual Differences," first of a series of six films on *How to Provide a Personalized Education in a Public School*. Special Purpose Films, Malibu, California.
[2]Some educators and child psychologists (e.g., Susan Isaacs) rejected Piaget's concept of "preoperational thought" on these grounds.

accomplished. In brief, she is constantly on the alert for the "teachable moment" for every child.

3. *Acceleration of the stages may be possible within broadly defined limits.* Piaget's age ranges for the appearance of particular stages are approximations, rather than statistical averages or developmental norms. Bright children, for example, may achieve aspects of a certain stage months ahead of their average counterparts. The question then arises as to what extent conceptualization may be speeded up by means of specially developed learning sequences. Attempts to induce the notion of conservation through the use of structured tasks, for example, have met with equivocal results but, in general, support Piaget's position on the ineffectiveness of training. However, this finding need not lead to the depressing conclusion that nothing can be done to enhance intellectual development. It is by no means apparent that everything is being done to stimulate children of any age to the highest intellectual functioning of which they are capable at the particular stage they have reached. Even the best home provides the necessary kinds of experiences for learning basic concepts and logical relationships only in a haphazard and unsystematic way. The long-range effects of a continuous program of sequential and wide-ranging activities geared to the child's interests, but designed to lay the foundation for conceptual growth, are as yet undetermined. Programs of educational stimulation based on Piagetian principles are relatively new and, for the most part, designed for children who lack either the customary home experiences, or the verbal labels to apply to them.

In general, what needs to be done is to enrich rather than accelerate. For even with the richest environment possible, given the young child's cognitive organization, it takes time to assimilate the numerous experiences necessary for growth. One may induce an appearance of learning, but true understanding takes time.

4. *Early childhood education should provide the foundation for later learning.* Conversely, there is an optimal period in the child's life for certain kinds of learning, and failure to capitalize on these periods may lead to difficulties at later stages. The early years, being those in which the child gains the experiences which form the whole basis of future logical thought, are especially crucial for *all* children, not just the disadvantaged, *if* the content of the preschool program is based on the concept of living learning, and is rich in cognitive content. "Good" nursery school programs have always attempted to provide a wide range of opportunities for learning within the context of activities chosen and planned by the child. Inferior programs by contrast have consisted either of child-care facilities without educational content, or of class-type activities based on the primary or kindergarten

model. Some day care centers are examples of the former kind of operation, while many Head Start programs would fit the latter description.

The question now arises whether even good preschool programs have gone far enough in providing experiences designed to develop children's intellectual functioning. In terms of Piaget's theory, the answer would appear to be negative. There are many things a child can learn, many ways in which he can develop broader and richer concepts which will give new dimensions and scope to later learning. In other words, cognitive growth need not be entirely dependent on fortuitous occurrences (though the alert teacher capitalizes on these also), but can be manipulated and ordered by the teacher to ensure maximum learning opportunities for children. By studying Piaget's description of concept development, the teacher may come to a new understanding of the process itself, and may emerge with many new ideas of ways to facilitate this process.

It would be unfortunate, however, if such a conclusion were construed as a call for a nursery school "curriculum" on the lines of the elementary and secondary curricula. Early childhood education has, above all other levels, been responsive to individual differences and attuned to individual needs. This flexibility and freedom of action need not be abandoned in light of the need for some kind of structured curriculum. Rather, ways must be sought to implement the newest findings on children's cognitive functioning within the traditional framework of early childhood education, and to develop materials which are both sequenced and adaptable to individual differences.

The necessity, or indeed the value, of early childhood education has been a controversial issue for many years. The issue has appeared in a number of related questions such as the effect of nursery school programs on IQ, or the immediate and long-range effects of "forcing," as well as the relative importance of the school and the family as spheres of influence in the child's life.

a. *The effects on IQ.* Starting with early Iowa studies (Wellman, 1940) and their critics (McNemar, 1945), it has been argued, on the one hand that a nursery school education may enhance the IQ as much as 20 points (Smilansky, undated), and on the other, that such gains are spurious or short-lived. This is not the place to discuss the recent controversy concerning racial differences in IQ (Jensen, 1969; Elkind, 1969; Hunt, 1969; Kagan, 1969) but the implied corollary that compensatory preschool education is thereby doomed to failure is worthy of comment. The most plausible conclusion to be drawn at present is that compensatory programs such as Head Start have provided "too little, too late," and should be expanded downward to earlier age levels rather than discontinued. Moreover, it is by no means the single, or even the most important objective of the preschool to raise IQ scores. The issue is further clouded by current dissatisfaction with traditional notions of intelligence, as major predictors of school achievement, and by increased attention to divergent and creative thinking.[3]

Hence, the mere proof or disproof of gain in IQ is insufficient to establish the worth of nursery school education, since the typical intelligence test does not tap those modes of functioning such as divergent thinking and problem-solving which the nursery school seeks to foster, and since maintenance of such gains in any case requires continuation of those conditions under which they were originally fostered.

b. *The immediate and long-range effects of forcing.* This question has often been viewed as a corollary of the nature–nurture issue. If growth is a process of gradual unfolding according to inner laws of development, it would appear futile, if not downright harmful, to seek to hasten this process. Evidence to support this view can be cited with respect to walking (Dennis and Dennis, 1940), climbing/crawling (McGraw, 1939), manual dexterity (J. R. Hilgard, 1932), vocabulary (Strayer, 1930), reading (Gardner, 1930), giving rise to popular notions concerning the need for pacing (Olson and Hughes, 1943), the emotional and social effects of "pressuring," and the loss of initial advantages with time. On first acquaintance, Piaget's theory would appear to support the view that intellectual growth is a long and gradual process which is resistant to acceleration by adult intervention. The cognitive stages are sometimes mistakenly seen as analogous to developmental norms on a Gesell-type scale, which indicate where a child of a certain age "ought" to be. In point of fact, the theory carries none of these connotations, nor is it logically necessary that a "stage" theory should imply these or similar propositions. There is of course the obvious answer that Piaget's conclusions are stated for children within an average age range, with nothing to invalidate the possibility that more intelligent children may reach a given stage sooner than average children. There is the further argument that it is the sequence, rather than the actual age limits, that really counts. All this is undoubtedly true. But what Piaget has added is the important factor of the continuity of intellectual growth, and the dependence of each stage upon the successful implementation of earlier ones, thus providing the thread of continuity and lawfulness of development which permits explanation and prediction of cognitive behavior.

An additional important aspect of Piaget's system is the emphasis on social interaction as a necessary condition for cognitive growth. Social transactions in fact supply a large portion of the environmental data the active inquiring

· · · · · · · ·

[3] Whether new scales based on Piaget's tasks (see *Section VI: Test Development*) will incorporate these new dimensions remains to be seen.

child (or adult, for that matter) must obtain to continue functioning intellectually; he manipulates both people and objects to obtain the information he needs. The preschool provides this important social dimension in the form of children and adults who are themselves both stimulated and stimulating.

It is appropriate to note at this point that the precise long-term effects of this kind of educational intervention on later intellectual functioning are presently unknown. While Piaget's theory would predict a broader and richer intellectual life providing its own motivating force for continuous development, the empirical test of such predictions may be found only in longitudinal research which provides the necessary and sufficient conditions for intellectual activity at all ages.

In this respect, Piaget's theory is progressive and optimistic. It sets no limits on the possibility for continued intellectual growth. But the possibilities may be enhanced by timely and proper attention to the nurturing of the process at every stage of its development, especially the early ones.

General Implications

Piaget is a prolific writer and his theory is scattered through some twenty volumes and innumerable articles. Moreover, his terminology and reasoning are not invariably easy for the layman to follow. Many authors have addressed themselves to the task of expounding and clarifying the theory, but not many of these have considered it from the particular viewpoint of education. Even those who are well acquainted with the theory should find the discussion from this perspective refreshing; and the student who is unfamiliar with Piaget's theory will find the readings in this section indispensable to an understanding of the remaining articles.

These introductory papers have been selected for their clarity and readability. They present an exposition of the basic concepts of the theory, Piaget's doctrine of the sequential development of intelligence, and their meaning for education in general.

Jean Piaget, School Organization, and Instruction

■■■ MARILYNNE ADLER

Although Piaget has been working on his theoretical principles since the 1920s, he is content to let others explore their significance for education. In this article, the author, after a brief review of the major aspects of the theory, illustrates some of the directions in which Piaget's ideas are beginning to have an impact on educational practice, and enumerates a number of questions requiring further exploration.

The Theory

As a self-styled "genetic epistemologist" Piaget has been concerning himself for the past forty years or so with the growth of conceptual structures in children, as a means of understanding the origin of knowledge. His aim has been the clarification of such ancient philosophical questions as the idea of time, space, causality, and especially logic and number. In fact, however,

• • • • • • •
SOURCE: *Principal's Journal*, 6 (1965), 32–51. (With permission of the author and the *Principal's Journal*.)

his use of a "clinical method" has yielded some of the richest and most comprehensive observations on children's thinking that are presently available in the psychological literature. His use of the language of mathematics and symbolic logic, on the other hand, has made his theory even more inaccessible than has its general unavailability in English.

1. Key Concepts

Perhaps the most important concept in Piaget's theory of cognitive growth is the "schema." By this term Piaget refers to an internalized mental representation of a particular action, an internal structure which is linked with a certain pattern of behavior. Piaget uses the analogy of a mathematical "operator," and in fact refers to the highest levels of mental organization as "operations." A schema directs the person toward a specific action or transformation upon a given domain of objects. For example, the internal schema for addition in arithmetic directs an individual to take two or more objects and gather them together. These objects may be concrete, as in the case where one actually puts two things together, or they may be symbolic, as in the case where one is adding together two algebraic symbols. The identity of these two situations as far as the role of the schema is concerned is important to Piaget's theory.

This last statement becomes clearer if we realize that Piaget conceives of the development of mental structures as the progressive internalization and symbolization of action. Through a series of more and more complex stages, the child gradually is able to free his thought processes from the motor activities upon which they are based. Piaget sees these internal structures as hierarchically organized. The earliest schemata are physical actions upon the child's immediate environment. These become internally represented as the child moves through symbolic and perceptual representation of action to fully abstract mental concepts. Each stage of schemata contains the preceding stage within its organization, but the earlier has been further broadened, complicated, and enriched by interaction with other schemata. The new level is a sensitively balanced "equilibrium" of interlocking mental structures.

Thought develops out of an encounter between the growing child and his environment. Piaget employs the biological concept of "adaptation" to account for change and growth in mental life. The two complementary principles of adaptation are "assimilation" and "accommodation." In assimilation, the child has an existing schema or rule of action towards a particular group of objects. For example, he knows how to grasp a number of objects with his hand. If a new object comes into his view which is not very different from the previous objects in the "grasping schema," he will assimilate the object to the schema; i.e., he will grasp the object. If he encounters an unexpected deviation from the norm, if he is unable to use an old schema on the object because it is too discrepant from the other members of the set of objects, then he must modify his existing schema, or accommodate his behavior, e.g., he may have to coordinate both hands to grasp the object simultaneously. He is then likely to exercise the new schema on the old objects in the domain, to see if it applies equally well to them. The critical difference between the two processes seems to be in the degree of "perturbation" or discrepancy between the newly discovered object and the old schema. The only real *change in behavior,* and thereby in mental structure, occurs in accommodation. Nevertheless, adaptation is a balancing off of both assimilation and accommodation. The result at any moment is a "semi-mobile equilibrium," an equilibrium in the sense of a balance between the two processes, and semi-mobile in the sense that it is always subject to reorganization whenever discrepancy forces the child to move to a new stage. The issue of degree of discrepancy will become rather important in the succeeding discussion.

2. Stages of Development

A. *Sensorimotor.*   Between the birth of the infant and the ages of one-and-one-half to two years, the child moves through six substages of sensorimotor intelligence. The scope of this development may be seen by comparing the earliest period, where the child has only a few reflexive schemata (e.g., looking, sucking, prehension) at his command, and the final period, where he is able to imitate an absent model, search for and find a hidden object, and show considerable evidence of internal mental activity. He realizes that objects which are no longer in the immediate here-and-now still continue to exist, but his appreciation of them is tied to concrete action.

B. *Preconceptual or Preoperational.*   From two to four years, the child increases his capacity for stable internal images of external events and actions. Imitation, play, and language development are the primary achievements of this period. Thought, however, is "transductive"; the child reasons from particular to particular, and his symbolic activity is frequently very idiosyncratic. In the "intuitive" phase, he begins to show the beginnings of logical thought, but thinking is highly unstable and is tied to perceptual arrangement. The issue of centration and decentration of thinking is relevant to this period, and is most clearly illustrated by reference to Piaget's studies of the concept of number. The investigator asks the child what will happen to a quantity of liquid which is poured from a short wide beaker into a tall thin one, and child promptly responds by saying that the quantity will increase ("because it is now taller") or decrease ("because it is thinner"), but never that it will stay the same (i.e., that the increase in one dimension is compensated for by a decrease in the other one). He is unable to decentrate his perception from the dimension upon which he is centrating (concentrating); he cannot think without reference to visual images, and when they mislead, his mental apparatus is not sufficiently developed to correct the distortion. Similarly, when two identical rows of counters are placed before him, he can count them and realize their equality. But if he is then asked to spread one row out so that it appears longer than the other, he says that the longer one has more counters in it, and seems undisturbed to discover that moving them back together again restores the equality. He cannot "conserve" number in the face of irrelevant perceived changes. Another way of viewing this stage is to say that the child thinks egocentrically; i.e., he is unable to take the point of view of another, and Piaget in fact has an experiment where he shows that children at this stage cannot accurately describe how a particular mountain would look if viewed from the other side. Nonconservation occurs at this stage with respect to number, space, duration, length, quantity, classes, series, weight, volume, etc.

C. *Concrete Operational.* Between the ages of seven to eight and eleven or twelve, an important development of thinking occurs. The child becomes capable for the first time of appreciating the following four kinds of logical or mathematical operations, without of course being able to state the principles formally:

(a) Combinativity or closure: two classes or operations can be combined to make a third; $(a + b = c)$.
(b) Associativity: different operations lead to the same result; $(a + b) + c = a + (b + c)$.
(c) Identity: the negation of an operation annuls it; $a + (-a) = 0$.
(d) Reversibility: each operation implies its converse; $a \times b = b \times a$.

Reversibility, for example, in the case of the counters is achieved when the child can think about the action of spreading them out and bringing them together again as perfectly complementary opposite activities; i.e., arrangement and rearrangement can lead back to the starting point. Piaget likens thought at this stage to a film, which can be run forwards, backwards, slower or faster, as desired. The child can thus realize that number, quantity, etc., are capable of "conservation," that nothing really changes when you reverse the action. However, this understanding is only effective in concrete situations, with concrete materials at hand. For example, the child can classify and order objects with respect to some dimension, but he is unable to perform the same operations on their verbal equivalents. His ability to synthesize dimensions such as length and width in the beaker task, or even such concepts as classification and ordering into number, still does not permit him to reason about *ideas.*

D. *Formal Operational.* The capacity for formal, perfectly logical, abstract thought appears fully at about age eleven or twelve. Reasoning about the "possible," about ideas and events which are in the past, the future, or the imagination, is now within the person's scope. Such conditional concepts as proportions, probabilities, permutation, combinations are available to the adolescent, as is the capacity to perform "logical experiments," to formulate hypotheses and test them, and to do all this without necessary reference to concrete materials or images. According to Piaget, thinking now manifests the qualities of pure mathematics or logic, in its capacity to appreciate such relations as identity, negation, reciprocity, and correlation. Thought is now "mobile, flexible, and free."

Applications

1. Assessing Development

A. *Validation of Piaget's Theory.* A number of psychological investigators have tried to assess the validity of Piaget's studies, since the original ones are often lacking in scientific control or statistical analysis. Indeed, many persons have started their work with the express intention of disproving many of Piaget's contentions about children's concepts of causality, number, etc. (e.g., Deutsche, 1937; Estes, 1956). It is for this reason that the evidence in favor of the theory is all the more impressive. The overwhelming majority of studies have shown that the *sequence* of development outlined above is an accurate portrayal of mental growth. Studies with the mentally retarded (Inhelder, 1943), children in other cultures (Price-Williams, 1961; Dodwell, 1960) have in general found the same stages of development occurring in the same chronological order. The relatively few exceptions (Estes, 1956) have tended to be less competent investigations.

Nevertheless, an important caution should be raised at this point. It is *not* the case that psychologists have uniformly found the exact *ages* of transition that Piaget reports from his own studies of children at the Institut Jean Jacques Rousseau in Geneva, or his own three children Laurent, Lucianne, and Jacqueline. For example, children from rural backgrounds or lower economic status do more poorly in tests of number concepts (Dodwell, 1960). A difference of as much as three years has been found between children in Martinique and Montreal in the age of attainment of certain levels of development, even though the school curriculum is very similar in both areas (Laurendeau and Pinard, 1962). Mental age appears to be a much more reliable indicator of Piaget stage than chronological age for some children on certain tasks, particularly in the case of retarded children (Hood, 1962; Carpenter, 1955). But Piaget himself has repeatedly emphasized the idea that his ages are only to be regarded as guidelines or estimates of the ages at which the majority of children are likely to show these changes. The general conclusion to be drawn from this line of research is that the sequence is invariant, but the ages may vary with circumstances.

B. *Test Development*. An important application of Piaget's theory lies in the area of developmental testing, or the more traditional interest in intelligence testing. If these stages of cognitive development form a reliable scale of progressively more complex mental activity, then the basis for an improved method of mental testing is provided. Three important criteria of such a test would be its reliability (stability), its validity (in terms of some criterion of mental development), and its scalability (whether the test items form a true ordered scale on which successful performance on one item implies a similar success on all preceding items). Two major test standardization projects are currently under way, one in Geneva under the direction of two of Piaget's assistants (Vinh–Bang, 1957) and one in Montreal under the supervision of Adrien Pinard. Both projects are nearing completion and promise to yield a most valuable testing instrument.

The importance of such tests for education cannot be overemphasized. The assessment of the overall level of ability of a child has long been recognized as vital in education, but most IQ tests have been pragmatic affairs, with little solid developmental theory behind them. A Piaget developmental test would have the added advantage of assessing those areas of intellectual development of most concern to educational planners — concepts of number, space, geometry, time–speed, etc. — in conjunction with providing a general index of ability. Both the specific and general scores would be useful for grade placement or ability grouping, but perhaps even more valuable for the diagnostic assessment of specific conceptual liabilities for the purpose of remedial teaching. Special aptitudes, strengths and weaknesses in particular conceptual areas, general concreteness of thinking might come to light. More interesting perhaps is the possibility of a new kind of "readiness" test; for example, a test of number readiness which assesses the child's understanding of the components of number, classes and asymmetrical relations, or his readiness for certain more formal kinds of mathematical problems.

2. Influencing Development

A. *Extent of Influence*. For a long time Piaget's work was viewed with suspicion by educators and others on the grounds that Piaget was treating development as the result of inner maturational changes so powerfully predetermined that no amount of training could make any difference. It is important to realize that the twin principles of assimilation and accommodation can only operate in terms of a constant interaction between the child and his environment. Piaget (1964) has recently reemphasized that mental development depends on at least four major factors: hereditary endowment and nervous maturation, social transmission through education and language, richness of environmental experience, and most important, equilibrium achieved through the child's own active transformation of the objects in his environment. Whereas the rate or even the final level of cognitive development may be determined by inner biological factors, nonetheless the onset of each higher stage is profoundly influenced by educational experiences. The few psychological studies which have been directed to this question have been somewhat ambiguous, but they have provided information about the nature of instruction which can influence development. These studies will be reviewed in the next section.

B. *Teaching Methods.*   If there is one conclusion to be drawn from Piaget's work, it is that thought grows out of the internalization of concrete motor activity. It follows logically that educational practice must respect this process by permitting the child multiple and varied opportunities in the early grades for direct action upon concrete objects. The child must be able to transform the objects and to perform his own operations upon them, if these operations are ever to form the basis of his fully developed mental structure. To understand classification, he must have had experience in grouping objects together on some dimension; to analyze, he should have pulled them apart; to understand the ordinal properties of numbers and series, he must have arranged objects in some order. Counting objects on a flash card is insufficient; many children in Piaget's studies have been able to count or passively understand a teacher's explanation of number facts, and have failed miserably in the tests of conservation of number, which demand more than parrotlike recitation of verbal labels. To understand that operations are reversible may perhaps only be possible if a child has actually performed an operation and its converse on the same series of objects, such as counting from right to left and left to right, or moving apart the counters and pushing them together again. The teacher must carefully analyze her material, in the primary grades especially, into its basic operations. And then she must permit the child to carry out these operations through his own activity. Commenting on Bruner's ideas about teaching the structure of a subject (1960), Piaget (1964) has recently stated that we must ". . . present the child with situations where he is active and creates the structures himself. . . . Teaching means creating situations where structures can be discovered; it does not mean transmitting structures which may be assimilated at nothing other than a verbal level."

Two examples of such teaching may be found in two studies concerned with introducing children to early concrete number experiences. Churchill (1958) matched two groups of children for number understanding, and then gave one group four weeks of special number experiences, i.e., she allowed them to use a variety of concrete objects for ordering, matching, comparing, sharing, and grouping. The concrete operational level of number understanding was attained considerably earlier in the experimental group, and appeared to be retained over several months of retesting. Hunt (1961) reports a similar study in a Rhode Island kindergarten. Children were encouraged to play a variety of block-stacking games, and to label two-dimensional arrays as areas, and three-dimensional ones as volumes. Early definitions of these children were in terms of action; for example, "area is when you put four blocks this way, and five that way, and fill them in, and count them." Addition and subtraction were introduced as complementary operations as soon as the games led to questions about the relationships previously explored through manipulation, as were multiplication and division. Although no clear-cut conceptual changes appeared at first in number understanding, by the fifth grade, these children had a deeper, richer, and more advanced understanding of number.

The relative success of these projects is somewhat in contrast with the results of several psychological investigations which have tried to accelerate the onset of certain stages. Wohlwill and Lowe (1962) succeeded in training a group of preoperational children to agree on the equivalence of sets of rearranged objects by repeated reinforced practice in counting, arranging, and recounting the objects. Morf (1959) on the other hand was unsuccessful in convincing children at this level of the principle of class inclusion (that class B is larger than class A where $B = A + A'$). Beilin and Franklin (1961) were able to train conservation of length and area, only to find that many children could not transfer their learning to a later test situation. A series of studies by Smedslund (1961a through 1961d) has yielded mixed results, but the most interesting of these points out the importance of the nature of the training experience — the match–mismatch problem.

It will be remembered that the notion of discrepancy was introduced in connection with the difference between assimilation and accommodation. Smedslund has been investigating the degree of discrepancy required to induce sufficient "cognitive conflict" such that a reorganization of mental structures must occur. His results are interesting if only for the fact that they indicate how very difficult it is to induce a preoperational child to adopt a conservation attitude even under specific training. Smedslund induced conflict by setting two contradictory transformations in opposition to one another. He used Piaget's test of conservation of substance — a ball of Plasticine which can be flattened out into a sausage shape. Whereas preoperational children usually insist that the quantity changes when the shape changes, a very few of the children changed their minds either when the ball was lengthened or when the experimenter removed a small piece from it. In other words, the two conflicting explanations of "something added — something subtracted" were resolved by *some* children in favor of the simpler nonconflicting operational level explanation.

Also relevant to the problem of matching the task to the child's conceptual level is the question of how much more (or less) advanced a task must be from the child's level for the maximum accommodation to occur. Only a very few psychological experiments have been done thus far on this problem. Turiel (1964) did a recent study of children's moral judgments using Piaget's method of testing these concepts. He presented the child with alternative solutions to the moral dilemmas which were: congruent with the child's present level of understanding, one stage behind, one stage ahead, and two stages ahead. The greatest amount of cognitive change occurred in those cases where the child received the alternative which was one step ahead of his own level. This study strongly implies that educative efforts are likeliest to lead the child to accommodate his mental structure when they are just far enough ahead of him to induce a moderate degree of mental discrepancy, but not so far ahead as to be beyond his range of understanding.

A rather interesting program of research on Piaget concepts conducted by Charlesworth (1964) attempted to evaluate the role of surprise, unexpected discrepancy, or violation of expectation in the development of mental structures. He argues that "focusing on unexpected and expected events appears to be important in the educational process. Creating environments in which expectancies can be established and confirmed or unconfirmed by new events seems to me to be an important part of the teacher's task . . . We should allow the child to construct correct but incomplete hypotheses or expectations about events before presenting him with a new single non-confirming instance which challenges his hypothesis to the extent that he seeks to expand it, or we allow him to pursue misleading ideas before presenting him with a carefully selected fact or event that will suddenly contradict and hopefully rectify them."

C. *Curriculum Development.* It is rather encouraging to discover that Piaget is beginning to be taken seriously by curriculum planners. In 1964, Piaget was invited by a group of persons interested in his work and in curriculum modification to be a guest consultant at two conferences on the subject (Ripple and Rockcastle, 1964), and it is clear from the report on these conferences that many areas of the curriculum are beginning to show his influence. Only a very few of the many possible changes will be mentioned here, partly because a great number of possibilities exist, but also partly because a great deal of careful and patient research is required to assess the effects of actual application of the theory to the classroom, before any massive reorganization takes place.

The first and most general principle of curriculum planning should be to respect the sequence of development of children in general, and of individual children in particular. It is clear from the preceding section that active transformation of the objects in the environment should be the beginning stage of any instruction in number, space, quantity, etc. It should also be emphasized that the curriculum should move gradually from the concrete to the symbolic and formal. It should be possible, following Bruner's idea of the "spiral curriculum" (1960), to teach any subject to any child at any age. Yet it is clear that the age at which we begin instruction in any concept will strongly determine the level of presentation of the material. This fact has long been familiar to educators, but the curriculum still indicates in many places that there is still an insufficient appreciation of the length of time it takes to reach the more abstract levels of understanding. The teaching of arithmetic, for example, has often been far too concerned with abstract symbols at too early an age, before the child has any "feel" for the operations and transformations on objects that the arithmetical signs imply. The recent interest in the use of structural materials for the teaching of primary school mathematics is a step in the right direction, but with the possible exception of the devices constructed by Dienes (1959) and tested in Bruner's laboratory at Harvard, they have not been assessed in conjunction with a carefully designed plan of instruction which would extend and enhance their value for cognitive development. One outstanding exception of a Piaget-like program is that of Montessori (1964a).

What has largely been neglected is the question of articulation from one level to the next; just as it is important to avoid premature accommodation and verbal parroting, so it is likewise important to guide the transition from concrete material through perceptual to formal reasoning. This does not mean what has traditionally been assumed to be appropriate — giving the primary school child a few concrete materials for a few weeks and then moving him quickly along to pencil and paper equivalents. Rather it may even require the complete absence of symbolic forms until such time as the child asks questions which indicate a readiness for the next stage, or such time as a Piaget developmental test indicates that his concrete understanding is firm enough to risk a new accommodation.

The question of the grade placement of traditional areas of instruction is an important one to curriculum planners, and one can get some guidance from Piaget's research. For example, Piaget finds that children only understand the meaning of number when they have first mastered classes and asymmetrical relations. Perhaps kindergarten would be an excellent time to introduce the child to the experience of grouping objects on the basis of similarities and differences *before* the exercises in counting and the like are introduced. Another interesting area for experimentation both in the laboratory and classroom is the question of space and geometry. Piaget has asked children to manipulate by hand various objects which were hidden behind a screen, and has discovered that children can discriminate topological features (open from closed figures, even from uneven surfaces) long before they can determine projective or Euclidean concepts (circles from squares, acute angles from right angles, etc.). His work indicates that there may be two major errors in our teaching of geometry: (a) The present order of instruction proceeds from Euclidean geometry through projective to topological; perhaps this should be reversed; (b) Formal geometry now begins in junior or senior high school; Piaget's subjects could make these early discriminations at five years of age. This does not mean that geometry could be taught in primary school in its formal structure. Rather it suggests that one could begin at a very concrete level to introduce some of the underlying concepts which could lead gradually to a fully formal understanding.

Ideas for science instruction abound in Piaget's work. For example, he finds that the attainment of the concrete operational stage appears first in connection with the conservation of substance (the Plasticine experiment), next with respect to the conservation of weight, and finally in the conservation of volume. A natural scale of development appears to exist with respect to mass, weight and volume, the first occurring at about age seven or eight, the second at nine or ten, and the third at eleven or twelve. While children of higher overall intelligence may reach the concepts at lower absolute ages, the order is the same (Kooistra, 1963). Thus it would appear that one could take advantage of the match–discrepancy principle by introducing instruction in these areas in this order, while always trying to keep just a little ahead of the child's level of understanding.

With respect to formal operations, it is clear that the present practice of not introducing formal scientific experimentation into the classroom until roughly the high school level is a good one. Nevertheless, students might benefit considerably from some practical experience at this time with proportions, probabilities, introductory logic problems, etc. The ideas of permutations and combinations could be forcefully introduced by adopting some of Piaget's own procedures. For example, his "chemistry experiment" requires adolescents to mix four jars of liquid, whose relation (unknown to the child and to be discovered by him) is such that Jar A plus Jar B, but NOT Jar C will produce the desired color of liquid, with Jar D being irrelevant to the combination. Encouraging the students to use a combination of mental deduction of possible results, with later hypothesis testing using the actual jars, would go a long way in giving a firm basis both to the nature of scientific method and to an understanding of the logical–mathematical principles involved.

3. Summary and Conclusions

As a theory of mental development, Piaget's formulation has much to say to education. Piaget himself has cautioned, however, against the hasty and ill-considered application of his work until much more specific research into the educational effect of his theory has been undertaken. He is not personally interested in this variety of research, so the task is in the hands of education and psychology, and it is a huge task indeed. He would, however, be satisfied to learn that educators are becoming aware of the general principles of cognitive growth as he has described them, and that they are beginning to become concerned about educating in these terms. The general issues still to be explored in more detail seem to be the following:

(a) Does educational practice influence, or even accelerate, development?
(b) Does the effect of a particular practice transfer to other aspects of mental growth?
(c) What are the long-term cognitive effects of a given practice?

Three general conclusions seem to be warranted from the work completed thus far:

(a) You must *match* the level of instruction and information to the level of cognitive development of the child. Matching will probably mean presenting situations that are congruent with, or slightly in advance of his assessed level.
(b) You must motivate the learner less with extrinsic rewards and more with the internal push of cognitive *discrepancy,* inconsistency, "perturbation." Motivation will probably be greatest when the discrepancy is large enough to be interesting, but not so large as to be beyond the child's scope of understanding.
(c) When deficiencies occur in learning, you may have to go back to the level of understanding (concrete, or even intuitive or sensorimotor) where the inadequate adaptations occurred, build up that level, and gradually progress again (Kephart, 1960).

What Piaget Suggests to Classroom Teachers

■■■ MARGARET SMART

In this paper, the author deals with Piaget's concept of conservation. In so doing, she reflects on the ingenious design of Piaget's experiments, Piaget's analysis of intellectual development, and implications of Piaget's findings for changing classroom procedures to bring about greater learning.

A teacher stopped me in the hall to remark, "Now that I have experimented in my classroom with some of Piaget's intellectual tasks, never again will I look at children in quite the same way — and the change is for the better." Her comment reflected my own feelings because it's heady stuff to become a student of Piaget's work. Suddenly one finds it necessary to be an astute observer of children's behavior; a critical listener of their speech; an assessor of their thinking abilities; a stimulus for provoking their thought; and, indeed, a player of a half dozen other roles, frequently all at once. Moreover, many long-valued teaching techniques appear trite and totally inappropriate in light of one's new knowledge about children.

What is there in Piaget's studies which makes one perceive children in such different ways? After reflection, I deduced that three aspects of Piaget's work hold special meaning for me: (1) the ingenious experiments he has designed for revealing the nature of children's thinking; (2) his astute analyzations of children's intellectual development; (3) his provocative findings which imply classroom changes to promote more meaningful learning. Let us examine these three aspects separately.

Experiment: Conservation of Area

My introduction to Piaget's experiments occurred last year when I interviewed individually forty Mexican–American children between six and eight years of age.[1] To replicate any of his experiments, however, it is necessary to understand his concept of conservation and its relationship to operational thought. Children conserve, Piaget tells us, when they recognize the equality or invariance of objects even if altered in shape, size or position. Prior to acquiring this ability, children's capacities for viewing things in their true relations are limited. They attend to only one attribute of an object or experience at a time and are unable to handle complex relationships or

• • • • • • • •

SOURCE: *Childhood Education*, 44 (1968), 194–300. (With permission of the author and the Association for Childhood Education International, 3615 Wisconsin Avenue, N.W., Washington, D.C. Copyright © 1968 by the Association.)

[1] The children interviewed are a sample of those with whom the author worked.

13

abstractions. The ability to conserve, then, is a prerequisite to the development of logical and systematic thought.

From among the many experiments Piaget (1964) designed to study children's acquisition of conservation, I chose one dealing with the composition of area. His purpose (and mine) was to find out if young children "think of an area as a stable attribute which may be conserved even while the shape of an object is altered."

The necessary materials consisted of two identical rectangular sheets of green cardboard, approximately 18″ × 24″; two farmers (plastic); two cows (plastic); thirty wooden blocks 2″ × 2″ × $\frac{1}{2}$″; and four wooden blocks 2″ × 4″ × $\frac{1}{2}$″.

Piaget's usual method of showing children an area (in this instance, one piece of cardboard), made up of subareas (the blocks grouped in one fashion on the cardboard), and then of modifying the visible structure of the total area (by taking the second sheet of cardboard and arranging in different positions an equal number of blocks on it) was replicated as the children looked on.

To stimulate the child's interest the interview followed a story pattern.

One of the farmers has decided to build a house on his field (a block is placed on field one). Do the cows still have the same amount of grass?

Following the child's response, the interview continued:

The other farmer decides to build a house on his field as well (place a block in a different position on field two). Will the cows have the same amount of grass to eat?

The next sequence introduced the central problem:

Each farmer decides to build another house (add a block to each field, spacing the houses on field two and placing alongside one another on field one). Do the cows have the same amount of grass to eat?

From this point on each additional house placed on the fields left the child with the perceptual impression of more grass to eat for the first cow. It became increasingly difficult for the child to perceive the equality of the two fields as more houses were added.

The point at which he succumbed, if he did, to the perceptual differences required a change in procedural strategy. The spaced houses on field two were gradually moved closer together, while the child was asked, "What about now?" Some children would not admit equality until the blocks were arranged identically on both fields. Children were asked to explain their responses during the interview. What meaning did these replies have?

Analysis of Children's Responses

Piaget considered his results in the conservation of area task extremely informative. "Each new block which can be added without disturbing the recognition of equality," he wrote, "marks a step forward in development, until the point is reached when the solution is generated to all possible situations." Some illustrations from my data will help perhaps to clarify Piaget's meaning.

Six-year-old Tony was confronted with just two houses on each field.

TONY: Field one has more grass because it has houses together and this one doesn't.

INTERVIEWER: What about now? (adding a third block to each field).

TONY: No, because field one has more. It's not all covered (with houses).

INTERVIEWER: What about now? (moving spaced houses closer together).

TONY: Yes, they're the same now because you moved them.

Piaget would label Tony at the intuitive level. Characteristically, the arrangement of the houses had to be identical for him to admit the equality of the remaining green space.

Then there were children who admitted the equality of the fields up to eight or ten houses, yet their language described their interest in the attributes and actions of the objects rather than in the task itself. For instance Gilbert, almost seven, agreed the fields were the same through twelve houses but he consistently reasoned their equality because "the grass is green." The attribute of color took precedence over any other aspects of the situation.

Six-and-a-half-year-old Susie, admitting equality at eight houses, illustrated a growing mobility in her language: "Yes, the fields are the same because they're the same size." Similarly, other children evidenced their growing articulation with such remarks as:

They don't look the same size.
The fields are the same because there's two squares of grass.
This is more spread out and this is more squeezed up.

Gilbert, Susie, and others were all caught up in the perceptual differences of the situation and vacillated from one aspect of the task to another. Still, the use of such words as size, square, look, spread out and squeezed up indicated a more mobile articulation.

Adelina, age six, was able to match five blocks on a one-to-one relationship. "Look," she remarked as she successively picked up a block from field one and placed it alongside its counterpart on field two, "they fit on my fingers. They're the same," However, she reverted to perceptual differences when she admitted, "This has more green (field one) than this one." Her eyes continue to take precedence over her mind, although she is in transition from one level to another.

Seven-and-a-half-year-old Mark has almost attained operational composition. Sixteen blocks were grouped on each field before he denied equality: "This field has more grass (field one) but there's the same amount of blocks."

Eventually there does come a time when the children are no longer misled by any changes in position. Ramon, age seven-and-a-half, remained confident throughout the interview. "The farmers," he responded, "are doing everything the same. They have grass the same and houses the same.

Six-year-old George also could not be shaken. "George," I queried, adding the seventeenth block, "are you watching what I'm doing with the blocks?" George, running his finger along a crack on the table, looked up and grinned: "No, but I know what you're doing. You're going to add one more block to each field."

Ramon and George relied upon an operational handling of the equality of the remainders. They were convinced of the necessity of their reasoning and thus were able to conserve area.

On the whole the children's responses fitted rather well Piaget's sequence for the development of operational thinking, but it is interesting to speculate why there were such discrepancies between their ages and their abilities to conserve. Why could six-year-old George conserve while Tony, his age counterpart, could operate only at the intuitive level? Piaget and others strongly suggest that the principal difference lies in the kinds of experiences children have. If this is true, what kinds of experiences should George, Tony and the others encounter if, as Piaget (1950) emphasized, "we wish to adapt teaching to the findings of developmental psychology as opposed to the logical bias of scholastic tradition."

Time and Experience

Planning appropriate situations to fit the psychological findings suggests a different concept of time. How often have we heard, "Wait until the child is ready." "Give the child time to grow." It is true still that the rate at which a particular nervous system is developing affects the selection of experiences, but should time be the central determinant of developmental change? Rather, it seems to me, the experiences which occur in time are more important. Time nurtures the development of logical thinking because it permits laying in a stock of those situations necessary for children to accommodate new ideas and assimilate them into their own repertoires.

With such a concept of time, the choice of classroom experiences becomes crucial. In the classrooms from which my data were gathered, the experiences were designed to nurture the development of logical thinking. Special attention was given to fitting the appropriate experiences to the children's conceptual abilities, ranging from the intuitive level through the conservation stage.

In planning these experiences, Piaget's work suggested the importance of keeping in mind:

At the intuitive level young children are not able to deal with more than one property of an object or situation at a time.

Children able to conserve in one task may be unable to conserve with different materials or tasks.

Children tend to revert to the intuitive level when the demands of the environment are too removed from concrete content.

Experiences must be tied to action and accompanied by speech.

Examples from our classrooms illustrate each of the above four points.

First, a touch box served as one of the vehicles to promote children's use of analogy, which would consider the attributes of objects.

SITUATION: Children were taking turns feeling inside the touch box and guessing what was there (before school the teacher had placed a wooden soldier nutcracker inside).

CHILDREN: "It feels like a doll." "No, it's like a monkey." "I think it's a soldier." "I think it's a man." "No, it's like a coffeepot." After all the children had guessed and the box was opened, Richard gleefully shouted, "I know what it is. It's a cracker's nut."

TEACHER: (Her role is to model the language, provide the correct labels when needed, and reinforce positively the children's behavior.) "You are right, Richard. It is a nutcracker shaped like a wooden soldier. There were many good guesses, for it is like a doll, a soldier and a man."

The second point implied many related opportunities for the children to classify objects and discriminate between their differences and likenesses. During the many walking trips around the neighborhood the children looked for differences in fences, roofs, gardens, and other aspects of their environment. One teacher walked her class to see the changes which occurred in the cottonwood trees during the fall, the winter and again in the spring. Floor maps were developed of the neighborhood. The children classified many objects as they talked about such attributes as softness versus hardness or curved versus flat surfaces.

Third, careful attention was paid to the educational setting. A variety of materials which would accommodate to many uses was used to extend the range of individual differences. For examples, large floor blocks, table blocks, Lego blocks, Play-Doh and, of course, all the art media were available for the children to manipulate and to work through their conceptualizing problems.

The final point has been described in the above illustrations because all the experiences permitted children to become actively involved and to learn what objects can do as they handle and discuss them.

It is hoped that these excerpts will suggest mapping out similar teaching strategies to promote children's intellectual growth.

The Equilibration Process: Some Implications for Instructional Research and Practice

■■■ EDWARD L. PALMER

Piaget's descriptions of the equilibration process employ subjective terminology. In this article, Dr. Palmer suggests an operational definition in terms of levels of confidence, and explores its implications for instruction.

The interest that Flavell (1963) described as "something of a contemporary Piaget revival" has continued to increase, particularly in the areas of educational research, curriculum development, and classroom practice, until today the fruits of this interest can be detected in almost any preschool or elementary program in the country. But while some of the major concepts contained in Piaget's broad and original theory of intellectual development are becoming increasingly well known, many of their implications for educational research and practice are yet to be explored. A set of constructs which have received far less than their due emphasis, considering their central role in Piaget's system, have to do with the process of equilibration.

This paper will review the most significant facets of the equilibration process, as well as the main body of instructionally relevant research based upon it. The major purposes will be (1) to propose an interpretation of Piaget's construct of equilibrium, both conceptually and operationally, in terms of subjective certainty, or confidence; and (2) to explore some of the potential implications of this interpretation, both for a theory of intelligence and for instructional research and practice.

The Process of Equilibration

Piaget distinguishes two complementary aspects of intellectual organization. The first is the structural aspect. In treating this aspect, he traces the

• • • • • • • •

SOURCE: Paper presented at the American Educational Research Association meeting, February, 1968. (With permission of the author.)

evolution of the sensorimotor prototypes of logical thinking through a series of stages and substages up to the level of formal, or logico–mathematical representation. Three of the principal factors that he recognizes to be involved in structure formation are maturation of the nervous system, experience acquired in interaction with the physical environment, and the influence of the social milieu.

The second complementary aspect of intellectual organization is the process of equilibration. Piaget invokes this process as the principal mechanism of transition from one level in the formation of the intellectual structures to the next. The intellectual structures may be viewed as a system which is subject to modification through external intrusions. Equilibration is the process whereby the individual compensates for these intrusions through his own intellectual activity. The progressive steps in the process of structure formation are achieved through this compensatory activity. New forms of experience that disturb the individual's equilibrium at one level of structuring initiate the compensatory process of equilibration, which terminates in a new level of structuring. Note that in invoking this process, Piaget places particularly strong emphasis upon the active role that the individual plays in organizing his own experiences, and in contributing thereby to his own intellectual progress.

Equilibration is held to be a psychological self-regulatory mechanism, analogous to the homeostatic, or steady-state mechanisms of biology. However, Piaget makes it clear that it is to be viewed not as an extrinsic or added characteristic, but as "an intrinsic or constitutive property of organic and mental life" (Piaget, 1967). Moreover, he views it as a perfectly general process, one upon which all intellectual progress depends (Piaget, 1964). In view of its fundamental character, he ranks it as the fourth — and principal — factor contributing to such progress, along with the maturation of the nervous system and physical and social experience.

Equilibrium states are not all of a kind. Piaget identifies a number of characteristics which distinguish one such state from another. One of these has to do with their relative stability. In general, the structures associated with the earlier stages of intellectual development tend to be characterized by less stable equilibrium, in that the probability of their modification through new experience is relatively high. As the structures evolve, they come into increasingly stable equilibrium, until those which have developed by the time the individual reaches the level of formal, or logico–mathematical thought, at around fourteen years of age, will undergo little fundamental modification throughout the remainder of his lifetime. This does not necessarily imply that all forms of intellectual development reach a plateau at this approximate age level. It only reflects Piaget's conclusion that the fundamental structures associated with this particular form of thought tend to be present by then (Inhelder and Piaget, 1958). Equilibrium states tend not only to exhibit increasing stability over the course of intellectual development, but also increasing mobility. Mobility is a property which has to do with the individual's facility in oscillating between one object characteristic and another, as between the increased length and the decreased thickness of a piece of clay which has been rolled from ball to sausage form. In Piaget's view, the ability to oscillate between such characteristics is a prerequisite to the development of a strategy which coordinates them (e.g., to the development of a strategy which recognizes that the increased length of the sausage compensates for its decreased thickness). Piaget applies the term "centering" to perception that is immobile, and refers to the development of increasingly mobile perception as "decentering". Equilibrium states are further distinguished in terms of their fields of application. Fields of application are said to be either more or less extensive. Over the course of development, the intellectual structures tend to accommodate to an increasingly wide range of objects or events with no essential displacement of equilibrium. A final distinguishing characteristic concerns the ability to compensate for actual versus anticipated intrusions. The individual compensates for anticipated intrusions, for instance, when he frames and "tests" hypotheses without actually carrying out the experiments. The acquisition of increased facility in this regard is especially prominent among the factors which Piaget takes to define the transition from concrete- to formal-operational thought (Inhelder and Piaget, 1958).

Toward an Operational Definition of Equilibrium

Although Piaget typically speaks of equilibrium states in normative terms, they are clearly subjective states of the individual. A state of disequilibrium is a state of "subjective dissatisfaction." In the present interpretation, equilibrium states, or levels, correspond to levels of confidence. There may be much to gain through following this interpretation. First, confidence may be viewed as the resultant of all the influences, from within and from without, which determine one's level of equilibrium in a given circumstance. Secondly, any measure of confidence will serve to provide an operational definition of equilibrium. And the additional information which confidence measurement provides is useful in many ways in the instructional context, as will be pointed up in a later section.

The Experimental Manipulation of Equilibrium States

Smedslund (1961e) made the first explicit attempt to facilitate intellectual progress through the manipulation of equilibrium states. In a part of one experiment, he trained children in conservation of continuous substance, or amount. The training procedure employed was designed to disturb the equilibrium of nonconservers of amount, or to induce a state of "cognitive conflict." He predicted that in resolving this conflict, the children would acquire conservation. An excerpt from one of his training procedures will lend clarification. After a child had agreed that two identical pieces of clay contained the same amount, one piece was deformed, and he was asked whether it now contained more, the same amount, or less clay. As a presumed result of the misleading perceptual distortion brought about by the deformation, the children tended to conclude either that the deformed piece contained more or that it contained less. At any given stage in the training sequence, if a child held that it contained more, Smedslund either removed a small bit of clay from it, or added a small bit to the nondeformed piece, and again called for a comparison. In this manner, the child was presumably induced to bring the addition–subtraction schema to bear in comparing two such objects. And the conclusion based upon this schema — that when nothing is added or taken away the amount must still be the same — conflicted with the conclusion based upon the perceptual distortion. Smedslund held that in resolving this conflict, the child would find the conclusion based upon the addition–subtraction schema more compelling, and would therefore subscribe to conservation. Smedslund explored the theoretical significance of the fact that the gains produced through this type of training occurred in the absence of external reinforcement. In particular, he proposed that equilibration theory offers a clear alternative to exclusive reliance upon traditional reinforcement learning theory relative to the facilitation of intellectual progress.

Gruen (1965) found a similar conflict-producing procedure to be effective in accelerating the acquisition of conservation of number among children, but only when it was coupled with pretraining in the discrimination between "number of objects" and "length of array." When the conflict-producing procedure and the discrimination training were administered separately, neither yielded significant improvement. These results point up the complementary nature of the relationship between structural factors and equilibration in the facilitation of intellectual growth. Specifically, they suggest that in order to promote intellectual progress by manipulating the equilibration process, it is necessary that certain prerequisite structural components be present. They also support the complementary position that in order for certain of the structural components which have been acquired by the individual to become organized, it is necessary that there be an occasion for him actively to organize them — i.e., it is necessary that the conditions which give rise to equilibration be present.

Beilin (1965) adapted Smedslund's conflict-producing procedure to the problem of inducing conservation of number and conservation of length, and found no significant improvement in either. However, his procedure omitted the addition–subtraction that had been present in Smedslund's. Recall that it was this addition–subtraction feature which Smedslund had held to be the effective factor in producing cognitive conflict. Further research is needed to determine whether a closer adaptation of Smedslund's procedure will be effective where Beilin's was not.

Palmer (1966) brought about gains in conservation of number by each of three conflict-producing procedures. Each one of these procedures was quite different from that employed by Smedslund. In two of the three, the conflict was produced by way of social interaction. In one case, this form of interaction consisted of no more than a verbal expression of surprise on the part of the experimenter whenever a child responded as a nonconserver. In the other, nonconservers were exposed to the contradictory conclusions of their own peers, who were already conservers. Delayed post-tests, administered after two months, showed that the gains produced through these forms of training were stable. However, it is not clear whether they were sustained through the effect of the training, or through intervening maturation or experience. A later study by Mermelstein, *et al.* (1967) showed no improvement in conservation of continuous or discontinuous quantity through the use of procedures that were intended to produce cognitive conflicts.

A problem in dealing with conflict-producing procedures is that of determining whether the intended state of conflict has, in fact, been produced. Palmer (1966) held that children who failed to understand the relationships denoted by the terms "more," "same," and "less" would fail to experience the intended state of conflict, and, accordingly, would fail to acquire conservation. One of his three training procedures provided an indication of the extent to which the children understood these terms. There was improvement on the part of eleven of the sixteen children who showed an understanding of them, but on the part of only one of the eleven who did not. These results further emphasize the instructional and developmental significance of the complementary relationship between structural components and the equilibration process in the facilitation of intellectual growth.

If the equilibration process applies as broadly as Piaget suggests, then it should be possible to interpret all attempts to facilitate intellectual growth in terms of it. Although, for obvious reasons, it is not within the scope of the present discussion to pursue this possibility very fully, a few selected examples will be mentioned below.

Implications for a Theory of Intelligence, and for Instructional Research and Practice

Useful criteria for evaluating any theoretical position are, first, the extent to which it lends organization and clarity to areas of prior knowledge, and secondly, the extent to which it is fruitful, in the sense of generating new research or new types of practice. The discussion which follows will take up in very general form some of the ways in which the equilibration position relates to areas of previous theory and research, and will also suggest further possible forms of extension.

The most detailed attempt to relate the equilibration position to previous research and theory appears in the work of Berlyne (Piaget and Berlyne, 1960). Berlyne has attempted to integrate Piaget's position with that of the American learning theorist, Hull. Of Berlyne's results, Piaget (1964) has this to say:

> Our findings can very well be translated into Hullian language, but only on the condition that two modifications are introduced. Berlyne himself found these modifications quite considerable, but they seemed to him to concern more the conceptualization than the Hullian theory itself. I am not so sure about that. The two modifications are these. First of all, Berlyne wants to distinguish two sorts of response in the S–R schema: (a) responses in the ordinary, classical sense, which I shall call "copy responses"; (b) responses which Berlyne calls "transformation responses." Transformation responses consist of transforming one response of the first type into another response of the first type. These transformation responses are what I call operations, and you can see right away that this is a rather serious modification of Hull's conceptualization because here you are introducing an element of transformation and thus of assimilation and no longer the simple association of stimulus–response theory.
>
> The second modification which Berlyne introduces into the stimulus–response language is the introduction of what he calls internal reinforcements. What are these internal reinforcements? They are what I call equilibration or self-regulation. The internal reinforcements are what enable the subject to eliminate contradictions, incompatibilities, and conflicts. All development is composed of momentary conflicts and incompatibilities which must be overcome to reach a higher level of equilibrium. Berlyne calls this elimination of incompatibilities internal reinforcements.
>
> So you see that it is indeed a stimulus–response theory, if you will, but first you add operations and then you add equilibration.

A more recent work by Berlyne (1965) further expands upon the integration of these two positions, and contains a number of instructionally relevant suggestions, particularly concerning the role of conflict and curiosity in the motivation of productive or creative forms of thinking.

An earlier section referred to a number of characteristics associated with equilibrium states. Some of these may be particularly worthy of further exploration in the instructional context. One has to do with the mobility of equilibrium states. While there has been little work that could be subsumed under the rubric of "mobility training," I am indebted to Smeds-lund (1966) for reference to one very excellent example. Actually, Smeds-lund refers to this example in the context of the social origins of decentration; however, as indicated in an earlier section, coming to decenter is interpreted here as equivalent to achieving increased mobility. Smedslund's example reviews the work of the physicist, Karplus, in teaching science to elementary-school children:

> The key device in Karplus's techniques is called Mr. O, a small stylized man with clearly marked right and left, front and back sides. The characteristic feature of Mr. O is his complete egocentrism. He thinks he is the most important thing in the world, and reports the phenomena around him consistently with reference to himself. He states that a thing is in front of him, underneath him, behind him, etc., irrespective of how he himself is oriented. If held with his head down over a table he reports, "the table is above me." When asked, "Where are you?" he always answers, "I am here." . . . Sometimes several Mr. O's are introduced, giving contradictory reports. Faced with the contradiction between the different Mr. O's and between Mr. O and himself, the child is assumed to become aware of the *relativity* of positions and movements, i.e., to become gradually decentered in his dealings with physical systems.

Smedslund underlines the conclusion that, "in order to teach physical concepts to young children, Karplus has found it necessary to introduce a social interaction framework" (Smedslund, 1966).

In a separate but related study, Feffer and Suchotliff (1966) used a role-taking test to measure the ability of college students to consider different perspectives simultaneously with respect to their own (i.e., the ability to decenter in the context of social interactions). This ability was found to relate positively to certain measures representing effectiveness and efficiency in interpersonal communication. However, the potential instructional impli-cations of this outcome remain to be explored.

The clearest evidence that it is possible to bring about decentration through training is that contained in a series of studies reported by Elkind and his associates. They have made the most systematic study to date concerning the particular constructs and conditions involved in this sort of training. An excellent review of their work focuses upon its applications to reading and special education (Elkind, 1967). The most recent study in this series (Elkind and Deblinger, in press) reports the effect of nonverbal exercises in perceptual decentering upon the reading performance of dis-advantaged children. In this study, the experimental group made signifi-cantly greater improvement on Word Form and Word Recognition than did the control groups, which had received practice in reading, and exercises in vocabulary, grammar, and comprehension.

The equilibration position is particularly compatible with the discovery-learning, inquiry-training, and problem-solving approaches to instruction. All rely for their effectiveness upon the learner's own constructive ability. In terms of the equilibration position, it could be said that these approaches provide the conditions which disturb the learner's equilibrium and initiate his own self-regulatory activity. Suchman alludes to this effect in somewhat different terms when describing a series of films that were designed to motivate inquiry on the part of children. As Suchman puts it (1964), these films "pose episodes which the children cannot assimilate without accommodating . . ." The intent of Suchman's work was not only to impart the principles with which the film episodes dealt, but more importantly, to train children in effective, generalized strategies of inquiry.

An earlier section proposed that confidence measurement may be taken as one means for operationally defining equilibrium.[1] If the conditions which initiate learning through discovery, inquiry, and problem solving are those that disturb the learner's equilibrium, then consistent with this interpretation, they are also those that disturb his confidence. In the present view, the individual's degree of confidence will have a strong influence, in turn, upon his persistence in such learning situations: all else being equal, the higher his confidence, the more likely he will be to terminate his search for a solution, and the lower, the more likely he will be to persist. It is particularly interesting to consider the manner in which over- or underconfidence may affect the individual's search for a solution. As the notions of over- and underconfidence suggest, the individual's degree of confidence in an attempted solution will not always be warranted by the degree of accuracy which can be objectively ascribed to that solution. In some cases, his degree of confidence and his degree of accuracy will be more congruent, and in other cases, less so. Theoretically, the condition of overconfidence will result in the premature termination of the search for a solution, while the condition of underconfidence will lead to the use of redundant searching strategies. The optimal, or ideal condition, then, would consist of perfect congruity between confidence and accuracy.

Palmer (1967) recently found overconfidence in the solution of science-related problems to be more prevalent among a group of rural first-grade children, whose parents had completed little formal schooling, than among

• • • • • • • •

[1]Due largely to the work of Shuford, Albert, and Massengill, it is now possible to measure confidence in a more sophisticated manner than ever before. See Shuford, E. H., A. Albert, and H. E. Massengill, "Admissible Probability Measurement Procedures." *Psychometrika, 31* (1966), 125–145. Shuford and Massengill are currently exploring the general application of these procedures, including their use with children (personal communications).

a group of urban children, whose parents had achieved a relatively high level of education. The difference in parental education across these two groups suggests that characteristic levels of confidence, either more or less nearly approaching the optimal level, may possibly be acquired through the process of social transmission. For instance, generalized overconfidence could conceivably be transmitted to a child by typically offering or accepting inadequate problem solutions. If the present position is correct, the effect would be to retard the child's intellectual progress, since as a result of his overconfidence he would characteristically terminate the search for problem solutions prematurely.

The theoretical condition of perfect congruity between confidence and accuracy is viewed here, not as an isolated ideal, holding only for the so-called Piagetian tasks, or only for children, but as a perfectly general one, whose degree of approximation may properly be counted among the characteristics which define the individual's level of intelligence. The line of theoretical consideration which links the degree of congruity between confidence and accuracy to the socialization process emphasizes once again the potential fruitfulness of looking to the social context for the conditions which facilitate or impede the individual's rate of intellectual progress. Hopefully, it will be possible for the schools to realize any possibilities this neglected approach may hold for planned, compensatory intervention in the socialization of intelligence.

Children's Conception of Reality: Some Implications for Education

▬ CHARLES D. SMOCK

In this article, Dr. Smock discusses several aspects of Piaget's position as they bear upon certain controversial issues in early childhood education, and examines the elementary curriculum in terms of the child's changing concept of reality.

I would not go so far as many experts in the area, but I do realize the tremendous role that education must play in the challenges that confront our society and the world today. Not only are we confronted with the challenge and magnificence of a knowledge explosion in many areas, but there is currently an increased awareness of the role that education must play in creating truly equal educational opportunities for all people, at home

• • • • • • • •

SOURCE: *Journal of Research and Development in Education*, 1 (1968), 30–37. (With permission of the author and the *Journal*.)

and abroad. The transformation our society is undergoing, we hope, will be directed on such a course that our traditional values and beliefs concerning the nature of human existence will be maintained.

These challenges make educational theory and practice the most exciting of all time. Certainly some of the most significant advances have been in the technological sector; e.g., the teaching machine. However, in my opinion, we have recently devoted relatively too much time to teaching machines and too little to the characteristics of our "learning machines"; that is, to the children who are the targets for educational innovation.

Fortunately, recent theoretical and research emphasis, particularly that of the Swiss psychologist Piaget, has begun to draw appropriate attention to the child once more.

During the past decade, psychologists have discovered or rediscovered three important aspects of the early phases of child development that are of central importance for education:

(1) The tremendous plasticity of the human organism: These discoveries range from the fact that infants are capable of form discrimination within the first few days of life (Fantz, 1963), to that of the tremendous effects of the structure of the environmental factors impinging on the infant, to intellectual growth, and to the realization that relatively young children can learn to read.

(2) The effects of early stimulation and early environmental systems on infant and early child development are tremendously complex. Some of these early experiences appear highly persistent, but many are not. The Head Start program is an excellent example. We now know a short period of intervention whether it be for three months or for a full year is not likely to have lasting effects on the child's ultimate intellectual level. In fact, the "follow through" and "upward bound" programs are insufficient as well. We also need programs of adult education that might be entitled "stay on top" and "operation retread."

Further, the possible delayed effects of many early experiences have been curiously ignored. The most dramatic example of this is derived from the work of Harlow and Zimmerman (1959) on the development of affective systems in mammals. The initial experiments indicated no undesirable consequences of substituting a piece of velvet for a biological mother during infancy. Follow-up studies, however, indicated behavior consistent with what clinicians might call a severe form of psychopathology. As adolescents and adults, the chimpanzees did not establish social emotional relations with other members of their species. While such procedures, at the human level, might help solve the population explosion, I'm quite sure that other desirable goals of society would be lost. In any case, it is important to approach all of these problems of early stimulation with the understanding that hardly anything is known about the long term effects of such experiential innovations.

(3) The third major discovery (or more correctly I should say rediscovery) of recent years is that children have a mode of reasoning that characterizes their understanding of reality that is different from that of adults (Piaget, 1954). To understand the child's conception of reality is the necessary ingredient for truly innovational education strategy. Until we do understand the principles underlying child thought, our innovations will not persist, will be neglected and misinterpreted and probably misused if used at all. Such has been the fate of most important educational innovations in the past.

The most dramatic of yesterday's discoveries about the child's world was the Freudian one that the child has an emotional life of fantasy more or less secret and inaccessible. Perhaps of equal or even more importance, however, was the discovery of people like John Dewey and G. Stanley Hall that a child has an intellectual life of his own. The idea was not entirely new. At the turn of the century, for example, Darwin had been concerned with early intellectual development, but previous educational thought had defined the child largely as a small replica of the adult. That is, the child differed from the adult mainly in terms of his lack of what he is not rather than what he is, in terms of ignorance, incompetence, and probably original sin.

Progressive education arose in opposition to these notions of the child as an unformed adult. In its initial stages, and certainly as it was formulated, it proposed that the objective of education was the cultivation and stimulation of the child's world so that the child would grow into an adult with an adult's understanding of his world in reality. Unfortunately the careful thought and research which would give substance to this vision has been very slow in coming. And, I might add, progressive education in its original form was never really tried in the public schools despite the fact it has become the whipping boy for all that is wrong in our society today. It did gain some foothold in preschool education but there it became transformed into an educational strategy that can be summed up by "be patient, be nice, don't push, let the child play."

Emerging from a number of social forces (e.g., Sputnik) and new theoretical and research knowledge we have recently been confronted with a contrasting point of view. A number of psychologists and educators are proposing that a child can be taught anything if only the right gimmicks, the right teaching techniques, and the "right" theory of learning are used (Bruner, et al., 1966). Such a position is embarrassing to me as a child psychologist and acceptance of it should be embarrassing to any educator. While some outstanding success and significant discoveries have been achieved by this approach, I anticipate little lasting good to come from uncritical acceptance of such a position. To anticipate my conclusion, I believe that no matter how clever our programs are for the teaching of specific skills at the sensory motor level (i.e., during the first three years) such as reading, they are secondary to the educational goals of general cognitive stimulation related to the natural world view and thought of the young child. Educational approaches designed to be consistent with this latter view will neither make the absurd mistake of separating the emotional–social development from the child's intellectual development nor ignore the importance of constructing an educational environment that instills a continuing desire to learn and particularly one that lasts beyond the second or third grade.

To return to my main theme. To give substance to the notion that a child has his own view of reality after so many years, we rely heavily on the forty years of child study by Jean Piaget. In innumerable books and research reports he and his colleagues have presented results of interviews, observations and experiments on young children dealing with the stages in the child's development of concepts of reality including space, time, number, logic, causality, and so on.

On the basis of these data Piaget concluded that a radical change occurs in the child's modes of reasoning at about the age of three and again at about five or six. According to his theory, the thinking or reasoning of the preschool child has a logic of its own; a logic that is quite different from the adult rather than being simply a weaker form of an adult logic or a reflection of ignorance of adult concepts.

Although American psychologists rejected Piaget's observations and conclusions for a number of years because of methodological inexactitude, today psychologists and educators are taking a new and very close look at his ideas, methods, and findings. In fact, it is not too strong to say he is the dominant force in child psychology and education today. Regardless of the outcome of attempts to verify his findings and the confirmation or disconfirmation of his theory, the strategy he has proposed in the study of cognitive development will at least, if followed, finally give substance to the idea that the child's world is different from that of the adult. Most specifically he emphasizes, and it cannot be overemphasized, that the child helps to build his own concepts of reality, the child participates in the construction of reality and will not accept the ready-made adult-imposed reality as his own.

Two aspects of children's reality concepts that are central to Piaget's thinking, albeit a limited aspect of his general theory, are: first, that children fail to make a distinction between "subjective" and "objective" aspects of the world; and secondly, that in acquiring an "objective" view or adult mode of reasoning, children move through an invariant sequence of cognitive structures that determine their learning characteristics (Inhelder, *et al.*, 1966). Both of these general ideas or working hypotheses are significant for educators and should be subjected to continual thought and analysis in terms of the various subject matter areas and goals of education.

The child's failure to differentiate subjective experiences from objective reality components of his experience pervades his behavior and thinking. A wide range of illustrative examples are available from current and past researches. Let's take first what may appear to be an irrelevant example. We all realize that children find it difficult, at times, to separate daydreams or night-dreams from real happenings. Piaget insists we should not dismiss the child's interpretation of his dream experience as due to the inadequacy of the child's mind, but rather as a product of the inherent logic of the child's thought processes and its consequent "realism" characteristic (Piaget, 1954). One aspect of realism is confusion of thoughts with things and things with that for which symbols stand. Children between ages two and three often seem to react to dreams, to pictures and toys of animals, and objects as though they were really the animals they represented. Perhaps you have had the experience of a young son or daughter who broke into tears as you cut the bunny off the Easter cake or who became quite upset that you were unwilling to accept his dream experience as real. These everyday examples of children's reactions to dreams are, then, quite relevant to what happens in other areas of their early learnings. The failure to differentiate subjective and objective realm components is characteristic of a child's adaptations to his environment including the educational environment and the concepts we attempt to teach them.

One of the major results of the differentiation of subjective and objective is the construction of a world of permanent and unchanging objects and events systems. The infant under eight to ten months has no conception of the permanent object when he is reaching toward a bright toy and, if the toy is covered with a handkerchief, he stops reaching. The toy no longer exists for him. By the age of one-and-one-half he knows objects permanently exist but he cannot see them. However, it is not until the age of six or seven that he begins to view physical dimensions and identity as unchangeable things that only appear to vary under different conditions.

For example, we could take a five-year-old from a kindergarten and seat her in front of a table with two brightly colored necklaces lying side by side. The necklaces are of equal length and their ends are neatly aligned. The child is told to pretend the blue one is "hers" and the red one is "mine" and our problem is to decide which necklace is longer. The little girl will probably be a little puzzled by the question since she replies with conviction that both necklaces are the "same length." I pick up one necklace and make a circle of it and ask her to tell me which necklace is "longer" or is mine still as "long as yours." The little girl stretches her arms to illustrate length and beams, "Mine is the longest. You made yours into a ring and mine is all this long."

Or a young child might be presented with two boards about two feet square, covered with green cloth. On each board there are several barns and a cow. The child is asked to pretend this is a countryside and to indicate which cow has the more grass to eat. Interestingly enough, but consistent with our earlier statements, when the barns on both fields are solidly packed in one corner the child answers "the cows have the same amount to eat in each field." However, if we spread the barns on one field into various locations and leave the barns on the other field grouped together, she then indicates that the cow on the field with the barns in various locations has less to eat than on that field where the barns are closely grouped (Piaget, 1950).

Examination of these kinds of ideas, including the child's conception of length, substance, and space, led Piaget to discover that the child's thought during this so-called prelogical stage is not due to the child being illogical in the adult sense but to the fact that he places too much trust in appearances (i.e., the child tends to respond to the perceptual and subjective elements of the situation). By the time the child is six or seven, however, she will know the length of a string of beads is conserved; that is the length will not change even if its "longness" disappears when its ends are joined in a circle. The basic question is how does she gain the concept of length as a dimension so that the perceptual cues presented by the changes in shape are ignored. Today most psychologists, along with Piaget, see that the child's mind is internally consistent and yet externally illogical, a kind of Alice in Wonderland where lengths, widths, weights, distances have as much consistency as Silly Putty.

This new picture has aroused widespread debates among psychologists and educators. It raises a host of questions about the understanding of mental processes in general and the education of young children in particular. For example, is intellectual development preset, as in the child's physical growth, or can it be speeded up by experience through teaching? Does the child develop through a series of specific stages on his way to adult reasoning? What are the long-range consequences of attempts to speed up the child's acquisition of adult forms of reasoning? Piaget's theory and research, and research of many American psychologists, has begun to give us some tentative answers. By the age of six or seven, children have developed the idea of logical necessity in the adult sense within a restricted range of their experience. This acquisition is manifested through the "conservation" of length and areas, as mentioned above, as well as a number of other concepts pertaining to the physical world. For example, at about age six or seven, the number of elements in a collection remains unchanged regardless of how the elements are displaced or arranged. Conservation of substance and length occurs at about age seven or eight, and weight and volume at ten to fourteen years of age. (These ages for the various acquisitions of conservation concepts are, of course, only gross averages but do not in any way detract from Piaget's major conclusion that the attainment of conservation points to the formation of a new stage in the child's mental development). Thus, most psychologists have been convinced these phenomena represent qualitative changes in the child's mode of reasoning and that the phenomena Piaget describes are stable and accurate descriptions of cognitive development processes.

A second aspect of Piaget's position has not been accepted so readily, however. He maintains the changes in thought processes are largely spontaneous and occur independently of teaching or specifically directed experiences. The controversy centers on two basic questions: (1) Can the child's logic, as indicated by the conservation acquisitions, be explained as resulting from qualitatively different modes of reasoning characteristic of the preoperational stage or is it merely the result of a naive trust in, and strong tendency to respond to, perceptual aspects of the situation? (2) Does the transformation from prelogical to logical modes of reasoning represent an invariant order or sequence of development? The answer to the first question now is fairly clear, in my opinion: the child's performance on the conservation task is not due merely to a naive trust in perceptual cues nor to inadequate development of language facility.

The answer to the second question must be more tentative but the evidence to date indicates that some sort of ordering or developmental sequencing is most probable. Cultural and environmental factors, or innate capabilities, may make one child or group of children reach a given stage of development earlier than another, but all children appear to go through the same order of modes of reasoning regardless of environmental structure or amount of direct teaching. It would appear the differentiation of the subjective from the objective world is a major developmental transformation (or task, if you wish) requiring considerable experience, time, and active participation of the child. Further, children appear to move through a series of qualitatively different modes of reasoning from birth through adolescence before there is adequate achievement of this distinction in a large number of areas.

We should mention one other factor. Besides the issues we've discussed so far, there is one major problem which must be faced before we can say a young child has a cognitively different experience of reality than the adult. The child's acceptance of the subjective as real may not be simply verbal or cultural ignorance but could be due to the child being more swayed by his wishes and fears than are adults. This is the explanation favored by psychoanalytic-oriented psychologists. The Freudian view sees the young child as dominated by the pleasure principle. Without denying that desire, wishes and fears are reflected in many problem-solving tasks, the explanation is inadequate. We find children's reality attitudes are highly consistent whether situations involve fears or wishes concerning quite neutral topics. The consistency across many levels of "emotional" involvement cannot be explained by the child's acceptance of "unreality" if it were only a product of wishes and fears.

The general conclusion to be drawn from recent research is largely confirmatory of Piaget's view that young children's mode of thinking and experience of reality are different than the adults' and that these differences are not due to the children's ignorance, or lack of teaching, or to lack of control over wishes and fears. If the young child's sense of reality is different than the adult's, should we exploit this difference by stimulating the child's exploration of the world he will later consider unreal, or should we stimulate his development of a more mature sense of reality? Often the young child's openness to the world of magic and the unreal is considered a unique capacity for imagination in creativity. Preschool could be considered as fundamentally the best time for such exploration through play. At the other extreme is the view the child should be taught objective skills (the three Rs) and knowledge as soon as possible.

Neither of the above views takes into account that the preschool orientation to reality is a developmental stage which needs to be integrated with later stages of development. To put off reality until elementary school is only to divorce the child's preschool world of the subjective from the elementary school child's world of the more objective.

To focus on training for specific skills during early cognitive development is to teach the child a body of information whose meaning to the child is full of subjective distortions. The child may invest these early verbal and number skills with magical meanings which interfere with later learning and, more important, may create the aversion to self-motivated learning we note so much of in adults and older children.

The controversy surrounding these issues has proven to be a healthy stimulant for educational innovation. Too often, however, the proponents of each position have taken an "all or none" stance and thus attracted nonthinking disciples to their particular fold. Education is devoted to multiple goals and I would like to see educators and psychologists continue to explore the multiple possibilities of generating optimal educational strategies for educating young children. Neither Piaget nor other modern theorists offer specifics; but there are many significant and far-ranging issues and problems to be solved that are not apparent in the polemics of the dogmatic "innovators." More innovations, more experimental approaches, more ideas — these we need from all educators whether teachers, curriculum advisors, or administrators.

The dogma of the three Rs needs to be replaced with a new set of principles (probably to become dogma in its own good time) which we might call the three Ts: Titillation, Time, and Tools. These terms describe an orientation and educational strategy that are independent of particular subject matter area. But they are, in my mind, three indispensible aspects of learning at any stage of development and are of particular importance in early childhood education. Taken together they can provide the kind of environmental–educational situation that promotes not only intellectual growth but the total organismic development of the child.

Titillation refers to a set of environmental conditions in which the teacher and curriculum materials together represent an educational strategy capitalizing on the particular prior experience and current cognitive development of children. The experiments in English schools have clearly demonstrated that if children are provided a sufficiently informal setting and broad range of educational activities, they will select the appropriate activities in much the same way that free selection of food results in children meeting appropriate nutrient requirements. Certainly we can force children to learn many kinds of things and have done so often. The consequences of such forcing techniques, however, have been generally undesirable, resulting in lethargy, lack of curiosity, and a continual need to force children to learn things by offering external and extrinsic rewards such as grades, money, and/or honors. Once again it is time that educators at all levels begin to recognize a dualism with respect to motivation: that is, the difference between intrinsic and extrinsic motivation (Smock and Holt, 1962). Children are always motivated to learn where the problems with which they are confronted represent areas designed to capitalize upon the adaptive requirements and capacities of the child at that particular stage of development. We too often confound the problem of motivating children by either failing to match the task with his current cognitive capacities or fail to recognize that many skills and much knowledge can be taught through many different media. We too often segregate subject matter into neat little compartments that fit our conception of reality, or that of our teachers, and fail to recognize that children can learn much about measuring or quantitative concepts while engaging in what we might term "art." Further, we are so fascinated by our own conversation and voice that we overly emphasize the value of verbal learning when much of the same material could be learned much more readily, easily, and with more permanent effects where we allow the child to participate in a concrete way and with concrete materials in solving problems requiring the same skills.

Time refers to two aspects of the educational problem: first, the timing of educational experiences; and secondly, the necessity for recognizing variation in amount of time children require to acquire certain skills or knowledge. The timing of educational experiences must be geared to the characteristics of the child (which I have emphasized so much in this paper); and secondly, it may involve a value decision. I know neither evidence nor reasons, from the point of view of our current knowledge of learning capacities of children, why children cannot be taught to read during preschool for example. Whether or not such early skill learning might have later undesirable side effects is yet to be determined. Nor do we know for sure that it has all the positive side effects that have been so emphasized. But certainly the time spent in such training should not deprive the child of opportunities for other kinds of acquisitions equally important for later learning whether they be in terms of a specific knowledge and skills or related to the personal–social characteristics that are desirable from the point of view of society (or the extent or persistence of motivation to learn.)

Time is also important with respect to variation in children's ability to solve particular problems. There is probably no ideal variation of optimum spacing of a particular task with respect to the amount of time necessary to all children to learn. The overemphasis on clock hours and definite temporal end points for "education" is as detrimental to the preschool child's cognitive growth as it is to that of the graduate student.

Finally, tools refer to the basic skills that are anticipatory of the child's adaptive requirements during later years. In later childhood and adulthood the child is confronted with complicated technical and cognitive problems as well as social, moral and political ones. Each child needs a certain set of specific tools such as reading and mathematics to be a constructive citizen and to live a good life. People may vary as to what these basic skills or tools might be, but I am sure we would all agree that reading, mathematics, logic, and understanding of social interaction dynamics are among the most important ones. Each of these, however, can be taught with an infinite variety of subject matter content. It is very difficult to separate economics from history or history from art or art from many other contents. The important thing is to provide a variety of possible contents which will tap the variety of interests, experiential backgrounds and cognitive level of the child. But in any case, the world of the child and the natural processes of his development to adulthood are such that an educational strategy is demanded which places appropriate emphasis upon titillation, time, and tools.

A final comment is, perhaps, in order. The new discoveries referred to earlier (relatively high-level capacity of young infants, plasticity of the human organism during early development, and the different modes of reasoning during early childhood) indicate the potentiality for accelerating cognitive development of children in diverse ways. Moving all or some of the three Rs, and other subjects, to the preschool level need not distress us, nor is it inconsistent with the broad generalizations to be drawn from the current theory and research on cognitive development. Such decisions, however, need to be viewed in the proper perspective of the multiple goals of education and more essentially, the nature of the thought process during the early stages of development.

Aspects of Piaget's Theory That Have Implications for Teacher Education

███ CELIA B. STENDLER–LAVATELLI

In this paper, the author discusses three aspects of Piaget's system which are particularly applicable to teacher education: the concept of intelligence, the properties of logical thought, and stages in the development of logical intelligence. The paper also elaborates on Piaget's guidelines for the acceleration of cognitive development through interaction of four factors: maturation, experience, social transmission, and equilibrium.

The past ten years have seen a tremendous upsurge of interest in the work of Piaget, due in large part to America's increasing concern following Sputnik, with the intellective development of children. The interest has centered not so much on Piaget's early work on language, judgment, and reasoning and moral development of the child (1950) as on his research into the psychology of intelligence (1957b) and, with Inhelder and others, the development of logical thinking (1958). This is not to leave the reader with the impression that there was a gap in Piaget's productivity or that his interests took a turn in the last two decades. A glance over his very impressive bibliography (Flavell, 1963) shows steady production and persistent interest in problems of epistemology. His main concern is and always has been with questions of how the child acquires knowledge and what happens to mental processes during the acquisition. Unfortunately, translations of his works have been limited to a few books, and publication involves an inevitable time lag. Gradual evolution of his theory has led him to his present investigations into the relations between perception and intelligence (1961) and the role of mental image in the development of cognitive structures, but reports on these investigations are not yet available in English.

• • • • • • • •

SOURCE: *Journal of Teacher Education, 16* (1965), 329–335. (With permission of the author and the *Journal.*)

Increased interest in Piaget has met with mixed reception. On the one hand, there are those who would dismiss his work as unworthy of the attention of either psychologists or professional educators because he has not tested an adequate sample and has not done carefully controlled research. But Piaget's theory is not founded on seemingly casual observations of children; research on large numbers of children has been conducted in Geneva, although only one report has been translated into English. Nor does his clinical method permit as much freedom to the experimenter as critics would make it appear. In the clinical method, a child is presented with a task to which he makes some kind of response; what the experimenter does next depends upon that response. But over the years, Piaget has discovered the type of response that is likely to be given, and directions for administering the task take into account the possibility of alternative responses.

On the other hand, there are critics who now attribute to Piaget every innovation in American education, from the emphasis upon teaching children the structure of subject matter to team teaching. The truth of the matter is that Piaget himself stoutly maintains in his lectures that he is not a pedagogue and that he does not concern himself with applications of his theory to problems of education. He acknowledges that there are, of course, implications for the education of children in what he has written, and he hopes that those in pedagogy will concern themselves with the task of searching out these implications. This paper considers those aspects of his theory that hold the most promise for application in the classroom.

From the wealth of ideas Piaget has given us, there are three in particular that are most relevant to problems of teacher education: his concept of intelligence, his concept of the properties of logical thought, and his concept of stages in the development of logical thinking.

Piaget's Concept of Intelligence

For Piaget, intelligence is a form of adaptation, a particular instance of biological adaptation involving a striving for equilibrium in mental organization.

As an individual acts upon his environment, certain elements from the experience are stored in mental structures. Construction of mental structures begins at birth, with new elements from fresh experiences being incorporated into those structures. These new elements upset equilibrium, but as old structures are altered according to the reality conditions being experienced at the time, equilibrium is restored. Piaget postulates twin processes — assimilation and accommodation — as being at work here, with assimilation the process by which information is taken into mental structures, and accommodation the modification of the thought patterns to adapt to reality. The reader of this paper may have brought to his reading a mental structure of what constitutes intelligence that is quite different from the concept being presented here. If he acts upon Piaget's notion and mentally digests its elements, equilibrium in mental organization will be upset. With a modification of the old concept to accommodate the new, a changed concept of what is intelligence emerges.

Self-activity is crucial in the adaptive process; for Piaget, *"Penser, c'est opérer."* If equilibrium is to be achieved at a higher level, then the child must be mentally active; he must transform the data. The elements to be incorporated may be present in an experience or the child may be told of the error in his thinking, but unless his mind is actively engaged in wrestling with data, no accommodation occurs. Children, like adults, are not convinced by being told they are wrong, nor by merely seeing evidence that contradicts their thinking. They have to act upon the data and transform them, and in so doing, make their own discoveries. As Piaget puts it, knowledge is not a copy of reality; to know something is to modify external reality. Knowledge always involves a mental operation which permits one to transform what one sees in the light of what one already knows. These operations are not the same at all ages; the thought of the young child and that of the adult are, hopefully, very different. Piaget describes the changes that occur with age in terms of stages; before turning to a description of the stages, it is necessary first to examine the properties of logical thought.

The Properties of Logical Thought

Piaget's model of logical thought is a logico-mathematical one. He sees the same properties in thought structures that have been identified in algebraic structures. What do we do when we think logically? We perform some mental action upon data; we shift data about in our minds, performing displacements upon them. We put two and two together, figuratively speaking, to arrive at a conclusion. Or, we arrange things in some kind of order — perhaps a temporal one — thinking of which event happened first, which next, and so on, so that we may think about a problem in a more systematic way. Or, someone makes a sweeping analogy in the course of conversation, comparing race relations in the South and in the North. The mind then does a one-to-one correspondence between elements in each racial situation in an attempt to see whether or not they are identical. Or, the problem comes up of what is responsible for an increase in language problems among children entering kindergarten. Not only must we check out certain obvious variables to see if each is a contributing factor, but we must also check to make sure that the less obvious is not a factor. We must ask ourselves how we know it isn't such-and-such a thing. All of these are examples of operations performed upon data to arrive at consistent, non-contradictory — that is to say, logical — conclusions.

Piaget has systematically analyzed logical operations and described for us a grouplike structure that mirrors the thought of the child. The structure is not the same for children of all ages. During some of the elementary school years (seven to twelve), certain mental operations are apparent in the child's thinking, operations which together form an ensemble or group.

One of the operations, reversibility, is for Piaget one of the most critical to develop. Every change, every displacement that we carry on mentally is reversible. We can combine robins and all-birds-not-robins to make up a class of birds, and we can also separate the class into the original sub-classes.

Several of the tasks developed by Piaget to discover how the child thinks about a problem involve the conservation principle. An illustration of the conservation principle is the fact that such properties of matter as amount of substance, weight, and volume are conserved even with a transformation in appearance. Thus a ball of clay rolled into a hot-dog shape will contain the same amount of substance and weigh the same as it did to begin with. How do we know? Logically, it has to be the same, for the rolling-out process can be reversed and the hot dog restored to the ball. This is exactly how the child solves the problem; he uses a reversible mental operation.

Logical operations, however, form a grouplike structure, and reversibility is not an isolated phenomenon. Present the conservation of weight problem to a nine-year-old, and his answer may go something like this: "They've got to weigh the same. The hot dog is longer, but it's skinnier, and that makes up for its being longer. Just put it back into a ball, and you'll see that it's the same." In other words, in shuffling the data about, not only is a reversible operation performed, but the child also sees that the hot dog is made of bits and pieces of clay (additive composition) that can be put together in various ways without a change in weight. The first is the operation of additive composition, and the second is the associative operation: the mind can reach the same goal by different paths. A change in one dimension can be compensated for by change in another.

Or, one can think about the clay-ball problem in still a different way. A child may say, "It's got to be the same. You didn't add anything, and you didn't take anything away, so there can't be a weight difference." Here the operation is one of identity.

What the child is doing here as he works on the problem is actually to perform one or more operations in his mind. He may reverse a process, or combine elements to make a whole, or put elements together in different ways, or perform an identity operation where two sets must be the same if there is a one-to-one correspondence between parts and all the parts are accounted for. To these four properties of logical thought — reversibility, additive composition, associativity, and identity — there is added a fifth, a case of special identities or tautology, which affirms the equivalence of members of a class. A class of red objects is still a class of red objects when more red objects are added. To call a spade a spade, figuratively speaking, means that we haven't changed the class with additions we make, provided the additions are identical in quality.

When a child is presented with one of the Piaget tasks, an analysis of his responses is made for evidence that his thinking is distinguished by these properties of logical thinking. Thus in the volumes by Piaget and those written with Inhelder we can find the gradual emergence of logical operations as the child matures. The most thorough and best analysis of the logic involved in the practical operations characteristic of seven-to-twelve-year-olds is to be found in Flavell (1963, Chapter 5).

The operations described above characterize the child's thinking during most of the elementary school years, but during adolescence, changes occur in modes of thinking. Piaget describes the thought processes that emerge at this time as propositional thinking. The adolescent states propositions in terms of the variables he has identified and then proceeds systematically to combine the propositions so as to test all possible combinations.

There are four ways in which propositions can be combined. We can combine by conjunction, as when we say, "It's got to be this and this"; by disjunction, "It's got to be this or this"; by negation, "It's neither this nor this"; and by implication, "If it's this, then this will be true." In addition to combining propositions in these four different ways, we can also transform each of the combinations in four different ways, yielding a possibility of sixteen different products.

Stages in Development of Logical Intelligence

From the foregoing analysis of logical thinking, it should be obvious that human beings are not capable of such thought processes at birth. For Piaget, they develop in stages; he regards logical thinking as the greatest attribute of man, and his account of stages in the development of mental operations is geared toward the individual's growth in ability to think in this fashion. There are four main stages: the sensorimotor, the preoperational, the stage of concrete operations, and the stage of formal operations.

Piaget finds the origins of logical intelligence in the sensorimotor period. The infant comes into the world with two kinds of reflexes: those like the knee jerk that are not altered by experience, and others like grasping and sucking that are modified as the infant exercises them. The modification occurs through assimilation and accommodation. The infant, for example, accommodates the grasping reflex to the shape of the object to be grasped, curving the fingers in one way for a long, narrow object, and in a different way for a plastic play ring. Later, looking and grasping become coordinated; the infant can put out his hand and grasp that which he sees. Each newly discovered experience brings with it a need to repeat the experience; activity begets activity. And as the infant operates upon the physical world with his sensorimotor system, he acquires notions of objects, space, time, and causality. Ask a ten-month-old baby, "Where's Mommy?" and he looks toward the door through which Mommy has just disappeared; he "thinks" about the concepts of time and objects with his motor system, i.e., Mommy was here but is not now. However, she still exists. Objects have a permanence and do not cease to exist when out of sight.

During the sensorimotor period, the infant lays the foundation for later representational thought. Structures are built which are essential for the mental operations carried on at a later stage of development. The sensorimotor foundation of one structure that adults recognize most easily is that involved in orienting ourselves in space. A person giving directions to a motorist will often turn his body and put out his hands as he "thinks" with his motor system which way to direct the questioner. With a mental map, the need for a motor accompaniment to thinking disappears; thought has become representational. But the structures which enable the school child to deal with space are laid in the sensorimotor period. The concept of a grid system, of an object being displaced in both horizontal and vertical direction, has its primitive beginnings in infant actions.

Gradually actions become internalized; the child can represent in thought processes that which was first developed on the sensorimotor system. This second stage begins at eighteen months and extends to seven years of age (roughly). It is in this stage that we find most kindergarten and first-grade children; some second-grade; and of course, some children even older than seven years. This stage is called preoperational because the child does not use logical operations in his thinking. Piaget characterizes mental processes at the preoperational stage as follows:

1. The child is perceptually oriented; he makes judgments in terms of how things look to him. Piaget has shown that perceptual judgment enters into the child's thinking about space, time, number, and causality. It is only as the child goes beyond his perceptions to perform displacements upon the data in his mind that conservation appears.
2. The child centers on one variable only, and usually the variable that stands out visually; he lacks the ability to coordinate variables.
3. The child has difficulty in realizing that an object can possess more than

one property, and that multiplicative classifications are possible. The operation of combining elements to form a whole and then seeing a part in relation to the whole has not yet developed, and so hierarchial relationships cannot be mastered.

So far this consideration of preoperational thinking has been largely negative. We have seen that the child lacks the ability to combine parts into a whole, to put parts together in different ways, and to reverse processes. What, then, can the child do. The development of logical processes is not at a standstill during this period and there are some positive accomplishments. We see, for example, the rudiments of classification; the child can make collections of things on the basis of some criterion. He can also shift that criterion. Thus, if we present a kindergarten child with a collection of pink and blue squares and circles, some large and some small, and ask him to sort them into two piles with those in each pile being alike in some way, he can usually make two different collections on the basis of color and shape (a few children discover the third criterion of size). Such an ability, of course, is essential to the formation of classes and eventually to the notion of hierarchy of classes.

The child is also beginning to arrange things in a series. He can compare two members of a set within a series when they are in consecutive order; he knows that Tuesday comes after Monday. But since Friday comes after Tuesday, which is after Monday, does Friday also come after Monday? This operation, involving seeing logical relations between things or events that are arranged in a series, is not yet possible to the preoperational child, but experiences with seriation are preparatory to the development of such operations.

By seven years of age, the logical operations of reversibility, associativity, etc., that I have already described, begin to appear. Piaget calls this the stage of concrete operations, because while the child uses logical operations, the content of his thinking is concrete rather than abstract. Fifth-grade pupils, if given a billiard-game problem when they are studying light, can do serial ordering, and establish a one-to-one correspondence between the two slopes of directions. "The more I put it like that (inclined to the right), the more the ball will go like that," a ten-year-old will explain. That the total angle can be divided into two equal angles does not occur to them, for they lack the formal operations necessary to such a discovery. They solve problems and give explanations in terms of the concrete data available to them; they do not try to state generalizations.

This stage of concrete operations lasts until twelve years, which is roughly the age for the onset of the stage of formal operations or propositional thinking. According to Piaget, most children at the high school level tend to do the if-this-happens-then-that-is-likely-to-happen (or not happen) kind of thinking. They are also more likely to think in terms of abstractions and can state, as in the case of the billiard game, the general principle involved.

Critics of Piaget have made this notion of development as occurring in stages one of their targets. Some mistakenly think that he uses the concept, as did Gesell, to refer to similarities among children of the same chronological age, with age being the critical antecedent of the similarities. As Kessen and Kuhlman (1962) point out, when the language of stages is used merely as a paraphrase for age variation, it is not useful. For Piaget, however, stages are convenient for helping us to think coherently about the course of development. His descriptions of stages are based upon changes in the child's comprehension of logic and emphasize sequence. They are not tied in any hard-and-fast way to age. In fact, as the students in Geneva discovered when they tried the Piaget tests on husbands, wives, or other adults, including themselves, adults are spotty in their logical development. Most adults have reached the stage of formal thought in solving many of the problems demanding logical solutions, but they may be a bit chagrined to discover that they are not even at the stage of concrete operations with respect to others. And with respect to operations at each of the stages, Piaget describes these in terms of probability; he would say that at a particular stage there is a probability which can be set at a certain figure that the child will select a particular strategy (not necessarily consciously) for solving a problem. Piaget explains the stage–age relationship in this fashion:

> The age of seven is a relative one in a double sense. In our research we say that a problem is solved by children of a certain age when three-quarters of the children of this age respond correctly. As a result, to say that a question is solved at seven years old means that already one-half of the six-year-olds can solve it, and a third of the five-year-olds, etc. So, it's essentially relative to a statistical convention. Secondly, it's relative to the society in which one is working. We did our work in Geneva and the ages that I quote are the ages we found there. I know that in certain societies, for instance in Martinique, where our experiments have been done by Monique Laurendeau and Father Pinard, we have found a systematic delay of three or four years. Consequently the age at which those problems are solved is also relative to the society in question. What is important about these stages is the order of the succession. The mean chronological age is variable.

The question arises, once we assume that age changes in logical thinking are not fixed, as to whether we can then speed up the development of logical thinking. This is a question that never fails to amuse students and faculty in Geneva, for they regard it as typically American. Tell an American that a child develops certain ways of thinking at seven, and he immediately sets about to try to develop those same ways of thinking at six or even five years of age. Actually investigators in other countries as well as in America have tried to accelerate the development of logical thinking, and we have available today a considerable body of research on what works and what doesn't work. Most of the research has not worked. Paper after paper reports the stubborn refusal of children to accept the conservation principle, despite a variety of training techniques. Efforts have not been successful because experimenters have not paid attention to the processes of assimilation and accommodation in equilibrium theory. The researchers have tried to teach a response rather than to develop operations. They have tried, for example, to teach the child that of course the hot dog will weigh as much as the clay ball; the subject can put both on a two-pan balance and get immediate feedback. But the child is completely unconvinced unless he acts upon the data in his mind, transforming them by means of one or more of the operations already described. In fact, an ingenious technique devised by Smedslund showed that external reinforcement leads only to a pseudo-concept. After children had been trained on the balance to give conservation responses, the experimenter tested each child by surreptitiously removing a piece of clay from the hot dog before it was put on the scale. The subjects who had learned the proper response immediately abandoned conservation in favor of perceptual judgment. Learning a fact by reinforcement does not in and of itself result in mental adaptation. Learning involves active assimilation resulting in momentary conflicts and compatibilities which the learner must himself resolve to reach a higher level of equilibrium.

What does work? Research by some investigators offers some promising leads. These might be summarized as follows:

1. It has been possible to accelerate the development of logical intelligence by inducing cognitive conflict in subjects. Smedslund (1961c) devised a training procedure with the balls of clay where he both elongated the clay and also took away a piece of it, thus forcing the child to choose between two conflicting explanations. Can the hot dog weigh more when a piece has been taken away? Given this kind of choice, the child veers toward consistency. The number of successful cases was small, but they offered tentative support for the cognitive-conflict hypothesis.

2. Training children to recognize that an object can belong to several different classes at once aids in the development of logical classification. Morf (1959) and Sigel (1965) have had some success with this procedure. Sigel has worked with bright preschool children on conservation tasks, training them on certain logical operations considered to be prerequisite to conservation. Children were trained on multiple labeling, multiple classification, and multiplicative relations. For example, the teacher would first have a child label a piece of fruit, then another and another; then search for a

class label; then define criteria of the class; and finally take the class apart and put it together according to various criteria. Only five children were trained, but four out of the five showed an increase in ability to deal with conservation tasks.

3. There is a tendency for conservation of number to be accelerated in children trained to see that addition and subtraction of elements change numerical value, and so, if nothing is added and nothing is taken away, number is conserved regardless of how the elements are arranged in space.

4. To help children move from the preoperational stage to the stage of concrete operations, it is helpful to make gradual transformations in the visual stimulus and to call the child's attention to the effects of a change in one dimension to a change in another.

Piaget himself has provided guidelines for acceleration of logical development in his identification of four factors that influence development from one stage to another. These factors help to explain individual differences in children's performance on the Piaget tasks:

1. *Maturation.* Maturation, defined as a ripening of neural structures with age, undoubtedly plays a part in the transformations in mental structures, and undoubtedly genes influence the ripening process. But maturation alone cannot account for changing mental structures. The Martinique studies (Laurendeau and Pinard, 1962), showing a four-year delay in development over the Geneva norms, reveal that maturation alone does not guarantee that children of a certain age will have reached a certain stage in logical development. And evidence from the Dennis studies in Teheran shows that maturation itself is dependent upon experience. Babies in an orphanage confined to cribs and terribly limited in motor experiences were shockingly retarded in age of onset of walking. Ripening of the nervous system is not something that is completely under control of the genes. A recent critical review by Moltz (1965) had this to say:

> An epigenetic approach holds that all response systems are synthe-sized during ontogeny and that this synthesis involves the integrative in-fluence of both intraorganic processes and extrinsic stimulative condi-tions. It considers gene effects to be contingent on environmental conditions and regards the genotype as capable of entering into different classes of relationships depending on the prevailing environmental context. In the epigeneticist's view, the environment is not benignly supportive, but actually implicated in determining the very structure and organization of each response system.

2. *Experience.* Piaget finds that experience alone is not enough to acceler-ate logical development, if experience is defined as exposure to objects or events only. There must be a logico–mathematical experience if logical

structure is to develop. There must be a "total coordination of actions, actions of joining things together or ordering things, etc."

3. *Social transmission.* Social transmission is linguistic or educational transmission. Like the two preceding factors, this, too, plays a part in logical development, but it is not enough. As Piaget points out, young children hear everyday expressions involving whole–part relationship ("Champaign, Illinois"; "Some Indians lived in tepees"), but they do not understand the logic involved. Some Indians are no different for them from all Indians, and Champaign is not physically contained in Illinois. Linguistic transmission is possible only when logical structures are present in children's thinking.

4. *Equilibrium.* For Piaget, this is the critical factor. The three previously mentioned factors are necessary, but it is the mental activity of the subject when confronted with cognitive conflict and operating to compensate that determines the development of logical structures. Compensation is achieved through the operations of reversibility, etc., already described.

No attempt will be made here to spell out the implications of Piaget's theory for educators. Certainly his account of stages should be useful to curriculum makers interested not only in attending to subject matter to be mastered but also in providing for development of logical structures. And Piaget's equilibration theory should shake the faith in external reinforcements of all but the most orthodox of learning theorists. For the doubting Thomas, some experience in using external reinforcements to try to teach a child the conservation principle will prove to be shattering but rewarding.

The Transition from Concrete to Abstract Cognitive Functioning: Theoretical Issues and Implications

■■■ DAVID P. AUSUBEL

Piaget's concept of developmental stages has been subjected to critical examination on both a theoretical and empirical level. In this article, Dr. Ausubel submits the concept to intensive analysis, and outlines the possibilities and limitations for developing children's thinking which may be inferred *a priori* from the theory.

The primary school child is by no means dependent on immediate concrete–empirical experience in understanding and manipulating simple abstractions or ideas about objects and phenomena. It is true, of course, that the emergence of such ideas must always be preceded by an adequate

• • • • • • • •

SOURCE: *Journal of Research in Science Teaching,* 2 (1964), 261–266. (With permission of the author and the *Journal.*)

background of direct, nonverbal experience with the empirical data from which they are abstracted. But once their meaning becomes firmly established as a result of this background of past experience, the child can meaningfully comprehend and use them without any current reference to concrete empirical data.

The meaningful understanding or manipulation of relationships between abstractions or of ideas about ideas, on the other hand, is quite another matter (Inhelder and Piaget, 1958). In this kind of operation the primary school pupil is still dependent upon current or recently prior concrete-empirical experience: when such experience is not available, he finds abstract relational propositions unrelatable to cognitive structure and hence devoid of meaning. This dependence upon concrete–empirical props self-evidently limits his ability meaningfully to grasp and manipulate relationships between abstractions, since he can only acquire those understandings and perform those logical operations which do not go beyond the concrete and particularized representation of reality implicit in his use of props. Thus, where complex relational propositions are involved, he is largely restricted to a subverbal, concrete, or intuitive level of cognitive functioning, a level that falls far short of the clarity, precision, explicitness, and generality associated with the more advanced abstract stage of intellectual development.

Beginning with the adolescent period, however, children become increasingly less dependent upon the availability of concrete–empirical experience in meaningfully relating complex abstract propositions to cognitive structure. Eventually, after sufficient gradual change in this direction, a qualitatively new capacity emerges: the intellectually mature individual becomes capable of understanding and manipulating relationships between abstractions directly, that is, without any reference whatsoever to concrete, empirical reality. Instead of reasoning directly from a particular set of data, he uses indirect, second-order logical operations for structuring the data; instead of merely grouping data into classes or arranging them serially in terms of a given variable, he formulates and tests hypotheses based on all possible combinations of variables. Since his logical operations are performed on verbal propositions, he can go beyond the operations that follow immediately from empirical reality (equivalence, distinctiveness, reversibility, and seriation), and deal with all possible or hypothetical relations between ideas. He can now transcend the previously achieved level of subverbal, intuitive thought and understanding, and formulate general laws relating general categories of variables that are divorced from the concrete–empirical data at hand. His concepts and generalizations, therefore, tend more to be second-order constructs derived from relationships between previously established verbal abstractions already one step removed from the data itself.

Validity of the Stage Concept

Many American psychologists and educators have been sharply critical of Piaget's designation of concrete and abstract stages of cognitive development. They argue that the transition between these stages occurs gradually rather than abruptly or discontinuously; that variability exists both between different cultures and within a given culture with respect to the age at which the transition takes place; that fluctuations occur over time in the level of cognitive functioning manifested by a given child; that the transition to the abstract stage occurs at different ages both for different subject-matter fields and for component subareas within a particular field; and that environmental as well as endogenous factors have a demonstrable influence on the rate of cognitive development. But although much more rigorous empirical data than have been presented to date are required to substantiate Piaget's conclusions with respect to the existence of these two particular stages of cognitive development, the aforementioned criticisms reflect many gratuitous and unwarranted assumptions regarding the criteria that any designated stage of development must meet.

Actually, developmental stages imply nothing more than identifiable sequential phases in an orderly progression of development that are qualitatively discriminable from adjacent phases and generally characteristic of most members of a broadly defined age range. As long as a given stage occupies the same sequential position in all individuals and cultures whenever it occurs, it is perfectly compatible with the existence of intraindividual, interindividual, and intercultural differences in age level of incidence and in subject-matter field. It reflects the influence of both genic and environmental determinants, and can occur either gradually or abruptly. Hence all of the aforementioned arguments disputing the legitimacy of Piaget's stages of intellectual development seem quite irrelevant.

Although stages of development are qualitatively discontinuous in process from preceding and succeeding stages, there is no reason why their manner of achievement must necessarily be abrupt or saltatory. This is particularly true when the factors that bring them into being are operative over many years and are cumulative in their impact. Unlike the situation in physical, emotional, and personality development, cognitive development is not marked by the sudden, dramatic appearance of discontinuously new determinants.

It is also unreasonable to insist that a given stage must always occur at the same age in every culture. Since rate of development is at least in part a function of environmental stimulation, the age range in which a stage occurs tends to vary from one culture to another. Thus, considering the marked differences between the Swiss and American school systems, it would be remarkable indeed if comparable stages of development took place at the same ages. Similarly, within a given culture, a particular stage cannot be expected to occur at the same age for all individuals. When a particular age level is designated for a given stage, it obviously refers to a mean value and implies that a normal range of variability prevails around the mean. This variability reflects differences in intellectual endowment, experiential background, education, and personality. Thus a certain amount of overlapping among age groups is inevitable. A particular stage may be generally characteristic of five- and six-year-olds, but also typically includes some four- and seven-year-olds and even some three- and eight-year-olds. Piaget's age levels, like Gesell's, are nothing more than average approximations set for purposes of convenience. Hence to attack the concept of developmental stages on the grounds that a given stage includes children of varying ages, instead of taking place at the precise age designated by Piaget, is simply to demolish a straw man.

One also cannot expect complete consistency and generality of stage behavior within an individual from one week or month to another, and from one subject matter or level of difficulty to another. Some overlapping and specificity are inevitable whenever development is determined by multiple variable factors. A particular twelve-year-old may use abstract logical operations in his science course in October, but may revert for no apparent reason to a concrete level of cognitive functioning in November, or even several years later when confronted with an extremely difficult and unfamiliar problem in the same field. Furthermore, he may characteristically continue to function at a concrete level for another year or two in social studies and literature. Since transitions to new stages do not occur instantaneously but over a period of time, fluctuations between stages are common until the newly emerging stage is consolidated. In addition, because of intrinsic differences in level of subject-matter difficulty, and because of intra- and interindividual differences in ability profiles and experiential background, it is hardly surprising that transitions from one stage to another do not occur simultaneously in all subject-matter areas and subareas. Abstract thinking, for example, generally emerges earlier in science than in social studies because children have more experience manipulating ideas about mass, time, and space than about government, social institutions, and historical events. However, in some children, depending on their special abilities and experience, the reverse may be true. In any developmental process where experiential factors are crucial, age *per se* is generally less important than degree of relevant experience. Finally, stages of development are always referable to a given range of difficulty and familiarity of the problem area. Beyond this range, individuals commonly revert (regress) to a former stage of development.

Neither is the concept of developmental stages invalidated by the demonstration that they are susceptible to environmental influence. It is erroneous to believe that stages of intellectual development are exclusively the products of "internal ripening," and hence that they primarily reflect the influence of endogenous factors. Gesell's embryological model of development has little applicability to human development beyond the first year of life when environmental factors become increasingly more important determinants of variability in developmental outcomes. In fact, as the educational system improves, we can confidently look forward to earlier mean emergence of the various stages of cognitive development.

Determinants of Change

It is hypothesized that the combined influence of three concomitant and mutually supportive developmental trends accounts for the transition from concrete to abstract cognitive functioning. In the first place, the developing individual gradually acquires a working vocabulary of transactional or mediating terms that makes possible the more efficient juxtaposition and combination of different relatable abstractions into potentially meaningful propositions. Second, he can relate these latter propositions more readily to cognitive structure, and hence render them more meaningful, in view of his growing fund of stable, higher-order concepts and principles encompassed by and made available within that structure. A sufficient body of abstract ideas that are clear and stable is obviously necessary before he can hope efficiently to manipulate relationships between them so as to develop meaningful general propositions. The possession of a working body of inclusive concepts also makes possible the formulation of more general statements of relationship that are less tied to specific instances; greater integration of related ideas and different aspects of the same problem; the elaboration of more precise distinctions and finer differentiations; and less dependence on complete concrete–empirical data in reaching warranted inferences. Finally, it seems reasonable to suppose that after many years of practice in meaningfully understanding and manipulating relationships with the aid of concrete–empirical props, he gradually develops greater facility in performing these operations, so that eventually (after acquiring the necessary transactional and higher-order concepts) he can perform the same operations just as effectively without relying on props. The same sequence of events is seen in acquiring many other neuromuscular and cognitive skills, e.g., walking without "holding on," bicycling "without hands," speaking a foreign language without internal translation from one's mother tongue, transmitting Morse code in sentences rather than in word or letter units.

General and Specific Aspects of the Transition

It is apparent from the previous discussion that the transition from concrete to abstract cognitive functioning takes place specifically in each separate subject-matter area, and invariably presupposes a certain necessary amount of sophistication in each of the areas involved. In the more general sense of the term, however, it is possible to designate the individual's overall developmental status as "concrete" or "abstract" on the basis of an estimate of his characteristic or predominant mode of cognitive functioning. This distinction is important for two reasons: First, the individual necessarily continues to undergo the same transition from concrete to abstract cognitive functioning in each new subject matter area he encounters — even after he reaches the abstract stage of development on an overall basis. Second, once he attains this latter general stage, however, the transition to abstract cognitive functioning in unfamiliar new subject-matter areas takes place much more readily.

Thus, even though an individual characteristically functions at the abstract level of cognitive development, when he is first introduced to a wholly unfamiliar subject-matter field, he tends initially to function at a concrete-intuitive level. But since he is able to draw on various transferable elements of his more general ability to function abstractly, he passes through the concrete stage of functioning in this particular subject-matter area much more rapidly than would be the case were he still generally in the concrete stage of cognitive development. These facilitating transferable elements presumably include transactional terms, higher-order concepts, and experience in directly understanding and manipulating relationships between abstractions, i.e., without the benefit of props, which, although acquired in specific subject-matter contexts, are generally applicable to other learning situations.

Acceleration of Intellectual Development

Is it possible to accelerate children's progress through the preoperational stage or the stage of concrete logical operations by taking account of their characteristic cognitive limitations, and by providing suitably contrived experience geared to their cognitive capacity and mode of functioning? Can we, for example, train them, as Inhelder (Inhelder and Piaget, 1958) suggests, to focus on more than one aspect of a problem at a time or to acquire genuine appreciation of the concept of conservation of mass? If stages of development have any true meaning, the answer to this question can only be that although some acceleration is possible, it is necessarily limited in extent.

Suitable training can undoubtedly accelerate to some extent the rate at which the various stages of intellectual development succeed each other. Inevitably, however, maturational considerations impose a limit on such acceleration. For example, training of children in the preoperational stage to appreciate the notion of conservation of mass tends to produce an unstable understanding of this principle which is hardly equivalent to that acquired by older children. Similarly, young children who receive laboratory training in learning the principle of a teeter-totter, i.e., that the longer side from the fulcrum falls when both ends are equally weighted, fail to acquire any resistance to learning a spurious causal relationship about the operation of a teeter-totter, i.e., that the color of the blocks placed at either end is the determining factor. Older children, on the other hand, who are both cognitively more mature and have more incidental experience with teeter-totters, resist learning the spurious causal relationship (Ausubel and Schiff, 1954).

In general, therefore, transitions from one stage of development to another presuppose the attainment of a critical threshold level of capacity that is reflective, in part, of extended and cumulative experience. In addition to the operation of genic patterning factors, the necessary environmental stimulation must be forthcoming; and as children increase in age and cognitive capacity, teaching methods can place increasingly less reliance on concrete–empirical props. Also, since rate of development is partly a function of quantity and appropriateness of relevant experience, it is conceivable that suitable long-term training procedures might produce greater evidence of stable developmental acceleration than the previously reported studies of short-term training have indicated.

By suitably adapting methods of teaching to the child's level of cognitive functioning, both Bruner (1960) and Inhelder (Inhelder and Piaget, 1958) believe that it is possible to teach preschool and primary school children any subject that can be taught to adolescent students. It is quite possible, of course, that prior intuitive understanding of certain concepts during childhood could facilitate their learning and stabilize their retention when they are taught at a more formal, abstract level during adolescence. In fact, this procedure may be the most effective means of discouraging rote memorization of verbally presented propositions in the secondary school.

However, it undoubtedly overstates the case to claim that any subject can be taught to children in the preoperational stage or in the stage of concrete operations provided that the material is presented in an informal, intuitive fashion with the aid of overt manipulation or concrete–empirical props. It is readily conceivable that some topics, such as "set theory" in mathematics, can be successfully learned by fourth-grade pupils when recast in accordance with their characteristic ways of thinking and conceptualizing experience. This hardly rules out the possibility, however, that the comprehension of many other ideas presupposes a certain minimal level of life experience, cognitive maturity, and subject-matter sophistication, or that some ideas simply cannot be expressed without the use of certain higher-order abstractions. These latter kinds of concepts would be intrinsically too difficult for preschool and primary school children irrespective of the method of presentation. Moreover, even assuming that all abstract–verbal concepts could be restructured on an intuitive basis, it would be unreasonable to expect that they could all be made comprehensible to children at any age level. Although the intuitive comprehensibility of any given restructured idea is best determined empirically, it would surely be plausible on a priori grounds to expect that a certain proportion of these ideas could not be rendered understandable to typical pupils in some of the preschool and elementary grades.

Finally, I think it is necessary to temper the enthusiasm of those educators who believe that children cannot only learn everything that adults can, but also do so more efficiently. Adolescents and adults, generally speaking, have a tremendous advantage in learning any new subject matter — even if they are just as unsophisticated as young children in that particular discipline. This advantage inheres in the fact that they are able to draw on various transferable elements of their overall ability to function at an abstract–verbal level of logical operations. Hence they are able to move through the concrete–intuitive phase of intellectual functioning very rapidly; and unlike the comparably unsophisticated child, who is tied to this latter stage developmentally, they are soon able to dispense entirely with concrete–empirical props and with intuitive understandings. Research findings suggest that as long as abstract–verbal understandings are meaningfully rather than rotely acquired, they constitute a more complete, explicit, inclusive, and transferable form of knowledge than their intuitive counterparts.

In conclusion, therefore, although prior intuitive understanding of many ideas during childhood may greatly extend the primary school child's horizon of useful knowledge and facilitate the learning and stabilize the retention of these same ideas when they are taught later at a more formal and abstract level, there is little warrant for believing that children can learn everything in this manner, or that this type of learning is more efficient than the verbal–abstract learning that succeeds it. The intellectual achievement of children can only be accelerated within the limits imposed by the prevailing stage of intellectual development. These limitations cannot be transcended through experience. One can, at best, take advantage of methods that are most appropriate and effective for exploiting the existing degree of readiness.

The Relation of Conservation to Emotional and Environmental Aspects of Development

■■■ MARCEL L. GOLDSCHMID

On a theoretical level, Piaget and others have attempted to relate Piaget's theory of cognitive development to theories of personality development, and in particular to psychoanalytic theory. There is, however, very little empirical research on this relationship. In this paper, the author has attempted to determine what empirical links might be present among cognitive, affective, and environmental factors in the child's development. Piaget's concept of conservation was chosen as the cognitive variable. Affective variables consisted of the child's anxiety and his conceptualizations of his actual and ideal self. Environmental factors included peer preference for the child, teacher's view of the child, and the parents' attitudes toward childrearing. The results are discussed in relation to theoretical issues.

Piaget and his associates have provided an impressive body of data and theory describing the intellectual growth of the child (cf. Flavell, 1963; Tuddenham, 1966). While Piaget's concern has been almost exclusively with cognitive structures, he acknowledges the importance of environmental and affective factors in the child's intellectual maturation. Piaget and others have attempted to relate his theory of cognitive development to theories of personality development, particularly the psychoanalytic theory (Anthony, 1956, 1957; Odier, 1956; Piaget, 1953; Wolff, 1960). These essays have been fruitful in demonstrating, at least theoretically, the possible implications of Piaget's findings for other areas of child development. Little empirical research on the relation among different aspects of development has been carried out, however, despite its significance for a comprehensive theory of psychological maturation.

The present research represents an attempt to relate Piaget's concept of conservation to significant affective and environmental factors in the child's development. The most important cognitive change, at the end of the second or preoperational stage in Piaget's theory, is the acquisition of the "schema of conservation," that is, the emergence of more abstract concepts, such as quantity, volume, and weight, with decreasing dependence on specific attributes of the stimulus object, such as form and shape. In a previous paper (Goldschmid, 1967), both the interrelations among different areas of conservation and the relation between conservation and age, sex, IQ, MA, and vocabulary were described. Boys demonstrated a higher level of conservation than girls, and older subjects outperformed younger subjects on every conservation task. Conservation was positively correlated with IQ, MA, and verbal ability. This paper focuses on the relations between con-

• • • • • • • •

SOURCE: Adapted and abridged from *Child Development*, 39 (1968), 579–589. (With permission of the author and The Society for Research in Child Development.)

servation and (a) the child's anxiety, (b) his actual and ideal self-descriptions, (c) teacher and peer ratings of the child, and (d) the parents' attitudes toward childrearing.

Method

The Conservation Experiments

Ten experiments, modeled after Piaget and others (cf. Flavell, 1963), were developed to assess the child's level of conservation of substance, weight, continuous quantity, discontinuous quantity, number, area, distance, length, and two- and three-dimensional space. Briefly, the children had to judge whether two objects were equivalent in volume, weight, length, etc., after the form or shape of one of the two objects had been changed by some manipulation. In addition, the subjects were asked to explain their responses. A detailed description of the experiments and the procedures employed were presented previously (Goldschmid, 1967).

Three scores were derived: one to measure the child's accuracy in perceiving conservation or nonconservation, a second for the child's explanation of his response, and a third for the total of the perceptual and explanation scores. The analysis for the total score of each individual experiment, and the total scores across all ten experiments for conservation (TS), explanation (TE), and the sum of TS and TE (TT), are presented below.

The Affective and Environmental Variables

Children's Manifest Anxiety Scale (CMAS). The CMAS (Castaneda, McCandless, and Palermo, 1956; Palermo, 1959) was administered orally to each child. Scores from the Anxiety Scale and the Lie Scale were analyzed separately.

Actual and ideal self-ratings. A specially-constructed adjective checklist for children, modeled after those by Domino, Goldschmid, and Kaplan (1964), Goldschmid and Domino (1965), and Gough (1960), was administered orally to each child twice to derive his conception of his actual self ("Tell me what you are like; are you . . .") and his ideal self ("Tell me the way you would like to be; would you like to be . . ."). The seventy words, included in the checklist for their easy understanding by young children, had previously been rated independently by two judges who had reached full agreement that half of the adjectives were positive, the other half, negative. The negative and positive words were distributed randomly throughout the entire list.

The following three scores were derived from this checklist: the total number of positive (*CA*+) and negative words (*CA*−) checked for the actual self, and the difference score between the actual self and ideal self (*CD*).

Teacher's rating.   Each subject was described on the same adjective check-list by his teacher. A total score for the teacher's positive adjectives (*TA*+) and negative adjectives (*TA*−) was computed. A third score consisted of the difference between the child's actual self-rating and the teacher's rating (*TCD*).

Sociometric choice.   Here, the procedure employed by McCandless and Marshall (1957) and Moore and Updegraff (1964) was followed. Each child was asked to look at photographs of his classmates and to pick out three children in his class whom he liked the most, and the three children whom he disliked the most. In addition, he was asked to state for each classmate whether he liked him (her) or not. Entire classes, not just the experimental subjects, were asked to perform this sociometric choice to insure a reliable peer rating of the subjects in this study.

For the free choice, a score of +3 (like most) or −3 (dislike most), and for the forced choice, a score of +1 (like) or −1 (dislike) was assigned to each classmate. These scores were summed for each experimental subject and then divided by the number of peer raters, since the latter varied from class to class.

Parental Attitude Survey (PAS).   The PAS (Shoben, 1949), a measure of parents' attitudes toward childrearing methods, was administered independently to both father and mother. Three scores, reflecting the degree of dominant, ignoring, and possessive attitudes, were derived for both parents. A score for the absolute difference between father and mother for each attitude was also computed.

IQ Scores.   IQ scores based on the Pintner–Cunningham (school *E*), Otis (school *P*), and Stanford–Binet (school *L*) tests were culled from the school records.

Subjects

Conservation in the ten areas, and the emotional and environmental variables described above, were assessed in 102 children in the first and second grades in the following urban schools: (a) a public school (E): $N = 43$ (22 boys, 21 girls), mean age = 87.35 months; (b) a private school (*P*): $N = 38$ (16 boys, 22 girls), mean age = 82.16 months; (c) a school for emotionally disturbed children (*L*): $N = 21$ (17 boys, 4 girls), mean age = 109.05 months.

The subjects were from predominantly upper-middle-class (schools *P* and *L*) and lower-middle-class (school *E*) families.

Results

The means and standard deviations for both the conservation and non-cognitive variables for all three schools combined were computed. A previous comparison (Goldschmid, 1967) demonstrated no significant differences among the three schools with respect to conservation, although it should be kept in mind that the children in school L were, on the average, two years older than those in schools E and P. The scores for the noncognitive variables are equally comparable across schools, except for the teachers' ratings in school L. As would be expected, the emotionally disturbed children were given less favorable adjectival descriptions than normal subjects; consequently, the difference between the teacher's and the child's rating was also largest for school L.

The scores on the CMAS correspond closely to the norms offered by Palermo (1959), despite the fact that in the present study the CMAS was administered orally and the subjects were in first and second grades, rather than fourth, fifth, and sixth grades. The results on the PAS were generally consistent with Shoben's (1949) findings. No reliable norms have yet been established for the adjective checklist and the sociometric choice task. It should be noted, though, that the results for both the peer ratings and the children's self-descriptions were consistent across schools.

Correlations between Piagetian and non-Piagetian tasks were also computed for each school separately, but in view of the consistency of scores across schools, only the results for all subjects are presented here.

Anxiety as measured by the CMAS was not related to conservation. The scores on the Lie Scale, on the other hand, were negatively correlated with conservation. Children with a high level of conservation tend to be less reluctant to admit anxiety than low scorers.

The self-ratings on the adjective checklist did not differentiate among children with high and low conservation scores. In view of the narrow range of scores and the consistently strong preference for positive self-description, this was to be expected. At least in the context of this study, ratings of actual and ideal self by young children do not appear very useful.

When obtained from teachers, the checklist data becomes more illuminating. The teachers, in describing those children who obtained high conservation scores, chose more positive and fewer negative adjectives. Furthermore, the smaller the difference between the teacher's and child's rating — a rough index of the child's objectivity in describing himself — the higher were the conservation scores. Peers' ratings tended to parallel the teachers' ratings; subjects with higher conservation scores were preferred by their classmates to those with lower scores.

Children whose mothers had strong dominant attitudes (PAS) tended to do poorly on the conservation tasks.

While most of the correlations, even the ones that were significant, accounted for only a small portion of the variance, they nevertheless suggest meaningful and internally consistent relations among cognitive, affective, and environmental factors in the child's development.

Five variables, dominant attitudes by the mothers (DM), the number of positive adjectives ($TA+$) and negative adjectives ($TA-$) chosen by the teachers, the difference between the child's and teacher's rating (TCD), and peer preference (SCh), were included in a stepwise regression analysis in order to generate equations which might more accurately predict conservation totals than single noncognitive variables. All three equations that were developed on school E ($N = 43$) predicted the conservation totals at a statistically significant level ($p < .01$). These equations, when subjected to cross-validation on school P ($N = 38$), yielded lower, but still significant ($p < .05$) correlations.

For the normal children (schools E and P) and with respect to the non-cognitive variables, a t test revealed no significant differences between younger (mean age: 79.13, $N = 40$) and older (mean age: 90.56, $N = 41$) subjects, except for the Lie Scale of the CMAS (Older subjects achieved lower scores on the Lie Scale than younger subjects; $p < .01$). Another t test comparison between boys and girls on the same variables indicated no sex differences. Thus, children who are preferred by their peers, rated favorably by their teachers, and not dominated by their mothers tended to achieve higher conservation scores regardless of their age and sex. The present findings, furthermore, demonstrate that the age and sex differences in conservation found previously (Goldschmid, 1967) are unrelated to the noncognitive factors assessed in this study.

Further inspection indicates that IQ is significantly correlated with five of the nonconservation variables ($CD, TA+$, $TA-$, TCD, and SCh). The question arises whether conservation is related to emotional and environmental factors, at least in part, because IQ is related to both conservation (Goldschmid, 1967) and some of the noncognitive variables. To answer this question, the entire correlation matrix was recomputed with the effects of IQ partialled out. The result of this new analysis indicated that for most of the correlations the changes were negligible.

These results suggest that IQ no doubt accounts for part of the variance in the correlations between conservation and a few of the noncognitive variables (especially SCh), but overall the general trends persist even when the effects of IQ are controlled for.

Finally, two composite teacher's ratings of children in schools E and P were derived: one for ten subjects with a high conservation level, and a second for ten subjects with a low conservation level. Adjectives assigned by teachers to high scorers two or more times more frequently than to low scorers made up the composite rating for the high scorers. Conversely, adjectives attributed twice or more often to the low scorers constituted the composite rating for the low scorers. The two groups were matched on sex, age, and IQ in order to eliminate any influence these variables might have had on the teachers' preference for certain pupils. The two composite ratings indicated that: Low scorers were characterized by greater physical prowess and energy (big, healthy, noisy, quick, restless, and tall) and unsociability (bossy, cruel, rough), but were also seen as "afraid" and "silly." High scorers, on the other hand, were judged to be more passive and reflective (lazy, quiet, worrying) and more attractive (cute, good-looking, handsome) and "clever."

Discussion

Piaget's views with regard to the indissociability of cognition and affect contribute to the understanding of the relations discovered in the present study. He asserts that "affective life, like intellectual life, is a continual adaptation, and the two are not only parallel but interdependent, since feelings express the interest and value given to actions of which intelligence provides the structure" (1951). Consistent with these notions, children achieving higher conservation scores tended to possess personality characteristics typically thought of as enhancing cognitive functioning. Children with a high level of conservation tended to see themselves more objectively and were described as being more reflective. A previous study (Goldschmid, 1967) indicated the possibility that emotionally unstable or disturbed children develop conservation later than normal children of the same age, suggesting that disruptive personality characteristics may delay cognitive development.

As to the relation between cognitive and social variables, there are undoubtedly environmental conditions which serve either to enhance or inhibit development of the child's cognitive structures. In this study, for example, it was found that children who are not dominated by their mothers tend to have higher conservation scores. Complex environments, providing age-relevant competency-building experiences for the young child may lead to increased exploratory and manipulatory behaviors (R. W. White, 1959) which very likely accompany the early acquisition of the conservation schema. A generally more successful and adaptive interchange with the environment would likely ensue, producing more differentiated understanding of self and others as well as the object world. Piaget (1952b) expresses similar intent by defining intelligence as adaptation to the environment in which processes of assimilation and accommodation play a significant role.

Hence, one might expect children with relatively high conservation scores also to maintain (conserve) a more consistent view of themselves and their social relations, perhaps enhancing thereby their interpersonal attractiveness. This expectation finds tentative support in the fact that children with a high level of conservation also tend to have a more objective self-image, are described more favorably by their teachers, and are preferred by their peers.

The results of this study do not challenge Piaget's age-dependent theory of cognitive development, but they do demonstrate significant individual differences in conservation within a given age group. The particular relations that were found suggest specific aspects of the child's personality and his environment which coexist with conservation and possibly foster its development. It is hoped that further research will serve to explicate the experiential conditions responsible for the development of conservation and, more generally, contribute to the development of a comprehensive theory of maturation through clarifying the relations among different facets of child development.

Early Childhood Education ▌▌

The theory of cognitive development is comprehensive in scope. It extends from the earliest reflexes of the neonate to the elaborations and nuances of scientific thought. Since development is essentially lawful, and in view of the dependence on the very earliest experiences of later cognitive growth, it is no accident that Piaget's statements have received wide attention in the field of early childhood education. Personnel in this field have long recognized the unique opportunities for young children's learning which arise in an informal setting where the child is presented with challenges to his thinking. As the articles in this section suggest, Piaget's concept of stage development does not conflict with the time-honored approach based on individual unstructured learning, but it does give the teacher greater insight into the child's degree of understanding of what he learns.

New Views on Intellectual Development in Early Childhood Education

▬▬ MILLIE ALMY

After describing Piaget's stages in terms of an information processing view of intelligence, and the principles governing transition from one stage to the next, Dr. Almy explores new trends in curriculum development which have emerged in response to this view.

Americans, according to anthropologists, are committed to change, to the notion that what is new, or at least different, is probably better. The pendulum of popular interest swings in wide arcs as people espouse first one, then another idea.

Psychologists and educators like their contemporaries are pendulum prone, though they do not always swing in the same direction at the same time. During the years I have spent as an educator and developmental

••••••••
SOURCE: A. Harry Passow and Robert R. Leeper, eds., *Intellectual Development: Another Look* (Washington: Association for Supervision and Curriculum Development, 12–26.) Copyright ©1964 by the Association. (With permission of the author and the publisher.)

psychologist I have noted three major swings beginning with the habit training and behavior inventories of the 'thirties. Next came a considerable preoccupation with the social and emotional aspects of development and, to a lesser extent, concern with the personal and subjective aspects of child behavior. Now interest centers on the intellectual aspects of development.

Concern with the cognitive or, as it is often phrased, with concept formation, is widely manifest in educational circles these days. Visit one kindergarten in which the children are playing with blocks, another in which a painting of a dinosaur is the big attraction, one in which the children are coloring flags for Washington's Birthday, or even one in which the curriculum is built around reading readiness workbooks. Each of the teachers will likely tell you his program is designed to build concepts. "Readiness" is no longer a fashionable term.

To catch up with psychological jargon is simple. Yet the challenge to education, implicit in emerging theories of intellectual development, cannot be met by mere lip service. It will demand teachers who are well-informed and thoughtful, and who understand as much about the ways children think as they do about the subjects they teach. Furthermore, the demands on early childhood education will be at least as great, perhaps greater, than for any other level of education. For it is at that level that children acquire and learn to process basic information that can either further or impede their later progress, that may indeed either enhance or stultify their intellectual powers.

Intelligence as Information Processing

Several popular definitions of intelligence have been stated, such as "the capacity to profit from experience," or even, "that which the intelligence test tests." Such statements imply something more global and more fixed than does the presently emerging view that intelligence is "the variety of ways an individual has available for processing or organizing incoming information." Such a view allows for a more adequate analysis of the varieties of thinking that underlie intelligent behavior, and of the role that experience plays in their development.

So many psychologists have contributed to this view of intelligence as information processing that one hesitates to begin to name them, although Guilford, Osgood, Hebb, and Bruner come immediately to mind. None of these has been so concerned with the development of these processes as has Piaget, although most of his theoretical formulations have been put in other terms. Since Piaget himself has speculated that information theory and game theory might provide a needed common language for those interested in various aspects of child development, it is not inappropriate for me to translate some of his concepts into these terms. In so doing I shall aim for common clarity with an emphasis on what I believe to be the implications of his theory rather than attempting to elucidate the theory precisely. Those who have struggled with Piaget's theory will, I hope, bear with me. Those who are less familiar will perhaps be grateful for an over-simplification. As someone has said, Piaget's writing is often difficult, perhaps because he does not wish to obscure the great darkness of his subject.

Essentially the view of intelligence that I shall present says that intelligence, rather than being fixed by genetic factors at birth, emerges as it is nurtured. Each stage of development carries with it possibilities for the acquisition of new abilities, new ways of processing information. Unless each of these abilities is sufficiently exercised as it emerges, it will not develop fully and it will contribute little if at all to the demands of the next stage.

Piaget's theory encompasses the development of information processing from the infant's earliest sucking, looking, and eventual reaching and grasping, to the adolescent's ability to manipulate logical propositions mentally. It is a theory wherein the person's grasp of the ideas encountered in algebra and geometry, chemistry, and physics represents the top level of a hierarchy of experiences beginning at birth. Along one dimension the person has moved from a completely subjective view of the world, to one that is increasingly objective. On another dimension, the concrete–abstract, he has moved from "a world of things present to a world of things possible."

The models Piaget has chosen to represent thought processes are the "operations" of logic and mathematics. Psychologists and educators who know Piaget only from such early volumes as *Language and Thought* (1957a) or *Judgment and Reasoning* (1928) may be shocked to find the discursive musings of the children in those volumes replaced in the *Growth of Logical Thinking* (1958) with experiments in which the child manipulates materials and both his actions and his comments are summarized in statements written in symbolic logic. We are not accustomed to thinking of children's thoughts in terms of P's and Q's, implications, and disjunctions. This child seems a different child, largely because Piaget and his collaborator, Inhelder, focus so exclusively on the concrete–abstract dimension of his thought, making reference to the subjective–objective dimension only to explain or clarify difficulties in the other dimension.

The present theory, then, takes explicit account only of the kind of thought that is clearly reality-adjusted. This theory deals primarily with the ways the person gains factual knowledge and the ways he orders facts, but not with the ways he feels about or values them.

Patterns of Action

Perhaps we can also say that the theory applies best in those instances in which the developing child's basic needs for emotional security are being adequately met. Piaget acknowledges the interaction between emotion and intellect, but his is not a dynamic theory in the usual sense. Wolff (1960), in a comparison of the developmental psychologies of Freud and Piaget, has pointed out that Piaget is not concerned with long-range forces or drives corresponding to physiologic or homeostatic imbalances, but rather with short-range forces involving a need to function. Similarly, Bruner (1959) has indicated that Piaget's theory of cognition will not be complete until he integrates into it the goals for which people strive. J. McV. Hunt (1961) on the other hand has suggested that Piaget's notions about the development of cognition can appropriately be integrated into emerging theories of motivation. Piaget's children, like Berlyne's rats and Harlow's monkeys, are intrinsically curious and active. They respond to the strange, the unfamiliar, and the incongruous in ways consonant with current models of cognitive dissonance, incongruity, or imbalance. Piaget himself (Tanner and Inhelder, 1960), has suggested that such diverse views on affective and personality development as those held by psychoanalysts such as Erikson, and Bowlby, and the anthropologist, Margaret Mead, could be synthesized with his (Piaget's) theory of intellectual development. Such a synthesis would involve the idea that the child acts on information derived from interpersonal situations and involving emotions and feelings in much the same way that he handles information conveyed from physical or impersonal sources. In either case the strategy is to obtain maximum information or gratification with minimum expenditure of cognitive or psychic pain.

Whether or not Piaget's formulations figure extensively in the emerging theories of psychology, it seems likely that motivation and cognition, emotion and intellect will eventually receive less disparate treatment than in the past. Perhaps when this happens we can at last put some specific meanings into the slippery concept of the "whole child," long used so glibly by so many educators.

For an elucidation of Piaget's views, however, it seems most feasible to look at the cognitive child, thinking of him as a youngster brought up by parents who are reasonably loving, who have some appreciation for his growing powers, and who have thoughtfully provided him with brothers and sisters with whom he is only moderately rivalrous. We shall consider him to be motivated at least as much by his own pleasure in functioning, his own satisfaction in solving problems or resolving contradictions as he is by his mother's smiles and pats, his father's praise, or the "goods" his teacher may write on his paper.

This child is born with receptors that bring him information, initially meaningless, about the sights, the sounds, the tastes of the world around him. Similarly he is endowed with motor equipment that soon enables him not only to focus visually but even to turn his head toward an object, a face, a sound. Gradually his hands follow the lead of his eyes, and impressions from visual and auditory modalities are coordinated with tactual information.

From the standpoint of developing intelligence, he may be regarded as storing information in patterns of action. Piaget calls these sensorimotor schemata, and sees them increasing in complexity and relatedness throughout the first eighteen months or so of life. The infant grasps the rattle that is thrust in front of him and brings it to his mouth. Vary the position of the rattle, place it further from his reach, change its size and its shape and the infant, finding that his original pattern is not adequate, varies it, in Piaget's terms, accommodating himself to it. In the process, the action patterns or schemata are modified. Again, in Piaget's terms, the information from the environment is assimilated into the schemata. Through an intricate series of such accommodations and assimilations the child becomes increasingly facile at manipulating his world, and the world in a sense becomes increasingly predictable for him. Indeed one of the landmarks of the period comes when the child's ability to apprehend an object, presumably through having explored it visually and manipulatively in a variety of settings, enables him to recognize it even after it has momentarily disappeared from view. This is the beginning of the ability to "conserve," to comprehend the essential stability or invariance of many aspects of the surrounding environment.

For a considerable part of the infancy period the child's intelligence reveals itself primarily in what he does to the things he encounters. There is relatively little evidence of planning or anticipating. Yet as his actions become better and better adapted, as his world is consequently enlarged, as he attempts more and more to imitate its aspects, it appears that he no longer needs to operate on it so directly. He remembers previous actions and he applies them mentally. Thus he enters into what Piaget has called representative intelligence. By now he has to some extent accommodated his own vocal productions to those he has heard around him and is beginning to assimilate a vocabulary. He has labels for some of his own actions. Such labels, and the ability to acquire more, tremendously speed up the rate at which he can store information and of course also speed up the process of information retrieval.

Let us pause at this point, marking the place where human intelligence departs from simian, and note three important aspects of the theory described thus far.

First, this is more than a maturation theory. The increasing complexity and adaptibility of the action patterns are dependent, not only on growth, but on the child's opportunities to act on something.

Second, what a child assimilates, what gets incorporated into the repertoire of action patterns in part depends on the patterns he already has available. Mothers recognize this when they match their expectations for independent spoon feeding to the way the baby grabs for the spoon. Similarly, parental attempts to teach baby a new word are usually contingent on the sounds he is already making, and most successful when the match between the baby's repertoire and the new syllables is fairly close.

Third, new patterns do not emerge full-blown and perfect. They are spontaneously practiced as the child plays in his crib, his pen, his bath. You have heard infants babbling a repertoire of sounds that are almost but not quite English, and the slightly older child putting himself to sleep going over all the words he knows.

In summary, the infant does not maximize his intellective power unless he is exposed to a rather wide variety of stimuli, unless the opportunities presented by these stimuli are relatively well matched by the complexity of the action patterns the child already has available, and unless these opportunities are followed by much time for spontaneous play.

Using Labels for Experience

Once he has begun to use language, the infant, now a toddler, enters into a new stage of development, during which his ways of thinking become progressively more like those of the adult. Partly, this is a result of the child's becoming more and more adept at acquiring labels for experience, and also at matching new experiences to already available labels, that is, at forming concepts. Partly this progress comes from an increasing ability to isolate particular aspects of experience and to deal with the relationships between those aspects mentally rather than directly. The toddler who tries the "kitty" label on all small furry creatures gradually takes note of the long ears and short tails of some of them and applies a new label. He has created a new category or schema for storing or classifying information. What labels do two- or three-year-olds attach to the first white rat, the first guinea pig or hamster they encounter? Note that their classification is concrete in that they appear to match the unknown instance against their recollection of other specific instances of kitty or bunny. And it appears that, for a considerable time, "animal" is a second name applicable to cats, rabbits, guinea pigs, and so on, rather than an overarching category into which many instances can be put.

Just as the young child acquires labels for the objects in the environment, so he also learns to label their properties and attributes. He notes color, shapes, sizes, textures, sounds, movement tendencies, and so on; but the concepts of properties apart from the objects implied in words like big and small, light and heavy, up and down, behind, beside, and before are complicated by the child's tendency to judge them more from their reference to himself than their reference to each other. Have you ever tried to explain a procedure for lining up to take turns on a slide to a group of young three-year-olds or inexperienced four-year-olds? Initially, Johnny's acceptance of the idea that placing himself always behind Dick and in front of Tom will bring his turn in orderly fashion is much more a matter of faith in the adult making the arrangement than in his own understanding of it.

Gradually, however, as the child checks his view of this and other situations with their actual outcomes, he modifies his thinking to obtain a better fit with outer reality. While at an earlier period he accommodated his actions to the size and shape of the objects he encountered, now he is accommodating thought patterns to more and more dimensions of his experience. He not only assimilates the new information into already established categories but creates new categories and gradually develops greater flexibility in categorizing.

The way young children deal with the problem of objects that float and objects that sink is illustrative. Although we might assume that young children with a moderate amount of experience with water play could predict adequately whether or not certain familiar objects placed in water would sink or float, many of them are surprisingly inaccurate. They have some notions about the objects but not about the objects in the water. We can question them about why they think a particular object will behave as they have predicted, seeking not for a scientific explanation but rather for an indication of which aspects of the objects they were attending. The young children (threes and fours) note whether the objects are large or small, or simply observe that an object goes up or down or that it "has to." As they grow older, the weight dimension of the objects is noted. The old notion that big objects float and little objects sink no longer accommodates adequately to the incoming information. The big–little schemata is gradually transformed into a fourfold categorization involving big–heavy and big–light objects as contrasted with little–heavy and little–light objects. Still later a notion of relative weight is assimilated into the thought pattern.

Arrival at the ability to deal simultaneously with relationships between two aspects of an object is preceded by the development of a new kind of conservation. Just as the child's encounters with his environment in the sensorimotor period led him to the discovery of the constancy of objects, so in the period of "concrete operations" he comes to the discovery of the invariance, or constancy, of an increasing number of *aspects* of objects. From these discoveries he eventually arrives at a grasp of the mathematical idea that quantity is not changed when a set of objects is partitioned into sub-groups and the physical idea that mass or substance does not change when the shape or appearance of an object is transformed. Piaget's tests for demonstrating whether or not a child has achieved this kind of conservation are fairly well known. One of them involves confronting the child with a ball of clay that is pulled out or flattened, or broken in small pieces, and testing to find out whether he thinks the amount of clay changes as its appearance changes. Another test involves establishing with the child the identity in number of two rows of objects — say cubes —then bunching one row together, or spreading it apart to test whether the child thinks quantity changes with change in configuration. Another test involves establishing identity between two amounts of liquid and then testing to see whether the child retains that identity when he sees the liquid in one vessel poured into another of different shape.

It is only recently that these tests have been tried with American children. To a considerable extent Piaget's findings have been verified. In a study in which I am currently involved, we tested some 330 children in kindergarten, first and second grade. In a middle-class school only nine per cent of kindergarteners were able to conserve a number of blocks and a given amount of liquid. At first grade this per cent rose to 32 and at second grade to 48. This gives some idea of the gradualness of the transition. In a lower-class school the trends were similar but the transition was much less rapid and only 23 per cent of the second graders in this school were able to conserve consistently.

More important than the mere fact of transition is the question of its meaning. To what extent is the ability to conserve related to or facilitating of the child's thinking in other areas?

The practical dilemma of the child who is not yet conserving can be illustrated by the case of the youngster who had been asked to count five bottles by her teacher when a visitor arrived. The visitor suggested that the counting continue. The child had counted the bottles going from left to right. When the teacher asked her to repeat the process she pointed to the right-hand bottle. The child was baffled, could not do it, finally in desperation turned to the left-hand bottle, named it "one," the next "two," and so on. Then the teacher further confused her by saying, "Now put the five away." This child had no notion of number as a concept apart from specific objects.

Our own research indicates that children who conserve early are also advanced on other maturity measures including a reading readiness test. They also do better on a test that purports to be a test of logical abilities, the Stencil Design Test. Further analysis of our data may shed additional light on the nature of these and other relationships. Longitudinal study of the kindergarten children is designed to indicate whether early conservers have any marked advantages over other children.

Piaget associates arrival at the ability to conserve amount or quantity with the ability to perform a variety of logical operations heretofore impossible. These include not only the addition and subtraction of mathematics but also the operations involved in constructing logical classes. While the child, as we have suggested, has long been categorizing his experience so that he has an awareness of objects belonging together, or a common general name adhering to a large number of instances, it is only now that he begins to be able to hold a large category constant while he manipulates subcategories. Thus he recognizes that such a general class as say "animal," can be sub-divided, for example, into land animals and sea animals, and that the totality of all animals will exceed that of either the land or the sea animals. Similarly he can conceive the same general class "animal" as made up of vertebrates and invertebrates.

Increasing flexibility also appears in the child's ability to comprehend mentally certain other relationships. For example, knowing that John is taller than Jim but shorter than George, he can arrive at the notion that Jim is the shortest or George the tallest without needing to see all three together. In somewhat similar fashion he can grasp the reciprocal nature of a left-hand relationship, understanding that a person who is a foreigner in one country is also a native in another, and so on.

Up to this point concrete operations, according to the Piaget theory, have been in formation. Beyond this, they are applied to more and more areas of experience. The turning point comes for most children around the ages of seven or eight years. Consequently, it is appropriate to regard the early childhood years, encompassing nursery school, kindergarten, first and second grades, as the years when thought is in transition between sensorimotor and concrete operations.

In other words, there is a hierarchy from the period when the sensorimotor schemata become integrated with the first words, through the period of early childhood when so much basic information is being stored and classified, and when new possibilities for classification develop so rapidly, into the period of middle and later childhood when concrete operational thinking facilitates a different grasp of reality, and finally to the time when formal operational thinking opens up the realm of possibility, and thinking can deal effectively in relationships among abstractions.

Now it is appropriate to review the principles discussed earlier when we considered the transition from infancy to toddlerhood.

First, more than maturation is involved. The increasing complexity and adaptability of the child's thought are contingent on his opportunities to think about something, to have appropriate new experiences.

Second, what a child assimilates, what gets incorporated into his repertoire of thought processes, what challenges him to reorganize or reclassify information is in part dependent on the processes and the systems he already has available. As one experimenter has put it, "The possibility of inducing a cognitive reorganization depends on the child's already available schemata. If he already has a structure which approaches the given notion the probability of the desired reorganization is high, whereas if he is still far from the notion the chances are small . . ." (Smedslund, 1961a).

Third, abstract patterns of thinking, like concrete patterns, do not emerge full-blown but are rather the product of a series of encounters with ideas in which the child's thought has accommodated itself to new relationships, and the ability to comprehend these has been somewhat assimilated into the repertoire of thought processes so that they can be applied more and more widely.

Views of Intellectual Development

How do these views of intellectual development differ from those that have been more generally held?

They would substitute for the psychometric notions of an intelligence sufficiently fixed by heredity so that a child's position relative to his peers should remain constant throughout the period of development, the notion of a natural ordinal scale of intelligence. The position a child had reached on such a scale would indicate the intellectual progress he had already made, but prediction of development from that point forward would have to be predicated on knowledge of the experiences in store for him.

Implicit in such a notion is the possibility of some degree of acceleration of the rate of intellectual development. If the existence of a natural ordinal scale can be established, then the way is open to measure the effects of varying kinds of experience on the rate of transition from one point on the scale to the next.

It may well be that interactions between perceptual and verbal experience, in the period when concepts are being formed, have considerable to do with the kind of general intellective ability the child displays later on. Further evidence of this may come from studies of enrichment for culturally deprived children whose general intellective ability is so often extremely low. These youngsters at the preschool level do not appear so much to lack perceptual experience as verbal labels to apply to it. On the basis of my own observations, I think it likely when nursery school teachers make a deliberate effort to help the child with such labeling, conceptualization may speed up considerably.

Hunt (1961) has described the possibilities in the new views on intellectual development:

> . . . it might be feasible to discover ways to govern the encounters that children have with their environments, especially during the early days of their development, to achieve a substantially faster rate of intellectual development and a substantially higher intellectual capacity. Moreover, inasmuch as the optimum rate of intellectual development would mean also self-directing interest and curiosity and genuine pleasure in intellectual activity, promoting intellectual development properly need imply nothing like the grim urgency which has been associated with "pushing" children. Furthermore, these procedures, insofar as they tended to maximize each child's potential for intellectual development would not decrease individual differences in intellectual capacity as assessed by tests but would increase them.

Hunt goes on to indicate that to discover effective ways of governing children's environmental encounters would require a tremendous amount of research, and that once those were found the task of changing childrearing practices and educational procedures would be Herculean.

Research that can throw light on some of the questions raised by the new theories is already under way. Numerous attempts to change educational procedures at the first and second grade levels, and to a lesser extent in kindergarten and nursery school, are in progress. If interest in the early childhood years continues, and if educational experimentation at that level involves sufficient awareness of the repercussions it may have on the development of children's thinking at later levels, future historians may refer to the 1960s as the beginning of the renaissance of early childhood education. Nursery and kindergarten education will emerge from the doldrums of the past ten or fifteen years and assume an importance equal to or perhaps even greater than first and second grades. In any event, it seems clear that education in the early childhood years can become more fruitful than is often the case at the present time.

Trends in Experimentation

It may be profitable to examine present curricular experimentation in early childhood in the light of the theory of intellectual development presented here. Unfortunately, almost none of the experimentation familiar to me includes provision for long-term follow-up, or adequate study of comparable children who were not involved in the experimental programs. Without such provision, present experimentation will contribute little to the understanding of intellectual development.

One trend in experimentation is to revive the use of an earlier system of instruction. The widespread interest in Montessori materials and methods is perhaps the best illustration. In many respects Montessori's ideas run parallel to those of Piaget. But questions of whether the materials provide sufficient diversity for adequate concept formation, whether imagination is given free enough rein, and whether sufficient attention is given to social and interpersonal concepts all need investigation.

A second trend, and one that seems very promising in some of its manifestations, involves making a cognitive analysis of the content of a given curriculum. On the basis of such analysis enriching opportunities are provided. The teacher's customary ways of working with the children do not change. How successful such ventures are seems to depend on the teacher's abilities to infer from the children's comments and other behavior the level of their understanding. For example in a program for so-called socially disadvantaged four-year-olds, a teacher, who was attempting to show some of the children the possibilities in block building, discovered that the word "wall" had no meaning for them. Moving from the block construction to the wall of the room she asked them to tell her what this was. They said, "paint." In somewhat similar fashion she discovered that for them "animal" was not even a second name for a horse, let alone a category in which horse might be put. Similarly a parakeet was not a bird. When teachers become aware of the hierarchy of experiences that are involved in concept formation, they are not so inclined to think that a child has a concept because he has been exposed to some examples of it. They learn to provide opportunities for him to demonstrate his understanding. They learn to use open-ended questions to find out where a child is in his thinking, and to reserve the more pointed, leading questions for the instances in which they can assume his understanding and want to reinforce it by having him make a correct response.

Another trend in curriculum experimentation involves attempts to break down specific disciplines into their component parts, and to match the learning of these to the developing intellectual abilities of the children. An especially happy example of this, according to reports, is the mathematics curriculum devised by Dienes in England. He has designed a set of materials, blocks of varying kinds, abacuses and so on, with which children in the infant school (kindergarteners and first graders in our system) can teach themselves the basic mathematical concepts. Teach themselves, that is, provided they have a teacher who understands how children think. Such a teacher never tells the child that he is right or wrong, but does provide him apparatus that enables him to make his own discoveries and to correct his own mistakes. In such situations the child moves at his own pace and is rewarded by his increasing mastery. This is exactly what Piaget's theory suggests should happen and appears to be an ideal way to enhance intellectual power.

In this country current experimentation involves not only mathematics and reading, but science, economics, linguistics, and foreign languages. Fortunately, as far as I know, no one has attempted to experiment in all these areas at the same time, with the same children. Yet the fact that there are so many different approaches to young children in so many different areas of the curriculum raises some important questions so far as the nature of intellectual development is concerned.

The problem is illustrated by the current experimentation in elementary science carried on by Robert Karplus. Karplus, who is himself a physicist, is attempting to teach first-graders some of the vocabulary and the concepts that are basic to modern science. In doing this he has children identify and describe objects and their properties, sort and match them on the basis of those properties, count them, measure them and so on. Clearly these activities involve mathematics, reading and language as well as science. Clearly some of them are as appropriate to kindergarten as to first grade, and all of them seem to have at least as much to do with the development of logical thinking as with science.

If the early childhood period is to capitalize more effectively on the learning and thinking propensities of children, more attention needs to be given to the question of which learnings are basic to later intellectual understanding in a particular area of the school curriculum and which are also generalizable to other areas.

Both current experimentation in schools and experimental studies of concept formation suggest that with superior teaching, children's understanding in a particular subject area or at least their ability to use vocabulary appropriately, can be considerably accelerated. Yet the net effect of such acceleration on intellectual development needs careful study. Some provocative work on Piaget concepts of conservation done by a Scandinavian psychologist, Smedslund (1961c), and a somewhat similar earlier investigation by Ausubel and Schiff (1954) suggest that such acceleration sometimes results in what may be called pseudo-concepts. The child knows the answers only under conditions similar to those in which he learned them. Vary the conditions and he varies his answers. In contrast, the concepts acquired when the child is more mature tend to be stable and can be applied appropriately in many different situations.

It seems doubtful, therefore, that early childhood education programs that are narrowly focused or designed primarily for acceleration in a particular area will have much beneficial effect on later intellectual development. On the contrary, there is considerable reason to believe that each level of the hierarchy of intellectual development serves its own purposes and contributes uniquely to the next level.

One aspect of the early childhood period so far not considered here is imagination. The young child's lack of clear-cut, logically consistent categories for information may hamper his thinking in certain respects, but it also frees him to structure his world as he pleases. The color cone so carefully designed to teach him to deal with serial relationships can be a tree to embellish his block building, or a place to hang his cowboy hat, or a roll of telephone cable to carry in his truck. He can take it apart and use the pieces for food, or as parts of a necklace, or as spare tires. Just how such free-ranging, playful thought relates itself to mature adult thinking is not very clear, though it is obvious that the highly intelligent adult who solves complex problems or arrives at new syntheses is by no means limited to the logical thinking described by Piaget. He muses, wonders, glimpses analogies, gets caught up in fantasy in ways not very different from those revealed by the young child when he plays or paints or chants. Of course, unlike the child, the adult can readily check the logic of the eventual outcome of his thought.

Perhaps metaphorical thought is too personal, too idiosyncratic to be nurtured in any particular way. Nevertheless, it is reassuring that current research in creativity and divergent thinking is beginning to move into the period of early childhood. Certainly no program intended to promote effective intellectual functioning in young children can overlook the importance of imagination in young children's thinking. Nor should it overlook the fact that the child's notion of play may differ from that of the adult. Indeed to plan only for the kind of play that the adult sees as a means to a particular end may be to stultify the initiative and interest that are essential to learning.

The point is illustrated by the four-year-old in an enrichment program in which the teacher, after noting that the child had successfully completed one puzzle, commented that he had learned that one well and inquired whether he would like to learn to do another one. The child, intent on his own purposes, replied, "No, but I'd like to play with it."

We come back thus to the cognitive child of our introduction. He is active, curious, interested; yet he is not completely manipulable. He has his own ways of thinking, his own ways of viewing the world. Whether or not he changes these ways depends only in part on what or whom he encounters. Change is equally dependent on what he thinks or feels he has to gain personally from his encounters.

New views on the nature of intellectual development open up new possibilities for influencing children's thinking, for guiding their encounters with the world in ways that will give them an increasingly better command over it. Such views need not, as some educators have feared, mean so exclusive a preoccupation with the intellect that other aspects of the child's being are necessarily neglected. Rather to the extent that teaching of this sort is based on understanding of the developing child and of his thinking and is able to free the child's intellect, it should also free him to be a more effective person.

Finding the Clue to Children's Thought Processes

■■■ ANNEMARIE ROEPER / IRVING SIGEL

The qualitative differences between adult and child thought delineated by Piaget may be responsible for some unexpected reactions on the part of children to commonplace events, and for the excessive difficulty adults may encounter in trying to communicate their explanations of these occurrences. Familiarity with Piaget's developmental stages may help the teacher to resolve some of these difficulties by identifying with the child's thought processes, and may point up teaching methods for developing better communication.

For centuries people have been both amused and impressed by children's remarks and observations. Nothing is more popular than the quotation "out of the mouths of babes." Nursery school educators are familiar with such remarks as "I know there are monsters in outer space, because I saw them on television," or "The whale is going to eat me," or "I see your Daddy," meaning the teacher's husband. But also, "I have a shadow, because light cannot shine through a thing, except for glass," or "Infinity is more than anything else."

Adults may chuckle at these childish expressions of foolishness or wisdom, but children are deeply convinced of their conclusions. This becomes obvious to anybody who has ever tried to change a child's mind about something he deeply believes in. The little boy, who knows there are monsters in outer space, may suffer from real fears. But much as he would like to be relieved of them, he will not accept the adult correction of his concept. Why not? Is it that the adults lack the clue to his reasoning? Is it that we do not know by what route he has arrived at his conclusion and therefore cannot bring any argument that will contradict his thinking? Perhaps we cannot prove anything to a child according to his own logic until we can understand his thought processes. Perhaps in this case we can

• • • • • • • •
SOURCE: *Young Children*, 21 (1966), 335–349. (With permission of the author and *Young Children*.)

only offer our protection from the monsters or get him to accept our thinking by virtue of our authority, not by our ability to convince him. Possibly we are not sharing a language of thought, and if this is true, it would constitute a serious lack of communication between adult and child that would pervade every area of contact. Until we find an answer to this fundamental question, our intellectual communication with children will continue to be based on trial and error rather than on active mutual understanding. Through advances in psychology we have learned to identify with the child's feeling. Through learning about his cognitive style, we may understand his "thoughts."

This article is concerned with an exploration of the following questions:

1. Do children actually have a different method of thinking?
2. What is their method?
3. Do all children use the same method?
4. Does children's style of thinking follow a definite sequence of development until it reaches the stage of abstract thinking used by adults?
5. Does each child reach this point only as he matures or can this process be influenced, that is, accelerated or slowed down, by outside factors?

We believe that the answers to these questions will give us some insight into:

— Children's reactions to daily life situations
— Unexpected emotional responses in children
— Methods of daily communication with the young child
— The child's approach to academic learning
— Ways in which to predict learning ability
— Ways in which to support learning ability
— Timing of teaching
— Methods of teaching
— Choice of subject matter in teaching
— Other aspects of teacher training
— Other aspects of parent education

We will begin with an example showing how different "intellectual conversations" may influence children's reactions to an experience: John's family owns a puppy. John is about four years old. Blacky has been his constant companion and is being referred to as Blacky Jones, just as he himself is known as Johnny Jones. One day the family car, parked on a hill, rolls backward and kills the puppy, who was sitting behind it. John is heartbroken. His mother tries to make him feel better, explaining that it was an accident. Someone forgot to pull the brakes, and so, the car, rolling backward, ran over Blacky and killed him. Blacky should not have been sitting behind the car. When mother sees that John is still very unhappy, she tells him that they may be able soon to get another dog just like Blacky.

How well does John understand what his mother is trying to tell him? How well is he equipped to understand the meaning of this experience?

Does John know what death means? Does he know what life means? How can he arrive at these concepts? Is everything that moves alive? Then the car that killed Blacky must be alive also and must have decided to do it. The car might want to kill him, John, too if he did something that was against the rules. Does John understand that human beings can only produce human beings? Or does he think Blacky Jones is as much a member of his family as he is? In that case, if he (John) was run over, would his parents soon get a new boy and forget him? How much do we know of his real thoughts and concepts?

One can find enormous variation in children's reactions to similar situations:

1. John may be deeply convinced that Blacky is a true member of the family, that the car is alive and therefore may decide to run over him also, and that his parents then might easily replace him. Thus the incident would create not only feelings of grief over his loss, but also strong fear of personal rejection, since he identifies completely with the dog. He feels great anxiety in addition to his grief.
2. John may have come to no conclusions, one way or another, about the identity of Blacky and of the car. (This is rare and the fact that it is rare signifies an important matter to be discussed more fully later, namely, that the child as a rule feels compelled to solve problems in some way. He wants to master his surroundings. He may therefore more likely arrive at a wrong conclusion than at no conclusion.)
3. John may believe the true and false at the same time (without being disturbed about it), leaning more toward one concept than the other depending on his frame of mind. He might feel at one moment that Blacky is his brother, while at the same time he may be aware that this is not true. His feelings also would vacillate.
4. John may have a true understanding of the situation. This would mean that he realizes Blacky was only a pet in the home — one who was loved but who was not identified with him as a person in any way. He also knows, then, that the car is not alive, that it ran over the dog by accident, and that there was no purpose behind the incident. In this case, he can view the incident realistically and concentrate his feelings where they actually belong, namely, in grief over the loss of his dog.

Why do we encounter this great variety of reactions? Again we find ourselves at a loss for an explanation, because we are only able to observe the end results of a thought process, not the road the child travels to arrive at his conclusions. In order to understand what the child thinks or why he thinks the way he does, we must find out how he thinks and what methods he uses.

Piaget, the Swiss psychologist, has done a great deal of research for many years to find the answers to these questions. Other psychologists have recently become interested in this area of investigation and have checked Piaget's work by repeating his experiments as well as elaborating on them. The results of these investigations are, of course, well known, but they have not generally been applied to our specific inquiry.

Is the infantile method of thinking different from the adult? Does the ability for logical thought develop in a predetermined order? Will the conclusions the child arrives at change according to the different stages he reaches during this process? Piaget answers these questions in the affirmative, and these contentions have been validated by Flavell (1963), Hunt (1961), Elkind (1961b), and Lovell (1961a), and by many others. There seems no doubt that the child's growth in thinking ability follows a certain predetermined sequence and that he cannot skip any of the developmental steps involved.

What is the predetermined sequence in which the child's capacity for logical thought grows? According to Piaget, this begins with the so-called preoperational stage within which the child goes through several predetermined steps until he reaches the operational stage, which is the ability of the adult to think in the abstract.

One basic prerequisite for abstract thinking is the ability to classify. How does a child attack this task? Here again he goes through different steps within the preoperational stage. In the beginning he is unable to use any significant criteria in order to put things into classification. Piaget, in his book, *The Early Growth of Logic in the Child*, uses the following example: A young child is asked, "What is a mother?" He may answer, "A mother is a lady who cooks supper." Or, to use our example, "Is a dog your brother?" may be answered by "Yes, because he lives in the same house." In other words, this child is not yet able to solve many of his daily problems intellectually because he does not have the mental tools that are necessary.

The next step shows a little more organization. A child is given a variety of different colored geometrical forms and told to put together those forms that are alike. He may put all red triangles in a row, then when he runs out of red triangles, add red circles, and when he runs out of red circles, add blue ones. He is able to use one single classification — namely the alikeness of the red triangles. Then forgetting his original criterion, he adds the red circles, and when there are no more red ones, again changing the criterion, he adds blue circles, which have nothing in common with the original red triangles. Yet this child has kept a significant criterion in mind and has applied it to several objects, namely, the alikeness of form or color, but he will move from one classification to another and forget the original classification.

This child is still not able to understand the story of Blacky. He might still believe that Blacky is his brother because he lives in the same house if this is his criterion for being a member of the family. If, however, it has been pointed out to him through various examples that people's brothers can only be people, he might find the correct solution by applying this realistic concept to his own situation rather than the incorrect concept he used before. In other words, the criterion has changed. "Put those things that are red together" can be the same as "put those things that are people together," rather than "those that live in the same house." He knows what people are from experience, just as he has learned what red is. This does not mean, of course, that he now understands family relationships or has acquired the skills to figure them out.

Bruner, in *The Process of Education,* maintains that children are often able to function in specific areas, such as mathematics, on a level of thinking above that which they are capable of in general. The children could collect certain geometrical forms on the basis of color but could not translate this classification to other life situations unless the criterion was specifically pointed out. They were taught one criterion and understood the concept in the particular context. This is an example of single classification.

The next step is the understanding of multiple classification and its application. The child at this stage has learned to put things together according to two or more criteria. He realizes that a geometrical figure can be both red and square. He can now put all the red squares with each other, or with forms that are square, or forms that are red, and can separate them using the same criteria.

John now can classify Blacky with his family when referring to all living beings in his home, but not when human beings are the criterion. For this reason Blacky could not be John's brother. John has learned the concept of multiple classification and he can apply this to some life situations, but others he will still be unable to classify. Further mental operations are necessary.

One of these operations is understanding the concept of reversibility. This is the phenomenon of characteristic things returning to their original condition: $5 + 3 = 8; 8 - 3 = 5$. An original situation can be recreated as long as no basic aspect has been changed. A child may turn a table upside down and use it as a boat, but since no change has been brought about in "tableness," it remains a table and can be used as one again by turning it right side up, back to its original condition. A black-and-white reversible skirt is still both black and white even though only the white may be visible at the moment. By reversing it, the black will be seen unchanged. To apply the concept to our example, Blacky was born a dog and this condition does not change, even though he lives with a family of human beings.

Another mental operation is the concept of seriation. Seriation means that things can be ordered. The child understands that things can be graduated from larger to smaller or vice versa. Seriation of objects can be based not only on their size but on any other common property that can be graduated along a continuum. For example, colors can be graduated on the basis of saturation or brightness.

When the child has mastered all these different operations, he has reached the stage at which he can understand the concept of conservation. Conservation, a term used by Piaget, can be thought of as ability to think in abstract terms. It marks the beginning of the operational stage. Conservation can be defined as "the cognition that certain properties (quality, number, length, etc.) remain invariant (are conserved in the face of certain transformations) displacing objects or object parts in space, sectioning an object into pieces, changing shapes, etc." (Flavell, 1963). For example, quantity does not change even though the form in which it appears does change: A piece of paper crumpled up contains the same amount of paper as before it was crumpled. Nothing has been added or taken away.

Piaget uses the following experiment to ascertain whether children are able to conserve quantity. The examiner takes two round balls of clay that are of equal size, weight, and volume. He then changes the one in front of the child's eyes into a cup-shaped object which looks bigger than the original ball. If the child understands conservation, he will be able to see that nothing has been added or taken away — the original volume, amount, or weight cannot have changed. In order for the child to understand this concept, he must understand that objects can have more than one classification — in fact, he must have the concepts of multiple classification, reversibility, and seriation.

In other words, the child must understand, first, that a piece of clay may acquire different shapes without changing its original qualities. Second, he must understand that it can be changed into one form and back again to the original form. Third, he must understand that, even if it looks bigger as compared to its previous shape, nothing has been added or taken away. In other words, the child must draw his conclusions according to a concept of reality, according to certain orderly laws that he has become aware of, and he must not let visual evidence overrule his judgment. John can now understand that Blacky was like a member of the family in some respects but not in others. Nothing of his dogness has changed. He conserves his dogness although other qualities are evident. Even though the car moved downhill, nothing of the fact that it is an object and not a living being has changed because these things are governed by natural laws that one knows and are not only determined by what one sees. He realizes, therefore, that the car could not decide to run over him. Since Blacky is not his brother, he can be sure that his parents would not react to his loss in the same way as they did to the loss of Blacky. He would understand that replacing Blacky would imply nothing about himself. This knowledge would keep him from identifying with Blacky too much.

If John had developed the incorrect concept described earlier, he would have an additional task to perform before being able to look at the circumstances with complete realism and before learning to build his concept on the important criteria. Not only must he believe what he knows rather than what he sees, he must also accept the fact that his previous way of thinking was wrong. It is in the absence of this last step that we occasionally find a child who cannot reconcile contradiction for a while, until he becomes completely convinced of the true facts of a situation.

Piaget also notes that conservation occurs at different times in different areas. Children can first understand the conservation of substance, then weight, and then volume. This sequence of development has generally been verified with some qualifications in studies by Elkind (1961b), Kooistra (1963), Lovell (1961a), and Smedslund (1961c).

The next question follows: Granted that these stages appear according to a certain order of development, are the ages at which they appear also definite or is there variation in this respect?

With regard to this question, the results of different researchers differ greatly. According to Piaget, conservation appears between the ages of eight and twelve, while Smedslund and Kooistra have reported it at younger ages. Kooistra, working with gifted children at City and Country School, where children had an IQ of 130 and higher, finds it as early as the age of four in a small number of children. This fact in itself is important for the program planning of nursery school teachers and teachers of early elementary school because these children perhaps can understand material that might previously have been considered beyond their scope.

The question that follows is: Can children be trained in these thinking tasks or is it merely a matter of maturation which cannot be influenced by education? Studies investigating the induction of conservation of other properties such as number (Wohlwill, 1960b; Beilen and Franklin, 1962) have shown that training in conservation is generally a failure (Flavell, 1963).

From these studies the general consensus, then, is that the training of children to conserve, be it quantity or number or area, is very difficult and for the most part results in failure. Flavell contends that these failures indicate that the training for conservation is built on a hollow core and, further, that these failures give evidence for the proposition that Piaget's concepts are not amenable to laboratory training (Flavell, 1963). In looking more deeply into these results we found that these investigators tried to teach conservation itself. Their failure might be explained by the method of approach rather than by a true inability of young children to acquire these concepts through training. Teaching conservation itself might fail because this would mean skipping some of the necessary prerequisite steps. The purpose of our investigation was therefore to determine whether the ability to conserve could be produced by training the child in the prerequisites: multiple classification, reversibility, and seriation.

In the pilot study, we worked with a group of twenty gifted children ranging in age from 4.9 to 5.1. Ten of these children were in the training group and ten were in the control group. The IQ as measured on the Stanford–Binet, was 149 for the training group and 152 for the nontraining group. All the children were enrolled as regular students in our nursery school for gifted children, which had an enriched curriculum. These children had been studying a number of concepts. Some of them could read, and the atmosphere could generally be classified as intellectually stimulating.

Teaching Procedure

The experimental group met with Mrs. Roeper three times a week for three weeks for about twenty minutes each session. The method used was the inquiry method. The children were never simply informed of a concept but were guided to discover it themselves through observation and discussion. The three processes described by Piaget were each introduced through simple examples. Each process was discussed and pointed out by different methods until the children's comments seemed to reflect a real understanding. It was impressive to observe the moment of recognition in one child, who was then able to convince the next. Where the children seemed to have grasped the idea in a specific context, other similar situations were introduced and finally they were led into generalizing their newly-found understanding. Verbalizing, according to Bruner, can protect the child against being overwhelmed by superficial and erroneous visual evidence. In other words, the discussion itself helps the child toward acquiring the ability to conserve.

We will describe each concept covered by examples taken from the verbatim transcript of our discussions.

A Verbatim Session on Classification

TEACHER: Can you tell me what this is, Mary?
MARY: A banana.

TEACHER: What else can you tell me about it?

MARY: It's straight.

TEACHER: It's straight. What else?

MARY: It has a peel.

TEACHER: It has a peel . . . Tom, what can you tell me about it?

TOM: Ummm . . . It has some dark lines on it.

TEACHER: Uh-huh.

TOM: It has some green on it.

TEACHER: What can you do with it?

TOM: You can eat it!

TEACHER: That's right! . . . Now let's . . .

CHILDREN: I love bananas!

TEACHER: What is this?

CHILDREN: An orange.

TEACHER: Is it really an orange?

CHILDREN: Uh-huh . . . yes.

TEACHER: Look at it closely.

CHILD: It's an artificial one.

TEACHER: Oh, that's right, it's an artificial one. . . . But what else can you tell me about it?

CHILDREN: You can eat it . . . it's round.

TEACHER: Uh-huh.

CHILDREN: Orange.

TEACHER: That's right!

CHILD: It has a stem.

TEACHER: Now, look at this one. What is this?

CHILDREN: An orange . . . orange.

TEACHER: And what can you do with it?

CHILDREN: You can eat it . . . and it's round.

TEACHER: It's round . . .

CHILD: It has a peel . . .

TEACHER: It has a peel . . . now, look at these two things. Are they the same?

CHILDREN: No!

TEACHER: What's different?

CHILDREN: This one . . . this one here is pressed in on the side a little . . . this one is lighter.

TEACHER: Do you know what this really is? This is a tangerine . . . and this is an orange. Now, tell me in what ways they are alike?

CHILDREN: This is smaller and that's bigger.

TEACHER: I said, in what way are they alike?

CHILDREN: They are both round . . . they both have a stem . . . both orange.

TEACHER: They both have a stem. Both round, both orange. Anything else alike about them?

CHILD: They're both fat.

TEACHER: Uh-huh. What can we do with them?

CHILDREN: We can eat them.

TEACHER: We can eat them. Now tell me, what's the same about all of these things?

CHILD: These are round, but this isn't.

TEACHER: I said, what is the same about them, not what's different about them.

CHILDREN: They're both round . . . they're round . . . they're round . . . and they are both artificial.

TEACHER: They are all artificial and . . . are they all round?

CHILD: No.

TEACHER: What about the banana?

CHILD: It's straight.

TEACHER: But . . . tell me something else that is the same about all of those things.

CHILD: They have . . . all have a peel.

TEACHER: That's right, too. But what can you do with all of them?

CHILDREN: You can eat them!

TEACHER: That's right! That's the same about every one of them. Do you have a name for all of them?

CHILDREN: Yes!

TEACHER: What?

CHILD: A banana.

TEACHER: A banana? No . . . is there something that you can call all of them?

CHILDREN: Fruit . . . fruit.

TEACHER: And what's the same about all fruit?

CHILDREN: They are all round except bananas.

TEACHER: No . . . why do you call all of these things fruit?

CHILDREN: Because you can eat them.

TEACHER: You can eat them.

CHILDREN: And they are food.

TEACHER: And they are food.

As you can see, we began by labeling the objects presented — bananas, oranges, or whatever — and we continued by discussing the differences, since differences can be grasped by young children before similarities. They moved from insignificant observations to significant ones. We then continued with discussion of similarities until the significant similarity was reached that made it possible to put them all in one important classification.

Another session was used to learn multiple classification. The discussion led to these conclusions: A pencil can be red and can be used for writing. When you need red objects, you put the pencil into the pile for red things; when you need to write you put it into the pile for writing utensils. Yet it is still only one pencil. Different classification does not change this at all. The multiple classification was acted out and tried out in many different ways. For example, different objects were put in the middle of the table. Each child was told to collect certain items that belonged together. One child was to take everything red — another, everything that writes. They found themselves reaching for the same object, which proved the point. From there we moved to the generalization: An object can be two things at the same time. This means: A person can be two things at the same time. Therefore, you can be a son and a brother at the same time.

The same method was used to show reversibility. Each child received five pennies. There were five children. They counted all their pennies and then were asked to put them in the middle of the table. The first comment was, "It is more"; then doubtfully, "It looks like more." Now they were asked, if each child were to take five pennies back, would there be any left on the table? The reaction was doubt and confusion. Next, the experiment was repeated with five pennies only. This time the process was obvious. They could see it better. Once they were convinced of the situation, the same procedure was used with the larger number of pennies. Objects can be grouped in different ways but can always return to their original form if nothing has been added or taken away. Thus the children were able to realize that sometimes things seem different from what they are.

Seriation

Seriation was approached again in a similar manner. By this time the children were already aware of the method and were able to react in faster and more sophisticated fashion. Can a block be big and little at the same time? The first answer was still no. It was pointed out that visually this is possible. This was then generalized and then again specified by showing that a person can be big and little at the same time — big compared to a small child, small compared to a big man.

It became apparent to us that it is important to prove these concepts by many different examples and to carry out with the children the thought processes that lead from the particular to the general and back again. Verbalizing and clarifying these processes made the children familiar with them and enabled them to apply the same processes independently. It seemed that being able to generalize did not automatically mean that the child could generalize to a new particular situation, but once he has experienced the process, he is better able to do it for himself.

Although the samples were small, the change in the training groups was most interesting and seemed significant. The degree to which the training experiences were assimilated by the training group is reflected in the type of response given to the inquiry questions in the posttraining session. The children verbalized their explanations in an articulate way, employing statements of reversibility, for example, as explanations. The explanations were of the level expected as a consequence of training experience. On the other hand with the children who did not have any training, there was little change in the explanatory level in the posttraining test situations.

All the children were given the conservation tasks of continuous quantity (Plasticene), substance, weight, and volume, and also the continuous liquid task. The procedure was the standard procedure described by Inhelder and Piaget (1964).

Further research is of course necessary, but it is our contention that training procedure may be one method that can help children toward the achievement of conservation, which means toward the abilities of realistic and abstract thinking.

These results and those of Piaget and of other researchers point to the following conclusions:

1. The development of logic in all young children proceeds according to definite stages.
2. The ability to conserve, that is, rational and abstract thinking, may appear as early as the age of four in children who have not been exposed to any systematic training. In most children, however, this so-called operational stage appears through experience at a later age.
3. Even in the preoperational stage, some kind of primitive sequential thought processes appear that may lead the child to either wrong or correct conclusions, depending on what criterion he happens to use. In the early part of the preoperational stage he may not be capable of understanding a significant criterion, because here again he will make use only of the most obvious. A little later on, however, his experience may make it possible for him to apply another obvious but more important criterion in order to come to more realistic appraisals of situations. It is important to realize that at no stage is his mind inactive. For psychological reasons he attempts mastery at any level and if his tools are primitive ones, his conclusions may also be primitive.
4. Training in prerequisites built on whatever stage at which the child actually functions also facilitates growth toward the ability to conserve.
5. The child may be taught to comprehend some of these concepts in

specific instances, even though he may not have reached this particular stage in his general development.

In summary, we can make three important points: a) Children's thought processes differ basically from those of the adult. b) Children's ability to think logically and abstractly, to conserve, develops according to definite stages. c) The ability to conserve can be reached through the process of growth but can be facilitated by carefully planned education.

What do these phenomena mean in terms of early childhood education? Their greatest importance lies in the fact that they open the door to mental territory so far largely unknown and uncomprehended: the young child's intellectual mind. The new discoveries possible seem unlimited. This knowledge can throw new light on specific situations as well as add new dimensions to our general educational plans.

Knowledge of the type of cognitive style used by young children will help us understand certain puzzling behavior patterns and emotional reactions. The problem of sibling rivalry, for instance — one of the most difficult and universal problems of early childhood — gains another dimension of understanding if seen in this context. A young child may not only feel emotionally rejected when his mother pays attention to a sibling but he may also be "intellectually" convinced that she cannot possibly love both of them at the same time, since he can only conceive of single classification. He believes that she cannot possibly be both his and his brother's mother simultaneously. If we understand this reaction, we may be able to find ways to help him at least toward a better intellectual grasp of the situation and this may then to some extent relieve his emotional reaction.

Another case in point: A young child may be completely surprised at the adult's negative reaction when he takes something off a shelf in the dimestore. He may not have reached the point at which he can put things into different categories. He therefore has no concept of ownership or "stealing" and cannot possibly understand why his mother thinks a policeman would be angry at him.

These examples may show us why it can be difficult for children to deal successfully with many life situations before some important concepts have been clarified. Knowledge of children's cognitive style may therefore lead to conscious intellectual guidance by the adult that provides the child with the correct clue to help him understand a specific situation even before he has reached the stage of conservation.

The following experiment with a group of four-year-olds may prove this point. Most of the children seemed to function on different levels with the preoperational stage. As explained in the Blacky story, the concept of what is alive is a most basic one in the child's daily life experiences. We therefore tried to give the children conscious guidance in understanding this concept. These children were in the habit of discussing problems with their teacher. Through the discussion method she was able to find out what their own concepts were and then guide them into their own discovery of usable criteria for more realistic conceptualization. The discussion method was amplified by movies, visits to a farm, books, and so on. We can only give here an overview of the procedure without describing the approach in great detail.

In order to find out the children's thinking in regard to the subject of "aliveness" the teacher would ask such questions as: "Is a book alive?" One of the answers to this inquiry was: "No, it cannot move." In this case, single classification (things that are alive move) leads to the correct answer. But it is precisely this concept built on single classification that brought an incorrect answer to the next question: "Is a car alive?" "Yes, because it moves." In this case a second classification is required and was finally arrived at by another child: "A car is not alive. It moves but cannot start itself." Out of this, then, emerged the following definition, which required the child's functioning within the concept of multiple classification: Things can move whether they are alive or not, but only things that are alive can do both — can move and can move by themselves. Other categories were then added: only things that are alive can grow and reproduce; and so forth. The children were then able to add categories of their own: "A cow is alive — it is made of flesh and blood; a car is not — it is made of steel." Or: "A cow is alive — it makes moo when he feels like it; a car is not alive — it can only sound its horn when you push it."

A second group of the same age and background was exposed to the same experiences — the same movies, stories, visits to the farm, and so on — but not to this specific type of discussion. These children were not able to give accurate definitions of aliveness. The first group was able to develop specific useful concepts based on the specific guided approach.

This brings up the issue of incidental learning. The young child is most eager for learning. Every experience therefore becomes a learning situation. Early childhood education has realized the child's great potential for learning by himself and it has become an integral part of preschool education. This type of learning, however, is unselective in the case of the child who functions on a preoperational level. He is not yet equipped to differentiate between different categories of facts and therefore to build his judgement on proper relevancy. In consequence he is apt to develop misconceptions, such as: A car is alive because it moves. Such conceptions may become deeply embedded in the child's thinking and stand in the way of further concept formation. In other words, the young child is deeply motivated toward understanding the world but is not yet mentally equipped for it.

The only solution for his dilemma seems to be knowledgeable adult guidance. It is for this reason that we believe the young child should be helped toward proper concept formation through an organized goal-directed approach built on knowledge of his cognitive style. The method described here may offer one approach.

Understanding children's cognitive style may provide an explanation for the failure of certain children to understand simple mathematical concepts. It may at the same time provide the means to help them overcome their problem. In addition, it may provide a method to keep such failures from occurring.

The greatest obstacle to such an approach to education is that it is most difficult for the adult to identify with the young child's manner of thinking. We have forgotten thoughts of early childhood, just as we cannot recall the feelings of that period. It actually requires translation of our method of thinking into another thought language. It may be difficult to learn a foreign language, but the more familiar we become with this one, the better we will understand the children, and, realizing our previous lack of communication with them, the more areas we will find that are affected by this new understanding.

In this article we were able to touch only briefly on some of the many possible applications of Piaget's concepts in our pilot study. Nevertheless we hope that it will stimulate other educators toward finding new ways of coordinating research results and education in this far-reaching field.

A Framework for a Preschool Curriculum Based on Some Piagetian Concepts

■■■ CONSTANCE K. KAMII / NORMA L. RADIN

In this article, the authors take the position that compensatory preschool can build a solid foundation for further intellectual development only by going back to the sensorimotor period as delineated by Piaget, and ensuring that intermediate stages are not skipped or only partially achieved. Portions of Piaget's theory which appear to be essential for future academic achievement are conceptualized into a framework for a preschool curriculum geared to the needs of disadvantaged
• • • • • • • •

SOURCE: This is a revision of an article by the same authors entitled "A Framework for a Preschool Curriculum Based on Some Piagetian Concepts," which appeared in the *Journal of Creative Behavior, 1* (1967), 314–324. With permission of the authors and the *Journal.* The paper was made possible by a grant from the U.S. Office of Education (Title III, No. 67–042490, Elementary and Secondary Education Act of 1965). However, the opinions expressed herein do not necessarily reflect the position or policy of the U.S. Office of Education, and no official endorsement by the U.S. Office of Education should be inferred. The authors wish to express appreciation to H. Sinclair of the University of Geneva for the many ideas she contributed to this paper.

children. The authors describe two areas of cognitive development which are necessary for logical thinking: representation of objects and understanding of relationships among objects. The implications of these concepts for teaching are discussed, with emphasis upon the importance of sequential mastery of prerequisite substages.

The need for compensatory preschool education has been widely accepted, and many such programs are in operation throughout the country. The question now is no longer whether or not preschool is desirable, but what to do with children once they are in school. Most preschools eclectically use a variety of traditional nursery-school activities, while some people are experimenting with distinctly new approaches. Bereiter and Engelmann (1966) emphasize language and logic with a unique method. Gotkin (1966, 1967) stresses programming at the representational level of pictures and language.

An alternative approach is to delineate the long-term cognitive goals of education and insure that the elementary levels are mastered during the preschool years. A curriculum based on such an approach would consist of a series of objectives which are prerequisites for subsequent learning. The theory of Jean Piaget appears particularly useful for the building of such a curriculum because it is the only coherent body of knowledge in existence which deals with the evolution of intelligence from infancy to adolescence along a variety of school-related dimensions.

Piaget described four major periods in the development of intelligence: The period of sensorimotor intelligence (the first two years of life), the preoperational period (two to seven years of age), the period of concrete operations (seven to twelve years of age), and the period of formal operations (twelve years of age and through adolescence).[1] He delineated various content areas such as classification, seriation, numbers, space, time, representation, etc., and described how intelligence evolves in each of these areas. Thus, we see in Piaget's writing (Piaget, 1954; Inhelder and Piaget, 1964; Inhelder and Piaget, 1958), for example, how classification is rooted in sensorimotor intelligence and takes diverse forms as it evolves through the three subsequent periods. Fundamental to Piaget's developmental theory is the view that cognitive growth is not an additive process but a continual reconstruction of existing cognitive structures. Growth is possible only if the child has the structures which are necessary for attaining the next stage.

Research has shown (Sigel and Anderson, 1965) that lower-class children appear to have cognitive lacunae. It is highly likely that such gaps in the foundation prevent them from developing fully in subsequent years. We

• • • • • • • •

[1] For a full description of the developmental period we would suggest Piaget (1967).

believe that compensatory preschools must build a solid foundation for further development by going back to the sensorimotor period, and making certain that intermediate stages are not skipped or only partially achieved. To this end, portions of Piaget's theory which seemed to be essential for future intellectual growth and academic achievement were selected and conceptualized into a framework for a preschool curriculum particularly geared to the needs of disadvantaged children.

The present paper gives only a theoretical framework for a preschool curriculum. No attempt will be made to describe the stages of development in any area; nor will there be a consideration of teaching methods which seem compatible with Piaget's theory. The few stages and teaching activities that are discussed are intended only as examples of how the framework might be implemented. It is hoped that the art of teaching will be applied by skilled preschool educators to the curriculum material presented below, and that the cognitive goals will be integrated with the socio-emotional goals which are so crucial for any meaningful preschool program.

A Framework for a Preschool Curriculum

Piaget delineates three areas of knowledge which have different modes of structuring, i.e., logical knowledge, physical knowledge, and social knowledge. The three are based on the feedback from different sources. Logical knowledge is based on the internal consistency of the system involved. Physical knowledge is based on feedback from the result of actions on objects. Social knowledge is derived from feedback from people.

From the standpoint of a curriculum designed for cognitive development, the areas which are crucial are logical knowledge and physical knowledge. Although social knowledge is essential for any child to get along, it is not indispensable for his cognitive development as such. Thus, the two major areas to be included in the present framework are logical knowledge and physical knowledge. A third area of the framework is representation, which helps the child to progressively structure his knowledge and symbolize it. Although the three areas will be discussed separately below, it should be remembered that they must constantly be integrated in actual teaching.

The most basic difference between logical and physical knowledge is that the former is based only on the internal consistency of what the child believes, whereas the latter is based on information from the external world. For example, in logical knowledge, if we start with the statement that all glass objects break when dropped, it follows that if a given object is made of glass, it will break when it is dropped. In logic, the veracity of the statement that all glass objects break when dropped does not matter. The only thing that matters is the internal consistency of a set of statements.

In physical knowledge, on the other hand, it does matter whether or not all glass objects really break when they are dropped. The truth of this statement is determined by the external world, and the child finds out about it by acting upon it. The curriculum implication of this distinction is that only in the realm of physical knowledge does the teacher have direct recourse to feedback from the external world. In logical knowledge, since the internal consistency of the system is the only criterion of right and wrong, teaching is more difficult. For example, if the child believes that eight objects arranged in a certain spatial configuration are "more" than eight identical objects arranged differently, the teacher does not have simple recourse to a physical phenomenon like breaking to contradict the child. Therefore, the only strategy available to her is work that builds on existing logical structures, such as the linear ordering of objects and the "renversabilité" of one-to-one correspondence. This statement will be clarified below when the teaching of numbers is discussed.

I. Logical Knowledge

Piaget makes the distinction between logico-mathematical relationships and spatio–temporal relationships. The former involve strictly logical relationships, which are independent of all spatial and temporal considerations. For example, in considering the class of "all glass objects," "bigger than," or "three," the spatial and temporal arrangement of objects does not matter. In spatio–temporal relationships, on the other hand, the spatial and temporal arrangement is all important. If an object A is to the left of B, and B is to the left of C on a straight line, A is to the left of C. If an event A comes after B, and B comes after C, it follows that A comes after C. The outline which follows summarizes the two types of logical knowledge and their subcategories.

A. Logico–mathematical operations
1. Classification
2. Seriation
3. Numbers
B. Spatio–temporal operations
1. Spatial reasoning
2. Temporal reasoning

The term "operation" has a uniquely Piagetian meaning, which can be translated as "reasoning" for the purposes of this paper. A full explanation of "operations" is beyond the scope of this article, but it can be said that in general the term refers to a logical form of reasoning which becomes possible around seven years of age.[2] The function of preschools is not to teach operations to four-year-olds but to teach their prerequisites so as to make operativity possible when the children reach first grade. To establish a foundation for classification, for example, preschools should teach the preoperational task of nongraphic collections (to be explained below) rather than the operation of class inclusion.

A. LOGICO-MATHEMATICAL OPERATIONS

1. *Classification.* "Classification" in a Piagetian sense means the ability to group things according to their similarities and differences, with the hierarchical structure and quantification of class inclusion. When the child groups similar things together, but without the cognitive structure of class inclusion, with the proper quantification of subclasses and larger classes, he is said to be in the preoperational period of "nongraphic collections" (Stage II). When he becomes capable of class inclusion, he is said to have attained the period of "classification" (Stage III).

This hierarchical structure can be seen in the following experiment. Almost all children at four years of age can dichotomize wooden beads which are identical in every way except for color (red and green). However, when we place six green beads and two red ones in front of the child, and ask him, "Are there more green beads, or more wooden beads?" some children at six years of age will say that there are more green beads. These children are at the "nongraphic-collection" level.[3] The children who answer that there are more wooden beads than green ones have attained the level of "classification," with the ability to coordinate the qualitative and quantitative aspects of a group of objects. (The qualitative aspect refers to the relationship among the redness, greenness, and woodness of the beads, and the quantitative aspect refers to whether there are more green beads or more wooden beads.)

At the preschool level, it seems appropriate to concentrate on the qualitative aspect of classification at the preoperational level of nongraphic collections. It is too much to expect four-year-olds to think about both the qualitative and quantitative aspects. The first step is for the child to become able to dichotomize objects by grouping together things that are *identical.* The next step is to move into grouping things that are *similar,* with a consistent criterion within each collection. Many four-year-olds tend to put

• • • • • • • •

[2] Many examples of operations can be found in Piaget (1965), Piaget and Inhelder (1967), and Inhelder and Piaget (1964).

[3] Before the stage of nongraphic collections comes the stage of "graphic collections," which is characterized by the children's use of spatial arrangements, or patterns, as the only basis for putting objects together.

together a blue square and a blue circle "because they are both blue," and then add a red circle "because they are circles." In order to maintain a consistent criterion, the child must develop mobility of thought, which makes it possible for him to remember why he put the first and second objects together, and use the same criterion for putting the eighth, ninth, and tenth objects in the same group.

2. *Seriation.*   While classification involves the grouping of similar objects without regard to how they are arranged within each group, seriation refers to the arranging of things according to a dimension along which they differ. An example is the ordering of ten sticks, all of different lengths, in a descending order. As in classification, the first prerequisite in seriation is the ability to dichotomize. The next prerequisite of trichotomies and arranging things in the proper order are also at the preoperational level, and therefore appropriate for four-year-olds.

With sizes, seriation begins with the dichotomy of "big" and "little" objects. This distinction in size can later be expanded to "long–short" and "fat–thin." With qualities, dichotomies are found in polar pairs such as "smooth–rough," "dark (blue)–light (blue)," etc. It is desirable to use a variety of materials and sensorimotor activities to teach the prerequisites for seriation because the essence of seriation is the *system* of relative sizes, darkness, and other attributes, which are not tied to a few limited objects. The child must become capable of seriating dolls, balls, sticks, various shades of colors, nesting cups, etc.

3. *Numbers.*   Piaget's theory of numbers explains the mechanism of the child's construction of numbers at a developmental level earlier than that at which set theory begins. His theory, therefore, makes a very valuable contribution to the very beginning of number work.

Before the number system of $1 < 2 < 3 \ldots$ is built, the child develops an intuition about groups of objects as containing "a lot" or "a little bit." This dichotomy is easy as long as the contrast is stark. Any four-year-old is likely to choose ten pieces of candy over a group containing only two pieces. The judgment becomes more difficult, however, when the comparison is between nine and ten pieces.

Piaget's theory has shown that a four-year-old's quantification of discontinuous quantities is usually based on spatial consideration. Many four-year-olds think that two rows of candy have "the same amount" as long as they are arranged in such a way that they have the same length. In actuality, one row may contain ten pieces, and the other, nine pieces. Since the judgment of "the same number" is impossible for a child who does not have the cognitive structure of numbers, the child uses what he can to make this judgment, i.e., the space occupied.

The first goal in the teaching of numbers according to Piaget's theory is the establishment of numerical equivalence by one-to-one correspondence.

The four-year-old child who uses the length of the rows to establish equivalence can be helped in two ways: By linear ordering of objects and by "provoked correspondence." The former involves two sets of heterogeneous elements (e.g., a cup, a saucer, a plate, a pan, etc., to correspond to a cup, a saucer, a plate, etc.). The latter uses two sets of homogeneous elements which correspond qualitatively with each other in such a way that there can be only one element of a set to correspond with an element in the other set (e.g., a set of cups to correspond with a set of saucers). In linear ordering the child is asked to make a copy of a set of objects that are arranged in a line. This task accentuates the distinctness of each element, and prevents the child from basing his judgment on the space occupied. In "provoked correspondence," the teacher can use instructions like "Give me enough cups for all the saucers, so that they will come out just right." The qualitative correspondence between the cup and the saucer facilitates the child's establishment of one-to-one correspondence.

It was stated in the introductory section of this paper that physical knowledge is easier to teach than logical knowledge because the former could be based on information from the external world, whereas the latter could be based only on the internal consistency of a logical system. The teaching of numerical equivalence by means of linear ordering and provoked correspondence is an example of using the child's current reasoning ability to facilitate the building of the next logical structure.

The second goal in the teaching of numbers according to Piaget's theory is conservation. Conservation is the result of mobility of thought, known as reversibility, which is preceded by *renversabilité*. *Renversabilité* refers to the child's belief that the objects can be returned to the original corresponding positions, and that when the spatial correspondence of two sets is physically resumed, the numerical equivalence will also be resumed. While *renversabilité* proceeds *successively* in only one direction, reversibility proceeds in two opposite directions *simultaneously*. Reversibility of thought makes conservation of numbers a logical necessity to a child who can think simultaneously of both destroying and reestablishing the one-to-one correspondence. Preoperational children have *renversabilité*, but not reversibility.

It is necessary to have children physically move equivalent sets and verify whether or not there are still "enough saucers for all the cups." Reversibility will come from the gradual building of internal operations which results from the speeding up and internalization of *renversabilité*.

B. SPATIO–TEMPORAL OPERATIONS

1. *Spatial reasoning.* The teaching of spatial reasoning includes such traditional topological content as "in-out," "on-off," "in front of-in back

of," etc. The playground and large-muscle equipment are especially well suited for sensorimotor activities to teach these concepts.

Piaget shows how space is progressively structured developing from topological space to Euclidean space.[4] In the four-year-old child, this structuring is much more advanced on the perceptual plane than on the representational plane. Thus, when he is asked to *copy* a square (i.e., to make a representation of a square), the child often produces a circle. On the other hand, when he is asked to *find* another square (a perceptual task), he is not likely to have trouble. Preschools must therefore work on the structuring of space on the representational plane.

The heart of spatial reasoning is more dynamic than static concepts like "in-out," and geometric shapes. Transformation is an example of dynamic spatial reasoning, and linear ordering of objects is another. To learn about the transformation of a shape into small parts and its transformation back to the original shape, the child can be asked to cut pictures and reassemble his homemade puzzle. To teach linear ordering, the teacher can ask the child to arrange his cupboard just like hers, with the cup coming first, then the plate, then the pan, etc.[5] As it has been discussed earlier, the teaching of linear ordering also facilitates the construction of numbers.

2. *Temporal reasoning.*   Temporal relationships have two aspects: Temporal order and intervals. Since Piaget has shown that intervals are structured much later than temporal order, it seems desirable at the preschool level to teach only sequence, such as "before-after" and "first, next, last."

The learning of causal relationships facilitates the learning of temporal order, and vice versa. Causal relationships can best be understood by the child when his own action on objects is the cause, and the effect is clearly visible. For example, the child can be asked to predict what will happen if he drops a glass jar, a piece of chalk, or a can. This way of teaching temporal sequence should be integrated with the teaching of physical knowledge, which is discussed below.

II. Physical Knowledge

Physical knowledge in the present context refers to knowledge about the nature of matter. Piaget states that the child learns about the nature of matter by acting on objects and observing and systematizing the results of these actions. Stretching, folding, cutting, floating, hitting, tapping, squeezing,

• • • • • • • •

[4]Topological space has such characteristics as openness and closure, and separation and proximity, but not Euclidean characteristics, such as angles, parallels, measurement, number of elements, etc. For a fuller explanation, see Piaget and Inhelder (1967), Chapter 1.

[5]For a fuller description, see Piaget and Inhelder (1967), Chapter 3.

breaking, and dropping are examples of actions the child can perform on any object in his environment. By acting on objects and observing the results of these actions, the child gradually becomes able to predict the result of certain given actions on particular objects. Thus, the child comes to know not only the properties of things but also the fact that the physical world has regularity.

The strategy of teaching physical knowledge is very different from that of teaching logical knowledge. In the teaching of logical knowledge, since internal consistency is the only criterion of truth, it is fruitless, and even detrimental, to contradict the child. In the teaching of physical knowledge, on the other hand, if the child predicts that a block will sink, all the teacher has to do is to ask him to prove that his prediction is correct. The physical world will respond in a clear-cut way.

It is important at the preschool level of physical knowledge to stay within the realm of predictions, and not go into explanation. The question for the teacher to ask is "What will happen if . . . ?" and not "Why did . . . happen?" For example, four-year-olds can predict exactly what will happen if a ball is dropped, but an explanation of the phenomenon is beyond their ability to comprehend.

III. Representation

Representation is necessary in logical knowledge for the child to become capable of concrete operations.[6] Representation is also necessary in physical knowledge to structure the feedback from actions on objects.[7] Representation is thus essential for the acquisition of knowledge, but it is not a sufficient condition, since representation as such is a static phenomenon. The ability to evoke static images and words does not insure the building of such structures as hierarchical classes, numbers, spatio–temporal relationships, and physical knowledge.

Basic to Piaget's theory of representation is the idea that representation is an active process, rather than a passive one like an afterimage or a photograph. In fact, even directly-observed objects must be constructed by the child in order to be recognized. The classic example of this statement is the baby's inability to recognize a bottle when only the bottom is visible. Until about nine months of age, the infant cannot recognize the bottle unless

• • • • • • • •

[6]For example, for the conservation of numbers, the child must become able to imagine (represent) the return of the elements to the original spatial correspondence. The preoperational child is not capable of this representation, which is made possible by mobility of thought.
[7]Without representation, it would be impossible to structure observations from the results of actions on objects. The child must be able to evoke what happened before when he dropped a ball, a fork, etc., in order to systematize the feedback from his actions on the objects.

he can see the nipple. Even when the nipple is visible, the three-dimensional object as such must be constructed, since the perception of all objects is always from a particular point of view. If the perception of an object requires such active construction, it follows that the representation of objects that are absent must require even more active internal construction.

The mechanism which provides the bridge between sensorimotor knowledge and representational knowledge is imitation. When a child pretends to hold a glass and to drink out of it, he is imitating, or accommodating to, the object. At first, he will need to engage externally in imitation, but later he will gradually internalize this imitation and becomes capable of evoking objects and events by imagining these actions. The result of this internalization is called the mental image, which is an internal reconstruction of the object having a visual, tactile, kinesthetic, auditory, and olfactory reality. The internal mental image is what makes it possible for the child to use such external representations as pictures and words.

Piaget distinguishes three types of external representations: Indices, symbols, and signs, which are summarized below.

A. Indices
    1. Part of the object (e.g., the bottom of the bottle)
    2. Marks causally related to the object (e.g., footmarks in the snow)
B. Symbols
    1. Imitation (the use of the body to represent objects, e.g., walking like a duck)
    2. Make-believe (the use of objects to represent other objects, e.g., using a box to represent a duck)
    3. Onomatopoeia (e.g., uttering "Quack, quack")
    4. Three-dimensional models (e.g., making clay ducks)
    5. Pictures (e.g., drawing ducks)
C. Signs
    Words and other signs (e.g., algebraic signs)

The index differs from symbols and signs in that it is part of the object being represented. Symbols and signs, in contrast, are differentiated from the objects. Symbols differ from signs in that they bear a resemblance to the object represented, whereas signs do not resemble the object at all.

A. INDICES

In the case of indices, the signifier is either a part of the object or linked very closely to it by a causal relationship. Examples of the former are the ringing of a telephone and the handle of a partially hidden brush. An example of the latter is footprints in the snow, which indicate that a child or a dog was there walking.

The teaching of representation at the index level involves giving children a great deal of experience in "constructing" the whole object (a) when only a small part is perceived, (b) when the object is perceived through senses other than the visual and (c) when a part is missing. Children enjoy guessing games. To have them guess the object when only a small part is perceived, the teacher can show objects that are partially hidden by a screen. To have children guess the object through senses other than the visual, the teacher can have the child put his hand in a bag containing an item, and let him feel the object without seeing it. For the construction of the "whole" when a part is missing, she can make a kit containing incomplete objects with the missing part (e.g., the fourth leg of a chair) readily available and attachable.

B. SYMBOLS

Symbols are the first true instruments of representation because, unlike indices, they are differentiated from the object. If preschools hope to strengthen children's ability to use language, it is at the symbol level that much work must be done to build a foundation for the use of signs.

Since imitation is the most crucial bridge between sensorimotor knowledge and representational knowledge, it must be particularly stressed throughout the year in motor-encoding activities and socio-dramatic play. Make-believe must also be stressed throughout the play. Onomatopoeia, clay models, block building, and pictures are part of any traditional nursery school, but Piaget's theory provides insight into how to sequence these activities.

C. SIGNS

The teaching of language (signs) is one of the most frequently stressed goals of preschools. Piaget believes that language is part of the semiotic function, i.e., the capacity to represent objects with things that are distinct from what they stand for. The position taken in this paper, therefore, is that along with verbalization, many other activities on the symbol level must be used to ensure the evocation of vivid, complete, and detailed mental images. For example, a trip to a farm must be reviewed not only verbally with pictures but also motorically with socio-dramatic play and with imitations of sounds that animals made.

From the perspective of Piaget's theory, language is neither the source of knowledge nor the foundation of children's ability to reason. However, a preschool curriculum based on Piaget's theory would attempt to develop children's language because of its unique functions in cognitive development. For example, compared to symbols, which represent objects without reference to the interrelationships of the symbols, signs form systems of relationships. Also, since language is much more communicable than symbols, it enables children to compare various points of view and hence to decenter. This ability is critical, for it is when children want to convince other children that their logic is truly mobilized. Language also serves to direct the child's attention to the relevant aspects of the environment, and facilitates the storage and retrieval of concepts (Inhelder, Bovet, Sinclair, and Smock, 1966). Thus, language development has a major role to play in a preschool curriculum, but not as the source of concept attainment.

The foregoing framework is intended only as an exploratory effort to seek in Piaget's theory specific ways of building a cognitive foundation for some of the abilities which appear essential for success in school. The framework needs to be developed in further detail by delineating a series of goals within each cognitive area.[8] The question of teaching methods which best enable children to attain these goals is a related but separate issue.[9]

In conclusion, we feel that the key to "readiness" lies in the mastery of prerequisites. Without a firm foundation, cognitive acquisitions can be only shaky and spotty at best. No matter how strong the student's motivation may be, and how healthy his social relationships, academic success is very unlikely without the prerequisite intellectual abilities to absorb classroom instruction. Academic success is crucial to the disadvantaged child, for unless he can perform adequately in the classroom, all efforts to enhance his self-image, increase his desire for further education, and enable him to participate fully in our society are likely to fail in the long run.

• • • • • • • •

[8] This work is currently in progress at the Ypsilanti Early Education Program, Ypsilanti, Michigan, Public Schools.

[9] Some teaching methods are discussed in an accompanying paper by Sonquist, Kamii, and Derman, immediately following this paper.

A Piaget-Derived Preschool Curriculum

■■■ HANNE SONQUIST / CONSTANCE KAMII / LOUISE DERMAN

This paper describes an exploratory attempt to construct a preschool curriculum based on Piaget's developmental stages. The emphasis is placed on organizing knowledge acquired during the sensorimotor period into a meaningful foundation for later cognitive development. In pursuit of this goal, the authors have taken a number of traditional nursery school activities and organized them into a logical sequence to achieve specific cognitive objectives.

Head Start and other similar prekindergarten programs are becoming an accepted part of public education. These programs attempt to prepare disadvantaged children for academic learning by enhancing all aspects of their development. While different programs stress one area of growth or another, there appears to be widespread agreement that what is needed now is a curriculum that could advance cognitive growth in addition to social, emotional, and physical development. The critical question has become what and how to teach.

The theory that seems to offer the most insight into the development of intelligence and to give a new perspective to the educational problems of disadvantaged children is that of Jean Piaget. One of the basic concepts of this theory is that intelligence develops by qualitatively distinct stages, each requiring solid attainment for the next stage to become possible. The developmental stages and substages suggested to the authors ways of delineating a curriculum that would move children step by step through the natural developmental course. A framework for a preschool curriculum for disadvantaged children was, therefore, derived from Piaget's theory (Kamii, Radin, et al., 1967). The approach suggested by this framework was initially explored at the Perry Preschool (Sonquist and Kamii, 1967) and Gale Preschool (Radin and Sonquist, 1968). The present paper describes the curriculum and some teaching methods currently being further developed at the Ypsilanti Early Education Program (Kamii, Radin, et al., 1967).

The fundamental function of preschools is seen as the facilitation of the

• • • • • • • •

SOURCE: Revised by the authors from Sonquist, H. and C. Kamii. "Applying Some Piagetian Concepts in the Classroom for the Disadvantaged," *Young Children, 22,* 231–245. Copyright © 1967 National Association for the Education of Young Children (With permission of the authors and the publisher.) The revision is based on work done at the Ypsilanti Early Education Program, which is supported by a grant from the U.S. Office of Education (Title III, No. 67-042490, Elementary and Secondary Education Act of 1965). However, the opinions expressed herein do not necessarily reflect the position or policy of the U.S. Office of Education, and no official endorsement by the U.S. Office of Education should be inferred. The authors wish to express appreciation to H. Sinclair of the University of Geneva for the many ideas she contributed to this paper.

transition from sensorimotor intelligence to operational intelligence.[1] Piaget describes this transitional stage as the preoperational period, a time when the young child begins to systematize his physical and social knowledge, to construct logical structures, and to reconstruct on a representational level[2] the practical knowledge he acquired during the sensorimotor period.

How to apply Piaget's theory to preschool education is not obvious. Piaget himself has said very little about education. The present paper describes an exploratory attempt to apply his developmental theory of knowledge to preschool education. The materials and activities presented below are often similar to those of a traditional nursery school, but they are used to achieve specific cognitive goals. In this preschool, an attempt is made first of all to consolidate the practical knowledge of objects, space, time, and causality which was acquired during the sensorimotor period, so that there will be a solid foundation upon which to build later structures. The teaching goals of the curriculum are not intended to extend children's experience quantitatively, but to help them integrate and elaborate their experiences so that they will have the cognitive structures into which future educational experiences can be assimilated. It is assumed in this paper that the reader has read the preceding paper in this book, titled, "A Framework for a Preschool Curriculum Based on Some Piagetian Concepts."

I. Physical Knowledge

Physical knowledge for the preschool child means learning about properties of objects by finding out how they react when acted upon in different ways. Young children discover the nature of matter by acting on things and observing and systematizing the results of their actions. Crushing, dropping, folding, pulling, pushing, stretching, squeezing, and tapping are examples of actions which the child can attempt on almost any object in his environment.

For example, one of the properties of matter is that after a certain transformation, some objects will return to their original state while others will not. The teacher can gather an assortment of objects (e.g., a pipe cleaner, sponge, paper, toothpick, crayon, plastic spoon, and rubber band) and have the children bend each one. They will soon find out that some of these objects will bend and then return to their original form, while others will

• • • • • • • •

[1] "Operational intelligence" refers to intelligence which has become capable of concrete operations. This stage is usually reached at about seven years of age. For a fuller explanation, see Piaget (1967).

[2] While "representation" in early elementary education refers only to toys, pictures, and words, this term has a broader meaning in Piaget's theory. In his theory, representation refers to evoking (or thinking about) any object that is not present.

break. Another example is trying to stretch assorted items such as thread, rubber band, cloth, ribbons, string, wool, and paper. Trying to flatten balls made of metal, clay, aluminum foil, and foam rubber is still another example. In all these activities, it has been found helpful to get children to compare the reactions of various objects in order to highlight their different properties.

As the children repeat the same action on the same object a number of times, they come to know the regularity of the objects' behavior and to predict the results of various actions. Through the structuring of this regularity, they also come to understand that objects will behave in certain ways regardless of what they want the objects to do (e.g., a metal ball cannot be flattened no matter how hard the child may try). Working with a group of children enhances their knowledge about the regularity of the physical world, since the children can see that the same action on the same object always produces the same result, regardless of who performs the action. Group activities also encourage the children to exchange views about what happened. This exchange of predictions and information strengthens the systematization of physical knowledge.

Two remarks must be made before concluding this section on the teaching of physical knowledge. At preschool age, children can observe simple mechanical changes that result from their own direct actions (e.g., breaking objects, bouncing them, and dropping them). However, a complicated change such as the transformation of water into steam is too difficult. Second, it is wise at the preschool level of physical knowledge to stay within the realm of predictions and not go into explanations. The better question for the teacher to ask is "What will happen if . . . ?" and not "Why did . . . happen?" For example, four-year-olds can learn to predict what will happen if they drop a Ping-Pong ball on water, but an explanation of why it will float would be beyond their ability to understand.

II. Logical Knowledge

The two kinds of logical constructions delineated by Piaget are logico-mathematical and infralogical (or spatio–temporal) relationships. Since each of these relationships has been described in the preceding "framework" paper, they are simply summarized below in outline form. It should perhaps be emphasized again that the role of preschool education is not to try to teach the operations but to lay the foundation for their eventual development.

A. Logico–mathematical relationships
   1. Classification (uniting, disuniting, and reuniting)

2. Seriation (comparing and ordering)
3. Numbers (arranging, disarranging, and rearranging)
B. Infralogical (spatio–temporal) relationships
1. Spatial relationships
2. Temporal relationships

A. LOGICO–MATHEMATICAL RELATIONSHIPS

While each specific object was all-important in the teaching of physical knowledge, the particular objects do not matter in the teaching of logico-mathematical relationships. What matters is the relationship among the objects. For example, grouping according to function is not tied to pencils, items of clothing, or foods. Therefore, a large variety of objects should be available for the child to group, to order, and to count.

1. *Classification.*   From the first day of school, at cleanup time, the children can put together things that are the same and separate those that are different. Games can be developed for them to find identical objects from an array of grossly different things (e.g., two cups, two sponges, and three crayons). Sorting games in which the children find identical objects by touch alone also strengthens awareness of similarities and differences.

Grouping identical objects is relatively easy, and the children soon become ready to group together things that are not exactly the same. Three types of reasons for grouping can be discerned from Piaget's theory. The first and easiest type is by situational belonging, e.g., the placement of a cake of soap with a washrag, and a man's shirt with a necktie. Grouping by situational belonging is based on spatial proximity, which is the child's first principle of unification. The second type of grouping is based on what the child does with the objects, e.g., the placement of a white crayon with a white pencil, and a cigarette with a white straw. The third type of grouping is by abstraction from the objects themselves, e.g., the placement of the cigarette with the crayon ("because they are both short"), and the straw with the pencil ("because they are both long"). Grouping by color, shape, size, and material are other examples of grouping by abstraction from the objects.

Kits can be put together containing objects that can be grouped according to any of the above principles. The objects used should be those with which the children have already played in school or at home. It is important to remember in the teaching of classification that there is no right or wrong grouping, since how the objects are grouped is determined by the child's wish. In physical knowledge, the outcome of an action is determined entirely by the object. A metal ball cannot be flattened no matter how hard the child tries. In classification, on the other hand, the outcome of the action is determined by what the child wants. If he wants to group objects by length, this response is just as correct as grouping them according to function or color.

Several techniques have been found to help the children who show the various problems that Piaget described. For the child who becomes involved and preoccupied with making graphic collections, sorting objects in a "mystery box"[3] by touch alone has been found to take the visual element away.

A successful way to solve the problem of children who are unable to move from the grouping of identical objects to the grouping of slightly different objects is the use of objects that can be grouped by function. In this method, children can be asked to show what they do with the objects, and to pretend to use them. For example, separating red and blue cups from big and small blocks can be taught by having the child pretend to drink out of the cups and to build with blocks. This use of "pretend" gestures facilitates not only the uniting of objects but also the explanation of the groupings in a nonverbal way.

Some children are unable to explain verbally the basis of their groupings. These same children are often quick to correct the teacher and explain *her* "mistake" in a classification game of Catch-the-Teacher-Making-a-Mistake.

Many preschool children cannot maintain a consistent criterion within a group. For example, they put a blue square and a blue circle together "because they are blue," and then add a red circle "because these are circles." For this kind of child who does not have enough backward mobility of thought to maintain a consistent criterion, covering the objects as they are placed in a box is sometimes helpful. When the box is covered and the child cannot see the objects that he put into it, he has to remember the reason for his grouping.

When the children can make nongraphic collections with ease, the shifting of criteria may be introduced. For example, given a kit of four red and blue combs and four red and blue cups, a child could make two groups according to use (the cups and combs) and then shift into grouping by color. Having four or five children working with the same kit helps them realize that there are different ways of classifying objects. The shifting of criteria is also facilitated by teamwork.

2. *Seriation.* The simplest seriation task involves sizes (e.g., the big, the bigger, and the biggest glass). A prerequisite for seriation according to size is the ability to make comparisons between two sizes. To teach this skill, it is necessary to begin with dichotomies of grossly different sizes of the same object (e.g., big and little square blocks). Similar tasks can be built

• • • • • • • •

[3] A mystery box is a covered box the size of a hat box with openings on two sides, so that the child can put his hands into it without being able to see the objects.

into the program to permeate the entire day. At first, equipment in all the activity areas can be provided in only two sizes. In the doll corner, the children use and arrange big and little pots, plates, spoons, dolls, etc. The block and truck area has shelves with two sizes of blocks, cars, trucks, and animal figures. In art, big and little brushes and paper are used. At juice time, cups and cookies can be of two different sizes. On the playground, children can take big and little steps, make long and short shadows, swing on swings of two sizes and heights, and play with big and little balls and hoops.

Later on in the school year, when two sizes have been mastered, the environment is enriched so that children can order objects of three or more sizes. Objects such as nesting cups and blocks are particularly good for beginning the ordering of many sizes because of their self-corrective nature. Making different sizes of an object with Play-Doh or clay is also good. Using dramatic play, such as making bowls and beds for the Papa Bear, Mama Bear, and Baby Bear, adds interest to seriation activities.

Comparisons can be taught about other qualities as well, such as hardness and loudness. These activities also begin with gross differences and insure that the children will be able to act on objects to compare their salient quality (e.g., learning about "hard" and "soft" by pressing down on a block and a piece of foam rubber having the same shape, size, and color). Rhythmics and instruments can be used to compare different degrees of loudness. Again, it is important that a large variety of materials and sensorimotor activities be used in the teaching of the prerequisites for seriation, as the essence of seriation is a system of relative differences which should not be tied to a few limited objects.

3. *Numbers.* The basic number goal in preschool for the teaching of numbers is to help the child construct a foundation for a logical system of numbers based on one-to-one correspondence, so that he will overcome his tendency to quantify a set of objects by the size of the space they occupy. The first strategy in helping the child to overcome his tendency to use space for numerical quantification is the establishment of equivalence by "provoked" one-to-one correspondence. "Provoked correspondence" uses two homogeneous sets which correspond qualitatively with each other in such a way that there can be only one element of a set to correspond with an element in the other set (e.g., a set of houses to correspond with a set of roofs). In using provoked correspondence, the teacher can ask the child to "find enough roofs for all the houses" without using words like "the same number" or "as many as," which the child often cannot understand. The qualitative correspondence between the house and the roof facilitates the child's establishment of one-to-one correspondence.

A second way to help the child overcome his tendency to base numerical judgment on space is through the teaching of linear ordering. This activity involves two identical sets of heterogeneous objects (e.g., a toy sock, shoe, dress, hat, etc.). Children are asked to make a copy of one of the sets arranged in a line. Interest can be added by having the children put paper clothes on a "clothesline" to look just like the teacher's line, or on a shelf to look just like the teacher's shelf. Linear ordering focuses the child on each object separately and prevents him from basing his judgment on the space occupied.

When children can establish numerical equivalence by one-to-one correspondence, games involving addition and subtraction are played. For example, after the child finds as many cups as saucers, the teacher adds an extra cup and asks him whether there are now enough saucers for all the cups, and what he should do to have enough. The child should be asked to justify his answer by his own manipulation of objects. If he decides that there are more cups than saucers, he will put one cup on (or next to) each saucer, and either take away the extra cup or add an extra saucer.

When a child can firmly establish equivalence, the teacher can change the spatial configuration of the sets and ask the child whether or not there are now enough saucers for all the cups. The next question about conservation is "how do you know?"

The teaching strategy for children who do not have conservation is the development of renversabilité. Renversabilité is prepared for at the sensorimotor level by the child's arranging sets of objects in one configuration (e.g., ten cups in a line), disarranging them (the same cups in a pile), and then rearranging them back to their original configuration. This practical knowledge can be used and extended in preschool by having the child begin considering such questions as "This doll wants to have a party. Put all the saucers in a line and then take out enough cups for all the saucers . . . Now, the doll wants to wash the cups; so put all the cups in a pile . . . Now, the cups are clean. Do you think you can put them back the way they were before? Do you think there will be a cup for each saucer? Let's put the cups back and see." This kind of activity is carried out numerous times using a large variety of different objects. Using dramatic play in number games has been found helpful in creating greater interest and involvement for the children.

A fundamental point to be gleaned from Piaget's theory of number is the importance of the child's own actions on objects. It is essential in all the activities described above that the child himself carry out the actions at all times. Games establishing or judging the numerical equivalence of two sets that the teacher arranged do not provide the full educational experience. Again, it is important that numerical equivalence not be tied to a few limited objects.

B. INFRALOGICAL (SPATIO-TEMPORAL) RELATIONSHIPS

1. *Spatial relationships.*   Three directions of programming can be discerned from Piaget's writings on spatial concepts. One aspect of development is the child's structuring of space from topological space to geometric space. Another aspect is the development of static space into more dynamic transformations. The third aspect is the reconstruction of sensorimotor space on a representational level.

Traditional topological spatial relationships such as "on," "off," "in," and "out" are taught through a sequence involving (a) motoric coordination with self-to-object relationships (e.g., getting on a block), (b) motoric coordination with object-to-object relationships (e.g., making a doll get on the block), and (c) motoric coordination of body parts in relation to each other (e.g., putting a finger on the nose).

An example of spatial transformation is that involving part–whole relationships. In order to learn part–whole transformations, the children disassemble objects into component parts, and reassemble them to their original form. An example is the cutting of apples into two, three, or four pieces and reassembling the proper pieces into the original apples. The "Fruit Bowl" marketed by Creative Playthings and construction toys such as Tinker Toys and Creative Snap Blocks are also useful for making three-dimensional part–whole transformations. Puzzles are ready-made materials for two-dimensional transformations, and the cutting up and pasting together of pictures and geometric shapes also teach spatial transformations. The most convincing evidence of the static nature of the four-year-old's space is his inability to reassemble a simple square that he has just cut into three pieces.

The four-year-old's sensorimotor space has developed into geometric space, but on the representational plane he tends to be still at the topological level. When he is asked to *find* another square (a perceptual task), the four-year-old can easily do this task. However, when he is asked to *copy* a square (a representational task), he is likely to produce either a circle or a kind of circle having one or two angles.

Two strategies may help the child to structure his representational space more geometrically. One is a variety of mystery-box games using perception by touch alone. When the child cannot see a shape, he is forced to structure his mental image of the shape. The other strategy is a variety of rhythmic activities involving the imitation of the teacher's body movements. When the child has to imitate the extending of one arm forward and the other arm to the side, for example, he has to mentally structure the $90°$ angle and the parallel of both arms in relation to the floor, thereby strengthening his geometric notions on the representational plane. Watching the movements of his body in a wide, full-length mirror has been found helpful to the child who has difficulty in these activities. The structuring of body image, too, results from imitation of body movements. Having the child assemble the pieces of a puzzle is by comparison not an effective way to teach body image.

Linear ordering has already been mentioned in connection with the teaching of numbers. This activity involves representation (i.e., copying) of topological relationships (i.e., the coordination of proximities, or the coordination of the relationship "next to"). While straight copying does not involve any transformation, two variations of linear ordering do. One such variation is ordering in a longer or shorter line than the model. For example, the teacher can put two sheets at both ends of the child's laundry line and ask him to hang up his clothes in exactly the same way as the teacher, even though his line has less empty space. The second variation is inverse order. In this task, the child is asked to begin with the last item of the teacher's line and end up with the first item of the model.

2. *Temporal relationships.* It has been stated in the accompanying "framework" paper that it is appropriate to try to structure the four-year-old's time into sequences but not into intervals. Another appropriate goal is the notion of speed at the sensorimotor level.

The school day offers numerous occasions for teaching sequence with the children's own activities. Some sequence involves large intervals, such as the daily schedule of going outside and then having juice, while others involve brief specific activities (e.g., planning together the sequences of cleanup). Rhythmics and large-motor activities are particularly good for games emphasizing temporal sequence, as these enable children to experience sequence in a vivid sensorimotor way (e.g., touching the eyes, the shoulders, and then the feet.).

The preceding sequences are arbitrary and therefore devoid of real meaning. Piaget points out that the notion of temporal sequence grows out of causal relationships, and vice versa. Thus, a good way to teach temporal sequence is in combination with the teaching of physical knowledge. For example, the action of dropping a ball precedes its bouncing. The means–end relationship, too, is a meaningful way to teach temporal sequence. For example, the children are asked what they have to do to make a big piece of paper for a big painting when only little pieces are available. Sociodramatic play is another way of teaching temporal order in a meaningful way. For example, the children have to buy their "groceries" before they start "cooking."

Speed is taught only in the sense of acting either slowly or fast in rhythmics. "Walk across the walking board as fast (or as slowly) as you can" is an example of the level that the children can understand. Pounding on the table faster, faster, and faster is another example, which has implications for the learning of seriation.

III. Representation

From the Piagetian standpoint, representation is a necessary but not a sufficient condition for the structuring of physical, social, and logical knowledge. As it was discussed in the accompanying "framework" paper, Piaget distinguished three forms of external representation: Indices, symbols, and signs. In the following discussion, it is useful to remember that teaching at the "index" level strengthens the child's knowledge of the object itself, that teaching at the "symbol" level strengthens his mental image, and that the "sign" (language) must be integrated into the child's knowledge at the levels of the index and the symbol.

A. REPRESENTATION AT THE "INDEX" LEVEL

Piaget states that even directly perceived objects must be "constructed" by intelligence, for an object is never seen in its entirety. Each perception is always from a particular point of view. For example, a car seen from the front looks different from one observed from the side. The child must, therefore, mentally put together the whole car from his limited point of view. This ability to construct three-dimensional objects that are in sight develops into the ability to reconstruct them when they are absent.

Teaching representation at the index level involves giving children a great deal of experience in "constructing" the whole object (a) when only a small part of it is perceived, (b) when the object is perceived through senses other than the visual, and (c) when a part of the object is missing. Numerous guessing games can be played in preschool. The teacher can partially hide objects behind a screen and ask the children to pick the same one out of a tray containing many things. Children can feel objects in a bag and guess what they are or what one can do with them. Kits containing incomplete objects and their missing parts can be put together, so that the children can find the missing parts for each object.

Another type of activity at the "index" level is the making of "prints" of objects in Play-Doh or clay, or with paint. The children's own footprints in the snow and handprints with fingerpaints is a good way to begin. The children can then move on to printing with objects such as a fork or a can. These printing activities prepare children for representation at the "symbol" level.

B. REPRESENTATION AT THE "SYMBOL" LEVEL

Symbols are the first true instruments of representation because, unlike indices, they are differentiated from the object. If preschools hope to strengthen children's ability to use language and to lay the foundation for reading, it is at the symbol level that much work must be done.

1. *The use of the body to represent objects (imitation).*   Piaget emphasized imitation as the child's first and most basic step into the symbolic world. In Piaget's theory of representation, the child's use of sensorimotor schemes in the absence of the object provides the transition between sensorimotor intelligence and representational intelligence (i.e., all the subsequent periods after the first two years). In imitation, the child expresses his mental image of objects directly with his sensorimotor schemes. Compared to make-believe, clay models, and pictures, which require an intermediary medium, imitation allows the direct externalization of the mental image. Therefore, the teaching of imitation is basic to a preschool basing its curriculum on Piaget's theory. Imitation should be heavily stressed throughout the school year.

In order to represent things with gestures, the child has to have mental images of what he tries to act out, and acting out in turn strengthens his mental image. Since mental images result from the internalization of sensorimotor actions, there is a circular, causal relationship between the strengthening of imitation and the strengthening of the mental image. Mental images are thus actively constructed. They are far from being passive residues of sensory stimuli.

Numerous "pretend" games can be played in school. The children are shown common articles such as an iron or a spoon and asked to "show us what you do with this." The objects should be the ones that the children have already played with, as the easiest level of imitation is self-imitation, i.e., the use of sensorimotor schemes outside of their practical context. At first, it is usually necessary for the child to imitate the teacher or another child who is actually using the object. Later, it will become necessary only to see the object, and eventually seeing a picture or hearing the name of an object will be sufficient for the child to make "pretend" gestures. The teaching of representation at this elementary level reveals how difficult it is for the lower-lower-class child to enter the symbolic world.

2. *The use of objects to represent other objects (make-believe).*   Piaget observed that children spontaneously use objects to symbolize other objects. The preschool environment can be structured to provide maximum opportunities to encourage this form of representation. The teacher can create an environment so that the child will use a block as a "car," line up chairs to make a "train," and pretend in his socio–dramatic play that pegs and beads are "food."

Games can be developed to stimulate the children to search for, and use, make-believe objects. Many children need to go through a sequence of using objects that closely resemble the real thing. For example, they need clamped-on wheels before becoming able to use a block alone to stand for a car. Making believe that a block is a car requires a mental image powerful enough for the block not to be seen as a block.

3. *The use of utterances to represent objects (onomatopoeia).*   Onomatopoeia is a vocal form of representation involving imitation of the sounds which characterize objects. For example, "ding-a-ling" means a telephone, and "quack, quack" means a duck. Games can be played where the teacher imitates characteristic sounds and asks the children to identify the things represented by these sounds. The answer can be given by finding a picture of the object or by giving the name. This game can later be made harder by having the children make the characteristic sounds for others to guess the objects.

4. *The constructing of three-dimensional models of objects.*   When children show ability to represent objects through imitation and make-believe, the construction of models is introduced. Block building and art activities are excellent ways to strengthen the child's ability to externalize his mental image of objects. Making models with Play-Doh, pipe cleaners, and wire offers children opportunities to represent objects that are familiar and important to them. Children usually need a period of sensorimotor experimentation with these media before going on to use them representationally.

5. *The making and recognition of objects in pictures.*   Every preschool program encourages children to recognize objects in pictures. What needs to be emphasized in a Piaget-derived curriculum is the fact that looking at pictures is passive representation, and that it is necessary to develop active representation with pictures. For this purpose, the teacher can draw a circle on the board and ask the children what it could be. One child may say, "A lollipop," and comes up to the blackboard to make the circle look like a lollipop. Another child may then say, "Now, it can be a girl," and makes the lollipop look like a girl, etc. Through activities of this sort, children not only develop active representation but also learn that symbols can be made to stand for whatever one wants them to.

C. REPRESENTATION AT THE "SIGN" LEVEL (LANGUAGE)

The unique role of language has been discussed in the "framework" paper. Exactly how to apply Piaget's theory of language to preschool education is a difficult question which still remains to be explored. It will be stated only that the two approaches to enhancing language development seem to be imitation (chanting, reciting nursery rhymes, etc.) and dialogues.

IV. The Integration of Physical, Logical, and Social Knowledge and Representation

An activity which fosters the integration of learning in all the above areas is socio–dramatic play. While playing "house," the children can group dishes and clothes, order them according to size, and practice one-to-one correspondence as they set the table. Temporal sequences are taught as the children put food in a pot, cook it, put it on the plates, and feed their "children." Spatial relationships are integrated as the children arrange things in the refrigerator, fold the tablecloth, and take the doll for a walk. Physical knowledge, too, enters the children's play. One child may take a pot off the stove and set it directly on the table, and another child may say, "Put it on a block. The pot is hot."

It is through socio–dramatic play that the child fully enters the world of representation. In playing "house," for example, he uses the "index" when he has to find things in the cupboard by seeing only a part of the objects. In imitating the roles of mother, father, baby, etc., he uses himself as a symbol of these people. He engages in make-believe by using round discs of cardboard that stand for dishes or sticks that stand for French fries. He uses onomatopoeia as he pretends to be a cat and says, "Meow." He constructs representations with blocks as he makes a bed to carry through his role play. When a teacher shows a picture of a kitchen scene, he gets ideas about how to elaborate his role. Finally, he has to use language to communicate the ideas and feelings which are appropriate to his role.

Socio–dramatic play requires that children engage in social collaboration, i.e., they must communicate with each other and adjust to each other's conception of their play roles. The ability to be aware of, and adjust to, viewpoints other than one's own is essential to the development of logical thinking. Language is crucial for these purposes.

Before concluding this paper, a general comment might be made regarding the structuring of the environment to maximize the child's chances for making discoveries. One of the few pedagogical principles Piaget has stated is the importance of the child's learning by his own discovery (Jennings, 1967). The teaching of cognitive content can be planned in any of the following three ways: (a) the manipulation of the environment to induce the child to "discover" the desired learning, (b) the manipulation of the environment to make "discovery" inevitable, and (c) direct teaching. An example of the first approach is to put measuring spoons in the doll corner in the hope that in using them the child might notice size differences. In this case, the teacher does not intervene in the child's play. An example of the second approach is having children return the measuring spoons to their outlines on a pegboard at cleanup time. In this situation, a preseriation activity becomes a necessary part of living at school. In direct teaching, the children are asked to give the biggest spoon to "Daddy," the next biggest spoon to "Mommy," etc. Preschools must use all three approaches either separately in a sequenced order or simultaneously. It appears best to begin with a period of free exploration and manipulation before direct teaching is attempted.

The curriculum described in this paper is still in the process of development as a research team attempts to read, understand, and apply Piaget's theory. It is a difficult theory to understand, and many misinterpretations have had to be corrected in the past. Many more changes will have to be made in the future. One thing that will not change, however, is that the kind of teaching described in this paper makes enormous demands on the teacher. It is hoped that skillful and creative teaching, combined with this theoretical framework, holds the promise that compensatory education can help the disadvantaged child to succeed in school, fulfill himself, and find a meaningful place in the world.

The Role of Experience in the Acquisition of Conservation

■■■■ MARCEL L. GOLDSCHMID

In recent years, much research has been directed toward testing the stability of such Piagetian concepts as conservation. While several investigators feel that conservation is exceedingly difficult to train into the child, others feel that conservation can be trained, and that a major factor is the training technique employed. In this article, Dr. Goldschmid describes a study of training conservation in which he evaluates the role of experience. He then goes on to relate his findings to the conservation controversy.

In Piaget's theory (cf. Flavell, 1963; Goldschmid, 1967) conservation represents a pivotal construct in the child's transition from a prelogical to a logical phase of development. When the child is able to conserve, he realizes that certain properties (e.g., substance, weight, volume) remain invariant in the face of certain transformations (e.g., changing the object's form or shape). Subsequent investigations (e.g., Fournier, 1967; Gellman, 1967) have suggested that the child's acquisition of conservation may be accelerated by special training. The purpose of this study was to assess the role of experience in the development of conservation by optimally incor-

● ● ● ● ● ● ● ●

SOURCE: *Proceedings*, 76th Annual Convention of the American Psychological Association, 1968, 361–362. (With permission of the author and the American Psychological Association.)

porating training variables which heretofore had been studied in isolation (comprehension of relational terms, transfer, stability) and variables which have not been investigated (training on several conservation tasks, different training techniques, and their interaction).

Method

Subjects.   The Ss were 110 English-speaking middle-class children in kindergarten in the Montreal Protestant School district.

Procedure

Relational terms test.   Previous studies (e.g., Brison, 1966) have indicated that a child's level of conservation may be a function of his capacity to understand relational terms. Each child was, therefore, first tested on his comprehension of the relational terms "as much," "not as much," and "more," the three phrases used in the conservation scales. Only those children who demonstrated an understanding of these terms participated in the experiment.

Conservation tasks.   Two conservation scales and a transfer test developed previously (Goldschmid and Bentler, 1968a, 1968b) were used to assess the level of conservation of the Ss. Scales A and B are parallel forms and include the following six tasks: conservation of substance, weight, two-dimensional space, continuous and discontinuous quantity, and number. The transfer test (Scale C) consists of two tasks: conservation of area and length. In all three scales S is asked to compare the relative quantity, weight, etc., of two objects after the shape or form of one of them has been transformed by a specific manipulation. The items are scored both with respect to the child's judgment (behavior) and his explanation.

Pretest on conservation. Prior to any training, all Ss were administered Scale A.

Training.   The training was designed to answer the following questions:

1. Can conservation be induced by providing specific training to nonconservers?
2. Do certain conservation tasks lend themselves more easily to effective training than others?
3. Are certain training procedures more successful than others?
4. Is there an optimal combination of conservation tasks and training procedures, i.e., is there an interaction effect between 2 and 3?

While these questions were couched in training variables, it should be noted that each of them was ultimately designed to elucidate the role that specific aspects of experience play in the acquisition of conservation.

All 110 Ss were randomly assigned to six experimental groups (each including 15 children) and a control group ($N = 20$). The experimental subjects were trained on two sets of tasks, half of them on discontinuous quantity, two-dimensional space, and substance; the other half on continuous quantity, number, and weight. Each half was further divided into three groups which were trained on reversibility, compensation, and a combination of reversibility and compensation, respectively. Thus, each combination of tasks and training procedure was represented in one of the experimental groups.

Reversibility training involved the repeated demonstration that after an object's shape has been changed, it may be returned to its original form, thereby enabling the child to make the inference that since an action can be reversed, the original quantity remains constant no matter how the object's shape is transformed.

Compensation training (emphasis on relevant perceptual cues) involved the step-by-step transformation of one of two objects of originally equal shape. For example, in conservation of substance, one of two balls of clay was gradually made into a long and thin sausage. This training procedure was used to show the child that, while one dimension was changed (e.g., the ball was flattened) there was a compensation factor (e.g., the ball became longer). Measuring rods were employed to concretely demonstrate the compensating factors in the two dimensions.

Combination of reversibility and compensation training involved aspects of both procedures outlined above.

In order to prevent a response set (i.e., "they are always the same") and to further enhance conservation behavior, the actual quantity of one of the two objects was also varied (addition and subtraction). Whenever possible the child assisted in the various manipulations and transformations. The order of the tasks in training was counterbalanced. Each experimental subject was given three one-half-hour training sessions, each session on a different task, spread over three days. None of the manipulations forming part of the three conservation scales were included in the training.

Post-tests and transfer test. The first post-test (Scale B) was administered after three weeks, and the second post-test (Scale A), preceded by the transfer test (Scale C), six weeks after training.

Results

Overall effects of training. In order to test training effects, analysis of covariance was used to remove any bias due to differences in performance on the pretest. The results on the first post-test indicated that the experimental groups did significantly better ($p < .001$) than the control group.

Additional *t* tests, furthermore, revealed that the experimental groups achieved significantly higher scores ($p < .001$) on the first post-test than on the pretest, on each of the six conservation tasks. In contrast, the control group obtained approximately the same scores on the first post-test as on the pretest. These overall findings clearly demonstrate that conservation can be induced in previously nonconserving children.

Stability of induced conservation. The data from the second post-test indicated that the gains the experimental group demonstrated on the first post-test were maintained on the second post-test, six weeks after training.

Transfer. The experimental *Ss* were trained on only three tasks, but obtained significantly higher scores than the control group on all six tasks. This result indicated specific transfer of training, since the six tasks of Scales *A* and *B* are highly intercorrelated (Goldschmid and Bentler, 1968*b*).

The experimental groups, furthermore, obtained significantly higher scores ($p < .001$) than the control group on Scale *C* which measures a somewhat different dimension of conservation than Scales *A* and *B*. These results demonstrated a more general transfer of training from one domain of conservation to another.

Comparison of training methods. An analysis of variance on the first post-test data indicated significant main effects ($p < .05$) for both tasks and training procedures and a significant interaction effect between tasks and procedures ($p < .01$). Additional analyses demonstrated that reversibility training was more effective than the compensation and combination training and that training on the first set of tasks (conservation of discontinuous quantity, two-dimensional space, and substance) was more successful than training on the second set (continuous quantity, number, and weight). The best combination was the reversibility training on the first set of tasks.

The results of the analysis of variance of the data from the second post-test data were similar to those obtained from the first post-test.

Discussion and Conclusions

These findings represent further evidence that the acquisition of conservation can be accelerated. Flavell (1963), after reviewing several learning studies, commented that "Piagetian concepts have so far proved inordinately difficult to stamp in, whatever the training procedure used." In the face of the present findings and those of recent studies, Flavell's conclusion no longer holds. Flavell further stated that "when one does succeed in inducing some behavioral change through this or that training procedure, it may not cut very deep." The results of this study suggest both stability of provoked conservation and specific and general transfer of conservation behavior to untrained tasks. The criteria for evaluating conservation behavior, furthermore, included not only the child's judgment of conservation or non-conservation after a specific manipulation, but also his explanation for his judgment. Piaget has insisted that the latter criterion be applied in judging whether a child has truly acquired the schema of conservation.

Flavell (1963) has also addressed himself to the question of how cognitive structures, such as conservation, are acquired. He points out that investigators who have applied Piaget's equilibration model have obtained better training results than those who have used a conventional learning approach. Results of subsequent studies (e.g., Fournier, 1967) and the present findings support this conclusion. Notions of reversibility and compensation, Piaget believes, are thought processes underlying conservation. A child may arrive at conservation behavior by different routes, i.e., by either applying the principle of reversibility or compensation, or his conservation behavior may be based on a simple unchanged quantity notion, i.e., on an inference that if nothing is added or subtracted to the objects, their quantity remains the same regardless of their shape. It would seem reasonable to assume that if a child, in his daily interactions with objects in his environment, acquires any one of these notions, he will spontaneously develop conservation. At a later stage he is able to combine different notions and give a more complete, multifaceted explanation for his conservation judgment (Goldschmid, 1967). The results of this study suggest that the acquisition of these three principles (reversibility, compensation, and/or addition–subtraction) are indeed effective in eliciting conservation behavior.

It remains to be explained why some of the training methods were more effective in inducing conservation than others. At least two alternative, but not mutually exclusive, explanations appear reasonable. It is possible that reversibility is a more rudimentary element of conservation than compensation. The other explanation is related to the specific training methods used. The manipulation and verbalizations were more complex and elaborate for the compensation and combination training than for the reversibility training. These same inferences may also serve to explain why training on the first set of conservation tasks was more successful than on the second.

In conclusion it may be stated that conservation can be induced by providing nonconservers with experiences involving elements of conservation which Piaget believes underlie or precede the spontaneous acquisition of conservation.

Concept Learning in Early Childhood

■■■ WILLIAM FOWLER

Interest in cognitive learning has increased sharply in the past few years, encouraging much research in early child development. Most of this research activity is centered around two conceptual models: the developmental theory of Piaget and the experimental child psychology following the classical S–R model. Discouraged by lack of basic research on long-range educational problems of cognitive development on the part of members of both camps, the author developed a conceptual model which has been used in a variety of educational projects with disadvantaged children and in infant learning. His description of the model in this paper is applied to concepts in community structure.

Today we seem to be witness to an explosion of interest in cognitive processes and their origins in early development that was hardly foreseeable a few years ago. There is a growing awareness of the possible importance of the early years as a foundation, if not critical, period for the establishment of basic learning sets and cognitive styles. There is also a widening of interest in the long-term, emergent and developmental character of complex thought processes.

Much of the impetus for the scientific popularity of these new foci has paralleled, if it cannot be entirely attributed to, the national and even international political sociology of our era. The race from Sputnik and the bottomless demands for education of underdeveloped world populations have seemingly contributed to the discovery that our own country is also inhabited by large populations of intellectually underprivileged people. With this discovery we have come to believe that poverty may be related to cultural deprivation and that social deprivation may be partly founded on certain root perceptual and conceptual deprivations, traceable to the earliest years of childhood.

Under such crash circumstances, it is hardly surprising to find that much of the research on problems of early cognitive development, deprivation and stimulation are in the nature of crash field projects aimed at developing viable educational settings for preschool, culturally disadvantaged children. More basic efforts to formulate and study the experiential–developmental course of concept formation in the beginning phases may be found in the writings of investigators like Deutsch and his colleagues (1964), Hunt (1961), Hess and Shipman (1963), Fowler (1962, 1965), and others.

• • • • • • • •

SOURCE: *Young Children, 21* (1965), 81–91. (With permission of the author and *Young Children.*)

Two Historical Frameworks

Notwithstanding this exponential growth of activity on these problems, much current research thinl ing on the emergence of cognitive processes remains encapsulated in either of two limiting frameworks. Both frameworks fail to concern themselves adequately with the etiology of concept development. Of these widely prevalent viewpoints, one tends merely to characterize and the other simply to measure intellectual processes at various ages, relating them, respectively, either to long-term, descriptive developmental theories or to short-term, general behavior theory models. In neither model is there much attempt to explain or control the course of development over time. On the one hand, the newer orientations which follow the molar, structural concepts of Piaget tend to be mired in ideal type, age–stage comparisons rather than tracing the specific, antecedent conditions and mechanisms which produce development. On the other hand, much of experimental child psychology, following the classical $S-R$ model, while not uninfluenced by the structural concepts of Piaget, continues to ignore the developmental history and life's circumstances of the subjects under study. In short, there is, as yet, little experimental effort to undertake basic research on long-range educational problems of cognitive development.

A Conceptual Model

In the course of attempting to grapple with some of these divergent orientations and explanatory gaps, I have evolved something of a model of developmental learning processes in the early years. The schema is aimed at pulling together a variety of poorly related concepts from the fields of learning and cognitive development for consideration in the little-developed area of systematic education and long-term programming of concept learning in early childhood.

Preliminary descriptions of the model have been derived in the main from my work on early reading (Fowler, 1962, 1965). More recently, I have been formulating the same type of conceptual organization in terms of broader subject areas of knowledge, formulations which I should like to present herein. As a means of general orientation, I shall furnish a brief overall picture of the schema. I shall then probe some of the central concepts in greater detail, illustrating their utility as we have been applying them at the Laboratory Nursery School and in projects with culturally disadvantaged preschoolers. At various points, I will also endeavor to relate them to some of the developmental issues and problems of (early) cognitive development.

Following the notion that development is a process of acquiring increasingly complex mental structures and modes of functioning through the cumulative interaction of the growing child with his environment, our approach is one of attempting (1) to program systematically concept learning and (2) to devise the most effective techniques and role for the teacher. To accomplish the first point, we can identify relatively focal structures in the social and physical world and set up learning programs which will enable a young child to learn specific features and relations of and between structures as well as lead him to the foundation of general concepts. To insure cumulative success for each child, we define functional units of analysis along continua of complexity.

Under the second main proposition, we establish a learning situation and style of relations to facilitate cue-guided stimulation. The general framework is founded on a discovery problem-solving approach but is liberally immersed in dramatic and play-oriented activities. Much of the activity entails physical manipulation of miniature or pictured objects by children in small group settings.

The Concept of Structure

Proceeding from this very brief summary to some elaboration, the concept of structure as used here applies both to the patterning of the external world and the organization of the child's mental processes in schemata, as Piaget calls them (1952b). It is assumed that it is the lawful ordering of reality in patterned and operating systems which makes possible the emergence of adaptive structures in the child's mind and patterned, interrelated systems of action. Meaning, in other words, has its basis in terms of the close and ordered relations of mental structures to reality structures.

At the beginning, in infancy, reality structures, as represented in the mind, are presumably grossly incomplete, immediate, and little generalized. Piaget makes much of this kind of distinction and the long developmental distance between what he defines as the early perception of infralogical structures and the only gradual and later emergence of classificatory mental structures (Flavell, 1963). By the former he means the direct perception of single objects and their components and the corresponding part–whole relations, spatio–temporal contiguity and physical continuity involved. Classificatory structures, on the other hand, are essentially constructions of the mind, although based on similarities and regularities among objects which are abstracted to form type structures. Physical proximity and continuity are not conditions for the formation of abstract or logical structures, according to Piaget.

In my organization of a schema for beginning conceptual learning, I consider it important to concentrate upon both single object structures (and their internal organization) and abstract classificatory structures. Direct, perceptual–motor manipulations of simple structures may well predominate in the intellectual modes of the infant and preschool child. From an educational point of view, however, the problem appears to be one of facilitating the developmental transformation of the child's intellectual operations from the level of these infralogical structures to more complex and abstract forms of logical functioning. According to Piaget and some evidence, the latter, complex structures typically evolve during the four- to seven-year-age span (Flavell, 1963; S. H. White, 1965). But virtually all of the evidence for Piaget's theories and the so-called "norms" of mental development have been gathered with little regard to prior experience, let alone the child's total life history (Fowler, 1962). In other words, there has been scarcely any assessment at all of the critical and cumulative role that learning plays in the development of concepts.

Planning and the Cumulative Nature of Learning

The importance of planning and guiding stimulation from the beginning and throughout the ontogenetic span of development is inherent in the cumulative nature of discrimination–generalization processes. The terms discrimination and generalization themselves imply processes of choosing among dimensions of reality to form concepts about it. They also imply the possibility of alternate paths along which a child can develop. The first discriminations and generalizations acquired become foundation concepts upon which subsequent discriminations and generalizations must be erected. All ensuing concepts formed serve as cumulative constraints determining which higher order paths to abstraction and which set of representations of reality we come to comprehend — or even whether we attain any at all. A central assumption, then, upon which my early concept learning model is founded is that we should concern ourselves with guiding and systematically programming a child's cognitive development from the earliest periods of life.

The first step in setting up a stimulation program is the selection of a particular subject area of reality, for example, modes of transportation, community structure, zoology, reading foreign languages, or almost any domain of reality which can be defined and presented in a form sufficiently simplified for a child to learn as Bruner has suggested (Bruner, 1960). Availability of materials and ease of obtaining pictures are likely to be important determinants of choice. Closeness of relation to the preschool child's interest, dominant in the culture, is secondary under the assumption that teaching techniques utilized are adequate to arouse and sustain interest in unfamiliar material, although this may influence learning gradients established.

Analytic–Synthesizing Approach

The act of selecting a specific area of reality for a learning program is *per se* a demonstration of one principle upon which the conceptual model is built, namely, the utility of an analytic, simplifying approach to studying the world. Having decided upon some area considered appropriate as a content area of value for children to learn, extension of this principle leads to an analysis of the structure into primary elements and infrastructural relationships as well as to charting a program according to levels of difficulty.

The approach is not one of merely studying elements as simplified and isolated bits, however. It is rather concentrating upon parts — both elements and simple relationships — to sharpen perceptual focus but also to study them as components subordinate to some supraordinate system or larger infralogical structure. The aims here are to simplify the intricacies of a structure through selecting out key dimensions while ignoring others. This, in turn, is assumed not only to facilitate learning about particular infralogical structures but to orient learning toward the development of abstracting processes.

A key principle represented here is the importance of steering between the extremes of molecular (S–R) versus molar (Gestalt) styles of learning, an unproductive polarization of alternatives which has long plagued theories of learning and education. By presenting material in a shifting but interrelated focus of attention on simplified parts and wholes, through a process of analysis and synthesis, the child is enabled to acquire a better conceptual grasp of both the forest and trees. Alternating analytic–synthesizing approaches toward stimulation facilitates learning simply because reality is organized in ways that parts bear some relation to one another and to a total structure, through the use they serve in the construction and operation of a structure. It is, in fact, the apparent organization and working of reality domains according to structural–functional mechanisms and relations which forms an important basis for this conceptual model of the stimulation process.

Learning Sequences

In our current experimentation there are a variety of alternate schemes for establishing sequential levels of difficulty which we have been exploring. The organization of levels which we have found more or less useful are, roughly: first, the gross perception of objects and their functions; second, focus upon salient features of objects, their functions and relations to the whole; third, ecological relations of the given structure and its components to other structures and aspects of the environmental context generally;

fourth, classificatory activities, which involve sorting and grouping of objects according to abstracted structures and functions of objects and in relation to the organization of larger supraordinate systems.

In general, while we may define certain kinds of organizational foci and related tasks in terms of "levels," much of this is a matter of convenience in outlining perspectives and guides for teachers. There is in actual practice considerable overlap among the levels in keeping with our analytic–synthetic approach, as well as in order to capitalize upon a child's curiosity to explore the various internal features and functions of objects and their relations to the ecological fabric. In some ways we are dealing as much with directions of analysis as we are with levels of difficulty.

There are, nevertheless, at least two ways in which gradients are followed. Aside from the presumably greater demands for conceptualizing and abstracting processes which the classificatory tasks impose, within each of the major levels or directions of structural analyses, certain definite gradients of difficulty are established and more or less followed. Among the criteria for setting up these gradients are degree of familarity or cultural commonness of objects; the complexity of a specific object structure, its parts and mechanisms; and the number of attributes, parts and objects and interrelations which are concentrated upon in a given event sequence or operation of a system or subsystem. There is the additional factor of ordering symbolic mediation in amount and kind of difficulty. This is more easily included in our description of the instructional techniques and situation.

An Illustration: The Structure of a Community

Having outlined our approach to defining the dimensions of a schema, it may be useful to illustrate their applicability to a domain such as the structure of a community. By community, here, I mean roughly some local unit of socio-economic organization which embraces clusters of residential, manufacturing, agricultural and distributive units of activity and the network of relations among them.

With respect to our own contemporary scene, therefore, some of the obvious conceptual units with which to start a program are a home, school, store, factory, farm, or community electrical circuits. Each of these concepts can be conveniently represented in concrete form — which draws in another major pillar of the model. Early stimulation programs are heavily built around the manipulation of real objects — usually in miniature or in pictures — in keeping with the low-power abstracting abilities of early development.

Starting with pictures and toy models and occasional excursions to stores, houses, factories, garages, parks, and people, at the first level, we explore a child's familiarity with the major dimensions of a community structure.

The type of cognitively oriented and developed child of middle-class professional parents who attends the Laboratory Nursery School is already familiar with most of the objects and many of their component features. One is likely, therefore, to find oneself almost at once launched somewhere on at least a second level series of discovering and discriminating such particulars as cash registers, greasing cars in a gas station, or money and checking accounts in a bank. But wherever one begins, gradients of complexity are selected and pursued on the basis of ordering in their number and complexity the typical structural–functional components of each community distribution unit, e.g., of a garage — pumps for serving gasoline, rack for servicing a car, and so on. The mechanisms for operating a gasoline pump are presumably more complicated than the process of gasoline flowing into an automobile's gas tank.

From these examples, it may be apparent that centering attention upon the internal structure of a community subordinate structure like a garage, as opposed to its external relations with the community, is a fairly arbitrary approach. It is here that the overlapping of units and relationships among structural levels becomes most evident. For instance, tools are standard components of a hardware store at one level of structural analysis; but tools also relate to and are synthesizable in terms of other categories, e.g., houses and home repair, and broader community concepts of maintenance, comfort and shelter. Structures at one level constitute the units at another level of analysis. The principle here, in sum, is merely to simplify the study of structural systems by momentarily isolating components from the network of internal–external relations of systems and subsystems. Components are sorted out, concentrated on and synthesized in one set of relations and directions, a step or so at a time.

In this maze of guided learning, further complexity is attained along two main arteries. One of these, again, involves the kind and number of relations toward which the child's understanding of the total community organization, operations and multilateral pattern of relationships is led. Ultimately, it is possible to conceive of sketching in for a child a still highly simplified but relatively complete picture of a community which embraces such concepts as the basic functions of money, the division of labor, socio–economic class and the like. To realize this goal, however, we must also traverse the second major arterial sequence, namely, classificatory concepts, or our fourth level of structural analysis.

Learning Classificatory Concepts

From one point of view, classificatory or generalizing activities, as with the three other directions of analysis, are not something entirely deferrable to a more advanced stage of the stimulation program. The moment we lead a child to distinguish a hardware store from a store in general, as a genre, we are introducing generality, or membership in a category. We thus overlook the fact that a hardware store sells tools and a grocery store, food, identifying only attributes they have in common, especially that of selling goods. When we do this, of course, we are introducing abstracting processes. Thus the supposedly simple labeling of individual stores — hardware, grocery, shoestore — in a community is in fact ranging across examples of a type concept. These roots of the language abstracting process through words begin very early according to Vygotsky (1962).

Notwithstanding, abstracting activities are treated in this structural model as a separate more complex type of activity. In a sense, word labeling and object discrimination activities probably do involve abstracting and generalizing. Yet, it is presumably a much simpler process to discriminate a single object from among a cluster of objects, to which a word label is associated, on the basis of gross configurations, than it is to sort objects — even those immediately perceivable — into groups on the basis of selected attributes which some but not all objects have in common. It is also evident that second and higher levels of hierarchial classification (e.g., a given individual works at a waitress type of job, which, in turn, is a class of semiskilled work within a still larger framework of working-class occupations) are even further removed from simple object discrimination, labeling type tasks. How far a child can progress through these levels remains to be determined since Welch (1940) and this writer (1961) found almost no second level hierarchy concepts available to three- and four-year-olds even following relatively long-term programs of stimulation continuing over several months or more. It is hoped that present attempts to analyze and program along the specific structural lines of the current model, however, may prove more successful than earlier crude attempts.

Teaching Techniques

The techniques employed for cognitive stimulation in the early years of child development may be described in terms of a situational setting and a few principles of interest arousal based on positive attitudes and styles in teaching relations, competence motivation (R. W. White, 1959) and incidental learning. It is productive to organize a stimulation program within the framework of a project unit of work for which the sequential guides and materials we have illustrated are prepared. The project is presented to a specific group of children over a period of several months on some regular basis, preferably no more than a few minutes or so per day. Brevity, frequency, and flexibility are important considerations in dealing with the brief attention and short recall spans and quasi-stable learning styles characteristic of the younger developmental periods. Small groups of four to eight children in a small area, visually and aurally separated from the valence of competing activities and attractions, is useful. The interest of groups of this size in insulated settings can be more easily corralled and group games managed. At the same time, the size permits individual tailoring and a loose framework of guidance for promoting productive self- and paired-direction of small projects.

The teaching approach itself rests on two types of techniques, one of these an atmosphere of play-game activities, the other a problem-solving orientation. The individual stimulus units — pictures and small objects (when available) — are presented to the children, singly and in small clusters (as more are learned), and spread out on a flat surface (table or floor) around which the children are seated. The basic forms of the learning tasks consist of three kinds of processes: discrimination–identification, matching–constructing, and sorting–grouping activities. Pictures or objects are discriminated from others in a set and/or identified (verbally labeled) at the teacher's request. Pictures are matched with other identical or similar pictures or put together with a pattern of other pictures to construct (synthesize) a larger structural scene. And pictures are sorted and arranged in groups according to criteria defined by the teacher for the abstract classificatory processes. All three types of activities are viewed as still rooted in the basic dimensions of discrimination–identification processes. The more complicated forms are merely extensions and elaborations which encompass multilateral relations, interrelations of parts to wholes, and discrimination of classes of objects and classes of ecological settings upon the basis of selected cues identifying type functions and structures.

There is a model question to be employed by a teacher which guides a child's attention effectively in the discrimination–generalization activities, while setting up for him a search task and an active role involving physical manipulation of concrete "things." The basic question or instruction follows some variant of the basic form, "Where is the bank?" or "Find all the pictures which show people working in factories." It may be seen that this question is readily adaptable to involving a child in specific tasks whose success is contingent upon performing higher level cognitive operations of a classificatory type. Thus, "Put the pictures of professional workers in this pile and the pictures of skilled workers in this pile."

Play orientations consist of "seek and find" and various targeting types of games, and other similar, competence challenging, means–end problem-solving tasks. In this category are included the finding of correct choice pictures hidden under one of a series of boxes or large cards; dropping a picture in a box after discriminating it correctly from among a cluster on a table; or pinning a discriminated picture at a correct position in an ecological mural painted on a broad expanse of paper on the wall. Open-ended ecological settings may be constructed from materials and pictures provided, or cut-up pictures may be assembled in a picture puzzle and used in synthesizing and matching tasks.

A second category of incentive technique used consists of a teacher narrating tales around the objects and scenes while she manipulates the stimuli in dramatic role play. The child is invited to participate along with the teacher in the course of the story development, which exposes him — incidentally — to further reinforcement experiences.

In every stimulation task, correction of "wrong" responses is avoided and liberal use of praise addressed to the child's effort is recommended. In this dramatic framework original and imaginative constructions can thus be encouraged. Yet, learning can also easily be channelized in definite directions of sequence and organization. The teacher simply has to redemonstrate a model associational task or to reask for a desired discrimination from time to time. Through varying widely the forms of the play activity in which the basic discrimination–sorting tasks are immersed, a large number of repetitions can easily be provided without the usual avoidance learning consequences of drill. Reinforcement is also multiplied in the small group setting, where each child observes the responses of the other children.

Gradient of Symbolic Mediation

While all play–instructional sessions are organized around discrimination-generalizing task activities, there is a further gradient of difficulty built into the program, namely the degree of symbolic mediation deriving from the arrangement of the tasks themselves. Initially, all new objects and relation-ships are labeled and defined for the child, as each is introduced. Immediately following this demonstration by the teacher, the next task or step in order of difficulty requires the child to discriminate the same item in response to an instruction which also provides a verbal label. His task at this beginning level is thus to associate this orally furnished label with the visual stimulus pattern placed immediately in front of him. Even at this stage, memory and, hence, mediation are involved in this perceptual–associative act. There is necessarily some time-lapse, however brief, between the model associative act performed by the teacher and the cognitive linkage between word and act performed by the child.

In subsequent stages, the gradient for the amount of symbolic mediation may be steepened through extending in time and space the distance between a teacher's demonstration model and a child's performance. Thus, at later stages of the program, a child might be asked (in review) to perform associational tasks which neither a teacher nor himself (self-reinforcement) had performed for some weeks.

Mediation also increases in proportion as the distance between the visual stimuli and the emission of a verbal concept is increased. Displacing a picture from a table at which a child is sitting to a blackboard may be one step. Bringing a picture from home, where the search cannot even be initiated until some hours after the verbalization is stated by a teacher at school, requires considerably longer memory storage. Similarly, in other ways, more complex mediation is demanded by removal of ecological context cues or by inserting objects in varied ecological scenes. In the same manner we may show other pictures of similar type objects whose structure or function may be similar but whose components, organization of structure, or mechanisms may vary. One may also increase the number, variety and spread of parts and relations which must be scanned and conceptualized, and so on. Again, each of these kinds of variations are introduced carefully, step-by-step, graded in terms of their degree of similarity, closeness and complexity in comparison with the original stimulus patterns and task requirements. We may also simply ask a child to identify a presented stimulus or set of relations, the teacher furnishing no verbal cues; the child must then rely entirely on his own internal mediation in response to the query, "What is ――― ?" This last form of task tends to test rather than teach a child and is generally minimized except in measurement sessions.

Positive Motivation, Flexible Sequences, and Inquiry Orientations

The important factor is to insure success at each step of the program, that is, to link each step in size and distance to the prior sequence of steps, always presenting bites of a size a child can chew. This is considered critical in order to minimize failure experiences, foster achievement motivation and a sense of intellectual mastery and autonomy, and produce progress in complexity of cognitive functioning and the extent of specific and general concepts absorbed.

Any of these sequences along a continuum — or in stages — of complexity need not be rigidly adhered to in the actual learning situation. Indeed overconcern with simplicity is likely to stultify teaching style and inhibit curiosity and exploration of structure, thus defeating a major educational goal. In addition to the active, physically manipulative search role which is continually set up for the child, an inquiry orientation is embedded into the nature of the guiding, stimulating process. Any given series of analytic construction and classification tasks requested of a child includes alternate and sometimes overlapping means and classificatory structures for conceptualizing. These shifts of foci are intended to convey to the child the idea of alternate pathways of inquiry about the world, while preserving the utility of guidance along and among particular paths and systems.

Within this kind of flexible framework, some rough approximation to a course graded according to levels of complexity is considered essential in setting instructional priorities if rates and degree of mastery are to be maximized. A balance between encouraging wider inquiry and insuring continuing progress through grading material to each child's level and style is attempted. The implications for producing a thoughtful citizenry are inherent in the developing of attitudes of inquiry. On the other hand, the value of programming lies in the fact that unless stimuli are ordered sequentially, it is difficult to regulate the flow of stimulation to conform to each child's rate, style, and level of acquisition. In the absence of the opportunity to pace and tune the presentation of stimulus patterns in close approximation to each child's evolving levels of comprehension, we offer less than ideal conditions to promote the operation of mechanisms for advancing cognitive development and mastery.

Problems of Disadvantaged Children

In closing, deficiencies in the grading and tuning process loom with the largest prominence in educational settings for culturally disadvantaged children, or any children who have experienced massive doses of sensory–cognitive deprivation or distortion. The difficulty of tuning into the non-productive and sometimes rigidly concrete psycho–cognitive styles of these types of children, even at the three-year level, has recently been most graphically displayed to this investigator (Fowler, 1961, 1965). Efforts to stimulate cognitive development in two such Negro children among a small group of identical twins and triplets over an eight-months' span in an experimental nursery school failed almost completely. There were no significant changes in cognitive functioning despite stress placed upon personal warmth, small group learning situations and the use of play–activity techniques. While all of the latter techniques may conceivably have been improved, the known lack of systematic programming has influenced my present efforts to proceed in this direction in projects on compensatory education.

Emphasis upon careful sequencing should not minimize the importance of emotionally supportive teaching attitudes and flexible teacher styles or the value of dramatic play activities and games. The curious fact, however, is that while these children often manifestly enjoyed the relations and the activity situations, they nevertheless made no real headway in learning. One question to which I am presently addressing myself is: to what degree can the introduction of systematic programming — while retaining the motivating techniques — reorient these essentially noncognitive learning styles and sets already apparently so ingrained by the age of three?

Young Children's Acquisition of Cognitive Skills under Various Conditions of Redundancy, Punishment, and Perceptual Input

■■■ WILLIAM J. MEYER

In tracing the course of normal intellectual growth, Piaget has also pointed to the nature of its interaction with environmental stimuli. The author of this paper explores the effects on concept identification of task-related stimuli, e.g., complexity, and various incentive conditions. He concludes that subject characteristics must also be considered, and identifies one which appears to have a relationship to both cognitive growth and social–emotional adjustment, namely motor impulsivity. The prevalence of this relationship among deprived children suggests retardation in terms of Piaget's schema, while the presence of biological deficiencies supports his view of the relationship between physical and mental functioning.

One obvious component of cognitive skills is the ability to adequately identify concepts in a variety of problem situations. Laboratory experiments typically provide the subjects with pairs of stimuli in which one dimension (color, form, etc.) is relevant and other dimensions are irrelevant. The child's task is to determine which dimension, and which value (red, square, etc.), is relevant and to associate that stimulus with a specific instrumental response. Another strategy provides the subjects with a variety of objects which can be sorted in a variety of ways. Typically, the subject is encouraged to continue sorting the stimuli until it is obvious no further categorizations are available to him.

Each procedure serves its purposes adequately but each relies on the subject's determining the salient aspects of the stimuli. This is particularly evident with the experimental strategy where the subject must figure out what the experimenter wants in order to receive an M & M. These studies are typically labeled "concept formation" or "discrimination learning," suggesting that the concept is acquired during the experiment. What is more likely to be the case is that the subject already has the concept and can, prior to the experiment, adequately discriminate among the various dimensions and values of the dimensions. A more accurate description of these studies is "concept identification" or "attribute identification" where it is assumed that the attribute already exists in the subject's response repertoire.

At least three attributes of the total task situation can be identified as contributing to the variability usually observed in such studies: (1) stimulus characteristics, (2) incentives employed, and (3) subject characteristics. I shall now examine each of these variables.

• • • • • • • •

SOURCE: Paper presented at the annual meeting of the American Educational Research Association, February 1968. (With permission of the author.)

Stimulus Characteristics. The term "stimulus characteristics" means the number of dimensions simultaneously present in the stimulus. For example, a pair of geometric blocks might include the dimensions of color, form, size, and, if they are paired, position. Clearly it is possible to vary the number of dimensions from two, where one is relevant and the other irrelevant, to n dimensions with one relevant and $n - 1$ irrelevant. Osler and Kofsky (1965, 1966) have shown that preschool kindergarten age children perform less well on any level of task complexity, but especially so with the more complex level. These investigators further showed that the older children dimensionalized the stimuli to a greater degree; that is, they tended to respond in terms of the available dimensions rather than in terms of the specific values of each dimension.

The fact that the older children spontaneously categorized to a greater extent than the younger children suggests that less of a memory load is placed on the older Ss; that is, failure to categorize required the S to recall the association between each separate stimulus and the correct response, while categorization of stimuli requires only that the child recall the association between a combination of stimuli and the correct response. Thus it seems plausible to expect that a memory aid would benefit both younger and older children, but benefit the young children to a greater degree. The following experiment, conducted by myself and David Hultsch, examined this possibility.

The subjects were 108 kindergarten and second grade children. There were 54 kindergarten children, mean $CA = 5.9$ years and 54 second graders, mean $CA = 8.0$ years. The children were from lower-middle-class homes and possessed average intellectual ability.

Concept identification tasks at three levels of stimulus complexity were constructed. Each level required the identification of one relevant concept and complexity was varied by including either zero, one, or two irrelevant concepts. The positions of the correct responses were sequenced so that within a block of trials each stimulus appeared equally often, right and left sides were correct equally often, and shifting sides resulted in reinforcement as often as staying on the same side. The dimensions were color, form, and size, each of which was relevant equally often.

For the memory load conditions in which one or two previous instances were available, a lighted display box was placed behind each of the response buttons. Following a correct response, a print identical in content and size to the projected stimulus was placed in the box behind the appropriate response button. In the condition where one instance was available, the print remained in the display box until the S made another correct response, at which time the new stimulus replaced it. The procedure was the same for the two-instance condition except that two prints were on display. Following a third correct response, the earliest print was removed.

The subject's task was to determine the relevant dimension and then associate each value of that dimension with the appropriate buttons. Relevant dimensions and values were randomized over subjects. Trials were terminated after ten successively correct responses or after 144 trials.

The design is a 3 × 3 × 2 model with three levels of stimulus complexity, three levels of memory load reduction and two age levels. There were six S's per cell. The stimuli consisted of pictures of geometric figures mounted on slides suitable for use with a Kodak 100 projector. The subject was seated at a table in front of a milk glass screen. Stimuli were rear-projected and terminated upon the subject's response. A successive-presentations procedure was used. Two buttons, one on the right and one on the left were on the table and in easy reach of the subject. Activation of the correct response button operated an M & M dispenser. The presentation of the stimuli and dispensing of reinforcers was controlled by means of a Gerbrands Program Timer.

Total errors to criterion were determined for each of the eighteen groups and served as the data for analysis. There were statistically significant effects, at the .05 level attributable to stimulus complexity ($F = 5.9$) and to memory load ($F = 6.7$). Thus the mean number of errors increased as a function of stimulus complexity and decreased as a function of memory load reduction. Chronological age was not statistically significant.

Although the age x memory reduction interaction was not statistically significant, a plot of the curves suggests that our hypothesis is incorrect; that is, the older Ss improved more as a result of the memory aids rather than the young Ss. It should be noted however, that the memory reduction variable did improve the performance of the young Ss.

Two aspects of this study have impressed us. First of all, the memory reduction variable was helpful in learning the task. It is also clear, however, that this variable is more beneficial when the Ss tend to dimensionalize the stimuli in the first place. We suspect the memory aid serves to remind the older Ss on what basis their previous decision was made, therefore providing a basis for the next response. Secondly, we were impressed by remarkable variability in performance. Our suspicion is that many children identified the correct concept very early because, indeed, it was highest in their hierarchy to begin with. Other children failed to learn altogether because of a willingness to accept low levels of reinforcement or an inability to attend to other stimulus dimensions. These alternatives are now being examined.

Incentive Conditions. In an earlier work where we ran concept identification experiments contrasting the effects of reward versus punishment, we found consistently, that under complex stimulus conditions as previously defined, the punishment groups always performed reliably better. When the level of complexity was low (one relevant, one irrelevant) there were no differences. Our interpretation of these data was that punishment, which obviously implies that the response was incorrect, was a more efficient means for helping the S identify the stimulus dimension and value we had in mind. In this connection, it should be noted that the variances for the blame groups were consistently smaller. However, these variances remained large enough to suggest that still other variables were operating.

Subject Characteristics. One of the behaviors readily observable in running these experiments is the number of children who do not seem to attend very adequately to the stimulus display before them. In the first study reported here, for example, we made a crude attempt to measure the amount of looking behavior. Although our data are quite incomplete, we did see children who examined the stimulus carefully, comparing it with the memory stimulus. Other children responded almost simultaneously with the presentation of the stimulus. It cannot be determined from this study whether this variation related to performance, but it makes sense that this occurred.

Clearly, what is referred to here is something like the notion of cognitive styles as described by Kagan, Moss, and Sigel (1963), among others. We believe, like many others, that nonanalytic or impulsive styles may serve, in fact, to limit the stimulus input from the environment and/or may operate in such a way that the child responds before adequately assessing the total situation. The study to be described is concerned with the relationships between two measures of motor impulsivity and Stanford–Binet IQ and was conducted by David Massari, Lois Hayweiser, and myself. Maccoby, Dawley, Kagan, and Degerman (1965) have recently reported a significant correlation ($r = .44$) between the ability to inhibit movement and performance on the Stanford–Binet. In that report, the investigators raised the question as to whether or not a similar relationship would exist among children from a lower socio–economic group or with lower average IQ scores (their sample was upper-middle-class with an average Binet IQ of 135). They further raised the question as to whether the greater impulse control of the high IQ children is attributable to their greater ability to follow instructions. In this brief report, the relationship between impulse control and Binet IQ is examined using a sample of deprived preschool children and a procedure for measuring impulse control, which at least partially answers the question about ability to follow instructions.

Method

Subjects. The sample consisted of thirty-three children whose families met the poverty criterion with respect to income and who were further known to the school district officials either through social service agencies or through prior encounters with the family. The mean chronological age of the children was 64.8 months and the SD was 6.9. The average Stanford–Binet IQ was 90.0 with an SD of 16.8.

Procedure.   As part of an overall evaluation of behavioral change resulting from the six-week intervention experience, the "Draw-A-Line-Slowly" (*DAL-S*) and the "Walk-A-Line-Slowly" (*WAL-S*) tests were administered during the first and last weeks of the program. These tests presumably measure a child's ability to inhibit motor activity.

The *DAL* requires the child to draw a line, beginning at the top of a plain 8½″ × 11″ piece of paper and proceeding to the bottom of the page, as slowly as possible. The following instructions were used: "I am going to draw a line on this paper as *fast* as I can. I will start here at the top and go to the bottom. Now, you try it, take the pencil and go as fast as you can to the bottom. Very good. Now, this time I am going to draw a line from the top to the bottom of the page as *slowly* as I can. Watch. Now you try it. Draw the line as slowly as you can. That was very good." These were practice trials designed to show and explain to the children the meanings of the terms "slow" and "fast." The children were then given the test trials in the following sequence of conditions:

1. The children were instructed to draw the line slowly using an 8½″ × 11″ piece of paper with no markings. The directions were simply to draw the line as slowly as possible starting at the top and going to the bottom of the page.
2. The children were instructed to draw the line slowly using an 8½″ × 11″ piece of paper on which there was an X at the top and at the bottom. The child was instructed to draw the line "even more slowly" and to connect the X's.
3. This was a repeat of condition Number 2.
4. The children were instructed to draw the line as fast as they could using an 8 ½″ × 11″ piece of paper with no markings.
5. The children were instructed to draw the line as fast as they could connecting the X's at the top and the bottom of the page.

The *WAL* task required the children to walk a path defined by two six-foot-long parallel lines of adhesive tape, five inches apart, which were placed on the floor. The children were instructed to place one foot on each tape. This task was given under three conditions in the following order:

1. *Regular (WAL-R).* In this condition the children were told: "I want you to walk to the end of the tape making sure you do not step off the lines." No instructions concerning speed were given.
2. *Slow (WAL-S).* In this condition the children were instructed: "Now I want you to walk the line as slowly as you can."
3. *Fast (WAL-F).* In the last condition the children were instructed: "Now I want you to walk the line as fast as you can."

The procedures for administering the *DAL* and the *WAL* have two features not included in the Maccoby, *et al.* procedures:

1. The instruction to perform the task "as fast as possible" which will provide a check on the children's ability to follow instructions.
2. The initial condition in each of the tasks whereby the children were simply instructed to draw the line or walk the line without directions relative to speed.

The Stanford–Binet was administered during the first and the last weeks of the intervention experience by trained, competent examiners. The examiners administering the Stanford–Binet, and the examiners administering the *DAL* and the *WAL* were different, and there was no communication between them with respect to the results on their particular tests.

Results

The data derived from the three administrations of the *DAL-S* were intercorrelated to determine consistency on the three measures. The median intercorrelation was .89, indicating a high level of consistency among the three measures. In treating the data it was decided, therefore, to pool performance on the three measures. Hence, elapsed time in drawing the lines could be a function of the length of lines. It was decided to use a rate measure; that is, length of line divided by time to draw the line. (Analyses involving the straight latency measure yield identical results.) It should be noted that a high score on the rate measure is indicative of high impulsivity. A rate measure was also determined for the *DAL-F* condition. Straight latency measures were used for the *WAL* test under each of the three conditions. Product moment correlations were run between each of the measures and performance on the Stanford–Binet.

With respect to the first question raised in this study, the correlation between two measures of impulsivity, the *DAL-S* and Binet is of the same order of magnitude as reported by Maccoby, *et al.* for the pre-test measures ($r = .45$), and somewhat higher for the posttest measures ($r = .56$). A similar degree of relationship was found for the *WAL-S* and the Binet with again a much higher correlation among the post-test measures.

The second question of concern in this study is the degree to which these measures correlate with Binet performance because of the inability of the poor performers on the Binet to understand the directions. Correlations between the *DAL-F* and the *WAL-F* measures with the Binet were all essentially zero. Since there is no apparent reason why children should understand the meaning of "fast" better than that of "slow," it would appear that the variation among children in the ability to control motor impulsivity has relatively little to do with understanding instructions. Two additional empirical arguments can be made for this conclusion. In the first place, there is a statistically significant difference between performance under the slow condition as opposed to the fast condition for both the DAL and the WAL on both pre- and post-tests (WAL: $t = 6.58, 8.94$; DAL: $t = 8.49, 11.55$; all t's $< .01$, $df = 23$). The second case can be made from inspection of the correlations between the Binet and performance under the WAL-R versus the WAL-S and WAL-F conditions. First, the correlation under the regular conditions and Binet are of the same order of magnitude as under the "slow" conditions. Second, the correlations between the regular condition and the slow condition are substantial and positive. These two sets of results suggest that for this task children's performance without any specific instructions is substantially related to their ability to conform to the "slow" instructions and that this behavioral tendency is related to performance on the Binet. Interpretation of the correlations involving the "fast" condition is difficult because of the comparatively low test–retest correlations for both the DAL and the WAL. With respect to the pretest correlations, however, the data indicate that the tendency to respond rapidly correlates moderately with performance under the slow and regular conditions. All correlations involving the fast condition for both the DAL and the WAL are essentially zero on the post-tests. In general terms, however, the predominant trend of the correlations suggests that the inability to inhibit motor behavior pervades all instructional conditions and is significantly related to performance on the Stanford–Binet.

Discussion

A comparison of the correlations between the measures of motor impulsivity and Stanford-Binet reported by Maccoby, et al. (1965) with those reported in this paper, suggests that their results were not simply a function of the properties of their sample. Thus, the results of the two studies suggest that measures of motor impulsivity may have meaning over a broad spectrum of children, at least with respect to intellectual ability.

The second objective of this study was to determine whether the significant correlations for the DAL-S and the WAL-S are, in fact, an artifact attributable to the inability of the less intelligent children's understanding of the instructions. With respect to the DAL, the children were required not only to draw the line slowly but also as fast as they could. It was reasoned that if the resulting correlations with the Binet were simply a matter of cognitive ability, significant correlations should have occurred with both the slow and fast conditions. This did not occur. With respect to the WAL, the children were required to walk the line slowly, fast, and under a condition of no instructions other than to simply walk the line. It can be argued that the "no instruction" condition would approximate the child's general tendency to respond impulsively and, therefore, this measure would correlate with performance on the Binet. Again, there was no reason to assume that children would understand the "fast" instructions better than the "slow" instructions. Here again the "fast" condition did not correlate significantly with Binet performance, but both the "slow" condition and the "no instruction" condition were significantly correlated with the Binet. Finally, it should be noted that there was a statistically significant difference between the time scores for the "slow" and "fast" condition. Although our procedures admittedly do not provide direct evidence concerning the question of cognitive competency, the trend of our correlations does not indicate that this is a highly important variable. To argue otherwise, incidentally, would be tantamount to saying that a significant proportion of Binet variance is related to the ability to understand the meaning of "slow" and "fast," which is a tenuous proposition at best.

One appropriate question is the degree to which the DAL and the WAL are intercorrelated, especially under the "slow" condition. The product–moment correlations are $-.40$ and $-.72$, for the pre- and post-test administrations, respectively. In addition, it will be recalled that the correlation between the "no instruction" and the "slow instruction" for the WAL was .81 and .60 for the pre-test and post-test administrations, respectively. These correlations lend support to the conclusion that lack of motor control may generalize across a broad spectrum of behaviors. There are additional data available from this study indicating that the DAL and WAL are significantly related to gain scores after a six-week intervention, measuring performance on such tasks as the Perceptual Speed Test (PST) of the Primary Mental Abilities Test, and teacher's perceptions of the adequacy of the social-emotional adjustment of the children. Thus, not only is lack of motor control related to performance on intellectual tasks, but this behavioral trait is apparently related to how children are perceived in terms of their social-emotional development.

A brief comment should be made on one aspect of this study which may have implications for the study of cognitive behavior among poor children. The issue is the nature of the antecedent conditions. Certainly, the extensive work of Hess and Shipman points to the fact that the parents of poor children tend to generate nonanalytic low-impulse control behaviors suggesting clearly that programs of parent education are crucial. And there is also reason to believe that the poor performance of these children on concept identification reflects, in part at least, their lack of awareness of what stimulus dimensions are likely to be salient to middle-class experimenters (or teachers). There is, however, another source of variation which is at least as important, namely the biological integrity of the organism. A recent survey by Birch, for example, shows the remarkable degree of malnutrition and anemia occurring in children from poverty areas, while the work of Pasamanick shows the high incidence of cerebral dysfunction among these children. One cannot speak with certainty about cause and effect in this area, but evidence suggests that the syndrome of hyperactivity and low impulse control is related to these biological deficiencies. Coupled with the stylistic patterns of their parents, we may well be seeing here an interaction effect which is overwhelming. The direction which must be taken is clearly one of fitting procedures to the child and this must also be the direction of future research.

Piaget on Play: A Critique

■■■ BRIAN SUTTON–SMITH

Piaget's well-known concepts of assimilation and accommodation find their purest form of expression in play and imitation, respectively. Dr. Sutton–Smith's purpose in this paper is to show how Piaget's dictum that in play there is "primacy of assimilation over accommodation" not only leads to certain contradictions within the system itself, but suggests a disjunction between affective and cognitive functions, which fails to accord with widely accepted views of the role of play in psychological development.

Piaget's *Play, Dreams and Imitation in Childhood* is the most recent of many attempts to make sense out of the theoretically anomalous subject matter of play. With the possible exception of psychoanalytic play theory, it is the most conceptually elaborate account of play yet to be presented and, in addition, includes the best available examples of the sequence of play activities in the first years of life. It is the intention of this paper to argue that Piaget's thesis, to the effect that play may be interpreted functionally as an activity subordinated to adaptive intelligence, leads to contradictions within his own system. The present analysis will maintain that Piaget's epistemological assumptions and his concern with directed thought lie at the base of his misconstrual of play.

Piaget's Epistemological Assumptions

Piaget's treatment of play is inseparable from his theorizing on intelligence. His root metaphor for the origins of intelligence in human beings

• • • • • • • •

SOURCE: Adapted and abridged from *Psychological Review, 73* (1966), 104–110. Copyright ©️ 1966 by the American Psychological Association. (With permission of the author and the publisher.)

is the process of biological adaptation in lower organisms. He is said to have been impressed in his earlier studies of mollusks by the way in which these lower organisms, while accommodating to the environment, also actively assimilated it in accord with their own schemas of action.

> An image of an active organism which both selects and incorporates stimuli in a manner determined by its structure, while at the same time adapting its structure to the stimuli, emerged from these early studies as a ready made model for cognitive development. (Flavell, 1963).

The concepts of assimilation and accommodation which were said to be applicable to lower organisms were also claimed to have applicability to the "intelligent" activities of higher organisms. These two became the indissociable functional invariants in Piaget's conceptual system for the description of intelligence:

> Accommodation of mental structure to reality implies the existence of assimilatory schemata apart from which any structures would be impossible. Inversely, the formation of schemata through assimilation entails the utilization of external realities to which the former must accommodate . . . (Piaget, 1950).

Having made assimilation and accommodation ultimate categories of adaptive intelligence, Piaget sought to express other (related) functions in these same terms. Imitation and play came to be formulated as particular types of relationships between accommodation and assimilation. When accommodation to external reality dominated over assimilation, there existed the state which Piaget termed imitation. Alternatively, if assimilation of external reality to preexisting concepts occurred, then there was the state to which the term play was given. Imitation and play were said to be polarized examples of the activity of intelligence: "Intelligent adaptation, imitation, and play are thus three possibilities and they result accordingly as there is a stable equilibrium between assimilation and accommodation or primacy of one of these two tendencies over the other" (Piaget, 1950). From this description, it follows that imitation and play should be explicable in terms of the same processes that determine adaptive or intellective functioning. Leaving aside whether Piaget has shown that imitation is explicable in terms of his categories of adaptive functioning, it will be argued that his attempt to treat play within these categories is inadequate.

The Asymmetry of Imitation and Play

There are Hegelian overtones in Piaget's view that imitation and play are dialectical opposites which are gradually reconciled in a higher synthesis as the adaptive intellectual structures of logic progressively succeed them. But closer examination of the respective roles of these two functions within his system suggests that imitation and play are not related as equipotent thesis and antithesis. Piaget verges, it is true, on the suggestion that in the origin of representative thought, imitation supplies the images and play supplies the symbols. But this antiphonal relationship is alluded to ambiguously and, for the greater part, only imitation is given a key role in the origin of concepts. Imitation is said to be a source of representation, but play is used largely as an illustration of what representation is like.

Piaget has criticized some of his predecessors, among other things, for their copy theory of knowledge or their naive realism. He has insisted that representative thinking is not merely a copy of external reality, but is rather the outcome of a long process of interaction between the organism and the environment with each modifying the other over time. As indicated above, he has stated this interaction in terms of the concepts of assimilation and accommodation. It is very clear from the corpus of his writings that he does not favor a copyist epistemology. Paradoxically enough, however, when the relationships between imitation and play are examined closely, the view emerges that Piaget has implicitly imported just such a copy theory into his own explanation of the processes of imitation, and that it is this implicit copyist notion of imitation which ultimately leaves play intellectually functionless within his system. To illustrate: The process of accommodation is portrayed as establishing for the subject a photographiclike negative of external reality. Imitation is said to be an extension of such negatives into positive action. "The function of imitation seems to be to produce this set of 'positives,' which correspond to the 'negatives' of accommodation and which, at each new 'printing,' make new reconstitutions and anticipations possible." In due course, it is said, these imitations become interiorized as images, and then, later, when these images become attached to, and differentiated from, external symbols during intelligent activity or during play, they are transformed into concepts. It follows that sustaining and initiating this whole process of representative activity are the encapsulated photographic negatives which occur during accommodation. It may be true to say, as Piaget does, that this accommodation is "an active copy and not a trace or a sensory residue of perceived objects," but accommodation is nonetheless conceived as a copy and given the initiating and sustaining role in his formulation of representative activity.

Now it is conceivable that Piaget intends to say that, when the interiorized images become attached to symbols in adaptive intelligent activity, this process of attachment changes the interiorized images. But whether or not this is the case, and this is not relevant here, it is certainly true that in Piaget's systematic accounts of play such an attachment of symbols is not said to bring about any such change in images. Piaget's definition of play as predomination of assimilation over accommodation specifically precludes any such change. Instead the encapsulated images derived from accommodation determine the character of the activity. Play merely diversifies the symbols. As "reproductive assimilation," or "assimilation of reality to the ego," play can merely repeat; it can never originate. We thus have a situation in which the symbols of play are merely the reproductions of images pre-established through the copyist activity of imitation following accommodation. On this interpretation then, imitation is an essential factor in the constitution of representative activity, whereas play is not. It has no essential role in the structure of intellect as conceived by Piaget. Intelligence cannot proceed without imitation. It can proceed without play. It is hardly necessary to emphasize that there are alternative points of view which grant to the processes of symbol formation a more active role in the constitution of thought than this copyist theory of Piaget's seems to imply (Werner and Kaplan, 1963). Greater internal cogency is given to the present critique, however, by showing that this implicit copyist notion of the origin of concepts leads to peculiarities within the system itself which are neither self-consistent nor consistent with the known data concerning play.

The Disjunction of Cognitive and Affective Functions

Having deprived play of an active, intellective role in the constitution of new concepts, Piaget is forced into a series of substitute explanations. Unlike imitation which has the one definition, play is provided with a variety of definitions. At times, it is referred to as "reproductive assimilation," as "generalizing assimilation," but also as "pure assimilation," "mere assimilation," and "distorting assimilation" (Piaget, 1951). The latter three terms do not occupy any systematic status within Piaget's theory of intelligence as do the first two. They are never defined, and it is not entirely clear just what they can mean. It is this lack of a functional role for play within the structure of intelligence which apparently forces Piaget to find alternative nonintellective functional explanations for play, which he does not have to provide for imitation. It is said, for example, that play exists in childhood because thought is not adequate to its tasks:

> The prevalence of play among children is therefore to be explained not by specific causes peculiar to the realm of play, but by the fact that the characteristics of all behaviors and all thought are less in equilibrium in the early stages of mental development than in the adult stage (Piaget, 1954).

But why is there assimilation of reality to the ego instead of immediate assimilation of the universe to experience and logical thought? It is simply because in early childhood this thought has not yet been constructed, and during its development it is inadequate to supply the needs of daily life (Piaget, 1951).

These quotations make it clear that play is not considered as making any intrinsic contribution to thought, but is instead some sort of compensation for thought's inadequacy. This interpretation is made explicit when Piaget says that the function of play is to serve ego continuity. "It follows that for the child assimilation of reality to the ego is a vital condition for continuity and development precisely because of the lack of equilibrium of this thought, and symbolic play satisfies this condition both as regard to signifier and signified." But, surely, it is difficult to maintain that play is merely a polarity of thought, that the "prevalence of play . . . is therefore to be explained not by . . . causes peculiar to the realm of play," and then to invoke this concept of ego continuity which is not a concept intrinsic to Piaget's account of the nature of intelligence. This invocation of "ego continuity" does, in fact, suggest that play has some other function to serve which is quite distinct from thought. The notion of ego continuity as the function of play bears close resemblance to the concept of ego mastery as presented in psychoanalytic accounts, particularly that of Erikson. But to rest play's positive contribution on such grounds is to lead to a disjunction of cognitive and affective functions, quite inconsistent with Piaget's own repeated stress that the two are not separable. If play has a constitutive affective function of this sort (ensuring ego continuity), Piaget's general position on affective–cognitive relations requires that it should also have a constitutive intellective function.

The Disjunction of Directed and Undirected Thinking

It would be wrong to imply that Piaget's particular treatment of play stems perhaps from an accident in his epistemology. The approach is more deep-seated than that for there is a consistency between his account of infant thought and his account of adult thought. It has been shown that in his treatment of infant thought he gives an initiating role to images which derive from accommodation to external reality. In adult thought also he is concerned with those coherent formal structures of intellect that have to do with accommodation to and control over the external world. In particular he is concerned with the correspondence between "the structures described by logic and the actual thought processes studied by psychology" (Piaget, 1957c). He is not concerned with those less directed aspects of adult thought usually referred to by such terms as reverie, creative imagination, or divergent thinking. Yet in the opinion of some, the latter have a great deal to do with novel forms of adaptation. It would not be farfetched to speculate, in fact, that if there is an intrinsic relationship between play and thought, it is more likely to be with these latter forms of divergent intellectual operations than with the directed forms which concern Piaget.

Piaget's formulation of adult thought has a number of consequences which are consistent with the epistemological orientation already outlined. For example, his view that the thinking of the young child is relatively disequilibrial is again similar to the empirical view which says that since thought copies reality, young children who are inexperienced will have more imperfect copies than older persons. Of course, stated in Piaget's terms, the young organism plays a more active role in acquiring its copies than was the case in the traditional empirical view, and unlike that view there is a telic quality to Piaget's formulation of the young child's operations. They appear to be "successive approximations to a kind of ideal equilibrium or end state never completely achieved" (Flavell, 1963). The difficulty with this approach for Piaget's own point of view is that it is not consistent with his stage theory which says that each stage of thinking has a characteristic organization and completeness of its own. It is difficult to see how there can be both "equilibration" of early stages and the view that these early stages are relatively less in equilibrium than later stages. The problem can be located in the different usages of the term "equilibrium" which Piaget employs both to refer to characteristics of intellectual organization at one time or stage and to refer to the ontogenetic status of the organism in general. Apart from the semantic confusion in having such entities as "disequilibrial equilibriums," either stage or ontogenetic usage leads to difficulties with respect to the definition of play as a polarity of thought.

If it is said that when an intellectual structure is disrupted by intractable data the lack of intellectual resources in childhood (the disequilibrial ontogenetic state) leads to the use of play as an affective holding action, this is again to give play no genuine cognitive function. Yet, if it is said that play is a true polarity of thought in the sense of reestablishing equilibrium through genuinely cognitive means at any one stage (the implied stage theory), this is equally unfortunate for the theory as it stands. If, for example, some divergent thinking function is attributed to the "distorting assimilations" of play, this requires a reconsideration of the role of divergent thinking not only in children's thinking but also in the development of adult thinking. If play does not simply "distort" old concepts but also originates new concepts, then the whole account of the genesis of intellectual structures from childhood through adulthood has to be changed.

Piaget appears to have chosen rather to make a disjunction between the operations of thought in adulthood and the operations of thought in childhood, in addition to the formal differences between sensorimotor, concrete, and abstract operations which are already a part of his theory. Thus it is said that childhood thinking is bolstered by the affective operations of play, but the thinking of adults is not. From Piaget's viewpoint as undirected thinking, fantasy, play, etc., are specifically childlike and mainly compensatory, that is, having nothing to do with the development of particular kinds of intellectual operations, they may be confined to the infantile stage and regarded as irrelevant to the nature of adult intellectual operations.

The Ontogenesis of Play

It is legitimate to ask whether the evidence on play supports Piaget's point of view. His view that play is merely a buttress to an inadequate intelligence leads to the corollary that as that intelligence increases in efficiency and adequacy, play will cease to be important in the development of the mind. In Piaget's unilinear account of the ontogenesis of intellectual structures, play has such a transient position. Thus it is said that from about the age of four years onward symbolic games decline because the child becomes capable of greater adaptive activity and is more realistic: " . . . progress in socialization instead of leading to an increase in symbolism transforms it more or less rapidly into an objective imitation of reality" (Piaget, 1951). "Rule games . . . mark the decline of children's games and the transition to adult play, which ceases to be a vital function of the mind when the individual is socialized" (Piaget, 1951). On the basis of the evidence about play several objections can be raised to the view that the symbolic games of childhood are simply replaced by more realism with age, and that play which is "vital" in childhood ceases to be vital in adulthood. In general it can be maintained with equal cogency that, rather than a decrease in the symbolic play function with age, what we actually find is a shift in the application and the differentiation of this function. First, the early rule games of children continue to be heavily loaded with symbolic elements which play a part in determining outcomes equal in importance to skill. In the host of singing games of young girls, for example, it is the one who is arbitrarily chosen as Punchinello or as Farmer-in-the-Dell who determines the outcome. Similarly, in the great group of central-person games of early childhood which model the family drama, it is the player chosen by the arbitrary counting-out processes or the player with the role vestments of Caesar or Red Rover who decides by fiat when the game will start, when the players will run, etc. (Sutton-Smith, 1959). Here the play symbolism has been collectivized, but it has hardly been decreased, or given way to greater realism. In Piaget's (1932) treatment of games he was concerned with a game (marbles) in which the symbolism was much less pronounced, marbles being more age appropriate at the end of early childhood, around nine or ten years, whereas these other games just mentioned tend to flourish from seven through nine years. Furthermore, in that treatise, play at games was used to illustrate moral and social development rather than to provide the basis for an understanding of the play function. In a sense, Piaget (1932) first uses games to illustrate the development of morality, while he later (1951) uses play to illustrate the development of thought. Neither time does he deal systematically with the peculiar functions of games or play in human development. Perhaps it is this tendentiousness of approach that leads Piaget to discount the continuing influence of play in psychological development. Even when children's games are mainly matters of physical or intellectual skill, as from ten years onward, however, it is difficult to accept Piaget's view that this is simply a matter of play being converted from a symbolic to a realistic application. The total game performance still remains basically a symbolic procedure. There is, after all, little that is precisely rational about a game of football or a game of basketball. In fact, there is support for the point of view that such sports are best conceived as modern ritualized dramas of success and failure (Sutton–Smith, Roberts, and Kozelka, 1963) and as such have little that is either rational or real about them. Furthermore, it is the thesis of Huizinga that play (if not sport) does continue to be a vital function of mind even in socialized adults and that it permeates all their vital activities including those of a cultural sort and those of an economic and political nature. Recent crosscultural work showing the full implication of games in culture would appear to substantiate this view (Roberts, Arth, and Bush, 1959; Roberts and Sutton–Smith, 1962; Sutton–Smith and Roberts, 1964). Though preschool egocentric symbolic play may decrease with age, play nevertheless finds expression in the midst of a variety of other cultural and social forms. It is thus not displaced by realism or by greater rationality, nor does it cease to be a vital function with age. Instead it becomes more differentiated and more representative in its contents of the other forms of human development. Without such a point of view it is difficult to understand the verbal play of adults, their social and sexual play, their rituals and their carnivals, their festivals and fairs, and their widespread and diversified playfulness.

This present criticism of Piaget's view of play as a transient, infantile stage in the emergence of thought parallels Vygotsky's (1962) criticism of Piaget's notion of egocentric speech as a transient, infantile stage in the emergence of socialized speech. Vygotsky maintained that in the course of ontogeny egocentric speech does not give way to socialized speech, but becomes transformed into inner speech which may itself be differentiated according to autistic or logical ends. Similarly, it has been maintained here that children's play does not give way to intelligent adaptation, but becomes differentiated in a variety of ways. The difference between Vygotsky's criticism and the present one, however, hinges on the fact that both Piaget and Vygotsky are talking about the ontogenesis of the same function — speech — whereas here two functions are involved, intelligence and play, which Piaget attempts to amalgamate into a single function (intelligence) and an aborted variant (play). It should be noted in conclusion that Piaget's various earlier treatments of undirected thinking in children, their animism, artificialism, etc., as transient, infantile stages in development are susceptible to similar criticism (Piaget, 1928, 1929, 1930).

Conclusion

It has been contended that Piaget's major concern with directed rather than undirected intellectual operations together with his implicit copyist epistemology have made it impossible for him to deal consistently with play. He has attempted to make it a function of thought without giving it any intellective function within thought. And he has been unable to give it such a function within thought because in his epistemology concepts are ultimately copies derived from and appropriate to an external reality. As play does not copy but "distorts" reality, it can have no intrinsic place in such an epistemology. As a result, Piaget is forced finally to explain play in terms of the type of affective and conative functions that are familiar in other play theories. (This is not to imply that there are not parallels between cognitive operations and play contents at given ages. It is the virtue of Piaget's observations that in this respect they complement those of psychoanalysts and sociologists which tend to be highly selective in terms of play content reflecting their own characteristic theoretical orientations. But the existence of such parallels between the operations of thought and the structures of play conveys nothing in itself about the function of play.)

While it has not been the purpose of this paper to propose any alternative theoretical approach to play or to criticize Piaget's play theory from alternative points of view, a brief mention of an alternative epistemology and the quite different approach to play which it entails may serve to highlight the legitimacy of the present criticism in epistemological terms. Ernst Cassirer (1953) explicitly opposes the view that concepts are copies of external reality. They are rather modes through which reality is constructed on a level transcending the simple sign functioning of lower organisms. From an epistemologically constructivist viewpoint of this sort, play might well be taken as a very positive illustration of the thinking process, because it involves the construction of symbols to create new conceptual domains. Though from Cassirer's point of view, play would have to be just one of many such symbolic modes with its own characteristic properties, others being art, myth, science, etc., for Cassirer's point of view with respect to symbolic development is not only constructionist, it is also multilinear.

Piaget with his contrasting copyist assumption and his unilinear notion of thought is forced to reduce all forms of symbolic activity to the single copyist form of adaptive thought. And on the evidence of the internal inconsistencies to which this leads, his approach does not appear to have been fruitful for the explanation of play.

The present criticism of Piaget's theoretical system which focuses on the inadequacy of his epistemology when applied to play probably has relevance for the interpretation of divergent-thinking activities in general, such as creativity, originality, expressiveness, etc. At the same time this criticism probably has less relevance to such convergent-thinking operations as the understanding of physical causality, spatial relations, etc., with which Piaget is mainly concerned and for which his copyist assumption may be more intrinsically relevant. For whatever may be said here about Piaget's theory of play, there is no intention to detract from the conceptual flexibility of his system when applied to the child's understanding of the operations of the physical world. In that area man and mollusk share a common concern, and Piaget's epistemology appears to be revealing.

The Educationally Handicapped   III

The statements preceding Section II are perhaps equally applicable here. Educators have become increasingly aware in the past few years that a larger portion of the national resources should be directed toward the elimination of all kinds of handicaps to learning. Piaget's theory, elaborating as it does the lawful growth of the intellect and the factors which contribute to its development, would seem to be particularly adaptable to the study of learning disorders. Yet applications of his theory in this area are, as yet, relatively meager. However, some of the articles in other sections (notably the work of Sonquist, Kamii, Radin, and Derman, Section II) might also be considered appropriate here.

Piaget and the Psychology of Thought: Some Implications for Teaching the Retarded

■■■ GLORIA F. WOLINSKY

Although Piaget's stages relate to the development of normal children, his theory will undoubtedly prove equally fruitful when applied to the education of exceptional children. In this paper, the author suggests several ways in which Piagetian concepts may be used in the measurement, diagnosis, and remediation of learning dysfunctions.

Jean Piaget's early efforts and recorded publications date back to the 1920s (1926, 1928, 1930, 1950, 1951, 1954b, 1957b). Not only is he an extremely prolific writer but one who uses his own work to modify or to expand his theory. His views and materials have met also with much critical comment, particulars of which he has acknowledged (Piaget, 1957c) and which, in further studies, he has attempted to clarify. Until rather recently, most of his materials were in French. His work is further complicated by the use of a particular system of logic to substantiate his arguments. However, within this often difficult but stimulating approach, there is an extremely

● ● ● ● ● ● ● ●

SOURCE: *American Journal of Mental Deficiency, 67* (1962), 250–256. (With permission of the author and the *Journal*.)

creative and potentially fruitful stream of thought that, in the years to come, will be particularly significant, for the concerns with which we are intimately involved are basically Piaget's.

Theory and Method

Briefly stated, Piaget's approach is a genetic one. It attempts to discover the processes that occur within the child's intellectual growth that culminate in "intelligence." This approach to intelligence, that is basically developmental, seeks to view the child as he proceeds through various biological and logical processes to mature thought.

Piaget's (1957b) earliest quests were concerned with the young child's development of thought. The material developed the thesis of the qualitative difference of the thought of the youngster from that of the adult. Early childhood is a period that is dominated by an egocentric attitude, being influenced by the wishes and inner needs of the child and the immediacies of the problem of perception rather than by an understanding of the environment and its needs. These early papers were critically received by the advocates of the then classical view of intelligence which saw no change in the qualitative aspect of intelligence between childhood and later years. Braine (1959), in a study to explore some of Piaget's formulations, surveying the extensive literature concerning "Test–Retest Correlations Obtained in the Longitudinal Studies of Intellectual Development," presents the evidence "for the existence of changes in the nature of intelligence during early childhood, which are not changes in quantity alone."

Some of the most severe criticism was directed to the methodology employed. Piaget's initial approach was and still is an extended interview in an attempt to arrive at an understanding of the thought and comprehension of an individual child as he faced particular problems. This "Clinical Method" is a system of observation which permits the child to talk and allows the examiner to observe in which way the thought of the child develops. The purpose is "to discover the actual operational mechanisms which govern such behavior and not simply to measure it" (Piaget, 1957c).

If we examine most efforts at research in the past and even today, we see attempts at the measurement of how much one understands; comparisons between groups on ability to perform certain tasks; concerns with the probability of duplicating certain responses under similar conditions; and confirmation of predictions made from other qualitative measures. There is great concern for rigorous design, problems of variance and degrees of confidence.

Recent work both here (Bobroff, 1960; Braine, 1959; Robinson, Katsushege, and McDowell, 1961) and in Europe (Bardecke, 1959; Lovell, 1959; Matalon,

1959; Morf, 1956; Page, 1959; Peel, 1959; Woodward, 1959), are attempts to elaborate his data for the sake of comparative studies, verification, and prediction. But the critics of Piaget, as well as those who look with great interest at his work, must come to grips with the basic idea of his approach, which is developmental and which sees complicated thought processes growing out of simpler ones. Intellectual operations, for Piaget, can never exist in a discontinuous state and, therefore, cannot be studied as such. Intelligence, too, cannot be studied in isolation but can only be seen as an inherent need for equilibrium. Piaget's intellectual heritage stems from the biological sciences and, more recently, mathematics. Because of this, there are usages and analogies that echo his interest and discipline. When he views intelligence as an inherent need for equilibrium, he incorporates a concept of "assimilation" and "accommodation." Intelligence as an act of "assimilation" involves an organization with the world about the individual. Therefore, a response must be made to the world, either in terms of past behavior or the incorporation of new acts of behavior into experimental meaning. Intelligence also is an aspect of "accommodation," which is the part the environment plays upon the individual. Intelligence, therefore, as adaptive behavior, seeks to find the equilibrium between "accommodation" and "assimilation."

As a vehicle for the study of what is actually a continuum of thought, Piaget and his associates since 1937 have developed a series of experiments that explores the sequence of certain logical and mathematical concepts. The research employs certain problem situations, but the instrument of analysis is that of the union of psychology with logic. Techniques of symbolic logic, therefore, have been used to study the intellectual behavior of children.

For, just as statistics have been of assistance to psychologists in examining quantitative data, symbolic logic and, more specifically, a variation of Boolean calculus can be useful for the analysis of the intellectual activities of the child.[1] This discussion will not concern itself with the intricacies of this calculus, but for now and for the sake of later statements, the point to remember is that in symbolic logic, while the variables that are used are similar to algebraic X Y Z, they do not refer to numbers but rather to propositions. "Operations and their groupings are the main thesis of Piaget's developmental approach to concept formation" (Thomson, 1959). What Piaget attempts to do, therefore, is to:

• • • • • • • •

[1] A detailed critical discussion of Piaget's use of logic is to be found in Parsons, C., "Inhelder and Piaget's 'The Growth of Logical Thinking II,' A Logician's Viewpoint," *The British Journal of Psychology, 51,* I (1960), 75–84.

1. " . . . construct a psychological theory of operations in terms of genesis and structure;
2. " . . . examine logical operations, treating them as algebraic calculus and as structured wholes;
3. " . . . compare the results of these two levels of enquiries" (Piaget, 1957c).

Therefore, our concerns lie in the observed behavior of the "stages" in the construction of operations, that are part of the aforementioned search for equilibrium, and the specific use of a tool of inquiry that permits the analysis of the development of this behavior. Furthermore, when we observe these developmental periods, we must look at them in terms of operational systems which have the following characteristics:

1. They can be internalized;
2. They can be reversed; and
3. They can be characterized by laws which apply to the system as a whole (Piaget, 1957c).

In other words, each stage develops and builds a permanency of its own that exists as a uniqueness which may eventually lose its identification but must exist if a more complicated process is to arise.

Implications for Teaching the Exceptional

Because this presentation's ultimate concern is with the meaning of Piaget's contribution to the education and care of children with learning difficulties, this introduction has been necessarily brief and has not concerned itself with issues and conceptual areas, which have been treated in some detail (Kessen, 1959) elsewhere. The abbreviated summary is to serve as a framework on which to build some pragmatic approaches to education by those who are not too familiar with Piaget's work. In view of the present state of affairs, as it concerns the affirmation or negation or comprehension of his material, two aspects of his work, which should give us immediate direction, will be discussed.

The first is the methodology of the clinical approach since the method implies analysis of the qualitative aspect of intellectual elaboration. The importance lies in the adult's ability to probe into the type of reasoning that underlies the child's conduct. The adult must record as well as provoke behavior, without projecting his ideas or losing sight of his goal. While admittedly there are weaknesses in this approach in terms of the substantive aspect of data collection, its use as a technique for the teacher of the exceptional is of paramount interest.

In working with children who present problems of learning, the teacher must often face the fact that the child is not learning at a specific rate or that material presumably learned is not fully understood. This approach to inquiry and analysis of response allows the teacher to analyze while she teaches. Since we are concerned with small classes and individual instruction, the methodology of presentation that implies instruction to a large group of children is hardly a suitable technique. Furthermore, the methodology of group instruction presumably implies a learning process that involves planned as well as incidental learning. Some recent research (Goldstein and Kass, 1961) indicates that incidental learning does take place but, because of the inaccuracies presented, instruction should be directed toward teaching "for facts and concepts related to objects, peoples and conditions," to reinforce the planned teaching unit. Even as we acknowledge that a teacher cannot teach every fact, what is taught must be linked to a method of diagnosis of content more accurate than the achievement test. The achievement test quantifies, whereas the exploraton of the meaning of the concept elucidates a response that indicates to the teacher wherein the misconception lies.

Teachers can be taught to use this approach in a modified form and the literature (Almy, 1961; Kaya, 1961; Lovell, 1959) indicates the results of some work by teachers who were so trained. For example, while not immediately concerned with the very slow, the following demonstration is given.

> . . . a highly verbal youngster demonstrated how extensively his thinking was dominated by his perception when he attempted an explanation of the reason certain objects stayed on the flannelboard when others did not. He volunteered the notion that the material on the board was rough and that the material on the back of the pictured objects was also rough. Not misled by his apparent logic, the teacher picked up a piece of paper and inquired as to whether he thought it would stick to the board. The child replied that it would not because it was "round" whereas the other objects were not (Almy, 1961).

One of the problems that plague workers in the field of education is the question of pupil–teacher ratio and pupil–teacher interaction. This question becomes most acute when discussed in light of the urgency the picture of retardation presents to us. The *"méthode clinique"* offers another fruitful dimension, for it implies a probing of demonstrated action that encompasses the "why" of unsuccessful activity. In the search for the genesis of a response, the correct and incorrect perception is explored. It must be remembered in this connection that while Piaget (1957b) has acknowledged a certain similarity to the analytic approach, it is analysis in terms of logical relationships and ontogenetic conception. Too long have we been concerned with size, selection and the "how" of group processes alone in terms of class instruction. The question ultimately to be faced is process, and process demands a look at operational mechanisms. What is best learned from Piaget is a conception of problem solving that attempts to pierce the miasma of tissues that surrounds group instruction.

The second point for immediate consideration is the concept of "stage." It matters little that some present research confirms (Bobroff, 1960; Braine, 1959; Lovell, 1959; Peel, 1959; Robinson, et al., 1961), for the most part, or does not confirm (Durkin, 1959a, 1959b; Mogar, 1960; Feigenbaum, 1961) the actual time of change, as Piaget indicates. The importance lies in realizing that change does take place, that children can understand things at certain times, and that the period of full realization does not spring spontaneously at a moment's urgency but rather is built up through the experiential world of the young child.

If we can see our youngsters as children who have not mastered certain stages in intellectual growth, we have potentially a more effective instrument for classroom use than an intelligence classification which may measure ability or capacity but does not actually give too much information as to the nature of the defect. Potentially, the development of scales of operational schemas can be one of the most stimulating and fruitful breakthroughs in the diagnosis of learning dysfunction. It can give to teachers an analysis of dysfunction similar to that which the laboratory analysis of biological dysfunction gives to the physician. The educational prescription, if you will, can then be filled and administered and then again evaluated as to efficacy.

Intrinsic to the utilization of "stage" is the Piaget formulation of the process of perception. Allport's (1955) work alone insures us of the complexity of the situation. In the present renaissance of concern with perception and the part it plays in the intellectual life of the crucial learning period of early childhood, Piaget's emphasis on the differentiation between perception and intelligence is worth noting. Perception is knowledge that we have of objects by direct or immediate contact. It, too, is developmental and includes activities that ultimately join up with intelligence as soon as it can free itself from the immediacy of the situation.

Though perception has always been investigated as part of sensorimotor development, specific aspects of perception as different but complementary to cognition are being explored as separate entities. As such, they are being approached from the same philosophical premise (genetic) but using the methodology of geometric figures as experimental variables. The mechanisms underlying the development of perception are being analyzed, and some interesting conclusions are being offered. Some of them are at variance with the approach of the Gestalt psychology. For instance, Piaget (1960), as the result of some experiments, notes that there are certain perceptual illusions that change with age.

Perseveration, for example, may thus be seen as a classification act, with inability to relate it to its proper place in a time and space continuum evolving from an incomplete attainment of stage. Perception, seen from the heritage of Gestalt psychology, concerns itself with the problems of configuration. The problem of whether children perceive globally or analytically is a controversy of long standing (Gibson and Olum, 1960), and some research indicates the process of perception may concern itself with operations rather than configurations. In other words, if this be so, in terms of providing curriculum experiences, we are faced with a problem in sequential operations rather than an inability to extract foreground from background. Again, pragmatically, it is not simply presenting structured material but rather exploring with the child what he sees and does with the material presented. Is it the problem of structure, or is it a question of unsuccessful mastery of a part of a particular developmental stage in cognition?

Current Use of Piaget's Premises and the Retarded

As far as the present use of Piaget's material and the retarded, the research reported indicates that the work being done is the quantification of his data and the confirmation of various phases of his concept. For instance, Inhelder has used the stage of intuitive thinking and concrete operations to distinguish certain cases of mental deficiency. The "imbecile" is not capable of concrete groupings; whereas in "slight backwardness" there exists the inability to reason informally, i.e., incomplete operational construction. Woodward (1959), in her observation of "idiots," noted that in spite of their ages, their sensorimotor activities are classified with the six main types of sensorimotor activity of the first two years of the infant's life and are not random or purposeless movements. Bobroff (1960), in his study, illustrates that educable mentally retarded children's "social behavior," thought, and ego development follows the Piaget formulation.

These efforts are similar to the work done by those who are concerned with the normative aspects of child growth and development. This, of course, is the important first step and actually is the "join" of the highly analytic Geneva School and the quantitative American approach. From this union we may anticipate a tomorrow that will substantially affect curriculum and research as it concerns the retarded.

Egocentrism in Institutionalized and Noninstitutionalized Children

■■■ JOHN M. NEALE

One characteristic of preoperational thought is egocentrism, or the inability to comprehend situations from other points of view. The socialization process is an important factor in leading children away from egocentric thought. In this paper, the author tests the hypothesis that institutionalized children who have been poorly socialized will show a correspondingly greater degree of egocentric thought.

In the developmental psychology of Jean Piaget, egocentrism is often used as a "core concept" in explaining aspects of the child's intellectual development. Piaget defines egocentrism as a cognitive state in which the world is perceived from a single viewpoint, that is, there is a lack of differentiation between one's own perspectives and viewpoints and those of others. An example of Piaget's use of egocentrism can be found in *The Language and Thought of the Child* (1957b). There Piaget has shown that children are unable to communicate fully because their egocentricity prevents them from taking the role of the listener and then adapting their output to fit the informational needs or input capacity of the listener. A second use of the concept can be found in Piaget and Inhelder's *The Child's Conception of Space* (1967). Here an operational measure of egocentrism was constructed involving the perception of different perspectives. The procedure consisted of presenting the child with a model of a mountain scene and then ascertaining whether the child could perceive that views of the mountains other than the particular view he was looking at were possible and could be identified.

The work of Piaget (1950), indicates that egocentrism as measured in the above-mentioned tasks exists in the seven-to eleven-year-old child with a gradual lessening of egocentrism as the child passes through this age range. By eleven most children are no longer egocentric as measured by these methods, but egocentrism does not entirely disappear. Piaget states that the mechanism whereby egocentrism is broken down during the seven-to eleven-year-old period consists mainly of interpersonal, and more especially, peer contacts. To the extent that the child feels a need to socialize, he must confront other viewpoints and perspectives differing from his own; through repeated and often frustrating interpersonal contacts, the child is forced to recognize that other views and perspectives are possible (Piaget, 1928).

Piaget's concept of egocentrism and his theory concerning its breakdown seem to be related to a role-theory approach to socialization. Role theory

• • • • • • • •

SOURCE: Adapted and abridged from *Child Development, 37* (1966), 97–101. (With permission of the author and the Society for Research in Child Development.)

states that socialization is a function of role-taking experiences and abilities. The basis for sociality is social interaction which itself is dependent on the individual's ability to look on himself as an object or to assume different roles (Mead, 1934; Gough, 1948). Gough further applied role theory to an analysis of psychopathy. The asocial behavior of the psychopath was conceptualized as being a result of a deficit in role-taking ability (Gough, 1948). As egocentrism represents the inability to see the world from the viewpoints of others (or a deficiency in role-taking ability) it would be expected that egocentrism would be inversely related to socialization.

The typical syndrome of the emotionally disturbed children found in Thistletown Hospital is that of an overaggressive, poorly socialized child. In fact, the basic reason for institutionalization of these children is their extremely poor socialization in the community. It was felt that due to this syndrome, the emotionally disturbed children would show a higher level of egocentrism than a control group of normal children.

The present experiment was designed to test this implication by measuring the egocentrism of a group of emotionally disturbed children and a control group of public school children.

Method

Subjects

Twenty Ss were used from each of Thistletown Hospital and Beaumonde Heights Public School. In each setting five subjects were chosen at each age level from eight to eleven; the institutionalized and noninstitutionalized groups were matched for MA, IQ, and sex. In total the mean IQ for both Thistletown and Beaumonde Heights children was 100 and the male/female ratio in each setting was 15:5. At Thistletown, Wechsler Intelligence Scale for Children (WISC) scores were available for all children; at Beaumonde WISC scores were used when available, but on a number of children the only scores available were those on the Dominion Test of Intelligence.

Apparatus

The apparatus was essentially that described by Piaget and Inhelder (1956). It consisted of a two-foot square board on which three papier-mâché mountains were constructed. The mountains were of different heights, shapes, and colors so as to provide easy discrimination. A series of nine coloured drawings of the mountains were made on 4 × 6-inch cards and all of these were mounted on a 2 × 4-foot sheet of cardboard. The drawings were made to represent the four "head-on" views from each side of the apparatus, two "corner views" and three impossible views. A plastic model of a man was used to illustrate the view that the child would have to attempt to take.

Procedure

Each S was seated in a chair located four feet from a table on which the apparatus had been placed. It was explained to each child by E that he was going to show him the model of the mountains from each side, and then E proceeded to do so, finally returning the model to a position such that S had a direct view of one side. The series of drawings was then shown to S, and E explained that the cards represented a number of drawings of the mountains that had been made from different sides of the apparatus. Instructions were then given to S to choose the card which showed the view that he was then looking at. After completion of this, the plastic man was shown to S, and the remainder of the task was explained. It was further explained to S that the man would be placed at different positions around the mountains, and that S's task would be to pick out the card showing what the man would see from his position. With the apparatus in the same position, the man was then placed opposite the middle of the left- and then the right-hand sides and then at the back directly opposite S. With each placement of the man S chose a card and was instructed to guess if not sure. The apparatus was then rotated and the man again placed in different positions; this procedure was then repeated, thus generating nine trials. Both the order of presentation of the various sides of the apparatus to S and the placements of the man were randomized. For the tenth trial the apparatus was placed so that one corner was directly opposite S's line of view and the man was placed behind this corner directly opposite S.

Each correct response by S was given two points. A response which was correct in that the correct viewpoint was ascertained, but the right–left transposition of mountains which occurs in changing sides was not given, was scored as one, that is, on the responses scored as one the S chose a card depicting a view from the side the "man" was on but did not get the correct positions of the mountains from left to right.

Results

The mean test scores for institutionalized and noninstitutionalized Ss may be seen in Table 1. From this it may be seen that the noninstitutionalized Ss scored higher than the institutionalized Ss at each age level (the higher the score, the less egocentric). The overall mean test score for the institutionalized Ss was 4.2, and for the noninstitutionalized Ss it was 6.9. By the

Table 1.   Mean Scores on Egocentrism for Institutionalized and Noninstitutionalized Groups

	8 years	9 years	10 years	11 years
Noninstitutionalized	6.4	4.4	8.0	9.0
Institutionalized	4.2	3.4	6.2	3.2

Mann–Whitney U test the differences between groups proved significant at beyond the .05 level.

Spearman rank-order correlations were used to test the effect of age on test scores. In the institutionalized group the correlation between age and test scores was .03 (not significant). For the noninstitutionalized group, this correlation was .40, which is significant at the .05 level. The relation between IQs and test scores was also examined. For the institutionalized group $p = .42$; for the noninstitutionalized group $p = .47$ (both significant at beyond the .05 level).

Discussion

The results may be seen as providing fairly strong support for the hypothesis, that is, emotionally disturbed children are more egocentric than normals. The fact then that significant differences in egocentrism were shown between the two groups offers support for a role-theory approach to socialization and childhood psychopathology. Piaget's theory regarding the breakdown of egocentrism through interpersonal contacts is also given correlational support.

A *post hoc* analysis was conducted, which gives further credence to this view. Children in the hospital are often found to be wards of Children's Aid Societies (CAS). These CAS children have had no stable home life or stable environment, and it was therefore felt that they would have had even less of an opportunity to form relations which would bring about a breakdown of egocentrism. The group of institutionalized children was then divided into two groups, and their egocentrism scores were compared by the Mann–Whitney U test. It was found that the CAS children were significantly more egocentric than the non-CAS children ($p < .05$). (IQs of both groups were also tested by a Mann–Whitney U test and no significant differences were found.)

The lack of correlation between age and egocentrism in the institutionalized sample may also be interpreted in light of the hypothesis. This absence of correlation would seem to indicate that emotional disturbances in children are strong enough to override the strong developmental trend in overcoming egocentrism noted by Piaget and Inhelder (1967).

Conceptual and Personality Factors Underlying Flexibility in Speed of Reading

In this article, the author discusses flexibility in speed of reading within the framework of Holmes's substrata-factor theory of reading. The essence of this theory lies in the notion that many different subabilities are continuously assembled and reassembled into that working system which best facilitates the reader's immediate purpose. Laycock is able to trace important parallels between this notion and Piaget's basic conception of equilibration, a finding that should be helpful in teaching slow readers to be more flexible.

What is Flexibility in Reading Rate?

As a goal of reading, flexibility is warmly applauded. Conferences regularly salute the reader who can adapt himself sensitively to his text. After all, a light magazine story and the directions for assembling a mail-order wheelbarrow are different, and anybody who treats them alike is a sorry reader. Reading rate is one of the clues to adaptability, and flexible rate is an elusive but highly desirable skill.

Fortunately there are some clear facts about rate flexibility, at least on the surface. It is fairly easy to measure, in both children and adults. There are some remarkable differences in voluntary flexibility that show up as early as the intermediate grades of elementary school (Laycock, 1958). That is, some people can read very quickly when they wish or when they are asked. Others read just about everything at the same plodding pace. And some poor souls actually slow down appreciably whenever they try to speed up. People also differ, of course, in their ability to recognize immediately which speed is appropriate. Flexibility control can even vary when there is no substantial content and therefore no shift in difficulty. For example, I have asked people to read lines of digits set up at random in pseudo-paragraphs. Some people readily alter the rate of this "reading" when asked to; others remain stuck at the same speed (Laycock, 1955).

There is even variation in the gross activity of the eyes (which, as Tinker often pointed out, is a superficial sign and must not be taken for the whole of reading). At the eye-movement camera I have found that persons who can alter their speed easily have better control of eye-movements, faster reaction time, and smoother progression through a sentence or a paragraph. Less flexible readers are more sluggish and awkward, whether under pressure or not (Laycock, 1955).

● ● ● ● ● ● ● ●

SOURCE: *New Frontiers in College-Adult Reading*, 15th Yearbook of the National Reading Conference. Milwaukee, Wisconsin: The National Reading Conference, Inc. (1966), 140–146. (With permission of the author and the publisher.)

At deeper levels, it is much harder to decide upon the facts or their significance. In particular, we should find out whether there is any general flexibility of mind and, if so, how reading flexibility may be part of it. Among children I have found a fair relationship between voluntary control of reading rate on the one hand, and, on the other, easy shifting from one method of solving certain arithmetic problems to a better method (Laycock, 1958). That is — in reverse — readers who stick to one reading rate tend to persist doggedly with a familiar arithmetic formula, even when the formula is less efficient or actually wrong. However, there is not very much systematic evidence for overall flexibility in the personality, partly because what the several investigators call flexibility or rigidity varies from study to study, or from one measure of it to another. We may someday find a substantial underlying trait, once our measurements agree; or we may find — as those who studied honesty did, for instance — that individual people vary in trait, as particular situations or intentions demand.

Now as for flexibility in reading rate, whatever its connection to other sorts of flexibility, there is a major question that transcends all these facts: how do children acquire this skill or miss it? Why do some of them, that is, become more flexible than others? I don't know, but I can specify three different possibilities:

(1) A child may consciously figure out how to vary his reading speed so as to fit the shifting demands of what he is reading. Just how he learns we don't know, nor whether flexibility itself can be taught somewhat separately from varying kinds of reading.
(2) Whenever flexibility appears, it is the unplanned result of accumulated experience with different kinds of reading matter. Many children who read this way have told me that they never had instructions in "how-to-vary-speed." But then, of course, neither had the ones who were not flexible!
(3) Flexibility may be taught, but within a broader framework or timetable that is neurologically or even genetically determined. That is, neither conscious development of flexibility nor Topsy-like emergence operates freely. Rather there must be prior maturation of necessary and under-lying skills before it does any good to train for or to expect flexibility.

Flexibility and the Substrata-Factor Theory

What help does the substrata-factor theory offer as we try to understand flexibility in reading rate? Since no direct measure of flexibility was included as the theory was put together, we cannot tell where flexibility goes into the flow charts for power and speed of reading. There are several relevant

aspects reported about speed and power, however. The decisive variable —
even though we are more directly concerned with speed — is power. The
many particular subabilities that have been extracted from the total act of
reading are mobilized, as Holmes puts it, into an "ordered hierarchy," and
"power" is crucial to this hierarchy. The primary contributors to power are
such factors as knowledge of word meanings and concepts. Thus we would
expect children to develop flexibility most readily by increasing their familiarity with the ideas behind the words that they read. Contrariwise, we can
slow them down by shifting to ideas that they do not understand or by
excessively complicating the prose, even though the individual words we
may use may be familiar to them and simple. According to Singer (1964),
speed of reading depends, in the substrata-factor theory, upon visual sensitivity in younger pupils (at the third grade). By sixth grade, visual properties
of words give way to the meaning itself, until a more judicious balance links
visual recognition and meaning.

In order, then, to shift reading rate easily, both speed and power must
be considered. With or without substrata factoring, it is plain that both
accurate sensing of a word's form and confident reaction to its meaning are
required. "Interfacilitation" of the various components for both speed and
power is thus the probable key to flexibility, and whatever increases interfacilitation (especially associations among ideas) should make possible
greater flexibility. Therefore I am impressed by the reports of Holmes, that
speed reading does not result from mere practice upon easy material, but
rather from persistent pressure to increase interfacilitation — that is, to
multiply associations among the several factors contributing to reading
(1962). The greater the number of associations, the more easily a reader
may reduce the individual cues he requires and still go fast. The richer will
be his understanding of the content if he prefers to attend to emotional
connotations, sounds, or conceptual complexities. It may be, as Singer's data
suggest, that a common source of inflexibility would show up in the child
whose natural approach to reading emphasized auditory cues. He may tend
to be a slow, if powerful reader, and thus relatively less flexible because
he does not easily speed up. Another pattern might appear in the more
typical child, whose natural avenue is visual. If he does not cultivate power
so faithfully as speed, his comprehension will suffer. He, too, would be
relatively inflexible, because he recognizes word forms without properly
comprehending the ideas they convey — and so he cannot shift smoothly
among the ideas.

Flexibility assumes that a reader can see the words correctly (and eye-
movements suggest that greater flexibility usually goes with more efficient
seeing). But it requires much more — a sure grasp of the ideas that the
words are there to convey, which the substrata-factor theory associates more

with power of reading. If so, then I find it helpful to see in flexible reading a form of reasoning: a reader is constantly examining what he is reading in order to decide how to go on, which ideas dominate the others, where it is safe to jump ahead because very familiar ideas are at hand, and so forth. All this goes on at the same time as thoughtful consideration of how clear or true or consistent the text itself is.

Piaget's elaboration of the critical skill of equilibration is helpful in thinking about reading flexibility. For it is necessary in both equilibration and flexibility for a reader to be constantly aware of how all the possible interpretations of a passage, for example, fit together. Past experience, various sections of the text, the purpose for the reading — all these rest upon each other, and the flexible person is probably the one who most effectively deals with their relationships. I also suspect that interfacilitation, in the Holmes formulation, refers to a similar critical activity that a child must eventually master.

Certain particular features of Piaget's system can be related to reading flexibility, although Piaget himself concentrates upon other problems, such as quantitative relationships and formal reasoning. First there are formal operations themselves, the most advanced stage in thinking. In reading, as elsewhere, there is the greatest freedom — hence the greatest boost to flexibility — when a reader can move out and away from the text that he is considering and even from his own direct experience. Second, three related mechanisms of thought that are critical to Piaget's system apply to reading flexibility: conservation, reversibility, and transitivity. They operate when a person notes constancy amid change, follows a process whether to or fro, and draws relationships among indirectly connected matters. These three skills begin to emerge in the intermediate period of concrete operations, but they do not really flower until — with formal operations — they can be employed without the need of specific objects to be present. In reading, to be flexible is to realize that an author's ideas may be put into more than one form, that a passage may serve various demands, that "reading" is more than a lockstep march from one word or phrase to another. At best, then, reading is "operational" when the ideas in the passage can be freely associated with each other and with all relevant material or experience.

To the extent, however, that Piaget's elaborate key to the development of thought turns upon an inviolate sequence of steps, he has been unable to convince all of his critics. Even in recent years, when he has made room alongside his clinical interview routine for careful sampling, statistical significance, and control groups, he has met resistance to the doctrine of stages. After all, whenever in the preschool years children can be found who are using abstractions (albeit, perhaps, easy ones), or who later on are solving problems hypothetically when they should still be working at a lower level, it is hard to believe in a stiff sequence. And it has been typical among American students of cognition to find a spiral rather than a straight-line sequence. That is, concrete and abstract elements complement each other, grow out of one another throughout most of the childhood years.

Now this controversy has special importance to the study of reading. Reading, by definition, is abstract, and children can learn this skill at a very tender age indeed. There have been inveterate admirers of Piaget who argued that abstract matters like reading belong in adolescence, and should therefore not be forced upon the young. We have, of course — especially among the look-and-say folk — an insistence upon "experience first, symbols second," which Piaget himself would applaud.

Experience

Those who find themselves unduly hampered by a sequence of stages in mental development argue that even when stages occur, they are the result of experience more often than of some inner unfolding. Direct instruction is for them not only desirable, but applicable whenever called for. If a child in a metropolitan slum has a little experience and less vocabulary, then we should try to make up lost time by providing him with sustained enrichment. That is, instruction, instead of waiting upon readiness, should in fact push it along. They would also argue, I suspect, that flexibility may be stimulated or inhibited more by experience than by an inner clock. Their best evidence probably comes from remedial teaching, where it is axiomatic to expect emotional disturbance to paralyze progress, or for deficient experience to limit meaning. Certainly a child will hardly become a flexible reader if his attention centers upon a personal problem or if he can't recognize what an article is all about. W. J. Moore (1962) reports, for instance, that tense or disturbed students do not skim, that skimming seems to require a certain inner freedom. It is lack of experience itself, or emotional tension, that must be directly responsible, rather than some previous and prerequisite stage that was missed.

Conclusion

Regardless of whether flexibility in reading has a determining sequential base or is a response to environment within a looser pattern, a few summary remarks are in order.

First, flexibility in both rate and more general attack is important enough to receive direct attention. If the substrata-factor theory does nothing else, it points out a remarkable array of contributing characteristics, that together constitute reading. As we find out which ones are most directly related to flexibility, we shall probably be able to set up diagnostic routines and pedagogic tools for fostering it.

Second, following the lead of developmentalists like Piaget, and of most contemporary specialists in learning and cognition, I think that a crucial contributor toward improvement in flexibility is active attention and vigorous practice. Whether as equilibrium (with Piaget) or as interfacilitation (with Holmes), a child makes strides toward independence and maturity as he actively seeks ever-widening connections. Both direct experience with concrete objects and vicarious experience with books or ideas yield confidence in working out one's own choices for dealing with concepts.

Third, there are apparently many, many ways in which individual children develop their reading skills. No single avenue toward flexibility exists. Therefore we must not only check among the many subfactors that may be suspected, but we must also assume that particular readers will display their own unique combinations of subfactors. If a beginning reader doesn't understand whole words presented visually, we long ago learned to try auditory approaches, and failing them even kinesthetic ones. Just as with the more advanced skills required for flexibility, we shall undoubtedly still have to help Johnny and Susie individually.

Finally, at the opposite pole from pedagogy, I look forward to learning more about the basic mechanisms that give rise to and sustain flexibility. Along the whole front from environmentally oriented sociologists to developmentally sensitive neurologists, there should come a wealth of new information. I recognize the substrata-factor approach as important not only for the information that it may provide, but even more for the stimulation and argument that it is provoking.

Piaget's Theory of Perception: Insights for Educational Practices with Children Who Have Perceptual Difficulties

■■■ GLORIA F. WOLINSKY

The study of perception has been one of the central themes in Piaget's work on cognitive development. In this article, the author presents an excellent discussion of the perceptual process as it relates to intellectual behavior, and provides some practical approaches to curriculum planning for children with perceptual difficulties.

● ● ● ● ● ● ● ●

SOURCE: *Training School Bulletin,* 62 (1965), 12–26. (With permission of the author and the *Training School Bulletin,* the American Institute for Mental Studies, Vineland, N. J.)

In a previous paper (Wolinsky, above) it was suggested that Jean Piaget's particular thoughts and approaches to the problem of perception could be of considerable assistance in understanding the child who is presenting a problem in emotional or intellectual behavior that is attributable to difficulties in perception. Beyond understanding the youngster, Piaget's theoretical constructs offer an approach to method and technique that may aid the youngster in making more meaningful responses to a complicated environment. This discussion, therefore, will concern itself with (1) Piaget's thinking on the phenomenon of perception, and (2) an attempt to derive some pragmatic approaches for instructional situations that are intrinsic to the learning process. It should be stated also that in no way is this paper to be viewed as exhaustive of Piaget's considerable theoretical and practical work on perception but rather conceived as a review in terms of the problems that face readers of this journal.

The Approach to the Study of Perception

In discussing Piaget's concept of perception, two important facts should be remembered. The first is that the major part of Piaget's endeavors, as well as those of his collaborators, has been guided by a philosophy of intellectual functioning that is developmental; the second is that much of his writing on perception is in direct response to, as well as a critique of, a viewpoint of preformation, most exemplified in the Gestalt approach to perceptual phenomena. In understanding his work, therefore, one is involved in a genetic approach to the development of thought that attempts to comprehend the relationships that perception has to the ontogenesis of cognition.

The problem of perception and the role it plays in cognition have always been studied, commented upon, and referred to in all observations in the thirty odd years of work that culminated in L'Épistemologie Génétique, the monumental investigations on cognitive development in children. Perception is viewed as an aspect of intelligence and was investigated as an important part of the sensorimotor period or of sensorimotor development. The sensorimotor period is that time, roughly from birth to twenty four months, when the infant proceeds from a neonatal reflex level of nondifferentiation between the self and the world to a relatively more sophisticated organization of his sensorimotor actions with his immediate environment.

Intelligence in human beings, according to Piaget, passes through various stages and, rather than being fixed in terms of actual age, continuities are characterized by an order of succession. Intelligent behavior has two poles (Piaget, 1960), a figurative and an operative; the figurative aspect precedes the operative and is particularly functional at the preoperative or sensorimotor stage. It serves as the basis for all operation or intelligent behavior. During the sensorimotor period, for example, there is considerable manipulation of objects in a trial-and-error pattern and an attempt at the formation of the behavioral concepts of permanent objects. Probably the most familiar of these observations on infantile perception is the apparent noninterest or nonpursuit of a vanished object. Studying the phenomenon phase by phase to the moment of actual retrieval, he concluded that object concept is developed.

The Nature of Perception

In studying perceptual phenomena, Piaget has contributed several interesting concepts that assume important theoretical foundations for his work. A major one is the idea of perception as different from intelligence. Perception is the knowledge we have of objects, as of movement, by direct or immediate contact (Piaget, 1960, 1950). During the sensorimotor period the child responds in a direct motor fashion to the immediacies in the environment. Each situation has a perceptual organization or equilibrium of its own that is distinct from the previous one. This phenomenon is illustrated by the Delboeuf illusion where the illusion increases or diminishes but does not conserve its own value (Piaget, Lambercier, et al., 1942). What actually occurs is a displacement of equilibrium which, according to the terminology of Piaget, obeys "Laws of Maxima." A particular relationship generates an illusion and produces an uncompensated change. This process is actually self-limiting, for the illusion diminishes when the limiting point is reached since the distortion then assumes the value of the new relationship, hence "maxima." In actual operation, therefore, the child reacts to the new value but does not incorporate the past knowledge. Incorporation of past experiences is a higher level process which is not involved in perceptual activity.

Furthermore, when intelligence or intelligent thought compares two objects, neither the standard nor the compared entity, the measure nor what is being measured, is in effect distorted by the comparison (Piaget, 1960, 1950). However, in perceptual comparison and, specifically, when one constituent serves as a fixed standard for the judgment of variables, a systematic distortion occurs which is called "the error of the standard." In effect, concentration on a specific aspect of the experience distorts the perceptual phenomenon. Perceptual space, in view of this explanation, is not homogeneous. It is, in Piaget's terms, "centralized from moment to moment." In other words, the child moves with the activity of an unstructured field, and the object at hand becomes the absorbed focus of the moment.

Centration as a Factor in Perceptual Behavior

The "Law of Relative Centralization or Centrations" is a further explication of the particularities that perception presents. Perceptual space, as has been stated, is "not homogeneous but is centralized from moment to moment." The area of centralization corresponds to a spatial expansion while the periphery of this area is progressively contracted as one proceeds outward from the center (Piaget, 1960, 1950). Centrations or centralizations cause distortions; whereas, decentrations or decentralizations act as correcting factors since they actually coordinate different centerings. The "Law of Centrations" is independent of the absolute value of the effects of centering and expresses the distortions in perception as a function of the figure. Even when the elements to be compared are equally centered in vision, the objective difference is subjectively accentuated by perception (the error of the standard), a problem in perception which is peculiar unto itself. Perception, which proceeds step by step from the immediate but still in partial contact with the object, distorts the object because of centration.

Perception as a Statistical Process

As for the initial aspects of perception, it is conceived as basically a process that is statistical in nature (Piaget, 1961). During the sensorimotor stage, the infant actually samples specific elements in his immediate awareness. This concept of sampling is stated in probabilistic terms. Piaget assumes that perception is a brief period from a state where there is no perception to a relatively stable one. In effect, there are intervals in the schema of perception. The young child is involved in a series of encounters set up by a stimulus. However, not all of the possible encounterable elements are engaged. A fraction or a random sampling is involved in the first encounter. What then follows is a second sampling, not of the entire possible area or stimulus, but rather of the remaining elements of the situation. This sampling procedure proceeds until the "sample" can be meaningfully utilized. It might be well to make a distinction here, too, between the perception of space, which is an aspect of early development and, according to Piaget, an aspect of perceptual behavior, and the representation of space, which is a later refinement and a part of cognitive or operational behavior (Piaget, 1955b).

This probabilistic sampling (recontres) in the early stages of development is incomplete because of previously stated inabilities to incorporate past experiences and complete absorption with the thing at hand. Therefore, error, particularly in early childhood, is caused by incomplete sampling (Piaget, 1961) which basically reflects time and space factors that are not fully realized. When the child is able to bring various sampling relationships into meaningful and more complex situations (*couplage*), error is corrected, for he is now able to utilize multiple encounters in time and space more effectively.

Perceptual Behavior as Sensorimotor Behavior

Piaget has indicated that perceptual activity is an intimate part of the sensorimotor period and sensorimotor intelligence; but intelligence or cognitive thought does not come about until the child can free himself from the immediacies of perceptual and motor activity and then concentrate on activities of the higher mental processes or operational behavior.

There exist " . . . partial isomorphisms between logical and perceptual structures" (Piaget and Morf, 1958), for the phenomenon of perception does not meet the fundamental operations of logic (reversibility, additivity, transitivity, inversion) that, according to Piaget, is "intelligent" thought, except for an approximate and rather limited sense. For example, in figure–ground reversals the perceptual inversion does not satisfy the logical criterion of inversion since the boundary always remains part of the figure. Furthermore, in perception there are "preinferences" that are "partially isomorphic" to the mechanisms of inference in logical reasoning; for inference in the logical state is based upon the knowledge of the situation while the decision that is involved in perceptual response is in terms of pure sensory data.

Sensorimotor "thought" responds to perception and motor activity. As the child develops intellectually, aided by his interaction with the world of people and things, the process of decentering becomes more viable. The central processes of thought become more autonomous, and the properties inherent in intellective function, classification, ordering, and numbering, that are basic to logical groupings, take over.

The Link Between Perceptual and Intellectual Behavior

If perceptual activity concerns the immediate and ultimately links up with intelligence as soon as it can free itself from the immediacy of the situation, what is the link that permits the higher intellectual process? The concept of "transportations" serves as the vehicle for understanding. When the child begins to respond to objects that are too distant to be included in the act of centering, perceptual activity is extended in the form of "transportation." What occurs is a reconciliation of "centerings" which leads the way to genuine comparisons. In effect, there is a decentralization that compensates for the distortion and, incidentally, also accounts for size and shape constancy. What actually happens in "transportations" is a coming to terms with spatial and temporal relationships that were difficult in the first stages of perceptual behavior. This is another aspect of *"couplage"* or more adequate sampling. This crucial step in the development of perceptual activity permits the individual to move toward an analysis of situations that is required for operational procedures.

What Piaget is saying, then, is that the complex of operations which have the characteristic of a Gestalt or *structure d'ensemble* are not preformed or innate in an individual. They actually evolve out of a history of a person's interaction with the environment, enabling him to use new experiences in terms of his past (assimilation) and to rearrange his response in terms of the demands of the environment (accommodation). Early in life the child acts without understanding or comprehension. It is the immediacies of his experience that fill his awareness. An example of this perceptual phenomenon is the young child's grasping of a geometric form and attempting to place it on a puzzle cutout that has no relationship to the size or shape of the form. The grasp response is perceptual and motor; whereas, the placement of the correct form in its proper spot is an aspect of the higher mental processes and comes later when the youngster is able to free himself from the preoccupation with the shape and notices similarities and makes generalizations concerning proper placement.

Piaget does not deny that these immediacies are "wholes" or "configurations," or that perceptual constancy does exist, or that in perceptual structure the whole is not reducible to the sum of its parts. Rather, he rejects that which the Gestaltists have considered to be there from the beginning, the laws of organization and the dismissal of the role of past experience.

> There are indeed complex structures or "configurations" in the infant's sensorimotor intelligence but, far from being static and nonhistorical, they constitute "schemata" which grow out of one another by means of successive differentiations and integrations and which must, therefore, be ceaselessly accommodated to situations by trial and error and corrections at the same time as they are assimilating the situations to themselves (Piaget, 1960, 1950).

So it is with perceptual structures. While they differ from intelligence or operational structures, in that the latter are mobile and permanent and changes within the system do not modify it, perceptual structures also show a change that is the product of progressive construction arising from "adaptive differentiations and combinative assimilations."

Experiments in Perception

In order to illustrate and maintain his position about perception, Piaget has undertaken a series of almost classical experiments of a psycho–physical nature and has been most concerned with the development of illusions as the underlying empirical evidence for his theory of perception as developmental. A system called the "concentric clinical method" (*méthode concentrique clinique*) has been devised. It is modifiable for the individual child and derives its name (*concentrique*) from the presentation of extreme values that are presented first, and then smaller differences are introduced. Values are shown on an alternating basis, above and below the standard, to determine upper and lower thresholds (Lambercier, 1946). Piaget and his collaborators have used this method to illustrate that fractionation or ratio judgments, as seen in the overestimation of acute angles and underestimation of obtuse angles, are a function of age (Piaget, 1949). Average errors show a clear decrease with age.

In a project designed to study the perception of intersecting and incomplete forms (Piaget and von Albertini, 1954), it was found that after four years of age, with unswerving accuracy, children could recognize intersecting forms. The recognition of incomplete forms was much more difficult. At nine years of age, all incomplete forms could be recognized.

Constancy, according to Gestalt psychology, is organized within a boundary, and this boundary, with invariant relationships between particular aspects of stimulation, is the basis of constancy in perception. Piaget argues that constancy is a part of developmental learning (Lambercier, 1946; Piaget and Lambercier, 1951, 1956) and explains this phenomenon as part of his theory of transportation.

The results of his work and those of his associates on illusions have been reported systematically since 1942 in "*Recherches sur le Développement des Perceptions*," *Archives de Psychologie*, Genève, and have recently been consolidated (Piaget, 1961). Flavell (1963) and Wohlwill (1960, 1962) have also made some valuable reviews of some of his work in this area. Basically, experiments on the developmental aspects of illusions are divided into three types: the ones that decrease with age, such as the Muller–Lyer (Piaget and von Albertini, 1950; Piaget, Lambercier, *et al.*, 1942; Piaget, Maire, and Prevat, 1954); those which increase with age, such as the size-weight illusions; and the ones that increase to the age of ten years or so and then begin to decrease as do certain aspects of the vertical–horizontal illusion. In making these differences concerning illusion, Piaget, as does Binet, distinguishes between the primary illusions (Binet's "innate") and secondary illusions (Binet's "acquired"). Primary illusions are examples of factors involved in centralization — the law of relative centrations — (Piaget, Lambercier, *et al.*, 1942; Piaget, Vinh–Bang, and Matalon, 1958). Illusions, such as Delboeuf, Muller–Lyer, diminish with age for they are caused by inadequate sampling. Secondary illusions are produced by the interaction between primary factors and perceptual activity and reflect more adequate samples. For perceptual activity has developed to the point where it becomes involved in decentralization and, therefore, is able to regulate any perceptual distortion. Secondary illusions involving acts of comparison and coordination are basic to intelligent thought and are formed differently than are primary illusions.

More recently there have been reports in the literature (Gaudreau, *et al.*, 1963; Stein, 1964) indicating that the nature of the perception of certain optical illusions is being explored with the retarded. Furthermore, studies utilizing some of the concepts derived from his work have been and are in the process of completion (Elkind and Scott, 1962; Elkind, Koegler, and Go, 1962, 1964; Robinson, 1964). These studies tend to substantiate his major premises.

Implications for Instructional Situations

The Educational Scene

It would be extremely difficult in the psychologically sophisticated times in which we live to avoid the word "perception" or words "perceptual processes" in discussing the problems of children who have difficulty in learning in the formal sense or who have difficulty in relating to the less formal but still demanding processes of daily living. Indeed, in view of the nature of man's intellectual organization, any discussion of adaptive behavior must imply a process of perception, even though not particularly specified at the time. In reading and listening to the current dialogue on malfunctioning of perceptual processes and the implication it has for the learning process, one cannot help but be aware at times of an intriguing naiveté that reflects the innocent as he surveys a still virgin field. Though the first flush of the "discovery of perception" as a problem area with the exceptional has somewhat abated, the problem of comprehension and utilization in terms of the pragmatics of the child who has "perceptual difficulties" is still very much with us.

Admittedly, this sounds harsh. However, it is not meant as indictment but rather a comment on an inevitable consequence of the complexities that the seemingly simple word "perception" actually presents. The study of perception has been and still is a problem that is basic to philosophy and has deep roots in the scientific aspect of validation of theory (Hochberg, 1962). Furthermore, one man's theoretical approach to the problem is not another's, in either problem to be studied or aspect to be explored. And so studies on perception may vary from the physiological to the cultural, with gradients between. In terms of children with presupposed perceptual difficulties, for the most part our philosophical and psychological focus has followed "holistic" or "organismic" theory best exemplified in Gestalt approaches, such as Goldstein, Lewin, Koffka, Kohler, and Wertheimer. However, it would be wise to remember that the theoretical positions and confirmations of these suppositions have found major support within the functioning or nonfunctioning of perceptual processes in the adult. While the insights derived *ex post facto* have been creative and fruitful, basically, the question is the problem of possible perceptual difficulty arising in what is a primarily undifferentiated period of life.

What does the meaning of perception as developmental and of perception as different from intelligence but yet an important part of intellectual activity imply for educational research and practice? What can Piaget and his collaborators offer a situation that is complex, both in terms of intellectual approaches and intellectual breakdown? How can a theory of perception as described be put into use so that benefits can be reaped? Woodward's work (1959; 1961; 1962a) has shown us that there is some indication retarded children and adults proceed through the Piaget developmental schema, albeit more slowly, and reach a termination point prior to complete development. Other studies (Hood, 1962; Lovell, *et al.,* 1960, 1962a, 1962b), utilizing retarded learners as part of their group of subjects, are presenting similar lines of evidence. Furthermore, Woodward (1962b) presents an interesting approach to the application of some of Piaget's work to the education of the retarded.

Perceptual Learning Within a Schema

What will be suggested here is that the position as presented, the interrelationship of the development of perceptual activity with the sensorimotor period, presents a schema for a possible sequence of learning experiences that will serve as an added dimension for corrected learning experiences. While Piaget's work is still to be quantified, no other psychologist offers us so detailed a description of different facets of development in the early years of life. While many of us have been successful in helping children who have difficulty in perception, most of our approaches have been intuitive — from the simple to the complex; however, the logical sequence, in terms of ontogenesis, has at times eluded us.

All human learning situations basically must be involved with a specified goal so that procedures and materials can be effectively utilized to achieve the goal. When there is no great pathology or obstruction, the goals may be broader or may assume a learning or an intellectual process that is in good use. However, with children who are presumed to have a basic deficit in the ability to organize themselves in relationship to the stimuli around them, the stated goals must always be specified in terms of the difficulties. A philosophical approach to curriculum planning, however comprehensive and/or specified in terms of methods and materials, is insufficient without a statement of suspected difficulties and a proper realization of how this particular approach is supposed to remedy the particular situation. When the diagnosis of perceptual difficulty is offered, this alone is not sufficient, for it must relate to the pragmatics of the effect of disturbance and then to the task of assistance. If learning experiences are to be built around the schema as presented by Piaget, we become involved with planning experiences on a developmental level that is quite specific in terms of ultimate intellectual or preintellectual goals. Furthermore, by planning in terms of specified sequence, a unique opportunity for analysis of nonlearning or stalemate is offered. While the dialogue concerning the ultimate meaning Piaget's work has for psychology will continue for some time, his preoccupation with the "why" and "how," the analysis of behavior, not simply "it is," may be crucial for those of us who are concerned with the education and care of exceptional children.

The sensorimotor stage, with its carefully analyzed stage sequences of development (Piaget, 1954, 1951, 1952b), presents a unique opportunity for curriculum development. Earlier it was noted that perception is tied up with sensorimotor activity and as such is basically an act of intelligence. It might be said that possibly what is seen in the behavioral activity of a brain-injured child is the activity of a child who has not completed the sensorimotor stage in certain areas and who is attempting to build acts of intelligence on a structure that is not yet free of the demands of the sensorimotor period. Since Piaget's work is detailed for these stages and since there exist at this time several fine analyses of this period (Flavell, 1963; McV. Hunt, 1961; Wolff, 1960), a detailed account of this period is not presented here.

The sensorimotor period, with its intricate subgrouping and substages, places our child with perceptual learning difficulties in a continuum that affords an analysis for the teacher–learner situation that I do not believe exists anywhere else. Nor, to my knowledge, is there a truly systematic hierarchy of the developmental aspects of perception and intellectual growth that we are presenting to teachers, in order to firmly base their classroom methods. Piaget's schema, coupled with experimental evidence of the perceptual development (Gibson and Olum, 1960; Vernon, 1962; Wohlwill, 1960a) of young children, now affords us the rationale and the sequence of corrective and meaningful learning experiences.

The Dimension of Perception

In helping children with perceptual difficulties are we fully realizing all that is involved in what Allport (1955) calls the six broad classes of perceptual phenomena: "sensory qualities, figural or configural aspects, constancy, dimensional frame of reference, concrete object, and effect of the prevailing set or state"? And, granting that we can come to grips with the meaning of perceptual phenomena, are we fully cognizant of each of the phenomenon's meanings, for example, on the development of space perception which, among other factors, involves visual size, depth and distance, tilt and tactual space? In methodology are we confusing the perception of space and the representation of space as Piaget feels experimenters are doing, because of our preoccupation with performance in terms of the normative demands of the school situation?

Insofar as the confusion of the perception of space and the representation of space is concerned, is our methodology so bound up with the heritage of the early experimental work on the perception of form that we are not responding as we should to the interesting insights of Piaget and Inhelder's work on the development of space concepts (1967)? (These have been substantially confirmed in a number of experiments done in England.) For example, it is a rare teacher who does not present her "perceptual training" material, however simple, within the framework of Euclidian geometry or projective geometry. Piaget has shown, however, that, in terms of the perception of form, the process is from the topological or the concern with being connected or bounded to an appreciation of the Euclidian metric properties of space. What the child initially seeks in form are the proximity, separation, order, enclosure, and continuity of structural elements; then he responds to curves, angles, lines, and parallels. These factors are similar to Gestalt concepts, and workers with children who display perceptual difficulties try to plan for experiences incorporating these concerns. Nevertheless, the materials that the children are usually given are of the third order of difficulty, for the developmental order of form perception appears to be topological, projective, and then Euclidian. So, while recognizing a basic deficit, an attempt at remedy is made at a more sophisticated level of recognition of form; this is an unfortunate paradox and a basic error in logic of presentation.

What is suggested again is a rationale for experiences that is based upon a sequence that has built within it the time for analysis of behavior even as learned.

A rarely-quoted study of E. Meyer (1940), concerning the development of the comprehension of spatial relationships in preschool children utilizing the major developmental insights of Piaget, brings dramatic evidence as to how the analyses of stage can assist in providing instructional techniques for children with perceptual difficulties. While her study did not concern itself with technique for teaching, it did try to analyze the process within the development of a particular phenomenon. In its analysis it can serve as the rationale for remedial or corrective experiences.

We are never sure of the "perceptual sample" in either the "normal" and even more uncertain in the atypical. However, by analysis that is inherently part of an educational sequence, we can react to what is necessary, in either freeing the child from a "sample" that is being responded to out of proportion to its functional use or because the child does not know how to respond. Children, we must remember, respond to many stimuli because of an insufficient understanding of the field to which they are being exposed. However, an understanding of the demands of the field and the problems of the child as he relates to it must be understood. The difficulty in the extraction, for example, of the important factor in a particular learning experience may be more a problem of immaturity of space perception or poor visual motor coordination than the pathological inability to separate foreground and background. While the overt behavior may be the same, the methodology may not be.

Since the basic perceptual process develops according to this schema during the sensorimotor period, any training must involve the emerging sensorimotor patterns and areas. Specific techniques must involve the child in terms of the interaction of the particular phenomenon that is to emerge, i.e., prehension and vision. One cannot educate for a particular defect alone, for it belies the basic integration or assimilatory aspects that the child is groping toward. Furthermore, deficit in one area does not preclude the effects it may have on another. It may well be that, in helping our youngsters to meet the demands of their environment, we have to take them back to the relatively undifferentiated period of the neonate and build with them the schema that they were not able to build themselves.

The Challenge — An Analysis of Interaction

Piaget's major contribution, aside from the obvious, is his addition of fuel to the always smoldering fire of thought that believes children are more than simply their biological heritage. His work extends further than classical developmental theory for, rather than waiting for this biological heritage to unfold, Piaget's work on perception, as well as most of his observations on cognitive development, leads us to the point where we can begin to examine the assistive aspects that an environment can afford to its children as they proceed through life. Though there will be replications of his studies, though his points of view will be debated and, indeed, there is much to understand and to debate, there is a liberating aspect in his work for teacher, student, and research worker. His whole approach to analysis, which is more than mere quantification of data, places this triad in a position where each one is involved in an intimate way with the process of how and why of the thought process. For research workers, if they follow this technique, must of necessity begin to explain why; the teacher must take this information and understand maladjustive thought processes and provide for a remediation in terms of an impairment of developmental function; and the child ultimately must come to terms with an environment that provides and involves thought and meaningful action.

The problem, then, is concerned not simply with an increased exposure to educational technique and academic content, but rather a correction or concern with a process that has not been completed or fully realized.

Communication
in Language and Art

IV

One of the major attractions of Piaget's theory stems from the wide range of disciplines to which it can be applied, thereby strengthening the theory itself and simultaneously clarifying the structure of the discipline itself. Piaget's own investigations have extended into the fields of science, logic, mathematics, and morality; hence, interest in his work has tended to focus on these areas. The articles in this section on the arts represent a comparatively new venture.

Implications of Piaget's Talks for Curriculum

■■■■ JONAS LANGER

In this paper, the author suggests several intriguing extensions of Piaget's equilibration theory, specifically the view that the transitional stages from gestural to symbolic representation are a function not only of the organism's activity, but also the conventional modes in which the community organizes and transmits its knowledge.

At the present time, there appears to be a gap between what the developmental psychologist of cognition is talking about and what the people responsible for the teaching of knowledge are doing. Piaget's and much work of its kind is primarily directed towards studying the development of cognitive functioning, i.e., the cognitive operations which emerge in the course of ontogenesis. These operations determine the forms of knowledge which the organism may construct at a given stage of development.

There is, however, the other side of the problem which has been relatively neglected in the psychology of cognitive development, namely, the operations whereby the community communicates the forms of knowledge which

• • • • • • • •

SOURCE: Abridged from *The Journal of Research in Science Teaching, 2* (1964), 208–213. (With permission of the author and the *Journal.*)

it has accumulated to the individual and vice versa. The means of expression utilized determine the forms of knowledge which may be communicated. This is particularly important to curriculum development since the goal must involve the creation of means of communication which increasingly facilitate the task of teacher and student, i.e., learning from each other.

In this connection it becomes necessary to review what is meant by development. Piaget characterizes cognitive development as equilibration rather than maturation, experience, or social transmission. Equilibration is defined as progressive interior organization of knowledge in stepwise fashion. Progressive development is the resultant of the interaction between the functions of assimilation and accommodation. It is the relationship between these two functions which makes for either disequilibrium or equilibrium and, consequently, developmental change and stabilization of knowledge. Yet the focus upon the formation of knowledge comes from an emphasis upon assimilation, i.e., with how things can become meaningful and interiorized in the first place, so that they can be dealt with. But if one is also concerned with the exterior fitting of oneself to the community and the community to oneself, then it becomes necessary to focus, in addition, upon organismic accommodation. Accommodation involves adapting to what is there and reorganizing it in such a fashion that it may be integrated with present schemata.

In attempting to understand, on the one hand, what it means to assert that a child is achieving knowledge, and on the other hand, that knowledge is being communicated to him and by him in the course of development, it is necessary to make certain distinctions. These distinctions will permit several issues to be raised for consideration with respect to (1) the growth of knowledge about other things and oneself, and (2) the process whereby knowledge is interiorized and exteriorized, i.e., communicated to oneself and to others.

The first distinction to be made is between what is knowledge and what is not knowledge. Piaget seems to reserve true, or at least the highest, forms of knowledge to those concepts which arise as a consequence of formal operations. He distinguishes conceptual knowledge, and even that which results from developmentally earlier operations, from those experiences which arise as a result of imaging, perceiving, and copying the environment. The development of this latter set of behaviors, according to Piaget, is independent of cognitive development.

A problem which may be raised in passing and which requires much further empirical investigation is whether other developmental relationships do not obtain between cognitive and noncognitive operations, such as imaging. It is particularly likely that relationships such as subordination may obtain where functions such as imagery subserve those of thought.

For example, visual imagery of spatial dimensions has often been used in the service of formal theory construction.

The distinction between cognition and noncognition hinges upon the operations involved. What is taken on in a passive fashion, as Smedslund has argued, what is impressed upon the child is not cognition. It is merely that experience which mirrors the environment. What is acted upon, what is created is cognition.

A further distinction has to be made between the means of achieving knowledge and the objects of knowledge. The means toward the formation of knowledge are always acts and they are always constructive acts. The assumption is that the organism is always involved in constructive schematization via the functional interaction of assimilation and accommodation. Piaget has characterized five stages of cognitive development and the functionally analogous operations which emerge at each stage. The first three are relatively external actions upon or with actualities. There are sensorimotor actions upon things; preoperational actions upon things; and intuitive operations, but not with things.

The first truly internal actions are concrete operations with things. Only at the highest stage of cognitive development do formal operations appear which involve contemplation about things. The last stage permits operating upon operations or the transcendent activity of being conscious of one's consciousness. It becomes possible to reason deductively, formulate hypotheses, and deal with possibilities in addition to mere actualities.

As a consequence of these various schematizing operations, different forms of knowledge arise in the course of development. The objects of knowledge, which are constituted via different schematizing operations, are qualitatively different in addition to possible quantitative changes.

Now it may be argued that these constructed objects of knowledge will always be intuited in spatial, temporal, numerical, and/or causal form. These categorical forms of intuition provide the continuity of cognitive organization even though it is constantly changing in the course of developmental growth.

Nevertheless, the various schematizing operations which emerge at different stages insure the discontinuity of cognitive development. For example, sensorimotor means result in different organizations of space than do formal operations. The forms of spatial knowledge, as a consequence of sensorimotor operations, are the resultants of actual manipulations by the organism within his environment. In this sense the organization of space is relatively egocentric, i.e., the intuition of space is not differentiated from the actions involved in its apprehension. It is grasped in an immediate, external fashion such that the spatial group achieved is that described by the action itself. Consequently, it will be a buccal space, a prehensile space, a visual space, etc. These spatial schemata are not even coordinated with each other in the earliest substages of sensorimotor activity; and are radically discontinuous from those constituted in the highest stage of cognitive development. Then spatial knowledge is differentiated from the operations involved and is the result of internal operations. Consequently, it becomes feasible to construct possible spatial systems in addition to those which are actually intuited, e.g., the conception that the earth revolves around the sun in addition to the immediate external intuition of the sun revolving around the earth.

I believe that this formulation of functional (sensorimotor actions through formal operational) discontinuity and organizational (spatial, temporal, etc.) continuity consistently complements the picture of functional (assimilatory: accommodatory) continuity and organizational (cognitive) discontinuity presented by Piaget in his *Psychology of Intelligence* (1950). It raises the major problem, however, of the processes whereby external forms of knowledge become interiorized as schemata. We shall return to this issue after briefly making certain distinctions with respect to the process of expressing and communicating knowledge. This should permit a fuller understanding of the ramifications of the problem of interiorizing and exteriorizing knowledge.

In order to communicate knowledge, whether to oneself as in inner speech or to others as in external speech, it is necessary to make reference to some object(s) of cognition. This requires the embodiment of the referent in some vehicle of expression. The process of depicting referents is representation. Now, the stages of schematizing operations involved in forming symbolic representations of knowledge are not well delineated. Much ontogenetic research analogous to that provided by Piaget on the development of knowledge is required. However, it is clear that the earliest representations are bodily gestures. Piaget himself has provided us with many examples of postural-gestural representation by preverbal children in *Play, Dreams, and Imitation in Childhood*. To cite but one example:

> At 1; 4 (0) L. tried to get a watch chain out of a matchbox when the box was not more than an eighth of an inch open. She gazed at the box with great attention, then opened and closed her mouth several times in succession, at first only slightly and then wider and wider. It is clear the child, in her effort to picture to herself the means of enlarging and opening, was using as "signifier" her own mouth, with the movements of which she was familiar tactually and kinesthetically as well as by analogy with the visual image of the mouths of others.

As can be seen from this example, the symbolizing operation involves making reference to a cognitive problem, i.e., getting the chain out of the box by gesturally representing it. The gesture schematically depicts the dynamics of the situation. There are at least two components to this schematic depiction, namely, pretending and imitating the dynamics of opening a box.

It is clear that the symbol, in this instance, is relatively little differentiated from the object of knowledge which it represents. It is a relatively natural form of expression since it closely mimics the object of reference. This is also characteristic of those vocal–gestural representations usually referred to as onomatopoeias.

At the opposite end of the developmental continuum the forms of schematizing expression are relatively conventional and artificial. The symbol is well differentiated from the referent which it represents. The name "cow" is arbitrarily assigned to a schema of knowledge. This makes it possible for me to communicate with you about that object of our knowledge, cow, without any actual exemplar being present.

There must, of course, be transitional stages between these extremes. For a more comprehensive treatment the reader is referred to a recent work by Werner and Kaplan, *Symbol Formation* (1963). I might just suggest that these transitional stages are partly natural and partly conventional. For example, when the child yells "mama," much of the meaning is represented by the vocal–gestural qualities of excitement. This is also an important quality, but to a lesser degree, of adult representation. Gestural expression may serve a conjunctive or substitutive function in adult verbal–linguistic communication.

Communication — exteriorizing and interiorizing knowledge — must be looked at not only from the viewpoint of the organism's representational activity, but also from the viewpoint of the community. The knowledge of a community is its scientific, ethico–religious, aesthetic, etc., cognitive systems. This knowledge is symbolized in its mythical, linguistic, mathematical, etc., codes. The problem of communication, then, becomes how the community's and the organism's symbolic codes match up. It cannot be emphasized too strongly that the problem is twofold. It is both a question of how the organism interiorizes knowledge, and how cognition is exteriorized by the organism and the community.

This is particularly interesting if we maintain with Piaget that the spatial, temporal, etc., categories of knowledge are already being constructed by preverbal, sensorimotor operations. (One might note that Piaget has reserved the title of *The Construction of Reality in the Child* for his study on the sensorimotor bases of cognition.) Then it is necessary to argue that both the basic forms and functions of cognition are interior as well as exterior in the first stages of development. In this respect sensorimotor actions are particularly suited to the simultaneous role of interiorizing and exteriorizing forms and operations of knowledge. Because of their bodily yet graphic nature they are little differentiated from the internal organization of knowledge and the external environment.

We may now directly face the question of what is becoming interiorized in the course of development. While the forms of knowledge are progressively becoming interiorized schemata, the forms of expression are increasingly becoming exteriorized symbols. It is this dual process which insures progressive communications. After all, if knowledge were merely interiorized how could any exterior correspondence, and consequently comprehension, occur between communicants. Yet we know that the course of development is characterized by progressive understanding between communicants.

It is, then, the exterior means of expression which facilitate increasing communicative correspondence between individuals whose knowledge is, at the same time, becoming progressively interiorized. Progressive development is characterized by (1) the increasing differentiation of these exterior forms of expression from the interior forms of knowledge, yet (2) their increasing integration by the establishment of arbitrary representational relationships rather than the fused relationships (as exemplified by gestural representation, word realism, etc.) which obtain in the early stages. It is this process of differentiation and integration between interior and exterior forms within the cognitive organization of individuals which is the necessary condition for correspondence between the exterior expressions of different individuals. That is, it is the condition whereby individuals may employ exterior forms to communicate their interior knowledge and achieve increasing understanding.

There is another issue with respect to the development of cognition. When one characterizes development as progressive it becomes necessary to speak about an organizing force. One may use the analogy of embryogenesis in speaking of an organizer which serves to direct the course of developmental organization, and from Piaget's works, the end stage to which development is directed seems to be that of perfect equilibration. This stage is characterized by formal operations. It involves operations upon operations and is consequently the highest possible stage of cognitive activity: dynamic equilibrium has been reached. The theoretical conception of cognitive development, then, is that of a closed system.

If development is truly a closed system, with formal operations as the last stage, then what happens in development when the last stage is achieved (at about fifteen years of age, according to Piaget)? What happens to cognitive development — is that the end? The initial answer to this problem must come from a characterization of development which goes beyond the formulation of analogous functions at different stages. Although Piaget has described cognitive development in terms of functionally analogous intellectual operations, he probably would not deny that other relationships between these operations may obtain which further characterize development.

In order to conceive of cognitive development as an open rather than a closed system, it seems to be necessary to speak of other relationships between cognitive operations. This should permit the theoretical conception of stages beyond formal operations. For example, one might have to consider exclusiveness, that is, functionally independent operations: when one achieves a new set of operations in the course of development, the earlier ones are no longer available. More interesting, however, would be a consideration of subsumption or the hierarchization of operations which emerge at different stages. This would mean the integration of the earlier, more rudimentary operations, by the later more sophisticated operations, such as formal operations. The resultant cognitive organization may be radically different and require the emergence of new cognitive operations. This theoretical issue takes on practical significance if we extend our consideration of curriculum development to higher education, at the undergraduate, graduate, and postgraduate levels.

Finally, I should like to raise a major problem, namely, the relationship of personal-emotional development to that of cognitive development. Let us briefly consider some of the genetic relationships between the organization of affect and intellect which are not typically dealt with. The organization of personality is largely a matter of identification. It is similar to the problem of the identification of any other object of knowledge in the course of development. In that sense one may draw very interesting genetic parallels for longitudinal study. This would involve the investigation of the development of permanence, conservation, etc., of personal identity in the course of the life cycle (Erikson, 1959). To put it plainly, we have yet to study the mechanisms of integration which insure developmental coherence of identity, e.g., that I am the same person now as when I was a child even though I have changed. On the other hand, we still have much to learn about the disintegration of identity in pathology, e.g., in dissociation, amnesia, etc.

There are also some striking differences between the operations involved in the formation of personal identity and of other objects of cognition. In conceptualizing the organization of objects of knowledge, one recognizes that in the course of development the individual gives different cognitive status to objects. In particular, the self takes on the cognitive status of a relatively subjective, i.e., internal, psychological, spiritual, object, while other things are made into relatively objective, i.e., external, physical, material, objects of knowledge. This is why, for example, scientists come to distrust their personal assessment of phenomena and place so much trust in "objective" analysis.

Piaget's (1930) distinction between efficacy and phenomenalism is particularly relevant in this regard. These are the two basic causal relation-ships which are formed. In the sensorimotor stage of development no differ-entiation is made between efficacious and phenomenalistic relationships, just as no distinction is made between objects as subjective or objective. With development, efficacious and phenomenalistic relationships progressively differentiate. Efficacy becomes the intentional mode and phenomenalism the physical–causal mode. The cognitive status of subjectivity is given to intentionality — the inner state or reason for doing something. If, for ex-ample, I made a noise by hitting the table, then the cause of that noise may be asked. If we mean by this, what is the reason for the noise's occurrence, we are asking a question of intention. That is, we are asking about the purpose for making the noise. On the other hand, if we are asking how the noise happened, then we are concerned with the physical relationships between objects which produce noise. The cognitive status of objectivity is given to the establishment of such physical–causal, external relationships.

The foregoing comments have been directed toward some of the impli-cations of Piaget's powerful theoretical–empirical model of cognitive devel-opment for curriculum development, and it is with this purpose in mind that some problems have been raised which may serve to stimulate con-sideration of the relationship of communication and personal development to cognitive development.

Role-Taking and Communication Skills in Children

JOHN H. FLAVELL

Meaningful communication presupposes a common system of stylized roles whose attributes are understood by both participants. This understanding implies role-taking skills which are acquired gradually as a function of the child's cognitive growth. Research into the development of role-taking and its relation to com-munication skills has been scanty to date. In this paper, the author describes several studies on this topic, and suggests that specific training for these skills might well constitute an important function of the school: through such techni-ques as programmed instruction, simulation, and educational games.

Thanks to the research efforts of Piaget and others, we are beginning to learn something about the child's developing intellectual skills with respect to the nonsocial environment, that is, the growth of his ability to order and

• • • • • • • •
SOURCE: *Young Children, 21* (1966), 164–177. (With permission of the author and publisher.) The experiments by the author and his coworkers reported in this paper were supported in part by Research Grant M-2268 from the National Institutes of Health, Public Health Service.

classify objects and events in the physical world, to reason and make inferences about them, and the like. We know far less, however, about the developmental course of those cognitive operations that are performed on human objects and that presumably mediate the genesis of various social skills. What sorts of cognitive operations and social skills are referred to here?

The Nature of Role Taking and Communication

A personal anecdote will illustrate one important member of the genre. This morning I met with my summer school undergraduate class in child psychology. There are sixty students enrolled in the course, and they are a heterogeneous lot indeed. Some have had many courses in psychology and some have had none. Some have regular jobs during the year (mostly teaching) and some are full-time students. Some are married and have children (and probably grandchildren, in one case), and some, I suspect, scarcely know what a young child looks like. In talking about child development to this mixed group, I find myself almost continuously shaping and tailoring what I say and how I say it in accordance with rough and quickly-made guesses as to what one or more segments of the class need to be told, will readily grasp on the basis of past experience, and so forth. In effect, I find myself engaged in two kinds of social–cognitive activity, one of which serves an instrumental function with respect to the other.

The instrumental activity is role taking: I keep trying to deduce or intuit what might be called the listener role attributes of the class as a whole or of some subgroup within it, that is, their current informational state, their information-processing capacities, their interests, and their biases with respect to child-development content — in short, that subset of their attributes or characteristics which is of relevance to their present role as students listening to a lecture on this particular topic. The cues which serve my role-taking activity here include those stemming from past teaching experience (for example, what subject matter most students in the past have had trouble grasping), normative information about these particular students (how much psychology they already know), and feedback gained from the questions they ask and the comments they make (not to mention the occasional disconcerting yawns and restless squirmings).

Role-taking activity in this setting serves as a means to the end of effective verbal communication. That is, what I learn from my attempts to "read" the students' listener-role attributes serves to monitor or control what I say to them. It serves to make me summarize quickly that which I think they already know something about, and to dwell at greater length on that which is likely to be unfamiliar and difficult. It serves to make me refer to something which they themselves have probably experienced in their everyday lives in order to illustrate some abstract principle, and to try to dramatize or otherwise enliven material of the "important but rather dull" variety. In short, I repeatedly engage in a species of social cognition (role-taking activity) for the purpose of governing or mediating a species of social behavior (verbal communication).

Role-taking activity can of course be instrumental to behavior other than that of social communication. For example, it may be a means to enacting or literally playing the role of another; the actor seeks to understand Hamlet's intellectual and personality characteristics, not to communicate with him, obviously, but to simulate him on the stage. Role-taking activity may also serve as a means to effective cooperation with another person in some joint enterprise (for example, with one's partner in bridge) or, conversely, to effective competition with the other (with one's opponents). In fact, role-taking activity may be and often is performed with no immediate end in mind at all, as when idle curiosity prompts us to try to guess the occupation and personality characteristics of the interesting looking stranger seated next to us on the plane. In sum, role-taking cognitions are often but not always instrumental acts, and when they are instrumental, they often — but again, not always — serve as means for communicative ends.

Previous Research

Role-Taking Development

There have been relatively few research studies which describe the ontogenesis of role-taking skills. Following is a brief summary of the more important of these studies. Milgram and Goodglass (1961) found a developmental trend from second through eighth grade in the child's ability to predict accurately the normative word associations of young children versus adults. Dymond, Hughes, and Raabe (1952) found that sixth-grade children are more disposed than second-graders to make inferences about covert attributes (thoughts and feelings) of the characters in TAT-like pictures.

Feffer has devised a Role-Taking Task (Feffer, 1959) which has been used to study role-taking development (Feffer and Gourevitch, 1960). His data suggest an increase across middle childhood, not only in the ability to take on (cognitively) a succession of different roles in a given depicted social situation, but also in the ability to keep each characterization in the series consistent with all the others — for example (the child's report of) how character A behaves according to character B's observation jibes with how A feels according to A's self report. Gollin (1954, 1958) has also devised a role-taking task which tests the subject's ability to maintain consistency in the face of change. It appears to demand more subtle and searching inferences about the other than does Feffer's, however, and it is therefore not surprising that only Gollin's middle-adolescence subjects performed well on it. A recent investigation by Wolfe (1963) using Feffer's and Gollin's role-taking measures also yielded developmental findings consistent with theirs.

Piaget and Inhelder (1956) have reported a study of what might be termed perceptual role taking in children, that is, the ability to estimate how the other person literally perceives a situation, rather than what he thinks or feels about it. Children four to eleven years of age were seated facing a scale model of three mountains and tested for their ability to predict how these mountains would look to an observer seated at various positions around the table. The ability to infer visual perspectives which differ from the child's own was shown to be strongly age-dependent in this study. O. K. Moore (1958) has demonstrated something analogous in the auditory sphere. Teams of children were given a problem whose solution would be facilitated if each team were to construct a private verbal code, one that would permit the members to communicate aloud to one another without at the same time informing the members of the opposing team, who were in a position to overhear everything they said. Moore found that twelve- to fourteen-year-olds were much more sensitive than nine- to eleven-year-olds to the necessity of constructing such a code, that is, they were more attuned to the probable listening and inferential activity of the other team.

All the studies mentioned deal with role-taking development during middle childhood and adolescence. An investigation by Piaget and Inhelder (1956), subsequently replicated by Lovell (1959), is almost the only existing study of the role-taking skills of younger children. The findings simply showed that preschoolers have considerable difficulty with less complex versions of the mountains problem, i.e., predicting the appearance, as seen from different points of view, of a single object.

So far as the writer knows, only Piaget (1957b) has investigated the child's verbal communicative behavior from the point of view described above, that is, as reflecting his level of role-taking skill. In one interesting study (Piaget, 1957b, Chapter 3), a child of six to eight years is given a body of information by the experimenter (e.g., a story) and told to relate it to a second child of the same age. The latter in turn attempts to convey what he has understood of the story back to the experimenter. The messages produced led Piaget to conclude that children in this age range (especially the younger ones) tend not to communicate very effectively, principally because they fail to take account of the listener's viewpoint. As in most of Piaget's studies, his verbatim protocols give a vivid picture of how the child actually performs. One of the stories told to the subject was the following:

> Once upon a time, there was a lady who was called Niobe, who had twelve sons and twelve daughters. She met a fairy who had only one son and no daughter. Then the lady laughed at the fairy because the fairy only had one boy. Then the fairy was very angry and fastened the lady to a rock. The lady cried for ten years. In the end she turned into a rock, and her tears made a stream which still runs today (1926).

Here is one child's account of the story, together with Piaget's commentary in parentheses:

> Gio (8 years old) tells the story of Niobe in the role of the explainer: "Once upon a time there was a lady who had twelve boys and twelve girls, and then a fairy a boy and a girl. And then Niobe wanted to have some more sons (than the fairy. Gio means by this that Niobe competed with the fairy, as was told in the text. But it will be seen how elliptical is his way of expressing it.) Then she (who?) was angry. She (who?) fastened her (whom?) to a stone. He (who?) turned into a rock, and then his tears (whose?) made a stream which is still running today."

The ellipses and indefinite pronouns in this message are taken as evidence of a basic failure on Gio's part to keep the listener's role in mind while communicating to him, that is, a failure to anticipate what he will and will not understand, what will and will not confuse him, and the like. Piaget obtained a number of messages of this ilk from his subjects, and concluded that it is not until age seven to eight years or later that budding role-taking skills make it possible for the child to engage in genuinely social, non-egocentric communicative behavior. As Piaget puts it, the younger child:

> . . . always gave us the impression of talking to himself, without bothering about the other child. Very rarely did he succeed in placing himself at the listeners' point of view.

Some Recent Research

During the past several years, the writer and his associates (Flavell, *et al.,* 1968) have conducted a series of studies on the development of role-taking skill, with particular attention to the instrumental value of such skill in verbal communication situations. The purpose of these investigations was simply to map out, in a descriptive–normative way, some of the developmental variety in this area. In other words, we were not so much concerned with showing how role-taking ability is attained, by searching for the factors and forces in the child and his milieu which accelerate or inhibit such attainment, as we were concerned with finding out what gets attained, and approximately when, on the average. Thus, our work would best be categorized as an exploratory, ground-breaking endeavor in a little-studied area of development. As such, it was primarily intended to provide some preliminary descriptive data upon which subsequent, more analytic research could build.

Findings from three of our studies will be reported here. In Study I, a series of tasks was given to 160 children, 10 boys and 10 girls at each of grades 2, 3, 4, 5, 6, 7, 8, and 11. In Study II, a different set of problems was administered to 60 girls, 20 at each of grades 3, 7, and 11. Two kinds of tasks were employed in each of these two studies. So-called communication tasks tapped the child's ability to assess the role attributes of others for the express purpose of composing an effective message. Role-taking tasks involved this same assessment either in isolation for its own sake, or in the service of some noncommunicative goal such as playing a competitive game or actually enacting the other's role. Study III was essentially a pilot investigation involving younger children. Several tasks were given to a group of 40 preschoolers, 10 at each of ages 3, 4, 5, and 6 (about half boys and half girls at each age level); a few of these tasks were subsequently revised and readministered to the three- and five year-olds. Unlike Studies I and II, Study III utilized only role-taking tasks. The present account of the three studies will of necessity be sketchy and abbreviated, with details of theory, method, and results omitted. Nevertheless it should be sufficient to convey how developmental–descriptive research in this area may be designed and carried out.

Role Taking in Middle Childhood and Adolescence

In order to test the child's ability to assess the role attributes of another person, the experimenter must of course make sure to arrange things so that these attributes clearly differ from the child's own. That is, the child should not be able to predict correctly the other's point of view simply by reporting his own. It seems likely that one of the chief obstacles to accurate prediction under these circumstances may be an everpresent tendency for one's own perspective to intrude upon and contaminate what one attributes to the other person. Particularly in certain role-taking problems, an active and continuous suppression of one's own point of view may be needed in order to avoid confusing it with that of the other.

In this connection, one of our tasks in Study I is germane to this point. The child is shown an ordered series of seven pictures which, comic-strip fashion, illustrate a story: A boy walks along, sees a dog pursuing him, climbs an apple tree to escape the dog, and eats an apple while awaiting the dog's departure. After the child has narrated the story (an easy task for all the subjects), the experimenter removes three of the pictures, leaving a four-picture sequence. The set of pictures was constructed in such a way that the four-picture sequence illustrates a story that is very different from the seven-picture sequence: A boy walks along, spies an apple tree, climbs it, and is shown eating an apple (with an innocent-looking dog in the background). A second experimenter then enters the room and the subject is told that this individual has never seen any of these pictures before. The subject is then asked to predict the story he thinks the adult would tell on the basis of seeing only the set of four pictures.

Most of our fourth grade and older children had little if any difficulty with this task. A number of the second- and third-graders, however, seemed to have trouble keeping their predictions uncontaminated by their previous experience with the seven-picture sequence. Some of them simply repeated the seven-picture story they themselves had given just previously. More of them gave what appeared to be a straightforward if rather skeletonized four-picture story but then "spoiled" it when the experimenter made certain standard inquiries. For example:

> "He's singing, and then he runs — he sees a tree. He climbs up it and he's eating an apple." (Fine. Why does Mr. X think that the boy wanted to climb the tree?) "So the dog don't get him — bite him."

Almost sixty per cent of the second- and third-graders showed one or the other of these two response patterns; the corresponding figure for the older groups varied from five to thirty per cent. As we see it, the younger children had more difficulty than the older ones in adopting — and especially, perhaps, maintaining over a sufficient period of time — the other's supposedly fresh and naive perspective vis-à-vis the four pictures. This difficulty stemmed precisely from the fact that the child's own perspective here was so utterly different. For him, these four stimuli had already been polarized in a certain way — semantically — and this polarization kept intruding on his efforts to take the role of the other. For some, the intrusion was apparent from the first; for others, it only became manifest when the crucial questions of the boy's motivation for climbing the tree and the role of the dog in the narrative had to be answered explicitly.

Role-taking activity undoubtedly exhibits a range of subtlety and complexity, just as do other kinds of cognition. Some attributes of the other person ought to require more intellectual maturity to detect and reason about than others. If this is true, one would expect that, given the opportunity to impute any one of several rather different characteristics to the other person, younger children would tend to discern only the more simple, superficial, or obvious characteristics, whereas older children should be more capable of finding the more complex, profound, and subtle ones.

A second task from Study I was designed to test this hypothesis. The child was presented with two opaque plastic cups turned face down on the table. One cup had a nickel glued to its bottom side; the other two nickels. These coins indicated the amount of money which might be hidden under each cup — one nickel under the first, two nickels under the second. The child was told that a man (as usual, one of the experimenters) would shortly come into the room, choose one of the cups, and get to keep any money found underneath. Before he entered, however, the child was to remove the money from either one of the two cups. The man's objective was structured as that of trying to choose the cup that covered the coin so that he could obtain the money. The subject's objective, on the other hand, was to try to guess which cup the man would choose and "fool him" — take the money out from under that one so he would not get any. It was stressed to the child that his opponent knows that the child intends to outwit him in this way and that the child should "think hard" before selecting the cup to empty. The subject then made his choice and was carefully questioned as to its rationale. The single choice-and-rationale comprised the only experimental datum; the task was terminated when the man entered the room and made a (random) choice.

Of the 160 subjects, 121 gave choices and rationales which could readily be categorized as reflecting either of two game strategies, one considerably more complex and searching than the other. A subject who adopts the simpler strategy apparently attributes to the other person nothing beyond cognitions and motives bearing on the game materials themselves. For instance, the child predicts that the man will choose the two-nickel cup because it contains more money; here, the child seems at most to represent to himself the other's monetary-gain motive and a cup selection governed by that motive. A child who follows the other strategy also represents these same cognitions and motives, but some others as well, namely, the man's representations of the child's own behavior, especially the child's cognitions concerning the man and what he might do. Here is an example:

> (The subject chooses the one-nickel cup.) (Why do you think he'll take the one-nickel cup?) "Well, I figured that, uh, if it was me I'd take this one (two-nickel cup) because of the money I'd get to keep. But he's gonna know we're gonna fool him — or try to fool him — and so he might think that we're gonna take the most money out so I took the small one (one-nickel cup). I'd go for the small one."

If one diagrams these two strategies, the difference in complexity becomes readily apparent. Let S, O, X, and $\rightarrow$ represent the child, his opponent, the game materials, and "cognizes" ("has motives regarding," etc.), respectively. The first strategy can be diagramed simply as $S \rightarrow O \rightarrow X$. The second, however, apparently cannot be adequately represented by anything briefer than the chain $S \rightarrow O \rightarrow S \rightarrow O \rightarrow X$ (S represents O's beliefs about what S thinks O is likely to decide regarding X).

The developmental data were clearly in accord with our expectations: The frequency of the simpler strategy decreased with age while that of the more complicated one increased. More than two-thirds of the subjects in the youngest three age groups followed the simpler strategy, while only one-tenth discovered the more complex one. For the three oldest groups, these fractions were approximately one-third and four-tenths, respectively. It may be that the essential hurdle in the more complex strategy for the younger child is the recognition that the other person's cognitive representations may subsume not only objects external to both the child and the other person, but the child and his cognitions as well. In other words, once he can achieve the component $S \rightarrow O \rightarrow S$ as well as $S \rightarrow O \rightarrow X$, the rest of the chain (an integration of the two, really) may be relatively easy.[1]

It is interesting to speculate about the relevance of these social-cognitive acquisitions to social behavior at large. The preadolescent or adolescent often seems to worry about how he appears to others, about what others think of him, and the like, whereas children in the preschool and early to middle childhood periods seldom appear to. We would venture that the sorts of role-taking capabilities illustrated in this study function as necessary (although surely not sufficient) conditions for such $S \rightarrow O \rightarrow S$ concerns.

Two other role-taking investigations can be quickly summarized, the first from Study I and the second from Study II. In the former, we were able to confirm Piaget and Inhelder's (1956) findings that the ability to predict the visual perspective of the other ("perceptual role-taking" ability) increases markedly during middle childhood. The latter investigation dealt with the ability to enact or play another's role. The subject played two roles in succession: first, a shy, inarticulate little girl reporting a recent visit to the zoo (with the experimenter taking the role of the teacher to whom the report is made); second, a bold, articulate little girl doing the same thing. Skill in role enactment was here defined as the extent to which these two verbal reports differed from one another — in length, in content, in vocal qualities (such as rate of speech), and the like. As expected, there was an overall

• • • • • • • •

[1] It might be mentioned in this connection that two fifth-graders and two eleventh-graders elected to remove the money from the two-nickel cup, according to a paranoid-looking strategy which could only be diagramed as $S \rightarrow O \rightarrow S \rightarrow O \rightarrow S \rightarrow O \rightarrow X$!

developmental increase in the ability to differentiate the two roles. Not surprisingly, however, individual differences at each age level were very marked, with the child's personality characteristics constituting an important determinant of her ability to perform on this kind of task.

Communication in Middle Childhood and Adolescence

Communication tasks have the same structural requirement as do the role-taking tasks we have been describing. That is, the experimenter must make sure that the listener's perspective vis-à-vis the content to be communicated is distinctly different from that of the speaker. When this requirement is met, the speaker will have to make special efforts if his message is to be adapted to the listener's needs; spontaneous "top of the head" verbalizations are almost guaranteed to be communicatively ineffective. Two of our tasks particularly well illustrate the uses of such a design in probing for developmental changes in this area. In both tasks the person to whom the child communicated had special, out-of-the-ordinary listener needs with respect to the subject matter of the message.

In the first (from Study I), the child is taught to play a simple competitive game by nonverbal means, that is, by actually playing it through with the experimenter, the latter making use of gestures wherever necessary. An adult then enters the room, and the child is instructed to tell him how the game is played. Two "rules" are in force during the ensuing communication: The child is not allowed to touch the game materials (thus ruling out a wholly nonverbal, demonstrational mode of explanation); the listener is not allowed to provide any feedback as to the adequacy of the message (he just sits there, looking acceptant, while the child talks to him). For half the children at each grade level, the adult was blindfolded during the session — a fact which was carefully brought to the child's attention. As such, he of course constituted a very special kind of audience in this situation, one whose listener needs were far greater than those of the ordinary listener, who could see at a glance what the game materials consisted of, who could easily follow the subject's gestural references to this or that game object, etc. For the other half of the group, the adult listened without the blindfold. The second- and eighth-grade subjects who talked to the sighted listener gave a second communication immediately afterward to a different, blindfolded adult.

We expected, of course, that the amount of useful information in the child's message would tend to increase with age, regardless of who the listener was. The more important prediction, however, was that the difference between sighted-listener and blindfolded-listener messages would augment with age, reflecting the older child's greater sensitivity to the differing listener requirements in the two cases. This prediction was confirmed by the data. For example, one of our measures of informational content was the number of different words the message contained. For both types of messages, number of different words increased with age. As predicted, however, the two curves had different shapes, the one for the blindfolded-listener messages rising faster than the one for the sighted-listener messages. This age-by-message type of interaction was especially clear-cut in the case of those subjects who composed two messages, the first to a sighted listener and the second to a blindfolded listener. In the eighth-grade group, the mean number of different words was substantially higher in the second message; for the second-graders, the two means were identical. The communicative consequences of failing to keep the listener's perspective in mind were most vividly illustrated in the performance of a few of the youngest subjects, who blithely spoke of picking up "this" and putting it "over there," and the like, when trying to explain the game to the unsighted adult.

The other task (from Study II) had a similar structure. The child was presented with a typed copy of the Aesop fable, "The Fox and the Grapes." After the child had familiarized himself with the story (and had been given help with any words she appeared not to be able to read or understand), she was given the task of explaining it to a four-year-old boy, represented by a photograph. The child was told that she could refer to the typed copy or not as she pleased — the important thing was to tell the story in such a way that the young boy would be sure to understand everything.

The subject's message was scored for the number of simplifying recodings it contained. These were defined as deviations from the text which appeared to represent attempts by the subject to make the story easier for her cognitively immature listener to grasp. There was a striking increase in the frequency of these recodings from third to seventh grade, with little change thereafter. The messages of these early-adolescent children make interesting reading because they give one the impression of actually "seeing" role-taking activity as it periodically occurs during the course of the message. Here is an example:

> "The Fox and the Grapes. One hot — one hot summer's day a fox was strolling, that means 'walking,' through the orchard, that's where there are lots of trees, till he came to a bunch of grapes just ripening on a vine which grew along a lofty branch, that means 'high.' 'Just the thing to quench his thirst,' that means 'satisfy' his thirst, quoth . . . that means . . . 'quote a little' or something like that. Drawing back his — drawing back a few paces, he took a running — a run and jump, but just missed the br–branch. Again and again he tried to get the tempting morsels, that means get the tempting . . . 'food.' But at last — last he had to give it up, and walked away with his nose in the air, saying 'I'm sure those . . . they are sour.'"

The remaining tasks explored the contributions of role-taking activity to several related communicative skills. Developmental changes were found, for example, in the ability to compose an effective message of the persuasive rather than simple information–transmission variety. Here again, the older child's ability to "read" the other's needs, attitudes, susceptibilities, etc., seemed to play a decisive role in her superior performance. The older child was likewise shown to be more skillful: in constructing barely adequate, minimally redundant messages under instructions to avoid overcommunication; in sending a single message of optimal redundancy to a group of individuals with differing listener needs; and in identifying the communicative inadequacies of a message composed by someone else.

Role Taking in Early Childhood

All but one of the Study III tasks were designed to measure very simple forms of perceptual role-taking ability. In one, for example, the subject and the experimenter sat facing each other across a table. The subject was to place a picture on the table in a position which would permit the experimenter to view the depicted figure right side up (in the original version of the task) or upside down (in the revised version). The perspectives of the subject and the experimenter were of course always opposed in this task: In orienting the picture so that the experimenter could see it right side up, the subject himself would perforce see it upside down, and vice versa.

There were several other tasks of the same type, one of which concerned tactual rather than visual perspectives. The equipment for this task consisted of an ordinary pencil, which was sharpened at one end and had a piece of absorbent cotton glued to the other end. The pencil was suspended in a horizontal position, the sharpened point in the experimenter's palm and the cotton in the child's. The experimenter first asked if "it felt soft" in the subject's hand, and then (test question) if it also felt soft in the experimenter's hand.

In the one task which did not involve perceptual role taking, the child was presented with a variety of objects and requested to select one which he might give to his mother (also tested: father, teacher, sibling, self) for a birthday present. Poor role-taking performance here was thought to be reflected in egocentric choices — for example, selecting a toy truck as an appropriate gift for the subject's mother.

The results of Study III were roughly as follows. Three-fourths to all of the oldest subjects performed correctly, depending upon the task, whereas only one-quarter to one-half of the youngest subjects did. It appeared that a number of three- to four-year-old children encountered real difficulties on these role-taking problems — the very simplest problems of the genre we would devise. But appearances are often untrustworthy when dealing with the formal test performance of very young children. There is always the lurking suspicion that the poor showing of the youngest children may have been at least partly due to misunderstanding of instructions, distractibility, and the like. Our confidence in the general tenor of the Study III findings is strengthened, however, by some ancillary data gathered in connection with another research project. Included in an interview schedule which we administered to parents of preschool children was a question about observed occurrences of role-taking difficulties in the child's everyday interactions. A number of parents were able to recall such instances, and many of these instances looked like the naturalistic counterparts of what we saw in Study III. For example:

> Sometimes, when the family is driving the car, the child (age 3:2) will suddenly ask "What was that?" although "that" is already out of sight. The mother says that she just cannot make the child understand that she (mother) cannot see "that" anymore.
>
> When the child (3:2) wants the mother to identify a picture in a book, she will hold the book pressed to her face and ask what it is, with the mother obviously unable to see it.
>
> The mother was drawing a statuette of a lion. The child (5:0) could not understand why the mother could not continue drawing it when the child turned it toward herself. The child's 6-year-old sister tried to explain the reason to her.

Retrospect and Prospect

As mentioned earlier, our own studies have largely been aimed at gathering preliminary data as to the what and the when of role-taking development, and the same has been true of previous work by others. We ought now to be able to make some speculations — likewise preliminary — about what this development consists of, and when in childhood its various constituents tend to appear. The nature of these constituents can be epitomized by considering what one needs to know, or know how to do, in order to engage in behavior which is mediated by role-taking activity. There are five such constituents:

(1) The understanding that there is such a thing as "perspective," that is, what you perceive, think, or feel in any given context need not coincide with what I perceive, think, or feel. (*Existence*)
(2) The realization that an analysis of the other person's perspective is warranted in this particular situation, that is, such an analysis would be a useful means to whatever one's goal is here. (*Relevance*)
(3) How actually to carry out this analysis, that is, possession of the ability to predict with accuracy the relevant attributes of the other. (*Ability*)

(4) How to maintain in awareness the fruits of this analysis, in competition with the unremitting press of one's own point of view, long enough for it to be able to fulfill its function as means or instrumentality for subsequent behavior. (*Performance*)

(5) How then to employ the fruits of this analysis as a means to some behavioral end, for example, as an effective monitor of verbal communication. (*Application*)

The evidence suggests that the development of existence is at least partly accomplished by the beginning school years. Young preschoolers often behave as if the very existence of perspective variation were foreign to them, whereas many older preschoolers clearly demonstrate an awareness of its existence, at least in task situations where the experimenter's instructions and the elemental nature of the role attributes in question conspire to facilitate such awareness. Correspondingly, there is some ability to predict with accuracy those perspectives whose existence the child is mature enough to recognize, but this ability appears to be extremely limited — limited primarily to the discrimination of the more obvious components of the other person's perceptual perspective.

On the other hand, really substantial prowess in ability, and in relevance, performance, and application as well, is probably not attained much before late middle childhood or early adolescence. We have been impressed with how rudimentary is the capacity, during the early school years, to tune in on the hidden role-taking requirements of ostensibly nonrole-taking (e.g., communication) tasks (relevance); to predict complex perceptual inputs and subtle or intricate intellectual processes in the other person (ability); to keep one's image of the other person's role attributes unsullied by one's own ongoing perspective (performance); and to translate what one knows or can guess about the other person into effective social behavior regarding him (application). In contrast, the child twelve to fourteen years old in our studies and in other studies shows himself to be a surprisingly adept role taker across a wide range of tasks and problems. Although the data are really not yet ample enough to justify it, one is tempted to predict that middle childhood will turn out to be the developmental epoch so far as basic role taking and allied skills are concerned, with the preschool period contributing the prologue and adolescence the epilogue. This assertion gains added interest in view of the fact that, until recently at least, developmental changes during middle childhood seem to have received less attention than those that occur during the periods which bracket it.

It should be pointed out that there are regions of certain ignorance in this area as well as areas of uncertain knowledge. What still remains to be learned about role-taking development?

First, additional descriptive information is needed regarding the factual course of role-taking development. That is, we should like to know more about just what particular skills in this domain get acquired in what order and at what ages. The tasks and problems that have been used so far for this purpose are, after all, but a small and doubtless unrepresentative sample of a whole population of possible assessment procedures.

Second, and related to the first, we presently know nothing about the "factor structure" of attainment in this area, that is, nothing about what abilities are and are not correlated (within individuals) with what other abilities. Does good role-taking performance in any one task setting imply good role-taking performance in any other task setting? Or is there, instead, a considerable amount of specificity and heterogeneity in skill structure here, leading us to think of role-taking skills rather than role-taking skill? The history of psychology is replete with unitary-looking abilities that, on closer examination, turned out to have a number of independent components. Role-taking "ability" may be another case in point.

Third, there is the whole question of the antecedents, correlates, and consequents of role-taking and related capabilities. What do we need to know about the individual, past and present, and about his milieu, past and present, in order to predict how well he will do on role-taking tasks? What kinds of children do better on what kinds of role-taking tasks vis-à-vis (and this could be an important variable) what kinds of other persons? What sorts of family histories and educational backgrounds are importantly associated with skill level as regards these tasks? And finally, what are the behavioral consequences of the child's skill level? One would be surprised indeed if the child's role-taking skill had no implications for his everyday social behavior, but there is as yet not a shred of research evidence on the question. To sum up, role-taking skill must certainly be embedded in a complex network of causes and effects, and it is an important task for future research to illuminate the structure and content of this network.

Finally, since role taking looks like a social–cognitive skill of considerable practical utility, one could well consider making it the subject of experimental educational research. Two of the writer's former associates have made beginnings in this direction. Fry (1961) tested the effectiveness of a series of small-group training sessions designed to heighten the child's sensitivity to listener role attributes when communicating. Botkin is currently completing a dissertation project at the University of Rochester in which attempts are made to inculcate role-taking and allied skills by means of programmed instruction. The eventual incorporation of an effective regimen of role-taking training into the school curriculum is a possibility worth thinking about. The writer believes that such training would constitute a most defensible form of Dewey's "education for life."

An Approach to Literature Through Cognitive Processes

▇▇▇ HERBERT KARL

Piaget's matrix of thought processes lends itself most readily to the scientific and mathematical disciplines, but its implications for teaching are not confined to these. The author of this paper demonstrates ways in which a teacher of English may use it to increase the student's awareness of the structural relationships of literary passages, and to construct and test his own hypotheses. In so doing, he may develop an awareness of the techniques of literary composition and sensitivity to the deeper symbolic levels of meaning.

The ideal student of literature must not only be perceptive; he must be conceptive as well. That is, he must be capable of transforming the surface qualities of literature into conceptual structures — patterns of deeper meaning which presumably will enable him to interpret, evaluate, and appreciate a given selection. With some notable exceptions, English teachers generally have not felt a conscious obligation to improve or, for that matter, identify the transformational processes which underlie learning and which therefore have specific relevance to the teaching of literature. Recognizing this problem as one which affects the entire English curriculum, Squire (1965) asserts that there is a growing need to consider recent contributions of psychologists, rhetoricians, and literary critics.

The psychological studies of Piaget might well provide the kind of rationale for literature study which could help students develop consciously the perceptual and conceptual skills necessary for a more complete awareness of the literary experience. What follows is an attempt to postulate an approach to literature study embodying the spirit of Piaget's theories. If some of the tentative conclusions stated later seem tenuous and highly speculative, the justification is that very little has been done in the past to use the methodology of psychologists in formulating an approach to literature study in the secondary school.

Before beginning to discuss Piaget, one must acknowledge his cognitive orientation. The cognitive psychologist, as Hilgard (1956) notes, prefers a learning situation which permits a "perceptual structuring leading to 'insight'; that is, the understanding of the essential relationships involved." To Piaget, the perceptual structuring of relationships must be regarded apart from simple perception. The former implies actual processes of thought (cognition), while the latter implies learning of a different kind. To give an example of learning which occurs through simple perception, consider the child who burns his finger on a hot stove. The child learns that it is

• • • • • • • •

SOURCE: *The English Journal*, 57 (1968), 181–187. (With permission of the author and the National Council of Teachers of English.)

the stove that burns him. This is an irreversible perception. What the child perceives (the hot stove) is the cause of his finger being burned; it is not his finger which causes the stove to be hot, nor will his finger be burned when the stove is not lighted. Perception in this case is directly related to learning. As Piaget points out, the child up to seven years of age continues to rely heavily on his perceptions as an index of what is true. The result is that the child experiences a number of misconceptions, since all learning is not a matter of simple perception (Berlyne, 1965).

The difference between simple perception and thought is simply that the latter depends on what Piaget calls the quality of reversibility. Reversibility can be explained graphically with an example from arithmetic. One might be asked to complete the equation: $2 + 2 = (?)$. The process involved in solving the problem is not inflexible; it is, in fact, reversible. We might form the answer $2 + 2 = 4$, and this would be true. But we could also reverse the elements and say that $4 = 2 + 2$. In the case of the child who burned his finger, we can say that the stove burned the finger, but we cannot say that the finger burned the stove. Solving the arithmetic problem is much more flexible. For example,

$$2 + 2 = 3 + 1$$
$$2 + 2 = 2 + 2$$
$$2 + 2 = \sqrt{16}$$
$$2 + 2 = 2^2$$

Piaget's theory of reversibility enabled him in *Logic and Psychology* (1957) to develop what he calls a lattice or group of concrete operations at the psychological level. The lattice can be taken to represent the womb of human thought processes, a kind of matrix which is, in itself, a finite structure. But like Chomsky's grammar, it is capable of producing an infinite number of thoughts. The matrix is not fully used by the child until he reaches the period of formal operations (eleven to fifteen years). At this point the adolescent is able to invoke intuitively the language of symbolic logic within the matrix to transform his perceptions into conceptual structures.

The matrix is composed of four processes which Piaget lists as identity, inversion, reciprocity, and correlation. Before attempting to define these processes in detail, it might be worthwhile to summarize what has been previously stated. Piaget recognizes first that simple perception and thought are two separate qualities. One may learn by perception alone, or one may transform his perceptions into conceptual structures, in short, he may think. Thinking depends on reversibility. A learning context is reversible when it can be restructured within the mind without losing its essential equilibrium. In other words, learning takes place when a learner is able (1) to perceive and (2) to restructure his perceptions into a relational pattern or multiple relational patterns.

Unlike mathematics, the quality of reversibility in literature does not stimulate the kind of relational patterning which can be easily checked and verified. The reason for this is obvious. Mathematics is a discipline which has a built-in capability of proving or disproving most of the hypotheses which are a product of mathematical thought. We know, for example, that $\sqrt{16} = 4$, because its inverse operation $4^2 = 16$. When we expect a student to structure certain details of a short story into a relational pattern which will enable him to form a hypothesis of possible meaning, we are asking for a statement which is unverifiable. The degree to which the hypothesis is valuable is not relative to its verifiability. Rather, its worth rests on the soundness of the relational pattern which the student perceives as underlying the hypothesis.

Since the processes which comprise the matrix are expressed in terms of logic and mathematics, it becomes necessary to translate Piaget's terminology into the language of literature study. Naturally, one cannot eliminate the concepts behind these terms by merely changing their names.

The four processes which make up the matrix, as was noted earlier, are identity, inversion, reciprocity, and correlation. The first — identity — has distinctive mathematical and logical connotations. Logicians introduce the sign $=$ as the identity sign. That is, $a = b$ means that a "is identical" with b. In a sense, identity is the fundamental process of all other structural relationships; any relational structuring usually begins and ends with identity. To use an example from literature, consider this poem by Wallace Stevens (1954) entitled "Life Is Motion":

> In Oklahoma,
> Bonnie and Josie,
> Dressed in calico,
> Danced around a stump.
> They cried,
> "Ohoyaho,
> Ohoo" . . .
> Celebrating the marriage
> Of flesh and air.[1]

We might want to pose the following question to a student: "Who is the poem about?" The student might respond: "The poem is about two girls." If we were to symbolize the foregoing question with letter a and the subsequent answer with the letter b, we could say that the relationship between

• • • • • • • •

[1]Wallace Stevens, "Life Is Motion," *The Collected Poems of Wallace Stevens* (New York: Alfred A. Knopf; London: Faber and Faber; 1954), 83.

the two is expressed as the identity $a = b$. This simple identity generates other structural relationships, enabling a more complete interpretation of the poem. We must be aware, however, that the identity, itself, is the product of deeper relational structures. To make this more clear, consider how the questioning could proceed:

TEACHER: Why do you say that the poem is about two girls rather than two boys?

STUDENT: The names of Bonnie and Josie are contracted forms of girls' names. I know a girl named Bonnie, and I think Josie is the shortened form of Josephine.

In essence, the student is forming an identity to explain his first identity. He is saying that Bonnie and Josie = girls. Credibility can be given this identity by structuring another identity which might be expressed: The Bonnie whom I know is a girl; thus the Bonnie in the poem might be a girl. In short: Bonnie I know = Bonnie in poem. And so forth. In tracing identity backward like this, we are actually bringing the entire matrix into play. As Piaget notes, NRC (the symbol for all the processes except identity) $= I$ (identity). There is a point where we accept identity without analyzing it as a transform of another process. We can identify, for example, Henry Fleming as the protagonist in *The Red Badge of Courage* without trying to determine the relational pattern which underlies this identity. Fleming's role thus can occupy a position in a more complex relational pattern intended to probe deeper into the novel.

Inversion, the second process, implies negation or elimination. In arithmetic, addition is negated by its reverse, subtraction ($2 + 2 = 4$, but $2 - 2 = 0$). Inversion, then, is a process which projects asymmetry. When a learner conceives a structural relationship in terms of inversion, meaning is achieved by recognition of the effect of opposing elements. Consider the third stanza of Stephen Crane's "Do Not Weep, Maiden, For War Is Kind":

> Do not weep, babe, for war is kind.
> Because your father tumbled in the yellow trenches,
> Raged at his breast, gulped and died,
> Do not weep.
> War is kind.

Assuming that certain preliminary hypotheses have already been aired, we might ask the student a question like this: "If, as the spokesman of the poem suggests, war is kind, what effect does the description of the death of the father have on you?" The student might reply: "The description of the father's death shows that war is not kind." To which the teacher might respond: "But the spokesman of the poem says in two distinct places that war is kind." The student has obviously perceived details of the stanza and transformed them into some kind of inverse or, to use the more familiar term, ironic relationship. Inversion thus arises from the perception of details which to the perceiver are necessarily incompatible, and from this incompatibility are born hypotheses of meaning. In describing an aspect of affective communication, Hayakawa (1964) makes a significant insight into the effects of inversion:

> Then there are such devices as antithesis, in which strongly opposed notions are placed together or even laid side by side in parallel phonetic or grammatical constructions, so that the reader feels the contrast and is stirred by it.

The inverse relationship can be identified with a number of terms which are bandied about by teachers of literature: paradox, contrast, dialectical argument, satire, and — of course — irony, to mention only a few.

The third process of the matrix is called reciprocity. To Piaget, reciprocity connotes symmetry. Symmetrical relationships, therefore, are those which are made up of details that are similar in some way. Simply put, reciprocity implies analogy. Teachers of literature are well aware of the importance of analogy. Such terms as metaphor, simile, symbol, and allegory are all extensions of analogical relationships. Poets such as Stevens and John Ciardi have expressed themselves on the effects of analogy in no uncertain terms. To Stevens (1951) any work of art — whether painting, poem, or what have you — is nothing more than an analogue of the artist's "sense of the world." And Ciardi (1963) writes:

> Every discovery of a true correspondence is an act of reason and an instruction to the mind. For intelligence does not consist of masses of factual detail. It consists of seeing essential likenesses and essential differences and of relating them, allowing for differences within the likenesses and likenesses within the differences. Mentality is born of analogy.

For an example of how a student of literature might transform his perception of details into a structured analogical relationship, consider again the poem, "Life Is Motion." The fact that the dancers are circling a stump — a central point of orientation — might be restructured by the sensitive reader in terms of such analogies as planets circling the sun, or electrons revolving about a nucleus. These analogies are not farfetched when one considers the themes which permeate much of Stevens' poetry. Regardless, such a conceptualization of the surface imagery of the poem by the student certainly merits consideration.

To use another example, consider these lines from a poem by Stephen Spender:

> The world maintained its traditional wall
> Round the dead with their gold sunk deep as a well,
> Whilst his life, intangible as a Stock Exchange rumor,
>   drifted outside.[2]

To the conceptive reader, the "wall" of the first line is not a wall like the one that surrounds the playground at school. It is a metaphoric wall, a wall that the reader might be able to transform into that "wall of tradition" (the system of values and mores) which separates the "in-group" from the "out-group" of the poem. In the last line appears the simile, "his life was like a Stock Exchange rumor." The reader must be able to structure a relationship between these seemingly unrelated quantities — life and Stock Exchange rumor — so that their point of comparison enables him to hypothesize meaning. One could continue to cite an infinite number of occurrences in literature which require the ability to conceptualize analogically.

The fourth and final process is correlation. For the purposes of literature study, we can consider correlation as the structuring of relationships between separate contexts. Correlation — like identity — intimates the simultaneous implementation of inversion and reciprocity. Piaget is careful to point out that all structured relationships are the product of transformations which "are always self-compensatory as a consequence of inversions and reciprocities."

Returning to the Stevens poem, we might wish to frame a question for the student which requires the structuring of a correlative relationship. We might ask him to relate the title of the poem, since the title can be regarded temporarily as a separate element, to the image of the dancers circling the stump. The interrelation of the two components (title and image) comprises a correlative relationship. The student might ideally reply: "Taken together, there is the suggestion that motion is the fundamental property of life. The dancers in this sense become symbolic. They are analogues of the essence of life." Using this hypothesis the student may wish to correlate another pair of elements. In the final line, the image of the dancers (flesh) is "married" to the image of the nonhuman universe (air), implying a fusion or explicit relationship between these seemingly unrelated images. From this inversion he may conceptualize a final hypothesis in which the poem becomes an attempt to express a unified vision — an attempt to reveal

• • • • • • • •
[2] Stephen Spender, "Ultima Ratio Regum," *Collected Poems, 1928–1953* (New York: Random House, 1955), 85.

motion as a kind of cosmic metaphor, having its analogues in such ordinary human activities as speech and dance.

But correlation should imply more than the structuring of relationships between contexts within the same generic whole. For example, the relationship between a reader and a given selection is correlative. The ability of the student to structure a correlative relationship based on the following passage from *The Red Badge of Courage* could well be vital to his appreciation of the novel.

> The youth *cried out savagely* at this statement. He *crouched* behind a little tree, with *his eyes burning hatefully* and *his teeth set in a curlike snarl* . . . His jacket and shirt were open at the throat, and exposed his young bronzed neck. There could be seen *spasmodic gulpings at his throat*.

The details in italics are individually part of an analogical pattern. The youth's behavior is compared to that of an animal's. Through correlating this obvious pattern of analogues, a hypothesis can be formed: The youth is an animal, implying that the hypothesis is itself an inversion. From what we learn of the youth's thoughts earlier in the novel, men are not animals; they have evolved beyond the "throat-grappling stage" and are calm, rational creatures. The inversion is of course ironic. The youth regards himself as completely unrelated to the animal world; yet his behavior is illustrated in animalistic terms.

The total relational process, however, does not stop here. The conceptive reader is capable — if he so desires — of sharing vicariously the youth's emotions, making, if you will, an imaginative entry. As described in the passage above, the youth is afraid and angry. He has taken part in a furious charge on enemy positions, and he has performed his duty admirably — or so he thinks. His efforts are subsequently scorned by his superiors. Although the reader may never have been involved in an identical situation, he may have experienced the wound of an undeserved insult, or maybe he has felt keenly the emotions of anger and fear on some occasion. The reader, on the basis of his own experience, has the option of accepting or rejecting — through his own correlative conceptualization — the emotional response of the youth. In short, his ability to identify with the youth is relative to his ability to mentally structure a correlative relationship. As Burton (1965) observes:

> . . . all students are capable of imaginative entry into vicarious experience merely because they are human and because they have had many experiences. The problem is to relate the experience recreated in the work to their own experience, and the answer, I think, lies in the identification of correlative experience.

Finally, correlation implies the imposition of unity through the structuring of relationships between seemingly different, yet somehow similar forms. We might call this process analogical correlation (no doubt inverse correlation is also possible in this sense) because it suggests the blending of two processes. For example, a student may read and hypothesize on a poem by Dylan Thomas. He may then view Marc Chagall's "I and the Village" and listen to an orchestral work by Debussy. From these varied perceptions, the student may be able to structure correlative relationships which enable him to express himself more intelligently on one of these contexts because of the conceptualizations which the others within the perceptual pattern have provided. Squire, quoted earlier, calls specific attention to the need and value of this kind of activity:

> Perception of form is basic to appreciation of all artistic expression.
> Whatever can be done to encourage perception of form in one medium
> of expression may reinforce and extend such awareness in others.

In employing the various processes of the matrix, the student should become aware of the changing levels of abstraction. In the Stevens poem, the structuring of a relationship in response to the question: "Who is the poem about?" will result in a hypothesis less abstract than one formed to conceptualize the analogical possibilities of the dancers circling the stump. Levels of abstraction suggest then, that conceptualization is not a limited faculty. Because the content of literature is largely imaginative, the student must also be aware of the function of inference. A source like Chapter III in Hayakawa's *Language in Thought and Action* contains the essentials to which the student should be consciously exposed. Conceptualization in literature study constantly demands that a student be able to structure relationships which are inferential. Since these relationships cannot be verified, they must reflect a high degree of logic. A student must be aware of the necessity to support his hypotheses by carefully structuring the underlying relationships. There is no doubt that formal instruction in semantics has a place in literature study. The implications of Piaget's processes, however, assume primary importance.

It is fitting that this discussion be drawn to a close by suggesting in more practical terms the ways in which Piaget's conception of a "thought" matrix can be implemented in the classroom by the teacher who is attempting to mold better readers of literature. Initially a student should be encouraged to react to his perceptions of literary contexts by forming hypotheses of meaning which are structured by one or more of the four processes. To accomplish this objective, a teacher might begin by presenting his students with a series of specialized problems which require the formation of basic or linear relational structures. The use of nonverbal models might even precede verbal contexts. The questioning method may at first be oral; this tends to focus attention on the minute and seemingly irrelevant details which contribute to the forming of accurate hypotheses. Questions must be constructed in such a way that the student is made conscious of the fact that he must conceptualize his thoughts in terms of underlying relational structures. As the student becomes more competent to conceptualize in this fashion, the teacher may turn to less precise techniques, allowing for more creative answers.

Thorough familiarity with the functional possibilities of analogy is an important part of the readiness activity for the complex phases of literature study. A student's sensitivity to inversion can be sharpened by presenting him with a context which evokes an obvious inverse relationship. Accompanying these basic activities should be a continual return to a more complex context, allowing the student to fully extend his ability to conceptualize.

The broad implications of this approach should by now be apparent. The student is initially trained to perceive a context in terms of structured relationships. In theory, the number of relationships which can be structured by the student are unlimited, but the kinds of relationships which he can structure are limited by the processes of thought which are at his command. By illustrating for the student the ways in which the finite processes of Piaget's matrix can transform his perceptions of the surface qualities of literature into deeper meanings, the teacher should be able to help the student transfer his new awareness to more difficult literary contexts.

The relationship of these processes to the areas of rhetoric and language study excites the imagination.

A Developmental Study of Word Definitions

■■■ RICHARD N. WOLMAN / EDWIN N. BARKER

In this article, the authors report the results of a study to determine whether or not Piaget's theoretical position of discontinuous cognitive development is tenable with respect to the way in which children define words. An alternative conclusion to Piaget's formulation is discussed in light of the findings.

In his book, *The Child's Conception of the World,* Jean Piaget makes the following observation:

• • • • • • • •

SOURCE: *Journal of Genetic Psychology, 107* (1965), 159–166. (With permission of the authors and the *Journal.*)

Binet, as is well known, has shown that if children of six to eight years are asked "what is a fork" or a "mummy" they reply "it is for eating with," or "it is for taking care of us," etc. The universality of the definition in terms of function has been confirmed by all who have checked the value of Binet's and Simon's tests. Yet these definitions, beginning with the words "it is for . . . (*c'est pour*)" cover the whole face of nature and do not apply only to the objects and persons in the child's immediate vicinity.

One of the general implications of Piaget's theory of the development of cognitive functioning in children is the idea that the transition from one type of definition to the other coincides with the development of levels of thought progressively "higher" than the previous ones. The various developmental stages are qualitatively different; each progressive stage embodies some unique aspect that characterizes it and that makes it distinctive. For example, Piaget (1950) discusses the development of "formal operations": i.e., formal logical thought. "The building up of formal operations . . . necessitates a complete reconstruction which seems to transpose concrete groupings to a new level of thought." And further: "Each of the transitions from one of these levels to the next is therefore characterized both by a new coordination and by a differentiation of the systems constituting the unit of the preceding level."

It would follow, therefore, that taken to apply to the way in which children define words, Piaget's theory could state the following: At one level of thought children define words, both familiar and unfamiliar, in terms of function or use. As they progress, however, toward the level of formal operations, their thinking makes a qualitative jump to the new way of defining words: i.e., in terms of some essential characteristic. The process is not a gradual trend of slowly learning the essential characteristics of first this word and then that; rather, the implication is that once they are cognitively equipped for higher-level definitions children will apply that ability to all words, just as previously they viewed all words in terms of function.

Purpose

The purpose of this study is to determine whether or not an empirical demonstration of Piaget's general hypotheses can be achieved.

Piaget's argument can be translated into statistical terms. A table of the frequencies with which various percentages of words are defined in terms of use should reveal a large cluster of children defining exclusively by use and a large cluster of children having made the complete change to the more mature type of definitions: i.e., roughly, a bimodal distribution.

It may turn out, however, that many children achieve a percentage of use definitions near the fifty per cent point or in a variety of proportions that show no overwhelming tendency one way or the other. This fact would tend to support an alternative hypothesis: namely, that children gradually learn to define words in terms of essence and eventually outgrow the tendency to view their world in terms of use only.

In addition to determining merely the percentage of words that children define in terms of use, other questions are raised. First, Piaget tends to regard his developmental stages in rather universal terms. Consequently, it might follow that the intelligence of any particular subject has no bearing on whether or not he defines words by use and that the only determining factor is the person's state of cognitive development. In both Piaget and Binet and Simon (1915) the question of the definitional form is not one of intelligence; rather, of maturation.

In this study, it was felt that the possibilities of the influence of intelligence upon the definition of the words could not be overlooked; therefore the tests that the children took were designed to include a means of estimating the IQ.

The second question is that of age. Piaget quotes Binet to the effect that, until age eight, children define words in terms of use. And Binet sets nine as the age level at which use definitions no longer predominate.

It would be unwise for us to attempt to make final judgments regarding the age at which the definitions that children employ change from use to nonuse. Consequently, even though the percentage of use definitions is demonstrated to change with age, no absolute cutting point is suggested because of the possible differences between populations.

The final question is in regard to the notion of cutting point or, perhaps, "the point of transition" from defining words by function to defining them by some other essential characteristic. It would seem that for each child the point of transition — if there is one — could be determined only by extensive longitudinal studies.

In this study the cross-sectional approach is taken. The purpose is not so much to determine for each child just where, in terms of developmental time, one stage stops and another begins as it is to test the basic proposition that such a discontinuous break exists. Age notwithstanding, if the theory is in accord with the facts, this "leap" or "complete regrouping" should be revealed by the data.

Method

The sample of subjects consisted of 117 children, ages four through twelve. These children were drawn from one socioeconomic grouping — the middle to upper-middle class.

A list of forty-three words was presented to each child, who was requested to define each word by answering the question "What does z mean?" or "What is an x?" The administration of the words was standardized by the same objective techniques as are used in the administration of the vocabulary portion of any intelligence test.

The selection of words was designed to fulfill, simultaneously, two functions. On the one hand, the lists included the "criterion" words for which the responses were judged as "definitions by use" or "definitions by basic qualities." On the other hand, from the full list of words, an estimate of the verbal intelligence quotient for each child was obtained. Consequently, the words chosen were the forty words of the vocabulary portion of the Wechsler Intelligence Scale for Children. According to Wechsler, the vocabulary portion of the verbal test has the highest correlation with the entire verbal test, both at the younger ages (.79) and also at the higher ages (.89). By scoring the vocabulary list according to Wechsler's criteria, an estimate of the individual verbal IQ could be determined.

An additional estimate of the IQ, from the Goodenough Draw-A-Person Test, was used along with the Wechsler. This addition served as a cross-check for the possible role of intelligence.

The words that were chosen as criterion words to determine the presence of use or nonuse definitions were chosen upon the basis of several criteria. First, the words were familiar, they appear early in the Wechsler list, and they have been standardized according to familiarity and facility.

Second, all of the criterion words were nouns. Often the form of definition for a verb or adjective, for example, is of the type "It is when . . . " Classification of this kind of definition is not only unclear but also not within the limits of the theoretical statements of either Piaget or Binet.

Third, all nouns included in the criterion words were tangible. No abstract nouns, such as "affliction" were used. The inclusion of such nouns might prejudice the issue or make scoring in terms of use or nonuse unwieldy or vague.

Fourth, some nouns (although tangible and familiar) are characterized exclusively by a single function or use. An umbrella, for example, is defined primarily as a protection against sun, rain, etc. In terms of the definitions that children would be likely to give, umbrella might always be viewed as "something that you use to keep dry when it is raining."

Fifth, some nouns that are familiar, tangible, and not recognizable in terms of some specific use were also excluded. These nouns, however, were also capable of being defined either as a noun or a verb — one clear example is "nail," which can be viewed as "a" nail or as "to" nail.

Sixth, inasmuch as there was an insufficient number of words in the Wechsler list to satisfy the criteria just outlined, three additional words were selected from the Stanford–Binet list. These words were chosen from the early portion of the Binet list, which (like the Wechsler) is standardized according to progressive difficulty. The total number of criterion words was 10: bicycle, orange, knife, hat, letter, puddle, cushion, donkey, diamond, and gown. For these ten words, the responses were scored as use or nonuse.

The list of ten criterion words is a list of familiar and tangible nouns that can be defined according to some function or in terms of other characteristics. According to Piaget, the child defines all or most of these words in terms either of use or nonuse, depending upon his level of cognitive development.

The scoring of a particular definition of a criterion word for use or nonuse was designed specifically for this study.

Several possibilities for the criteria of use or nonuse were available. One guide was that supplied by Binet, who formulated a distinction as early as 1915. Binet divided definitions into categories of "definitions in terms of use only" and "definitions in terms superior to use."

For Binet, the definition in terms of use only is always of the infinitive form. For example, "bicycle is to ride, orange is to eat," etc. The definition in terms superior to use is of a more mature "state of mind" and is exemplified by "A bicycle is something to ride" or "An orange is something to eat."

Feifel and Lorge (1950), in their qualitative analysis of the various kinds of definitions that children give, find one of them to be use (others are synonyms, explanations, demonstrations, etc.). Feifel's use category is explained by the example of "Orange — You eat it" and is similar to Binet's concept.

With one change, Binet's and Feifel's criteria of use were employed in this study. The one alteration applies to the precise distinction between the two types of definitions. It was felt that a definition of the type "An orange is to eat" is clearly a definition in terms of use; yet it was also felt that defining orange as "Something you eat" is also a definition in terms of use insofar as the notion of "Something you . . . " is a convenient colloquialism of neutral value. However, if a child responded with "An orange is a fruit you eat," this response was scored as nonuse because the child had recognized and stated not only a use but some other essential characteristic.

Results

The first and most general finding of the study is that no evidence was found in support of that interpretation of Piaget's theory that views cognitive development in terms of a discrete or discontinuous progression from one level of development to the next. The relevant data are presented in Table 1.

Table 1 shows that the frequency distribution of the percentage of words defined by use in no way resembles the bimodal distribution that would be necessary to support Piaget's hypothesis. Instead of massing near zero per cent and one hundred per cent, essentially a rectangular distribution was obtained, with the central tendency in the middle (forty per cent to seventy per cent) range.

Table 1.   Frequency Distribution of Use Definitions

Percentage of Use Definitions	Frequency	Percentage of Use Definitions	Frequency
91–100	4	41–50	19
81– 90	18	31–40	9
71– 80	12	21–30	12
61– 70	16	11–20	10
51– 60	11	0–10	6

As age increases, the per cent of use definitions tends to decrease: e.g., four-year-olds define seventy-eight per cent of the words by use; eight-year-olds, sixty-three per cent; and twelve-year-olds, twenty-five per cent.

The degree of this relationship was determined by a Kendall rank-correlation coefficient, tau, to be −.93, significant at the .001 level. The relationship between age and words defined by use also agrees with Feifel's finding. The regression lines are quite similar in shape.

The transition point (fifty per cent) for the two types of definitions in this study was between ages eight and nine. This fact is in agreement with Binet's postulation.

As the number of words that the child knows increases, the percentage of use definitions decreases. The degree of association was found to be −.81 (using Kendall's tau) and is significant at the .005 level.

Correlations were computed between the Wechsler verbal IQ estimate and percentage of use and between the Goodenough IQ estimate and percentage of use. In both cases, the correlations (determined by tau) were not significantly different from zero. It may be concluded, therefore, that intelligence plays a small role, if any, in influencing the percentage of words defined by use.

Our final finding was the lack of any significant difference between the means of males and females on any of the variables in the study. In addition, correlations were computed separately for males and females, and no differences were found.

Discussion

The major finding of this study is that there is no empirical evidence for a sudden or discontinuous progression in children's definitions of words. In the light of Piaget's theory, this finding has many implications. Piaget's theory of cognitive development implies progressive "qualitative reorganization." The findings of this study challenge that implication. The study supports, rather, the notion that children learn progressively to define their words in a more "mature" and more "essential" way.

This study, of course, covers only a very small range compared to Piaget's theory in general. It may be that with regard to the notions of causality, space, time, nature, etc., children's explanations do follow the pattern that Piaget outlines. Perhaps further studies based on the paradigm of the present one could verify empirically whether or not Piaget is correct.

In a chapter of *The Psychology of Intelligence,* entitled "Social Factors in Intellectual Development," Piaget states that ". . . logic [logical thought] requires common rules or nouns; it is a morality of thinking imposed and sanctioned by others." In other words, the way we think and speak is shaped by, directed by, and taught by others. In terms of the present study, Piaget supports the learning notion that has been empirically demonstrated and which is diametrically opposed to the position that the majority of his arguments imply. While it is true that Piaget attempts to present both the "nature" and the "nurture" of cognitive development, Piaget's sympathies seem to lie with the innate view — i.e., with the view that all men necessarily advance toward "operational" or logico–scientific thought, no matter what their environmental situation.

Whatever the repercussions for the theory that the notion of a morality of logic and thought may have, the implications for further research in this area are manifold. For example, one of the limitations of the present study is that it was restricted to middle-class children. The question may be asked, with justification, if it is not possible that the thought and language of middle-class children have been influenced by a particular middle-class "linguistic ethic." What of children who belong to lower classes? It is clear that the latter's social environment imposes different sanctions for grammar than are imposed by any middle-class ethic. Only additional research can determine the extent of this sociocultural force.

Finally, no matter what the form of future research in this and related areas, it is clear that account will have to be taken of the interaction of environmental influences as well as natural-growth tendencies. The extent of those influences in a study such as this has not been determined nor was it determined in Piaget's theoretical formulation. However, while the complexity of such a comprehensive analysis is great, its importance is self-evident and fundamental to a full understanding of cognitive development.

Summary

A sample of children was studied to determine whether or not Piaget's theoretical position of discontinuous cognitive development is tenable with regard to the way in which children define words. The findings support an alternative conclusion: namely, that the transition from the infantile mode of defining words to the more mature form is gradual and slow. It was also found that intelligence and sex play no important role in this development. Factors that do correlate with the mode of defining are (a) age and (b) number of words known.

Children's Conceptions of Psychological Causality

■■■ MARTIN WHITEMAN

In an interesting extrapolation of Piaget's view of the child's conception of physical causality, the author examines the development of understanding psychological events, and speculates on its relationship to other cognitive and personality variables.

Piaget's pioneering explorations have brought forth a number of investigations of the child's conception of physical causality. However, there has been relatively little investigation of the child's conceptions of psychological causality. It would seem as appropriate to ask a child "What makes people angry?" as it is to ask him, "What makes clouds move?" Yet, systematic explorations of the child's developing awareness of the causes of another person's behavior are lacking. This lack is particularly poignant since, as adults, we are continually making inferences about the causes of other people's behavior. An important problem, then, is how and when such causal inferences are learned.

A major set of concepts used by people in explaining behavior comprises the so-called mechanisms of adjustment. People, in their everyday behavior, do seem to use as explanatory devices those behaviors that psychologists

• • • • • • • •

SOURCE: Adapted and abridged from *Child Development, 38* (1967), 143–155. (With permission of the author and the Society for Research in Child Development.) This research was supported by a grant from the National Institute of Mental Health (No. MH-10578-01). The scoring criteria, interview guide, item analyses, and reliability data have been deposited with the American Documentation Institute, Document No. 9148, which may be obtained by remitting $1.75 for 35 mm microfilm or $2.50 for 6 × 8-inch photocopies.

have conceptualized as rationalizations or displacements or projections, for example, rationalization ("He's using that as an excuse"), displacement ("He is just taking out all his troubles on me"), projection ("Well, that's the way he is himself and he thinks everybody is that way"). From a theoretical point of view, it is important to understand how and when such explanatory ideas become part of the conceptual repertoire of the child. Psychologists of such widely differing theoretical persuasion as Anna Freud (1946) and Hilgard (1949) have pointed to the importance of such mechanisms for maintenance of self-esteem. However, there has been no attempt to study directly the cognitive development of such notions, which are as important in their own right as the development by the child of conceptions of space, time, and physical causality.

Piaget has drawn a basic distinction between the preoperational intuitive stage (around four to seven years) and the concrete operational stage (around seven to eleven years). According to Piaget (1950) and Flavell (1963), there is a major revision in the child's thought at around seven years, enabling him to conceptualize certain types of relations and classes. A major achievement of the operational child is his ability to decenter from a focus on the perceptually dominant to an emphasis on the more invariant but less salient properties of stimulus displays, as illustrated by the operational child's ability to conserve conceptually an object's substance or length despite changes in the object's appearance or location. Similarly, one would expect that the operational as compared to the younger preoperational child should have greater ease in decentering from the more obvious overt behaviors to the less obvious underlying motivations as described by the adjustment mechanisms. Furthermore, Laurendeau and Pinard (1962), replicating early Piaget investigations (1929, 1930), have shown striking differences between these two age levels in their explanations of psychological causality as well as to relate such differences to conceptions of physical causality.

The general aim of this study is to explore the feasibility of using interviews with children at two age levels, the five- to six-year range and the eight- to nine-year-old span, in order to study developing conceptions of psychological causality.

The study comprised two separate phases. The specific aims of Phase 1 were to (a) devise usable categorizations and scoring systems for the assessment of psychological causality, (b) study the homogeneity among items in order to determine whether reliable and meaningful indexes might be formed, and (c) study developmental and intellectual differences with respect to such indexes of psychological causality. The second phase had as its purposes: (a) the objectification and standardization of the interviewing procedure devised in Phase 1, (b) the replication of Phase 1 with comparable but somewhat larger samples to assess the reliability of Phase 1 findings with respect to developmental and intellectual differences in the understanding of psychological causality, and (c) the extension of Phase 1 results through the study of the relation between grasp of psychological causality and understanding of physical causality.

Phase 1

Method

Subjects. The subjects comprised forty-two children. The twenty-one younger children comprised an experimental kindergarten class in Harlem, New York City. Stanford–Binet IQs were available for these children. For each kindergarten child, a separate roster of third-grade children from the same school was prepared. The third-graders on each roster had been matched with the kindergarten child with respect to sex and IQ as assessed by group test. For each kindergarten child, a third-grader was then selected from the appropriate roster by random sampling. For each grade, the average IQ was 101 with a standard deviation of 10. All children were Negro or Puerto Rican. The kindergarten children were in the five- to six-year range, while the third graders fell in the eight- to nine-year span.

The interview. The interviews were conducted by the writer and dealt with the child's tape-recorded responses to questions about each of seven stories. Each story read to the child exemplified in rudimentary form a different mechanism of adjustment, that is, displacement, wishful dreaming, projection, regression, repression, rationalization, and denial. The instructions to the child and the stories themselves were as follows:

> "I'm going to tell you some stories about a little girl called Jane. In each of these stories Jane does something different from what she usually does. I want you to tell me why she did it. Here's the first story." (For boys, "Johnnie" was substituted for "Jane" in all of the stories, and "toy soldiers" for "dolls" in the first story.)
>
> 1. *Displacement:* "There was once a little girl named Jane. One day her mother promised that Jane's favorite dessert, ice cream, would be served at supper. But Jane's mother forgot to buy the ice cream, so there wasn't any ice cream for dessert. Jane didn't say anything to her mother about the ice cream. After supper Jane went to play with her dolls and did something she never did before. She spanked her dolls. Why did she spank her dolls?"
>
> 2. *Wishful dreaming:* "One day Jane looked at TV and saw a girl who had a wonderful bicycle. Jane herself didn't have a bicycle and couldn't even ride one. That night Jane dreamed that her father bought her

a bicycle and that she was riding all over the block on it. How come she had such a dream?"

3. *Projection:* "Jane was a good girl, but there was one thing she never liked to do. She didn't like to share her toys with the other kids. She always wanted to keep her toys to herself and not let the other kids use them. One day Jane's mother told her that they were going to visit another family where there was another little girl who was Jane's age. Jane and this other little girl could play together. But Jane looked unhappy and said, 'I bet she won't want to share any of her games and toys.' Why did Jane say this when she didn't even know the other little girl?"

4. *Regression:* "One day Jane didn't feel well. She had a headache and didn't want to eat. She began to act just like her baby brother. She talked baby talk; she wanted to suck her baby brother's milk bottle; and she even wanted to be held in her mother's arms just like a baby. Why did she act this way?"

5. *Repression:* "One day Jane's mother bought her a new pair of gloves. She warned Jane not to lose the gloves, because Jane had lost the last pair. One afternoon Jane lost her gloves coming back from school. She knew she had to tell her mother. But when she got home, she forgot to tell her. When Jane went out to play in the afternoon, she told her friends about the lost gloves. But that night she forgot to tell her mother. The next morning at breakfast Jane again forgot to tell her mother. Why did she keep forgetting to tell her mother about the lost gloves?"

6. *Rationalization:* "One day Jane's mother gave her a big bowl of spinach. Jane said, 'I'm not going to eat the spinach because it makes you very fat!' Why did Jane say that about the spinach when she liked to eat fattening things like ice cream and candy?"

7. *Denial:* "Jane wanted very much to go to her friend's birthday party. On the day of the party she felt sick and couldn't go. But Jane said, 'I didn't want to go to that party anyway!' Why did Jane say that?"

There was an attempt in each story to focus questions or probes on certain key elements, for example, whether the child grasped the role of the ice cream disappointment in arousing anger in the displacement story, or whether the child saw Jane as really wanting to go to the party in the denial story.

In order to gain some control on memory and language differences, an attempt was made to pose alternatives, to recapitulate part of the stories in the questions, and in some cases to suggest causal possibilities as a kind of testing-of-the-limits procedure.

Each story was coded according to the degree in which the motivation of the child in the story situation was grasped. Thus, in the displacement story, the highest score was given to the children who attributed the spanking of the doll to the ice cream deprivation, who spontaneously or in response to probes cited an appropriate emotional reaction to the ice cream deprivation, that is, being mad or sad, and had some psychological explanation for spanking the doll rather than the mother. A lower score was assigned to sequences which related the ice cream deprivation to the spanking, but offered no psychological reason for spanking the doll rather than the mother. At a lower level, the spanking was conceived as the doll's fault, with no apprehension of the possible causal role of the ice cream incident. Thus, the doll was conceived as bad or dirty or ugly or jumping too much.

Statistical treatment. The feasibility of combining the responses to the various stories into an index was explored. A Motivation Index was constructed by cumulating weights for each of the seven stories. For the entire group, this total index score was then correlated with each of the subscores derived from particular stories. Each of the groups of seven subscores was dichotomized at the median and correlated with the highest and lowest trichotomies of the Index. A χ^2 analysis based on correlated proportions was used to evaluate the significance of the differences between age groups for each of the stories. In addition, a three-way analysis of variance was performed on the Motivation Index using the method of unweighted means for unequal cell frequencies as described by Winer (1962).

Results

The individual stories. The stories proved difficult even for the older children. The percentage of older children showing the highest level of understanding ranges from 5 per cent for the rationalization story to 38 per cent for the displacement story, with a median of 19 per cent. The repression and displacement stories proved the easiest for the older children, while the rationalization and regression stories proved the most difficult. For the younger children, the highest level could be reached only in the case of the repression story, and this with only one child. With more lenient criteria, the percentage of success for the younger children ranged from 48 per cent in the case of the repression story to 0 per cent for the rationalization story, with a median of 10 per cent. Rationalization and projection were the most difficult stories for the younger children while repression, regression, and wishful dreaming proved relatively easier. Most of the older children (71 per cent as compared to 10 per cent of the younger children) were able to show comprehension of Jane's underlying motivation in at least three stories (using the more lenient criteria). The application of more rigorous criteria for comprehension, with greater concentration on the spontaneous answers of the child disclosed that 76 per cent of the older children were able to reach the highest level on at least one story as compared to 5 per cent of the younger group.

When the scores for each story were dichotomized at the median, significant age differences appeared in the case of the displacement, projection, regression, and rationalization stories.

With respect to the displacement story, the older children tended to attribute the spanking to the ice cream deprivation. The younger children tended to attribute the spanking to the intrinsic naughtiness of the doll. In the projection story, some of the older children tended to attribute Jane's statement about the other girl's not sharing to Jane's own behavior. Thus, Jane's remark is seen as a projection of her own disinclination to share. As one child put it: "Just because she don't share her things, she might believe that girls would be as evil as she." More usually, however, Jane's remark was seen as occasioned by the other girl's reaction to Jane's own habit of not sharing. The younger children had difficulty seeing Jane's own nonsharing as the direct or indirect cause of her thinking the other child would not share. The younger children tended to refer more to the other girl as directly causing Jane's remark, for example: "Jane says the other girl won't share because the girl was strange." In the regression story, the older children more readily perceived the advantages of acting like a baby. The younger children may have mentioned the illness as cause, but had difficulty in seeing the child wanting to be treated as a baby when ill. Finally, in the rationalization story, the younger child was more prone to believe that Jane said she would not eat the spinach because it makes you very fat because Jane actually thought that the spinach made you very fat, that she did not just say it but really believed it. The older child tended to attribute Jane's saying that spinach makes you very fat because she didn't want to eat it.

Item homogeneity. For each of the individual stories, the weighted responses were significantly associated with the cumulative index derived from all the stories. The ϕ coefficients ranged from .41 (for the repression story) to .66 (for the projection story), with a median ϕ of .57.

The Motivation Index. The analysis of variance of the Motivation Index revealed the expected and highly significant age differences. Ninety per cent of the younger children scored below the median score of the older children. The more intelligent children tended to score significantly higher when the dichotomies of those above 100 IQ and those at 100 or below were used. Rhos of .40 and .15 between IQ and Motivation Index were found for the older and younger children, respectively. Neither of these coefficients is significant. However, the analysis of variance revealed a significant interaction between grade and IQ. Thus, IQ differences on the Motivation Index were stronger among the older children than among the younger children. Sex differences on the Motivation Index were not significant, but there was a significant interaction between sex and intelligence. Differences between intelligence levels were more clearly related to the Motivation Index in the case of the boys, with the less intelligent boys scoring lower. However, among the girls, the difference between intelligence levels on the Motivation Index was minimal and in a reversed direction, with the less intelligent girls scoring slightly but not significantly higher.

Phase 2

Method

Subjects. The Phase 2 subjects comprised 70 children — 36 kindergarten children and 34 third-graders. As in Phase 1, the younger children were in the 5- to 6-year range, the older in the 8- to 9-year span, and all children were Negro or Puerto Rican. Two kindergarten classes were used, both taught by the same teacher. Of the 47 kindergarten children interviewed, the records of 11 children were not used either because of difficulty in comprehending their answers or, more frequently, because they simply replied "don't know" to most of the questions on the psychological causality interview. The 34 third-grade children were randomly selected from the entire third-grade roster of this particular school. The IQ data based on group tests were available for 27 of the 34 third graders. The mean IQ was 97, with a range from 75 to 133. For the kindergarten group, Stanford-Binet IQ data were available, but only for 24 out of the 36 children. However, these IQs were based on a random sample of children from the two kindergarten classes. For the kindergarten group, the mean IQ was 94, with a range from 71 to 116. Forty-two per cent and 53 per cent of the kindergarten and third-graders, respectively, were male. In order to replicate an analysis performed on twenty-one matched pairs in Phase 1, twenty pairs of kindergarten and third-grade children matched in IQ were selected. The mean IQ of the twenty Phase 2 kindergarten and twenty matched third-graders was 93.

Procedure. Six of the seven stories used in Phase 1 were administered to the two groups. The repression story was omitted in order to shorten the administration time. In addition, the projection story was revised so as to impress upon the respondent that Jane did not know the other child. However, the paramount change in Phase 2 was the use of a standardized interview with standardized probes and a standard sequence of probes. The standardized probes were explicit wordings of questions to be asked the child. The sequence of such probes was also specified for the inter-viewers. Directions were given to the interviewers about when to probe for a new element of the concept in question and when to stay with the same point, altering the question in order to see whether the child could succeed with more information. The stories were administered in a ran-domized order.

In contrast to Phase 1, the interviews were not conducted by the writer but by four graduate students of the Columbia University School of Social Work. A number of sessions were devoted to a discussion of the specific rationale of the study, of underlying theoretical issues, and of methodological problems in interviewing young children. Pilot interviewing was conducted by three of the students at a neighboring day-care center, after which further discussion was held regarding ambiguities or difficulties arising in the interviewing situation.

Scoring categories were devised, both for the initial responses to the story and the responses to questions by the interviewer. As in Phase 1, there was an attempt to arrange the categories in each story hierarchically, with the higher-numbered categories including more of the elements of the concept studied. The scoring system involved categorizing the children for each story at three levels. Level 3 was assigned to children whose responses at any point in the interview included all of the elements of the concept for any particular story, whether or not the grasp of the concept was maintained or lost following further questioning. Level 2 included children whose responses at any point showed comprehension of some but not all elements of the concept, while Level 1 was assigned to children whose responses at no point showed an understanding of any of the key elements of the explanatory concept.

In addition to the questionnaire on psychological causality, a series of questions dealing with physical causality was also posed. These questions dealt with the attribution of life to various objects and were designed to reveal animistic tendencies in the child. The questionnaire was originally constructed by Laurendeau and Pinard (1962) in their replication of Piaget's work on physical causality. The child was asked whether each of twenty-one objects was alive. In the present study, the score of this Animism Scale was the number of correct responses given by the child. The reliability of this measure for the combined group was .84 as assessed by the Kuder–Richardson Formula 20.

Results and Discussion

The individual stories.   The stories were scored independently by two sets of raters. For the coding of the elements of each story based on the initial response of thirty-six children, the percentage of agreement was 96 per cent. The percentage of agreement ranged from 89 per cent for the denial story to 100 per cent for the wishful dreaming story. For the coding of the elements of each story based on both initial and probed-for responses of 28 children, the overall percentage of agreement was 85 per cent, with a range from 75 per cent for rationalization to 93 per cent for the wishful dreaming story. The older children consistently scored higher than the younger group, with five of the six items significant at the .01 or .001 level. The failure of the rationalization story to yield significant differences between the two grades may be due to the relatively low interrater reliability of coding for this item. From the point of view of age differentiation, the new interview procedure seems at least as effective as the one reported in Phase 1. However, the increment in significant age differentiation on the part of the stories may be at least partly due to the increased sample size in Phase 2. The displacement, projection, and regression stories which were significant differentiators between age levels in Phase 1 also show significant differentiation in Phase 2. Additionally, the denial and wishful dreaming stories which did not yield significant differences in Phase 1 do so in Phase 2.

Item homogeneity.   The ϕ coefficients, representing the associations between particular item scores and the composite score derived from all six items, were all significant and ranged from a high of .89 in the case of the projection story to .35 for rationalization. The median ϕ was .45 as contrasted with a median ϕ of .57 derived from the item analysis of stories in Phase 1. The writer has been unable to find a test of significance of difference between ϕ coefficients. However, it is doubtful whether the difference between the two ϕ coefficients is significant with these sample sizes.

The reliability of Motivation Index 2, as assessed by the Kuder–Richardson Formula 20, was .68 as compared with the comparable coefficient of .76 derived from the Phase 1 sample. Again, it is quite likely that this discrepancy is attributable to sampling error rather than to real differences between the two indexes. The reliability of the Motivation Indexes was attenuated when computed within grade because of restriction in range. Although there is a drop in the reliability within age groups as compared to the total group, the error of measurement which is relatively independent of heterogeneity of talent remains at a moderately consistent level as we move from total group to younger and to older age groups for each of the Motivation Indexes. This indicates a fairly consistent pattern of measurement reliability for the Motivation Indexes as groups of children within the five- to eight-year-old range are being compared. It also suggests, however, that increased reliability may be required for differentiation among individuals within age-grades as compared to the differentiation of individuals between age-grades.

Focusing on the most significant results in both phases, we find that the items most sharply differentiating between the two ages (significant at the .001 level) are displacement (from Phase 1), and wishful dreaming, projection, and denial (from Phase 2). The projection story is the only one which is significant, at least at the .01 level, in both phases and at the same time shows the highest correlation with the Motivation Index in each sample.

The special difficulty of the projection story for the younger children may be traceable to the confluence of two factors. First, the story involves the difficult perception of incongruence between overt behavior and inner intent; Jane says that Mary will not share where her intent is really the reverse — she does not want to share with Mary. Second, the projection story also demands a difficult shift from a given locus of effect (Mary's not sharing) to a new causal locus (Jane's own nonsharing). A similar factor appears in the displacement story where the younger child finds it more difficult to assume a cause (the mother and her behavior) which is distal to behavior located elsewhere (child spanking doll).

Motivation Index 2. The age differences on Motivation Index 2 were highly significant. As anticipated, the older children scored considerably higher than the younger. Ninety-four per cent of the kindergarten group fell below the median score of the third graders, which parallels the comparable figure of 90 per cent found with Motivation Index 1. However, this and a separate analysis of variance failed to reveal significant IQ differences, nor IQ interactions with age and sex — contrary to the results of Phase 1. The younger children were significantly more animistic than the older ones. Twice as many kindergarten children as third graders fell into a high animism group ($p < .01$). The above analyses suggest that conceptions of psychological causality (as assessed by Motivation Index 2) and of physical causality (as assessed by the Animism Scale) both develop with age. However, the limited relation between the two measures points to independence in the rate and timing of their respective development within the individual child.

The relation between age and conceptions of psychological causality appears stronger than the relation between age and conceptions of physical causality. Thus when one selects children who are relatively homogeneous with respect to the Motivation Index, the relation between age and the Animism Scale is not statistically significant. However, when the selection is of children who are relatively homogeneous on animism score, the relation between age and Motivation Index is still highly significant. Similarly, a comparison of the five kindergarten children and eight third graders with comparable MA's (about seven years) revealed that the younger children averaged about four points below the older on the Motivation Index but about four points above the older on the Animism Scale. This suggests the importance of chronological rather than mental age in the development of conceptions of psychological causality.

Some Concluding Points

The relative difficulty of the younger child in (a) differentiating between observed locus of effect and inferred locus of cause and (b) decentering from a focus on overt behavior to a more covert intent would not be inconsistent with Piaget's distinction between the "intuitive" child (ages four to seven) and the "concrete operational" child (ages seven to eleven). It would therefore be worthwhile to explore the Motivation Index scores of children who have and have not attained conservation of substance, for example, since the latter is a criterion for the concrete operation stage. However, the operation of more specific experiential factors is suggested by the differential ease of the items within age groups, the lack of strong or consistent correlations of the Motivation Indexes with IQ, the importance of chronological age over and above mental age differences, the relative independence of the Motivation Indexes from the Animism Scale, and the sex differences on Motivation Index 1. It is also possible that age differences in psychological causality may take a different form within groups of higher socioeconomic standing where the child's linguistic experiences and explanatory encounters with adults are differently patterned.

Behavioral correlates need exploration. Certain patternings of responses to the stories may be related to particular behavioral patterns. Thus, ease in grasping projection stories, where blame is externalized, may be related to acting-out behavior. The Motivation Index might be correlated with measures of ability to shift role, to understand the other's viewpoint, and with avoidance of what Piaget (1932) has conceptualized as objective morality. One would expect the growth of understanding of psychological causality to parallel the growth of moral judgments based on the other's underlying intentions, rather than on his overt behaviors.

The Research of Jean Piaget and Its Implications for Art Education in the Elementary School

■ KENNETH M. LANSING

Many of the qualities of children's drawings which have long been familiar to art educators, can be seen to be compatible with Piaget's formulations. The author of this article illustrates a number of these points of correspondence, and draws implications for the teaching of art which should be interesting both to teachers and child psychologists.

Jean Piaget was born on August 9, 1896, in Neuchâtel, Switzerland. At an early age he exhibited a precociousness in science and other forms of studious inquiry that would classify him as a gifted child, and by 1918 he had obtained a baccalaureate degree and a doctorate in natural science from the University of Neuchatel.

In 1921, Piaget embarked upon a program of research that made him world-famous as a developmental psychologist, a philosopher, a logician, and an educator. His fame was earned before he was thirty years old, but he has continued to do research and to make significant contributions to our knowledge of child development for more than forty years. In fact, his work has produced one of our most systematic and comprehensive theories of cognitive development. The theory describes and offers an explanation for the evolution of language and thought in children. It covers the child's conception of the world, of physical causality, of number, of time, of geometry, and of space, as well as other dimensions of intellectual development.

Because of the overwhelming amount of research that Piaget has done, it seems most logical for us to consider only that portion of his work that seems most important for art education. Probably, his investigation into the child's conception of space is most pertinent, so this account of his work will concentrate on that aspect of his research.

To begin, Piaget's investigations led him to conclude that there are three major stages in the child's cognitive development: the sensorimotor period, the concrete operations period, and the period of formal operations. By subjecting children to a series of special tasks, and by observing them carefully, he also has been able to show that youngsters pass through three successive stages in their perception of spatial relationships, and they do so during the first, or sensorimotor, stage of development. Thus, Piaget concludes that young children perceive things differently from adults. This

• • • • • • •

SOURCE: *Art Education*, 7 (1966), 33–45. (With permission of the author and the National Art Education Association.)

is not a new notion, of course, but it is different from the layman's idea that youngsters and adults perceive the same things.

In addition, Piaget makes a clear distinction between perceptual images, representational images, and conceptual schemas. It would seem that the perceptual images are the ones that we have as we look at an object; representational images are the ones that we retain (as memory images) after our experience with the object has passed; and conceptual schemas are the informational materials about the object that we retain in the mind in the form of words. Piaget shows that the representational images pass through the same stages of development as the perceptual ones, and he indicates that they do so during the second period of child development, which he calls the concrete operations period. Because drawings are based upon representational images, Piaget's findings suggest that children's drawings exhibiting certain spatial relationships will appear quite some time after the child is able to perceive those relationships. Perhaps it would help to consider these ideas in more detail.

First Stage

Piaget's first stage of human development is called the sensorimotor period, and it lasts from birth to about the age of two. It involves a perceptual and motor adjustment to the world, but it does not involve drawing or visual symbolic manipulation of any kind. At the very beginning of the period, the child is unable to coordinate vision and grasping, and he is not capable of perceiving the permanence of solid objects nor the constancy of shape and size. In other words, he does not perceive a bottle as the same object when it is turned around and he does not see a nearby item as being the same size when it is far away. Instead, he sees the bottle and the departing object as changing their shapes and sizes.

The first spatial relationships that the child does grasp perceptually are topological in nature. This means that he can detect relationships of proximity, separation, order, enclosure, and continuity before he can see other spatial characteristics. To perceive the proximity of objects is to see how close they are to each other within the perceptual field. But, sometimes, things that are close together appear in the young child's perception as a hazy, diffuse unit. When the child detects separation, he does not see these objects as a unit, but he perceives them as being distinct and separate. As he perceives order, he sees things that appear in succession, such as the beads on a playpen or the opening of a door — the appearance of a person — and a bottle. Being able to detect relationships of enclosure means that the child can see things as being surrounded by something else. He is able to see an object in a box, features in a face, and his sister between his two brothers. Seeing relationships of continuity is perceiving something as being uninterrupted. Thus a child is able to detect the uninterrupted nature of a line or surface.

As the child moves further into the period of sensorimotor development (five to twelve months), he is able to coordinate vision with grasping, and his movements are controlled by vision. As a result, the child can explore objects systematically by fingering them, by passing them from one hand to another, and by moving his eyes around them. This increase in visual and tactile exploration helps him to do a better job of perceiving the permanency of shape and the constancy of shape and size as well as spatial relationships of a Euclidean and projective nature. To see such relationships is to perceive straight lines, angles, circles, and other geometric forms, as well as proportions or metric relationships and perspective.

One of the highly significant points that Piaget makes is that the perception of Euclidean forms is made possible by perceptual activity. This means that the perception of Euclidean or geometric forms is an outgrowth of movement by the eyes and the hands, two of our primary sense organs. Piaget also contends that such perceptual movement is as important as, if not more important than, the perceptual image in the formation of the representational or conceptual images that we retain after the originating experience has passed. Such ideas are contrary to the Gestalt theory that all relationships are given in an immobile percept, and that percepts are visual concepts. Gestaltists seem to suggest that our representational or conceptual images are the equivalent of the percept; what we know visually is what we perceive. All relationships are given in the percept, and we do not learn them. Piaget, on the other hand, contends that we build our conceptual images out of the perceptual image plus perceptual movement and the coordination of perceptual movements. Consequently, the formation of conceptual or representational images lags behind perception and recognition by a considerable period of time.

During the sensorimotor period, however, the child merely develops his perceptual images. He does not construct conceptual images. His gradual increase in perceptual exploration merely allows him to see the Euclidean relationships that we have already mentioned, and it makes possible the perception of relationships between objects. Finally, as extensive perceptual activity continues, and as visual and tactile movements become more highly coordinated, the child begins to develop a mental image. This signals the beginning of the next period of development.

Second Stage

The second stage of development is called the concrete operations period, and it lasts from about the age of two to the age of eleven. According to Piaget, the child has been able to perceive topological and Euclidean spatial relationships and coordinated perspective up to this point, but the lack of a mental image that he can retain prevents him from drawing and from thinking intelligently. As he acquires representational or conceptual images during the present period of development, he is able to draw and to think about concrete objects and events. But changes in thinking and drawing that are very evident occur within this period of development. Consequently, the period is divided into three substages.

The first of the substages within the concrete operations period is called the preparatory or preoperational substage and it extends from about the age of two to the age of four. This is the time during which the child makes his first unorganized attempts at symbolic representation. Piaget asked children between two and seven years to copy a few simple circles, triangles, squares, crosses, and other geometric and nongeometric figures. Up to the age of three, the youngsters were unable to do anything but scribble. Between three and four, however, they were able to indicate the open or closed quality of the forms being copied, and they could make irregular circles as well as shapes that enclose other shapes. Triangles, squares, crosses, and other Euclidean forms were drawn as circular figures. This means that the earliest aspects of forms that they could conceive and draw were the topological aspects. We also find this to be true in spontaneous drawing. Children follow their earliest controlled scribbles with loops, whirls, and irregular circular forms, but they do not begin making Euclidean shapes until a little later. They make drawings of men by attaching four lines to an irregular circle, and sometimes they put other circles inside a large one to represent eyes and other facial features. But, when the child attempts a complicated human being at this stage, it is clear that his concepts of topological relationships are not fully developed, because he may place the mouth over the nose or draw the ears detached from the body. Although his visual concept of proximity, separation, and enclosure is fairly well formed, his mental image of order and continuity is still poor. Thus, he cannot retain in his mind the correct sequence of mouth and nose along a vertical axis, nor can he imagine a man wearing a hat to be a continuous unit. Consequently, he draws the hat above the figure but not on it.

The second substage within the concrete operations period is the stage of intuitive thought, and it lasts from the age of four to the age of seven. During the previous substage, the early drawings of a man display a rudimentary concept of topological spatial relationships because parts of the body are frequently scattered over a sheet of paper. Between the ages of four and seven, however, the topological relationships within the human figure are more clearly understood, and they are drawn convincingly, while the forms that contain Euclidean relationships are just beginning to emerge.

This means that the child is beginning to make straight lines, squares, triangles, houses, and tables in his drawings. He makes these simple geometric forms by interrupting the rhythmical movements used in making topological forms. The earliest triangles, therefore, might have slightly curved sides and angles of imperfect inclination. Such figures and collections of figures are assembled intuitively, without thoughtful organization.

By the age of six or seven, however, the child's perceptual activity and his drawing have been extensive enough so that he develops a more coordinated mental image of the world. This signals his arrival at the next substage of the concrete operations period.

The third substage of the concrete operations period is called the concrete operations substage, and it lasts from about the age of seven to the age of eleven. Perhaps it would help, at this point, to give the meaning of the term "operation." To Piaget, an operation may be defined as a perceptual action, or a perceptual movement, or a perceptual decentration which can return to its starting point, and which can be integrated with other actions also possessing this feature of reversibility (reversibility is the ability to retrace action to its starting point). A concrete operation is, therefore, the coordination and the internalization of perceptual actions that have been made on a concrete object. To become fully coordinated and internalized as an accurate concept of a concrete object, the perceptual actions that we perform on that object must be reversible. The reversibility implies one or more stable points of reference, such as a starting point, and a person must have a stable perceptual reference point if he is to achieve a full understanding of the world from his perceptions. If he does not have a reference point he merely receives a number of unrelated perceptual images.

The concrete operations substage is the period during which the child achieves reversibility in his actions. Thus, it is the first time that he is able to imagine the relationships between concrete objects and organize those objects meaningfully in his drawings. Piaget's description of this stage of conceptual development is especially important for public school teachers because it covers the years spent in the elementary school. The child's progress in perceptual exploration during this period yields the kind of pictorial synthesis that we see in pictures from the stage of symbolic development that Lowenfeld has called the schematic stage. He begins to draw objects in a more natural relationship to each other because he is drawing what he conceives rather than what he perceives. The child perceives such meaningful relationships during the first two years of life, according to Piaget. Consequently, if he were drawing his percepts, his work would have been spatially organized for quite some time. Describing his present work as a kind of visual realism would, therefore, be inaccurate. It would be more correct to speak of it as conceptual realism.

The topological relationships within single objects in the child's drawing are well-developed, and the same kind of relationships are maintained throughout the total picture. In other words, the spatial relationships within the symbol for a house will be topologically well-developed, and that same house will be placed on a baseline in proximity to other houses and to trees, yet separate from them. The houses may be placed on the baseline in an order that is correct and continuous, and some of them may show occupants enclosed in the rooms. Thus, the child's total pictorial organization is topological.

Although Euclidean shapes appear as the triangles, rectangles, and squares in houses and other such objects during this period, there are many Euclidean and projective relationships that do not exist in the child's work until the age of eight or nine. The proportions of objects are likely to be different from visual reality, for example, and there is no perspective or depth in the drawings. Because of the lack of a coordinated perspective, single drawings often contain a number of irreconcilable views of an object. You might see three sides of a cubical house or its top and front all at the same time. In other words, things are drawn without any attention being given to the angle from which they are viewed.

Series of Experiments

Piaget developed a series of tasks for children that demonstrate how they develop toward a concept of Euclidean and projective relationships that is fully coordinated. In one experiment he placed matchsticks with Plasticine bases on square, oblong, and round tables. "The child was told that each matchstick represented a telegraph pole and that each must be arranged to form a perfectly straight line running along a straight road. To start with, the first and last posts were placed in position, and both were equidistant from the edge of the table." In most cases, children under four years of age were incapable of making a straight line. Between four and seven they could make straight lines parallel to the table. But it was not until the children were seven years old that they could make a truly straight line (the shortest distance) between two points. They were able to do this by sighting along a line that projects through the two end poles. According to Piaget, younger children are not able to make the straight line because they cannot distinguish between the various possible views of the matchsticks and thus relate the placement of the matchsticks to their own positions in space.

In another experiment, he placed a child and a doll in positions that would cause them to view the same object from different angles. He asked the child to draw or construct her view of the object and to select from a number

of prepared pictures the view that she saw. The prepared drawings elimi-
nated any effects that might have been caused by motor ability. Piaget also
asked the child to draw and select pictures of the view the doll would get
of the object. Apparently, the children were able to see and to say that
things look different from the doll's viewpoint. They also seemed to know
that things look smaller as they become more distant. But these same
children drew and selected pictures for the doll's view that were the same
as the pictures they drew and selected for their own view. During this same
period, the children drew pictures without perspective although they could
see and say that objects appear smaller in the distance and that railroad
tracks appear to converge in the distance.

In Piaget's words,

> The explanation for these difficulties must be sought in the basic
> difference between perception and representation of perspective. To
> see an object with a given perspective is to view it from a particular
> viewpoint, but it is not necessary to be consciously aware of this view-
> point in order to perceive the object accurately. On the other hand,
> to represent this object in perspective by means of a mental image or
> a drawing necessitates a conscious awareness of the percipient's view-
> point, together with the transformations induced in the perceptual object
> by this viewpoint. Thus, in contrast to perception, representation of
> perspective implies operational, or at least conscious, coordination
> between object and subject; or in other words, a recognition of the fact
> that they both occupy the same projective space extending beyond the
> object and including the observer himself . . .

It is apparent from the foregoing explanation and from his explanations
of other phenomena that Piaget considers such characteristics as single and
double baselines, folding over, and mixtures of plane and elevation to be
caused by the creator's lack of a conscious awareness of his own viewpoint.
Not until the child reaches the age of nine, or thereabouts, does he develop
the conscious awareness of his own point of view that allows him to draw
what he sees and to give his work a single perspective. To develop such
a personal perspective an individual must not only be aware of other points
of view, but he must be able to coordinate his visual knowledge of them.
When a child uses a combination of plane and elevation or "folding over"
in his work, he is not aware of the highly unique quality of his own views
of things. He knows that there are different things to see in a given object,
but he is unable to coordinate the different views in such a way that he
understands his own unique relationship to the object; this is a highly
egocentric attitude. It is interesting to note that both Piaget and Lowenfeld
attribute "folding over" to the egocentricity of the child, but Piaget goes

a step further when he connects most other graphic characteristics to the same basic cause.

Piaget has shown experimentally that a child cannot accurately conceive of a cross-sectional drawing until he reaches the age of nine. For that reason, the x-ray drawings that he makes are not true cross sections, but they are merely topological concepts of enclosure. A real sectional drawing is made from a recognized point of view while "x-ray" drawings are often a jumble of several points of view. The child stops making such drawings about the age of nine because he has become conscious of his own perceptual position, and he recognizes the impossibility of his earlier x-ray views. Subsequent to the age of nine, the child might conceivably make a drawing that resembles an x-ray picture, but it is likely to be much more of a true cross section.

During Lowenfeld's schematic stage of development, the baseline is a prominent element in the child's visual symbols, and it is common to see objects placed on this baseline and perpendicular to it. This seems reasonable enough, but chimneys on houses and objects on a mountainside remain perpendicular to the line that forms the surface of the roof or the mountain. Children who draw such things would probably feel that the chimneys or trees were tilted if they were drawn in a vertical position. The reason for this, according to Piaget, is that the child, prior to the age of nine, does not establish a vertical and horizontal frame of reference that is outside of the object he is drawing. Suppose, for example, that we replicate one of Piaget's experiments by partially filling a jar with water, and capping it. Then we ask a child of six or seven to draw the jar and its water as if it were lying on its side. Chances are that the child will draw the water line parallel to the bottom of the jar. His frame of reference is the jar itself, and he assumes that the water will have the same relationship to the jar in any position that the jar happens to take. Not until he is about nine years of age will he use a table, the floor, or the ground as a reference to determine the position of the water.

Thus, between the ages of nine and eleven, the child's visual symbolization becomes more highly naturalistic than it ever has been before. This is because the child's concept of spatial relationships is more accurate than it has ever been in the past. Distortions of reality are rare, but when they do occur, they are apt to mean that the child is approaching a higher level of conceptual development.

Final Stage of Development

Piaget's final stage of development is called the formal operations period, and it lasts from the age of eleven to the age of fifteen. Between the ages of two and eleven, the child becomes increasingly capable of conceiving concrete objects and of thinking about them. The spatial relationships within them and among them become clearer to the child, allowing him to draw objects more naturalistically and more accurately in relationship to each other. But his thinking and his visual symbols are usually confined to concrete objects and events. There is little or no evidence of abstract ideas either in his thinking or in his creative productions. By the age of eleven, however, we notice that the child's drawings begin to deal with abstract concepts, and this indicates that the child has entered the formal operations period of conceptual development. Piaget does not discuss the child's visual symbols during this period of philosophical thinking. Ideas that go beyond references to matter-of-fact objects and relationships can be entertained, and an argument can be followed while disregarding its concrete content. When an individual reaches this level of conceptual development, it seems reasonable that his visual symbols might become equally as abstract. In fact, this would be the first time during which it would be appropriate to consider the possibility of conscious abstraction in his work.

Implications for Art Education

Now that we have given a small amount of attention to Piaget's work, what meaning does it have for art education in the public schools? In the first place, Piaget's work gives further substance to the notion that a child's visual symbols are intimately related to his conceptual growth. If this is the case, there is plenty of justification for saying that we do the child no good by criticizing the visual forms that he produces. If we wish him to change the shape of his work, we must change his concepts first.

Second, Piaget has shown that youngsters between the ages of two and eleven are in the concrete operations stage of conceptual development. This means that they can entertain concepts that deal with concrete objects and events, but they cannot entertain abstract ideas. It means that a teacher's stimulation is more apt to be successful in the elementary school if it deals with concrete objects and events. It means that a justification for art based on a philosophical position would be hard to explain to children. It means that we can go only so far in teaching aesthetics to children.

Third, Piaget's work suggests that we might speed the development of the child's concept of space by causing him to engage in selected perceptual activities. We could give him problems that involve an understanding of projective space, such as the one with the matchsticks. We could do things that would cause him to follow the contour of an object very closely. We could ask him to draw a given object or scene from more than one point of view. There are a number of such things that might be done. But, there is a question in my mind about whether we should do them. As far as art is concerned there is no apparent virtue in a pictorial organization that imitates the spatial relationships found in nature. In fact, such organizations have not been fashionable for quite some time.

If there is an artistic importance attached to the development of the child's concept of space, it might be that such concepts give the artist more freedom in selecting a visual form to suit a particular purpose. In other words, a child might have sufficient perceptual experiences to want to do something more naturalistic than his concepts will permit. In such cases, a few perceptual exercises aimed at the development of spatial concepts might be helpful to the child.

Piaget's work also suggests another possibility. If children develop spatial concepts as a result of visual and motor action, then drawing itself should help to improve an individual's concept of space, if he draws from nature. Drawing a model or a natural scene would encourage the child to increase his looking and to look more carefully, and it would reinforce his looking.

Still another possibility is that youngsters could improve their concepts of space by tracing photographs or other naturalistic reproductions. Tracing is a dirty word in art education, but I sometimes think that we are so quick to throw out the undesirable bath water that we throw out the baby along with it.

Finally, it is interesting to recall Viktor Lowenfeld's idea that there are visual and nonvisual personalities. The nonvisual, in Lowenfeld's opinion, is a person who cannot coordinate his partial impressions to form a mental image. The tendency is apparently an inherited one. Now, Piaget says that a coordinated concept of the world depends upon perceptual action in relation to a point of reference. This would suggest that Lowenfeld's haptic or nonvisual person could have his spatial concepts developed. At any rate, the possibilities are interesting to contemplate.

Science and Mathematics V

Piaget's long-standing interest in science is reflected in his many investigations into the nature of children's scientific thinking, including the child's concepts of causation, probability, reality, space, and time. The well-known operations of conservation and reversibility, which may be considered fundamental to scientific thinking, are likewise essential to the basic structure of mathematics. Hence, his research into the growth of these concepts has stimulated the interest of science and mathematics educators to inquire into the appropriate time and sequencing of such items. The controversial question as to whether the learning of these concepts may be accelerated is of special importance in these areas, where the tendency in recent years has been to advance the presentation of scientific and mathematical material to earlier levels of the curriculum.

Piagetian Theory into Inquiry Action

■■■ ROBERT R. BUELL

The author presents evidence to suggest that, in the realm of science teaching at least, the use of discovery methods may be most effective at the secondary school level. Inquiry action in the adolescent is seen not only as a psychological process but also "as a sequence of principles which the student may rediscover in context." This view accords with Piaget's notion of the rapprochement between logical and psychological operations during the period of formal thought.

Cronbach, in a recent discussion of the gap between theory and practice in science and mathematics curricula, points out that current curriculum revisions are (i) "innovations and reforms having nothing to do with the psychology of learning" designed to update or replace trivial items with items of greater significance, and (ii) "tangential to notions that Piaget has been presenting out of his own investigations." This is an attempt to summarize some findings, in this country and Great Britain, which bear on

● ● ● ● ● ● ● ●

SOURCE: Adapted and abridged from *Science Education*, 51 (1967), 21–24. (With permission of the author and *Science Education*.)

science teaching and the teaching of the necessary mathematics for science.

Piaget outlines five stages of cognitive development, the first three of which are relatively external actions upon or with real things (actualities), the latter two being internalized actions:

i.   sensorimotor actions upon things
ii.   preoperational actions upon things
iii. intuitive operations with things
iv.   concrete operations with things
v.   contemplation about things

It is with the latter two (characteristic of postpubertal youth) with which secondary school teachers of science are concerned. Much more research is available on the scientific behavior of the elementary school child during the first three cognitive development stages indicated.

Gabel (1940), in an early study which, both as to design and creativity of idea, should be replicated with other materials, contrasted the type of quantitative terms (definite versus indefinite) which best aided comprehension and retention of social studies material. Using nine school systems in northern Illinois, and four grades (viz., grades 6, 8, 10, and 12) in each system, he presented students with two methods of teaching (definite versus indefinite, i.e., "1492" versus "late in the fifteenth century") and two methods of testing (definite versus indefinite). He concluded that "the definite method of presentation of quantitative terms in social studies material is more effective than the indefinite method," and that scores were larger on tests using definite quantitative terms (regardless of mode of instruction) than on tests using indefinite terms. But, most important, he shows that "the percentages of correct responses increase in size from grade to grade in all forms and in all types of quantitative concepts" and concludes that this may be due to "a natural maturation in the ability to synthesize definite and indefinite meetings which manifests itself at about the age of the average pupil who is at seventh grade level" since there was a wider increase in score on all concepts (time, area, distance and size) "between the sixth grade and the eighth grade than between the eighth and tenth or tenth and twelfth." With respect to mental age, he suggests the strong probability that "the more intelligent pupils" at any age level (i.e., higher MA) "are more likely to comprehend and retain quantitative concepts . . . than the less intelligent ones." If, as Piaget holds, maturation during the first three periods culminates during Stage IV and V (in Gabel's study, the latter) in internalized thought, we see striking evidence here of its effect upon the quantification of science (at least in terms of area, time, distance and size) as opposed to earlier search for qualities by external action.

The many Illinois studies reported by Suchman (1961) with his sixth grade pupils failed to show any significant effect of training in inquiry by verbalization of inquiring questions; Gabel's results would indicate that, until puberty (i.e., about seventh grade), there is little interest in, nor in Piagetian terms, structures for, inquiry process. If Suchman's sequence were to be repeated with children at or above eighth grade, it would seem from Gabel's findings that results might be more meaningful.

Banks (1958), in an unpublished dissertation at Birmingham University, based his study of formal reasoning in students approximating our junior high level, upon Piaget's *The Child's Conception of Physical Causality* and later studies of Inhelder and Piaget, using their experiments. Younger children, as Piaget explains, tend to base explanation of events in terms of magical significance, or finalistic (i.e., purposiveness in Nature) terms, or in other precausal forms of reasoning. In Banks' work, modern secondary school pupils in England experimented with material, and careful notations were made of the way in which they verified hypotheses. Success in verification was more closely correlated with "science ability" (as determined by previous marks) than with IQ. All children, regardless of success in building and verifying hypotheses, showed genuine interest in the experiments — both the manipulation and the cognitive resultants. On the basis of his results, Banks concludes that modern secondary school children should, whenever possible, be encouraged to elaborate their own interpretations of scientific demonstrations rather than being presented with the theories, ready-made, before seeing the illustration.

Peel (1959) reviews studies by four of his students, the one by Lodwick being of interest here. Lodwick investigated inferences drawn from reading historical passages, and answers given by pupils, based on their inferences, could be classified into three stages, corresponding to the three Piagetian levels. The first group, reasoning intuitively, merely assimilated the stories to their own childish notions and failed to understand them. The second group attained the "concrete reasoning" level and were able to make isolated links between elements given in the text. The third group, who attained Piaget's "formal reasoning" level, were able to compare different propositions and to make valid inferences. Peel deduces that maturation, experience and learning all enter into this development, and Lodwick infers that Piaget and Inhelder's kind of development of scientific reasoning may have relevance in other fields (here, social studies).

Some data from a study by Neal (1959) with children of CA 8 to 11 (and MA 12 to 13 as the upper group with which we are concerned) deal with Piaget's sharply raised question as to whether science should reasonably be introduced into the curriculum before children have attained sufficient maturity to understand and utilize the hypothetico–deductive mode of reasoning. Using a technique similar to Washburne's arithmetic studies, Neal gave children CA 8 to 11 a series of science demonstrations on magnetism, burning, sound, heat, electricity, water pressure and balance. There were eighty children in the study, all given a multiple-choice answer sheet to test achievement. Simple magnetism was understood by boys CA 8, but "magnetic induction" and "expansion of metals" were not understood until CA 10 to 11 and MA 12 to 13, with English girls about eighteen months in arrears of boys on such understanding.

Working with 193 English children drawn from two junior schools and one secondary modern school, Ross (1959) used a demonstration method with principles of sound, covering situations: relations between sound and movement of the vibrating body; frequency and length; length and pitch; conduction of sound; and interrelated topics. The majority of his subjects, from the two junior schools, were not yet at puberty; the rest were just at it. In his results, the majority understood little of sound, grasping only that it was connected with movement. Throughout, in getting these results, the students were, after being shown a demonstration, asked to imagine what the results would be if certain variations in procedure were followed, so it was a test of internalized experimentation, in which we are interested.

Lunzer (1960) has investigated Piaget's findings concerning spatial relationships (*The Child's Conception of Geometry*) using twenty-four children CA 6 to 14. Most of the clinical findings of Piaget were borne out in classroom research. The conservation of displacement does not appear until about CA 12, nor does the multiplication of three dimensions to give volume appear until this CA. In another experiment to examine Piaget's thesis that notions of infinity and continuity determine conservation of "space occupied" and "displacement volume," using forty children CA 12 to 13, Lunzer built a test of understanding of infinity and continuity, plus a laboratory situation demanding understanding of the role of multiplication of linear dimensions to calculate volume, plus questions to the students relating to equivalence of volume of water displaced by equal volume, plus a list in which they identified "contradictory proverbs." It was argued that the first three tests should show more interrelationship among themselves than any test should show to the fourth test. His results do not bear this out. Lunzer concludes that each process should be examined separately and that it is dangerous to deduce from the fact that "certain processes are logically interdependent" just what their psychological relationship may be to each other.

Prior (1959) studied school children up to CA 12 with respect to space concepts. He asked his subjects to draw a model village, using the Piaget–Inhelder technique. Children younger than CA 8 showed what one might imagine of confusion (except for topological sense), but at CA 8 relations of orientation were carefully preserved, though children, on the whole, drew plans far from satisfactory as indicating spatial perception. Inability to coordinate two dimensions, and inability to reproduce distances with accuracy were both noted. By CA 10, full-scale reproductions were quite reasonable, but minor inaccuracies were seen, viz., proportionality, particularly in reduced-scale plans. By CA 12, all these were overcome. Since Piaget describes his cutting point for achievement at that CA where seventy-five per cent have mastered a conservation; in the case of drawing a model village, this would lie at CA $10\frac{1}{2}$.

We may summarize this body of research as indicating the following: (1) The drop in Basal Metabolic Rate (BMR) between childhood and adolescence, as marked by onset of puberty, would seem to result in certain physiological changes which affect thought patterns, and which are borne out in the few studies cited. (2) The scanty findings to date of the psychological approach to inquiry as a means of concept mastery would seem to be at extreme variance with practice in science education. (3) Attention to psychological arrangement (including maturation principles) would aid greatly in utilization of inquiry processes with secondary school students; one needs to consider both inquiry as a psychological process (i.e., a cognitive process growing out of contemplation about things) and inquiry as a (perhaps historical) sequence of principles which the student may rediscover in context. Ross's (1959) work with sound (in which the events were arranged logically) would seem to indicate that perhaps a psychological arrangement might be used in a replication of this study.

The Science Curriculum Improvement Study — Report to the Piaget Conference

███ ROBERT KARPLUS

The question of spontaneous development from preoperational to formal thinking as opposed to deliberate instruction,to insure and accelerate this development is the topic of this paper. The aim of the Science Curriculum Improvement Study is described as that of fostering the development of thinking to the formal operational level, from natural philosophy to scientific literacy, an aim which lends itself to the use of Piagetian concepts.

I think you will probably all agree that there is a transition between children's preoperational thinking at kindergarten age and some of their thinking in terms of propositions when the pupils leave elementary school

• • • • • • • •

SOURCE: *Journal of Research in Science Teaching,* 2 (1964), 236–240. (With permission of the author and the *Journal.*)

at twelve years or so. It seems to me that in general this transition in children's thinking is not recognized by present educational practice in the United States. Teachers with whom I have been in contact have not seemed to be much aware that there is such a change taking place. And I would say that most instruction above kindergarten takes place on what one might call the formal level. As an unfortunate consequence of this fact, many students never understand the intent of instruction and become dissatisfied with school by the time they are fourteen or sixteen. There are, of course, a substantial minority who make transitions from preoperational to formal thinking due to their own intellectual capacity. Piaget has studied many examples of such children. But I maintain that there are persons who grow to adulthood without attaining the capacity to think on the formal level in very many areas of their experience. They do attain the capacity in some areas, but not in nearly so many as one should like. From my contacts with teachers, I should also say that stimulus–response theory seems to have a powerful hold on them — in terms of what the teachers are accustomed to do in order to achieve the teaching aims and objectives as they see them.

There are two ways in which a curriculum effort can attempt to modify this situation. One way is to help teachers recognize the fact that if one explains matters to young children in terms of "if–then" statements, they may not understand, even though they may be able to make check marks in the correct "if" or correct "then" column of a test. It is important for teachers to learn this, to become aware of Piaget's experiments and their outcome. I think his conservation of volume study is one of the most impressive demonstrations that any teacher can carry out with children at five, six, or seven. Those teachers to whom we have suggested this study and who have tried it have been amazed. They would not have believed the results ahead of time.

A second way is to develop the children's ability to use formal operations. Piaget has found that this ability develops in some respects without special instruction, but it does not seem adequate to encompass the results or thinking or attitudes of modern science. Instead, there develops what I would like to call a kind of common sense or natural philosophy. The formal thinking of most youngsters in high school does not in general enable them to recognize the type of relationship one has to recognize when one makes a scientific study.

The program of the Science Curriculum Improvement Study is aimed at the second of these problems, to help the children's intellectual development reach the formal operational level with a repertory of concepts that to a certain extent is different from the repertory which is part of the common sense and the natural philosophy in the population at large. The first item, that of leading teachers to a more sensitive recognition of different stages of intellectual development, is part, I think, of a teacher education program that is much broader than our own intentions.

The premise of our program is that it is possible for the school to have a conscious influence on the development of its pupils in order to produce a more significant and a more useful understanding of natural phenomena by the time they are in their teens. To this outcome we give the name "scientific literacy." Of course, one needs to define the meaning of scientific literacy or explore it in considerably more detail than I have time to do. I trust you will nevertheless recognize that it is a desirable quality. We try to go about this program by fostering development along a broad front during this roughly six-year period of quite rapid intellectual maturation — a speed of maturation which I think is not repeated later. And the fact that some of this seems to push down problems from later educational to earlier educational levels is a misunderstanding of what we do. If children do not receive appropriate early schooling, there are many items that they never learn — even as adults. For example, I would say that Mr. O, the concept of relativity, is one that many adults never learn. Whether we accept it as concrete or formal is not the point. There are intellectuals and university faculty members and social scientists like us who may take it for granted that such an obvious idea as relativity is grasped by adults in general. But my contact with many members of the general public makes me realize that this is not the case. Mr. O is not something that is learned as a matter of course in the absence of special instruction. Teaching relativity in the elementary school, therefore, does not imply an acceleration of learning that is accomplished more slowly now; it implies a qualitative change in learning. And this is the way the school's influence can be most significant: the curriculum planning can include ideas which are considered to be important and which are not normally attained. Here is where I would contrast the scientific point of view with the commonsense or natural philosophy point of view. They are different, and I would like the science program in the school to develop the scientific point of view.

Our program reflects the breadth of natural phenomena at the early stages as we try to develop in children's thinking about natural phenomena a hierarchical structure of concepts that later becomes more and more sophisticated (Karplus, 1963a). Each topic in this program represents an application of previous elements of study and at the same time lays a foundation for subsequent elements of study. For this reason our teaching experiment has to be carried out in a rather carefully controlled manner. In other words, it is impossible for us to work with a fifth-grade topic in a school in which the children have not had the previous four years of instruction. In fact, if it were possible for us to work in an "untutored" fifth grade, then it would be pretty obvious that what we were doing in the fifth grade was not significantly dependent on the previous four years. Since we believe that there is a dependence, and I think we have some evidence to support our belief, we are conducting our experiment by starting with the kindergarten — primary grades, and then adding to the experimental teaching program a higher grade each year as the children are promoted. Thus, we shall have a third-year program, then a fourth-year program, and so on.

Let me now describe some of the topics that we have considered. The first is "Material Objects" (SCIS, 1963) in the kindergarten and first-grade program. Here the children become aware of what is material in our environment and what conservation properties material objects have. By contrast, there are very many real and important things which are not material; for instance, relations of objects to one another are not themselves objects. In our experience the children are not able to distinguish very clearly among properties, relations, and the objects that are involved in these relations. In the program the children manipulate many objects having different properties. There are metals and wood, shiny objects, smooth ones, sharp ones, soft ones, liquids, powders, and gases. I would say that it is a kind of natural history of material objects themselves rather than of their manufacture, or their use, or something else. A basis for this kind of unit is, of course, that the children have some concept of the conservation of objects. Since this appears to be formed when the children are very much younger, age one or two, we are, I think, fairly safe in taking this intellectual accomplishment for granted.

When we come to "Variation and Measurement" (SCIS, 1964), the next topic for the first grade, the tasks are much more difficult because measurement involves conservation of an object's property with respect to various transformations — transformations that might involve displacement from one point in space to some other point, as when we move a ruler from one point to another. The ruler's invariant length has to be recognized; otherwise comparing one ruler to many objects when measuring them does not particularly make sense. Piaget has shed much light on the development of these concepts. The development of concepts of variation, however, is something I have never seen discussed in the psychological literature. Our teaching program today is, again, a kind of natural history in which one does not look at a single object only, but rather at a whole collection or sample of objects that are fairly similar to each other but which are different in some way. The objects may differ in length, or, to reduce the tasks to counting or measurement in natural units, they may be pea pods and differ in the number of peas. Then the children make histograms of distributions of specific cases they encounter and find by observation that certain specimens are much more likely to be found than others.

For the second-grade program, we have a unit that is called "Interaction and Systems" (SCIS, 1963). Dr. Cronbach said that it was important to have attention-directing devices as a part of teaching. A system is a grouping of objects which belong together in some way. By choosing a system in which the children are interested and allowing them to follow this choice or selection or definition, one can direct the children's attention to certain objects and their relation. At the same time, comparison of two distinct systems is facilitated. The scientist conceptualizes a system for exactly the same reason — to confine his attention to what appears to be significant or important right now, and to suppress, for the time being at least, those elements that appear distracting rather than significant. "Belonging together" is a quite subjective criterion. One sometimes, therefore, has to change his definition of "system" because experiment or observation reveals that the initial choice was inadequate.

Interaction is an interpretive concept. It is another concept that I have not seen discussed in the psychological literature, and just what role it plays in the transition from preoperational, informal thinking is a question I would like to ask all of you, including Professor Piaget. It is a relation between objects. It is not an object itself. It is an interpretive concept and is important for the following reasons. As one makes observations, as one accumulates a natural history of objects or phenomena, it is possible to attach significance to the phenomena in very many different ways. (As you know, some societies attach significance to rainfall in terms of certain mythological interpretations. I daresay you cannot rationally convince someone who holds this viewpoint that it is not correct.) Modern science is characterized by a certain hierarchy of interpretations. We would like children to learn to make a scientific interpretation rather than a mythological or a superstitious interpretation of natural phenomena. We feel that it is a responsibility of the teaching program to introduce these scientific interpretations. One of these is to interpret any change as evidence of interaction. Interaction is a fundamental scientific explanatory concept. We do not say that a change, a happening, is evidence of mythological processes as it was once thought to be, but we say it is evidence of interaction, interaction being a certain relationship. In other words, interaction of certain objects is the cause of a happening. This, then, is our second-grade interpretation of Newton's second law.

In order to introduce this idea into the curriculum, we have used a pedagogical device which is called "Invention and Discovery" (Atkin and Karplus, 1963). The way in which this pedagogical device (and again I am not quite sure about identifying the relationship between this and various SR or non-SR learning theories), functions is this: there is an instructional period consisting of several class sessions, in which the children are engaged in observation on a natural history level of some new or some familiar materials with which they "play." There is then a suggestion (invention) of a way to think about the observations. Finally, there is further experimentation in which the children can explore the consequences of using the suggestion (discovery). In "Interaction and Systems" the materials might be magnets and nails, some dry cells and light bulbs, etc. — more or less common materials with which one can do simple experiments. We then suggest to the children that they should think about the changes they observe as being evidence of interaction. The remarkable thing is that the children do learn to think of it this way, and that during a later experiment, they run up to the teacher and say, "Look, there is some evidence of interaction." Thus, "invention" is an introduction of an interpretive construct, and "discovery" is a recognition of the usefulness of the construct. What we have here is a guided discovery, a process of going from observation at the beginning to interpretation at the end through the device of "Invention and Discovery."

Now, I believe Piaget has pointed out that in the natural development of a child his own initiative to shape his explorations and to decide what he will do is dependent upon the child — the child decides. I think that this economy of decision is a significant element which determines the quality of the learning that occurs. The question we therefore face is, how much help can one give the child without depriving him of his decision-making initiative to such a large extent that he would never recognize when a particular idea really works out? The Science Curriculum Improvement Study's compromise is to have the teacher provide the construct, but to leave ample opportunity for the children to apply the construct to many cases in their own manipulation.

The second item for the second grade is the unit on relativity (SCIS, 1964; Karplus, 1963b). Since this has already been discussed a number of times, I will not go into further detail. Instead, I should like to present a more speculative discussion.

Let me consider the distinction between observation and interpretation in general. Is this distinction meaningful? For example, I mentioned earlier that interaction is an interpretive concept. It is not something that can be directly observed evidence. I think the distinction is meaningful, but I also think it must be kept flexible and that it may not hold for all individuals in the same way. What is an interpretation for one individual may be completely assimilated and an obvious part of an observation for another. If this is correct, then it raises another obstacle to effective communication between teacher and students, whose different degrees of sophistication make them distinguish differently between observation and interpretation. In science, where the distinction between objective, observable fact and hypothetical, interpretive theory is frequently made, the difficulty is likely to be particularly acute.

Cognitive Theory and the School Mathematics Study Group Program

■ JEREMY KILPATRICK

In this paper, the author describes the curriculum program of the School Mathematics Study Group and its philosophy. As in most other areas of curriculum development, the structure of the subject, rather than psychological theory, has played the major role in shaping the program. The issue of spontaneous development in children's thinking versus acceleration of this development through formal instruction and experience is discussed. While certain features of the SMSG curriculum are compatible with the results of Piaget's studies, the mathematicians participating in this program believe that the child's ability to understand may be changed by new curricula, and that the issue of stages, therefore, remains an open question.

Now that the first wave of curriculum reform in school science and mathematics has reached and passed its crest, those of us involved in curriculum development are beginning to investigate some of the psychological assumptions implicit in what we have done. The School Mathematics Study Group, in particular, is now attempting to identify components of mathematical abilities, both to assess the new mathematics curricula and to give direction to further reform. I would like to sketch for you some of the aspects of SMSG's work which are related to recent developments in cognitive theory. First, I will discuss briefly the philosophy of the SMSG curriculum program; then I will describe SMSG's National Longitudinal Study of Mathematical Abilities.

SMSG was initiated in the spring of 1958 as a nationwide project for the improvement of the teaching of mathematics in the schools. Until recently, its chief concern has been the preparation of textbooks for grade levels from kindergarten through grade twelve. Other activities have included the production of teacher-training materials, publication of a series of monographs on various mathematical topics, and the translation of certain SMSG texts into Spanish. But the preparation of textbooks was SMSG's first, and for a long time its major, activity.

The procedure used by SMSG in the preparation of these texts has been a novel one. Large teams composed of equal numbers of mathematicians and classroom teachers work intensively for a relatively short time, usually a summer session of about eight weeks, on the development of an experimental text. This preliminary version of the text is tried out during the school year at experimental centers across the country and revised by a similar team during the following summer. The general pattern has been for the mathematicians to suggest the mathematical content to be included

• • • • • • • •

SOURCE: *Journal of Research in Science Teaching*, 2 (1964), 247–251. (With permission of the author and the *Journal*.)

in the texts and for the classroom teachers to suggest how it might be presented at a given grade level.

The philosophy of the writing teams is suggested by the following excerpt from the first SMSG *Newsletter*, March 1959:

> We need an improved curriculum which will offer students not only the basic mathematical skills but also a deeper understanding of the basic concepts and structure of mathematics.

These writing teams have not worked in ignorance of contemporary learning theory; it cannot be said that they have been guided at every step by any explicit body of psychological knowledge. Their goals have been more logical than psychological. They have attempted at every point to make mathematical structure the focus of their concern, and they have made their own experience rather than predictions from psychological theory the test of whether and how a given topic can be taught at a given grade level. It is significant, I think, that none of the changes made in the revised SMSG texts are changes in the basic mathematics or philosophy of the original material.

In a sense, the mathematicians who have guided the recent curriculum reforms have been waiting to be shown that psychological theories of learning and intelligence have something relevant to say about how mathematics shall be taught in the schools. These reformers (and I speak now not only of SMSG) have been so successful in teaching relatively complex mathematical ideas to young children, thus doing considerable violence to some old notions about readiness, that they have become highly optimistic about what mathematics can and should be taught in the early grades. This optimism, if I may call it that, is reflected in the recent publication, "Goals for School Mathematics," the report of the Cambridge Conference on School Mathematics, held last summer at Cambridge, Massachusetts. This report calls for a major reorganization of the grade school curriculum and a compression of high school and college offerings. It deals only with the problem of organizing the mathematics curriculum, not with teaching methods. Its purpose is to anticipate another major curriculum reform to start in the next twenty to thirty years. I quote from the introduction to the report:

> We made no attempt to take account of recent researches in cognitive psychology. It has been argued by Piaget and others that certain ideas and degrees of abstraction cannot be learned until certain ages. We regard this question as open, partly because there are cognitive psychologists on both sides of it, and partly because the investigations of Piaget, taken at face value, do not justify any conclusion relevant to our task. The point is that Piaget is not a teacher but an observer — he

has tried to find out what it is that children understand, at a given age, when they have been taught in conventional ways. The essence of our enterprise is to alter the data which have formed, so far, the basis of his research. If teaching furnishes experiences which few children now have, then in the future such observers as Piaget may observe quite different things. We therefore believe that no predictions, either positive or negative, are justified, and that the only way to find out when and how various things can be taught is to try various ways of teaching them.

I think this quotation reveals the attitude of many mathematicians as they approach the problems of curriculum reform, and it also indicates some of the questions that educational psychology will have to face in the near future.

Jerome S. Bruner, in his book, *The Process of Education,* has provided a psychological rationale for the major ideas of the new mathematics curricula. Since much of his interpretation of new concepts and methods in education is made in the light of what Piaget has said about intellectual development, Bruner has stimulated considerable interest among mathematics educators and mathematicians in Piaget's recent work. Bruner's discussion of the spiral curriculum and the importance of emphasizing the structure of a subject has been especially well received.

Let us look briefly at those features of the SMSG curriculum that are most harmonious with the results of Piaget's studies. First, there is the grade placement of certain topics. Piaget's evidence that the child of nine or ten can handle many of the basic concepts of Euclidean spatial representation and measurement is mirrored in SMSG's placement of such topics in the elementary curriculum. His findings on the development of the concept of number are similarly shown in the emphasis on correspondences and relations among sets in the SMSG elementary curriculum, although we may have failed to anticipate some of the subtle misconstructions of a concept which Piaget has demonstrated can and do occur. Next, there is Piaget's emphasis on the participation of the learner as he performs real actions on the learning materials. This is shown in SMSG's use of discovery exercises in all of its text materials, but we have certainly not begun to realize the possibilities in concrete sensory aids. The work of Z. P. Dienes (1959) of the University of Adelaide is especially promising in this regard. We are looking forward with interest to Bruner's report on the recent research he and Dienes have done at Harvard's Center for Cognitive Studies. A final parallel between Piaget's studies and the SMSG curriculum can be found in SMSG's emphasis upon learning the structure of the subject matter. For example, the properties of reversibility and associativity are, in Piaget's theory, important features of operational systems. The SMSG curriculum gives the student ample opportunity to practice operations with these properties in the expectation that he will then become sensitive to cause–effect relations in mathematics and to the idea that there can be many routes to a goal.

Before leaving the subject of the SMSG curriculum, may I point again to the mathematician's belief in the possibility of radically altering the stages Piaget has observed in intellectual development by changing the child's previous experience. It would be no profound blow to Piaget's theory if the age levels of the stages were influenced by experimental manipulation, but it would be a serious matter if the sequence of stages was somehow rearranged. Considerable research in the near future is certain to be centered on this issue of finding "elastic limits" in children's cognitive processes.

Now I should like to discuss SMSG's testing program, in particular, the National Longitudinal Study of Mathematical Abilities.

There has been in recent years a growing recognition that the mathematics which students study in school is a continuous stream rather than a collection of discrete units and that detailed information about the processes involved in school learning is best gathered through a longitudinal study. Piaget's and Inhelder's work amply testifies to the value of a longitudinal approach.

The National Longitudinal Study of Mathematical Abilities, or NLSMA, was undertaken in 1962 as a five-year study. Its purpose is to discover the variables which affect mathematical learning and, in particular, to assess the effectiveness of various curricula.

During the fall of 1962, schools participating in NLSMA gave an initial battery of four inventories to a total of 122,000 fourth-, seventh-, and tenth-grade students in both conventional and new mathematics curricula. The battery consisted of standard intelligence test items, together with tests of attitudes with respect to mathematics and preferred conceptualization strategies. These variables were chosen as salient for assessing some of the individual difference variables which may interact with the growth of mathematical skills.

Jerome Kagan, a member of the SMSG Panel on Tests, the group responsible for the design of the study and for the selection and construction of tests, has provided the following rationale for the choice of instruments in this initial battery:

> . . . ease of learning new material — and this is the major variable in the NLSMA — is the function of three major classes of psychological variables: (a) degree of attention given to new material; (b) possession of those cognitive structures necessary for comprehension of new material; and (c) conditions of presentation of material, e.g., tempo of presentation (and) feedback of results . . .

The degree of attention invested in material to be learned is a function of motivational variables, anxiety, identification with specific (sex) role models, and cognitive strategies. The variables of importance with respect to possession of structures include vocabulary level and knowledge of the transformational rules appropriate to the material. The conditions of presentation have to do with the speed of presenting new materials, the degree of structuring of material, e.g., how big a unit is presented, and the importance of immediate reward or feedback of results.

It is, of course, impossible to assess all of these variables, and we chose to concentrate upon those that appeared to be most relevant for the differential mastery of mathematics and chose tests that were amenable to large-scale group administration.

Additional individual difference variables were measured last fall when the NLSMA population was divided into three subpopulations matched on demographic and intellectual characteristics. Each subpopulation was given tests of arithmetic reasoning, general reasoning, and other tests taken primarily from French's *Revised Kit of Reference Tests for Cognitive Factors.* The tests which were used were tests which had shown up as relevant in previous factor-analytic studies of mathematical abilities.

Measures of mathematical abilities had been given to the NLSMA population in the spring of 1963 when the mathematics section of the Sequential Tests of Educational Progress and other mathematics inventories were administered.

This spring we are attempting an even more comprehensive assessment of mathematical abilities. Three class hours of testing time will be devoted to the assessment of all levels of mathematical skills. The tests that will be given are the culmination of over a year's efforts. First, we tried to identify the basic mathematical topics that students are expected to master at each grade level. Then, we classified test items on these topics according to a system of cognitive skills based on the *Taxonomy of Educational Objectives: Handbook 1: Cognitive Domain.* The taxonomy orders cognitive skills into six levels: knowledge, comprehension, application, analysis, synthesis, and evaluation. Our ordering of mathematical abilities differs only slightly: knowing, translating, manipulating, choosing, analyzing, synthesizing, and evaluating.

When we examined test items from standard mathematics tests, we found that only a few of them tested skills above the level of choosing. We wrote a group of items illustrative of the various levels, and then last summer at Stanford we held a writing session. During the month of July a group composed of six college teachers of mathematics, six high school teachers of mathematics, and a psychologist met to create test items. They presented ideas for testing the higher cognitive skills, including aspects of problem solving and of creativity. Most of the ideas submitted for tests deal with topics in mathematics unfamiliar to students. In such tests, students would be asked to read and analyze new mathematical information and then to apply it to a problem. Some of the tests were pretested with students during the summer.

At a Chicago meeting in September, forty college mathematicians and educators reviewed the preliminary study and the work of the Summer Writing Session. They clarified the taxonomy and the mathematical topics for each grade level and selected forty-five of the sixty-four tests developed during the summer as being worth development.

In October the SMSG Sub-Committee on Mathematical Tests met and approved the work of this conference. In addition, the Committee decided to construct tests emphasizing number systems for the fifth grade; number systems, informal geometry, and algebraic concepts for the eighth grade; and algebraic sentences and formal geometry for the eleventh grade. Tentative items were collected from the Summer Writing Session, the University of Illinois Committee on School Mathematics, the Minnesota Testing Laboratory, the Educational Testing Service, and individual writers.

The subcommittee, along with several consultants, met again in January to review the items and to place them into tests for pilot-testing. More than sixty tests were devised and administered to 25,000 students in thirty-four states. These pilot tests have been analyzed, and we have just concluded the preparation of the spring battery of tests using those items which showed up well in the pilot-testing.

Soon we will be making plans for the final three years of the study. Analysis of data already collected will be used to guide future testing. We also plan a number of small-scale research studies which may then be incorporated into the longitudinal study.

One area of present concern to us is the detection of cognitive styles of handling mathematical concepts. We are particularly interested in systematic versus nonsystematic styles. We have developed some tests designed to detect students who approach mathematical problems in a systematic manner, but these tests will require a great deal of work before we can make inferences about cognitive styles with any confidence. This is, nonetheless, an area in which we have reason to feel some hope of uncovering cognitive variables associated with mathematical abilities. The work of John W. French on "The Relationship of Problem-Solving Styles to the Factor Composition of Tests," in which he found that the use of a systematic style on a test frequently reduced its loading on the factor with which it is usually associated, has been of great interest to us.

Three years of the longitudinal study remain. We hope that in that time we can gather information about the processes involved in mathematical performance that will contribute to cognitive theory as well as lead to a better and more satisfying mathematics program for future generations of students.

The Psychology of Piaget and Its Educational Applications

■■■ HARDI FISCHER

John Dewey familiarized educators with the notion that learning by doing is the best way to achieve true understanding. In this article, Dr. Fischer points out that Piaget's findings show the need for following a plan designed in accordance with the child's developing thought structures. Providing the requisite concrete experiences which undergird abstract and symbolic learning presents a challenge to the teacher, and calls for changes in much of the traditional curriculum.

If you know the meaning of assimilation and accommodation in biology, if you are familiar with grouping, reversibility, and equilibrium in logic, then Piaget's theory will be more easily understandable for you. Piaget is perhaps the best known Swiss psychologist. Other names of Swiss psychologists may be familiar to you: Claparède, Binswanger, Bleuler, Rorschach, Meili, Jung, Sechehaye. But with his more than 50 books, Piaget is, in comparison to the others, much more difficult to understand, because he gives us always a sort of synthesis of different theories: Piaget studied biology, he taught experimental psychology (especially visual perception problems) and sociology, and became increasingly interested in symbolic logic and genetic epistemology, fields in which he has published more and more in the last few years.

Piaget teaches psychology at the University of Geneva, a university of about 3,000 students, more than 50 per cent of whom come from other parts of the world. This small city which is the center of so many international organizations — the International Committee of the Red Cross, the World Health Organization, the International Labor Organization, the International Bureau of Education (directed since 1929 by Jean Piaget) — is pervaded by a mixture of the ideas expressed by Calvin and Rousseau. No wonder, then, that this atmosphere gave Piaget the chance for his studies in child development, which were already started before him by Claparède in the light of strict logical thinking.

● ● ● ● ● ● ● ●

SOURCE: Adapted from the *International Review of Education, 10* (1964), 431–439. (With permission of the author and the *Review.*)

For Piaget, intelligence is the field in which he is especially interested and means simply adaptation between the organism and the environment, as in biology one should look for an equilibrium between assimilation and accommodation. Assimilation means action of the organism on surrounding objects. Accommodation means action of the environment on the organism. If the assimilation is much stronger than the accommodation, we observe an egocentrism. This happens to the younger child when he explores the world. If accommodation is too strong, we have then an excessive imitation. It takes a long time for the child to feel the necessity to search for an equilibrium. This equilibrium is never stable and we need new adaptations. These needs have the function of motivations.

The function of his research often seems to be to investigate, measure, and categorize for its own sake. The value of Piaget's theory and work seems to be that it attempts an integrated understanding of the whole of the child's thought, not just fragments. He examines it from all aspects, but with an especial interest in cognition, and the entire developmental sequence. He does this always with definite hypotheses in mind.

What is his method of research? He uses a clinical method of investigation, similar perhaps to a psychiatric interview. The questions of course vary within certain limits. The use of concrete materials for examination serves as a point of departure for discussion. There are no time limits or right answers with higher or lower scores. What is important is the answer of why, rather than the performance. Intelligence tests do not help us to see how the answers are worked out. They are too stereotyped, and neglect the spontaneous answers of the subject.

The information given by the child is analyzed qualitatively. Protocols are taken of everything: manipulation of the material, verbalizations, expressions. In spite of differences in explanations and so on, one can still categorize results. Piaget applies symbolic logic to analysis, introducing means for describing and analyzing that which, in a highly connected way, a child does at different stages of his development.

The originality of the method consists of the search for developmental transitions between different levels of behavior, expressed through schemata. On the other hand, Piaget gives demonstrations of networks of related behaviors which can be regarded as elementary structures of the intelligence.

Piaget is interested in many areas of research, but here only his interest in the study of cognitive functions from birth to adolescence might be described.

His early investigations into the nature of a child's conception of the external world should be mentioned first. Conversations with children aged between four and eight, at the Maison des Petits, on such topics as causality, origins of names and relations to object named, movements of stars and clouds, and attribution of life and consciousness to living beings or to objects, resulted in the subsequent publication of numerous books and papers. All these observations on children's play, dreams, imitation, language and thought, and concept of reality, judgment and reasoning, and moral judgment of the child are characteristic of his early investigations.

With the birth of his own three children, he started detailed observations of preverbal behavior from earliest reflex activity to the first inventive, or, if you prefer, the first intelligent behaviors. During this period he elaborated his theory of intelligence as an adaptation between assimilation and accommodation. He described the genesis of the permanent object in space and time during the first stage of development, the sensorimotor–intelligence level (zero to two years).

At that time, he began further studies of logical thinking in children up to adolescence through the use of experimental setups. He studied concept formation with respect to the structure of thinking, in connection with time, speed, movement, space, weight, volume, number, quantity, etc. By doing this, he was able to consider the idea of cognition in its higher levels. For him, forms became the primary concern; distinction could be mainly between two stages, concrete operations (two to seven years) and formal or propositional operations (eleven to fifteen years).

Finally, Piaget developed his ideas of genetic epistemology, which stemmed from his observations of the similarity of the child's conception of physical phenomena to that of the early Greek philosophers. He then started to examine the relationship of the individual to the world of objects through a systematic, chronological inventory of complete and incomplete answers to so-called natural questions.

In discussing the different stages of development posited by Piaget and elaborated through his experiments, it must be kept in mind that these problems are being reexamined in a longitudinal study currently in progress. This study is based on a selected group of children who are well-balanced emotionally and who are examined with the consent of parents. They are tested every four to six months, so that progress on differences related to concept formation can be observed. During these sessions complete films and tapes are made. No results are given to teachers, so no importance is attached to scoring high. Some replications of test situations may have an influence on the stages, because learning is probably involved. This question and others being raised by Piaget, coworkers and critics, may as a result of the current studies be answered — the answers perhaps will bring about revisions in the system or strengthen existing notions.

When one considers the flexibility of the clinical method and the enormous heterogeneity of the testers — foreign students at different levels of understanding of the problems involved, and differently gifted for this rather difficult type of research — one is surprised by the homogeneity of the results.

Piaget stopped his genetic investigations at the fifteen-year-old level. We are actually trying in the field of language to find out if the development is similar between fifteen and twenty years.

Geneva, where these research projects have been worked out, is the city of Rousseau. Another Swiss educator who tried to interest the population in education was Pestalozzi. Today Geneva's schools are one very large laboratory for research in child psychology and in education. But relatively few applications of Piaget's psychology are observed there or elsewhere.

At first, one may have the impression that Piaget's stages imply teaching according to these developmental levels; for instance numerical operations should not be introduced before the age of seven. I remember, when I was a student in Geneva, we often discussed the results of Carleton Washburne, who was then superintendent of the Winnetka schools near Chicago. He published statistics showing at which level mathematical or other concepts could be introduced with success into the children's thinking. Today, a higher developed teaching, a little bit similar to that tried out by Washburne, the method of programmed learning, radically destroyed this older stage theory. What then is the difference to the stages described by Piaget?

If a child changes from one stage to the next one, he integrates not only the earlier stage in the following, but he restructures the whole. In other words: if the problems are similar, they are nevertheless expressed in a new form. I would like to give you an example from my own son. When he was five years old he developed in a very concrete situation the algebraic law that the product of two negative digits will be positive. Teachers in high school generally have some difficulty explaining this law. They often use diagrams or they introduce the law by induction or they do it axiomatically. I think, they may learn more about their teaching by observing children's behavior.

My boy got a toy automobile with a battery inside. A lever gave him the possibility of moving it forward (positive) and backward (negative). One day his battery was used up and I bought him a new one, but asked him to install it himself. He worked for a long time and came back somewhat confused, because now when he put the lever in the forward position, his automobile moved backward and when he put the lever in the backward position it moved forward. It took a long time until he found out that he had to turn his battery. He was very happy with the following new game and showed it to his friends:

battery right position (+) and lever forward (+):
movement forward (+)

battery right position (+) and lever backward (−):
movement backward (−)
battery false position (−) and lever forward (+):
movement backward (−)
battery false position (−) and lever backward (−):
movement forward (+)

But this is exactly the qualitative meaning of the well-known law in algebra, already mentioned before. Why not then start early enough with these discoveries for the child by giving him the right educational material? Learning by doing, as John Dewey told us sixty years ago, is necessary for understanding. But we know today that this doing has to follow a specific plan according to the structures to be developed in the child's mind. Piaget is convinced that the child's understanding depends on what he is doing at an earlier stage. Acceleration will probably be possible, if we observe the necessity for the young child to manipulate by himself and if we give him the chance to go through all the stages by doing it himself. All that we can do is to prepare the educational material for classification, for setting up correspondences, for ordering, etc. Many children count before they are admitted to the first grade of school, but they didn't discover by their own actions the operational concept of the number. Telling my boy how the battery in his automobile works is again useless; he had to explore himself, after which I was certain that he really understood.

On the level of concrete operations he can then study the problem again. For instance: what is the contrary of the contrary of beautiful, and so on, with other classes and relations. On the level of the formal operations he will again explore the problem by formal logic, introducing the structure of equivalence perhaps, similar to a structure of a strong correlation in statistics.

Educators should know that the younger child is able to reason in qualitative rather than in quantitative structures. Why then not start in the primary school or even in kindergarten with topology instead of Euclidean properties of the world's spatial relations? Why not discuss first qualitative properties of time, speed, measurement, number, etc. so preparing a better understanding? Using the methodology of programmed learning, one should pay attention to the fact that this teaching will finally only be successful when the pupil has previously had the possibility to structure his thinking. While Gestalt psychology saw a similarity between cortical and perceptual structures, we should now consider the fact that the meaningful coordination of our actions flows into a mental structure characterized by a mobility in it. For Gestalt psychology representation was never reversible because there were just static pictures collected in the mind. In the operational psychology of Piaget the pictures as such are not important, but the actions changing their position, so that representation is active and makes anticipation possible.

There is another application of Piaget's psychology to consider. The different experiments could serve as a new technique in developmental testing. As a matter of fact, most of the Binet-scale type tests are not based on a consistent theory in child development.

The longitudinal study mentioned will probably show which of the experiments give follow-up solutions. These experiments, when transformed into tests, could then be ordered with the help of a Guttman-scale. Unfortunately for those who are interested in testing, I must confess that I cannot yet see how to quantify the typically clinical experiments. On the other hand, each clinical use of these tests gives us the opportunity for the construction of psychopathology from normative genetic data.

Most of the well-known intelligence tests are too verbal, also containing numerical tasks, or they depend on scholastic performances. Piaget's experiments, when used clinically, present a broader situation. In tests you have mostly a sort of performance to judge, but you don't know the underlying reasoning processes. Piaget's experiments give this information and also permit an evaluation of educability. They have in general more motivational makeup and this is important for young people. Perhaps they have a greater predictability of the child's future development?

Because the experiments in Piaget's psychology are mostly explainable in terms of a bivalent symbolic logic, it should be possible to connect his system with logic machines. Piaget is himself interested in these problems and in the ideas of cybernetics. It should also be possible to judge children's or adults' behavior not in a statistically differential, but in a logically differential way.

An Analysis of the Effects of a Structured Teaching Approach Developed from the Work of Piaget, Bruner, and Others

■■■ HENRY P. COLE

Most educators are aware of the necessity for negative instances in teaching new concepts to students, but are probably less aware of the need in problem solving to learn the technique of rejecting the more obvious explanations which, for children, are often the perceptually dominant features of the situation. This paper

• • • • • • • •

SOURCE: Adapted and abridged from a paper presented at the annual meeting of the American Educational Research Association, February 10, 1968. The research reported in this paper was part of a dissertation completed under the direction of Dr. Ronald R. Raven, State University of New York at Buffalo. (With permission of the author.)

describing an experiment designed to test the efficacy of an instructional sequence based on this notion with respect to the problem of floating bodies, is of special interest to science teachers, and may well suggest new ways of introducing scientific principles in the classroom.

Statement of the Problem

Inhelder and Piaget (1958) report that subjects younger than thirteen or fourteen years use four common irrelevant principles to explain why objects float or sink. The four irrelevant principles state that an object will float or sink because of: (1) its absolute weight; (2) its absolute volume; (3) its absolute surface area toward the liquid; or (4) the absolute volume of the liquid into which the object is placed. Children frequently believe heavy objects sink, lightweight objects float, objects with a large volume sink, objects with a small volume float, flat objects float, nonflat objects sink, and that objects which sink in a small volume of liquid will float in a larger volume of the same liquid. Before a subject can correctly predict or explain why an object floats or sinks he must (1) learn to exclude the irrelevant principles and (2) learn to separate and form the correct principle by the appropriate conjunction of the relevant variables.

It should be noted that each of the four irrelevant principles is based upon one dominant perceptual dimension. Each of these irrelevant rules corresponds to the "noisy" and "nondefining" attributes in an attribute-learning concept attainment task which cause what Bruner calls "perceptual seduction" and which prevents concept attainment (Bruner, et al., 1966). In this rule-learning concept-attainment task, there are four "noisy," "nondefining" rules which lead to perceptual seduction and hinder correct formation of the rule.

In learning the solution to the floating bodies problem there are initially two perceptually apparent defining attributes: weight and volume. However, the two truly relevant dimensions in this task are not the perceptual dimensions of weight and volume but the conceptual dimensions of "density" and "specific gravity," which are what Bruner calls "configurational attributes," i.e., dependent upon the association or combination of two or more perceptually-apparent, defining attributes. The conceptual dimensions of "density" and "specific gravity" are good examples of this type of attribute. The "density" dimension is a relationship between the weight and volume attributes of an object. The "specific gravity" dimension is a relationship between the "density" dimension values of an object and a standard (usually water in Piaget's experiments). Solution of the floating bodies problem depends not upon the dimension of weight or the dimension of volume, but upon the two conceptual dimensions formed by the conjunction of weight and volume values. This is why weight and volume may be said to be irrelevant perceptual dimensions in this task even though they are necessary to the formation of the two relevant conceptual dimensions. To be able to use these conceptual dimensions in a criterial manner, an individual must first reject the "perceptual seduction" influence of the four "noisy" singularly nondefining attributes, and next form the conjunctive, configurational attribute concepts of "density" and "specific gravity." After this, an individual can determine the appropriate criterial attributes in an object–liquid situation, correctly predict if the object will float or sink, and/or correctly explain (on an empirical basis) why it floats or sinks. The two criterial attributes become, of course, the ratio of the weight of an object to its volume ("density") and the ratio of the "density" of the object to the "density" of the liquid ("specific gravity"). According to Inhelder and Piaget, these two relationships *must* be conceptualized and accepted as the relevant dimensions before the floating bodies problem can be solved. This statement would, at first, seem to be in error, since the principle to be learned in the floating bodies problem is, "an object will float if it weighs less than an equal volume of the liquid into which it is placed," and "an object will sink if it weighs more than an equal volume of the liquid into which it is placed." This rule is sometimes referred to as the flotation principle. However, according to Inhelder and Piaget, the criterial use of this rule depends upon the use of the concepts of "density" and "specific gravity" where all the resulting relationships between the weights and volumes of objects and the liquid are grouped into two, and only two, large classes; "that of bodies whose density is less than the density of water and that of bodies whose density is greater" (Inhelder and Piaget, 1958).

The implication of the above statements for the teaching of the principle of flotation in junior high science is striking. Science teachers are typically concerned with teaching only the correct principle. Attempts are not made to force students to logically exclude the common irrelevant principles. Yet, Inhelder and Piaget have shown that it is precisely this logical exclusion of irrelevant principles which must occur before the correct principle can be attained in a stable form. Their findings are consistent with the formulations of Bruner relating to the perceptual seduction effects of dominant irrelevant dimensions in concept and rule-learning tasks.

Assessment of Concept Stability

A criterion instrument to determine the stability of the conceptualization of the correct principle was developed. The idea for the basic design of this instrument grew out of a consideration of Smedslund's (1961a) trick test in his conservation of weight studies. The test consists of ten written, five option multiple-choice items. Each item requires the subject to observe a series of demonstrations and explain why objects float or sink. The demonstrations involve changing the shape, weight, and volume of a solid substance and the volume of liquid in several containers. The demonstrations are designed such that the objects which are heavier, have a larger volume, or are nonflat, all sink relative to a group of floating objects of lighter weight, smaller volume or flat shape. In addition, certain objects which sink in containers with a small volume of liquid appear to be made to float by increasing the volume of liquid in the container or by transfer of the object to a larger container with a greater volume of liquid. Verbalization by the demonstrator accompanies the demonstrations and serves the purpose of emphasizing the four singularly irrelevant dimensions. The five options consist of the correct "specific gravity" explanation, and four irrelevant principle explanations. In each item one of the four irrelevant principles is emphasized in the demonstration and made to seem a likely choice. It was reasoned that a person who had truly conceptualized the correct principle would resist the strong "perceptual seduction" feature of each demonstration and maintain the use of the correct principle in his explanation. The instrument was shown to be valid and reliable.

Early work with the instrument showed that nearly all college junior and senior nonscience majors studied had not attained the concept in a stable form even though they had received conventional instruction in the content area in science courses. The test was next administered to a group of sixty-one college students who were currently enrolled in a physical science course which had provided conventional instruction in the content area. The criterion instrument showed this group had not attained the concept in stable form. It was reasoned that poor performance on the criterion instrument after conventional instruction could be due to the selection of the four common irrelevant principles which the subjects had never learned to reject.

Development of an Instructional Sequence

The next question was whether the findings of Piaget, Bruner and others could be used in the development of a highly structured instructional sequence, designed to enhance stable concept attainment in the content area as measured by the criterion instrument.

A seventy-two-minute instructional sequence consisting of 35 mm color slides, tape-recorded verbal statements and student response booklets was developed, based primarily upon the typical sequence that Inhelder and Piaget report subjects use in the solution of the floating bodies problem. Part I was designed to force the exclusion of the four common false principles; Part II was designed to develop the correct principle. Both parts were constructed so as to require the student to progress through the same logical sequence described by Inhelder and Piaget. The entire instructional sequence was validated in terms of Piaget's logical analysis.

Treatment Conditions

In all samples studied there were five treatment conditions: I — A no-treatment or control condition. IIA (PG) and IIB (NPG) — Instruction in only the correct principle. III (PG) and IV (NPG) — Instruction in both the exclusion of the four common false principles as well as in the correct principle.

The only difference between conditions III and IV concerns the statement of the correct verbal principle in the response booklet. The subjects in treatment group III repeatedly receive the correctly stated principle, are instructed to use it repeatedly, and are reinforced for doing so. The measured performance of this group on the concept criterion test could be due to either one of two factors. High scores would indicate that the subjects had either attained the concept or had been verbally conditioned to the correct response. Certainly one could not say that a high score indicated stable concept attainment. However, for the subjects in treatment IV there would be no such ambiguity. Since these subjects are never given the correct verbalized principle, they cannot be verbally conditioned to it. If they select the correct response they do so not on the basis of a rotely learned verbal chain but because its meaning approximates a rule they have discovered to be true. It is for the same reason that a similar difference exists between treatment conditions IIA and IIB.

Samples

Three samples were studied: (1) 97 seventh-grade students enrolled in a middle-class suburban junior high school; (2) 259 eighth-grade students enrolled in another middle-class suburban junior high school; (3) 38 college junior and senior nonscience majors enrolled in an education course at the State University of New York at Buffalo. In all samples, subjects were randomly assigned to treatment conditions.

Design

The design for the seventh-grade sample consisted of a three-way fixed analysis of covariance. The main effects were sex $\times$ school ability group $\times$ treatment condition ($2 \times 3 \times 5$). The three covariates were a general knowledge test dealing with the content area, a nine-item conservation of weight, volume, and substance test, and the short form California Test of Mental Maturity total score.

The design for the eighth-grade sample was also a three-way fixed analysis of covariance. The main effects were the same as for the seventh-grade sample. However, there were four school ability groups in this sample ($2 \times 4 \times 5$). The three covariates were the general knowledge test, the conservation test, and the Lorge–Thorndike total score.

In the adult sample, the design consisted of a two-way fixed analysis of covariance. The main effects were sex $\times$ treatment (2×5). Only two covariates, the conservation test and the general knowledge test, were used, since all subjects were assumed to belong to one upper ability level.

Behavioral Hypotheses

The following behavioral hypotheses were made, based upon a consideration of appropriate literature:

Hypothesis 1. There will be an overall significant relationship between performance scores on the pretests (covariates) and the criterion instrument.

Hypothesis 2. The performance of males will be significantly higher than the performance of females on all measures except the intelligence test.

Hypothesis 3. High ability groups will exhibit significantly better performance on all measures than will low ability groups.

Hypothesis 4. There will be no significant difference between the mean performance of the two partially treated groups, which have not been taught to reject the four irrelevant principles, and the control group with respect to the criterion instrument.

Hypothesis 5. The two fully treated groups, which have been taught both the rejection of the four irrelevant principles and the correct principle, will perform significantly better than the control group on the criterion instrument.

Hypothesis 6. The two full instructional treatments will be most effective for the adult group and least effective for the seventh-grade group. The degree of effectiveness will be judged in terms of the magnitude of the contrasts between means of the treatment groups and the control group on the criterion instrument.

Results

Hypothesis 1: Value of the Covariates. The covariates were found to function effectively for only the eighth-grade sample. There was a 10.89 per cent reduction in the variance of the criterion instrument by the three covariates. Nearly all of this total variance (8.92 per cent) was accounted for by the general knowledge test. On the basis of these findings the analyses of the data from the seventh-grade and adult samples were carried out as exact analyses of variance, while the analysis of the data from the eighth-grade sample was carried out as an exact analysis of covariance.

Hypothesis 2: Sex Effects.   As predicted, no significant sex effects were found on the intelligence measure for the seventh- and eighth-grade sample. Significant sex differences were found on the conservation and general knowledge tests in the eighth-grade sample, though, in both cases, the magnitude of these effects was slight. The expected sex differences on the other measures were not observed in either the seventh-grade or the adult sample, and no significant sex differences were observed in the eighth-grade sample on the criterion instrument.

Hypothesis 3: Ability Group Effects.   Ability group effects could not be studied in the adult sample. However, significant and large ability group effects were found on all instruments for the eighth-grade sample, and also for all instruments except the general knowledge test in the seventh-grade sample.

Hypothesis 4: Ineffectiveness of Partial Treatment.   The prediction that the two partial treatment conditions would be entirely ineffective in developing stable concept attainment was fully confirmed in only the seventh-grade sample. Here, the subjects in both partial treatment conditions did not perform significantly better than the control group. However, it should be pointed out that no significant overall treatment conditions were found for this sample.

In the eighth-grade sample there was no significant difference between the partial treatment (IIB–NPG) group and the control group on the criterion instrument. However, the partial treatment (IIA–PG) group did perform significantly better than the control group on the instrument. Verbal conditioning of the correct response may have been the reason for the apparent success of this treatment condition.

In the adult sample the two partial treatment conditions, contrary to the prediction, proved to be quite effective. The subjects in both partial treatment conditions (IIB–NPG and IIA–PG) performed significantly better than the control group subjects on the criterion test. In all cases, the magnitude of the significant effects was quite large. However, it should be pointed out that the magnitude of the contrasts between means of the two fully treated groups and the control group was even larger.

Hypothesis 5: Effectiveness of the Full Treatment Conditions.   The prediction that the two full treatment conditions would prove effective in improving performance on the criterion and application tests was confirmed for the eighth-grade and adult but not the seventh-grade sample. As judged by the magnitude of contrasts between means of the treated and control groups, the two full treatment conditions proved most effective for the adults, somewhat effective for the eighth-graders, and *not* effective for the seventh-graders. In both the eighth-grade and the adult sample, the two full treatment conditions proved to be more effective than the partial treatment conditions. In the seventh-grade sample none of the four treatment conditions proved to be effective.

Hypothesis 6: Effectiveness of the Instructional Sequence for Various Age Levels.   As predicted, the two full treatment conditions were most effective for the adult group and least effective for the seventh-grade group. The instructional sequence proved to be highly effective for the adult sample, moderately effective for the eighth-grade sample, and completely ineffective for the seventh-grade sample.

It should be pointed out that the difference in the effectiveness of the full instructional sequence for the seventh- and eighth-grade samples was probably not due to a greater pretreatment knowledge of the correct principle by the eighth-graders since the observed means of their respective control groups on the criterion instrument are nearly identical (1.64 versus 1.66).

It should also be pointed out that for both the adult and eighth-grade samples the full treatment condition (III–PG) was more effective than the full treatment (IV–NPG) condition.

Summary and Conclusion

This study was concerned with the application of basic psychological research to the design and structure of an instructional sequence. Most of the structure and direction has been gained from Inhelder and Piaget's account and logical analysis of the natural and spontaneous sequence children use to solve the floating bodies problem. The reported research of many other investigators has been used to relate student characteristics, other than age, to performance in the task.

A series of instruments was developed, two of which were based on earlier instruments used by psychologists conducting cognition studies. The concept–criterion test, which grew out of a consideration of Smedslund's work, was intended to be a rigorous instrument capable of identifying subjects who have attained the concept in a stable form.

Early use of the criterion instrument suggested that conventional instruction does not lead to the conceptualization of the principle of "specific gravity." This conclusion is apparent from several sources, but emerges most clearly from the results of sixty-one college students enrolled in a physical science course.

The concept criterion instrument was used to assess the effectiveness of an instructional sequence which was developed and tested in public schools. It was found to be moderately successful for eighth-grade students and highly effective for adults in terms of both immediate and delayed criterion test performance. The results suggest that part of the effectiveness of the instructional sequence may be related to the effort made to teach students to reject the common false principles before being introduced to the correct principle.

It should be noted that the instructional sequence does nothing that a typical effective classroom teacher could not do, and could not do better! However, the full instructional sequence does contain material the teacher would probably not teach. Teachers have not generally been aware of the serious problems which arise in connection with the false perceptual principles commonly used by students in the floating bodies problem. Consequently, little effort has been made to combat the notions which arise from the highly dominant perceptual features of the problem. It would seem that instruction in the much less apparent and more abstract conceptual rule, without an effort to force the logical exclusion of the dominant false perceptual rules, is not sufficient.

One cannot but suspect that this same problem exists with respect to many of the constructs which are stated as content objects in science courses. Traditionally we have not been consistently aware of the great dominance of direct perceptual principles, which frequently obscure the much more useful, but less obvious, conceptual principles. Further, one cannot help but suspect that the problem goes unnoticed much of the time.

It would seem wise to develop instruments similar in design and intent to Smedslund's criterion instrument. Such instruments could, perhaps, help us to more realistically assess our educational programs and methods. There is also a need to conduct further basic psychological research about specific problem solving situations, as Inhelder and Piaget, Bruner, and many others have done. But if this type of work is to have any lasting educational significance, then it is even more necessary that an attempt be made to apply what has been and will be learned about human concept and rule learning in psychological laboratories, to the development of instructional methods and techniques designed to be used in real classroom situations.

Learning and Thinking in the School Situation

■■■■ E. A. PEEL

In this article, the author, who is a British educational psychologist, explores implications of Piaget's theory for learning in science, mathematics, history, and geography, and concludes that his basic ideas are valid for all school subjects.

The position in Great Britain with respect to applying Piaget's psychological theory to education is slightly different from what it is in the U. S. A. In the first place, most of the people who have studied Piaget's psychology have been educators as well as psychologists. Secondly, our contact with the teachers is different. We have been slower in forming curriculum study groups on the large scale, but now it is different as seen by the Nuffield Foundation's interest in the curriculum and by the work of the Southampton mathematical study group. On the other hand, we may have much closer personal contact with our teachers, which is usually made through courses given by the local authorities in which they invite someone knowledgeable to lecture about the findings of research into children's thinking. Usually such a person will illustrate the findings and ideas by reference to school situations and then leave it to the teacher to relate the results and ideas to his classroom work.

In the comments which follow, I shall begin with a few educational consequences of the Geneva researches and then follow with some ideas and inquiries resulting from my own work at Birmingham.

The revisions suggested in the teaching of science in primary schools and those for teaching mathematics in the infant and the lower part of the elementary schools are not concerned with any desire to accelerate, but to give the appropriate teaching at the right stage in the belief that ultimately the understanding of science and mathematics will be bettered. This is very true of infant school mathematics where conservation experiments are quite well-known and where teaching on their basis is becoming more evident. The use of the apparatus of Cuisenaire, Dienes, and Shaw is independent of the influence of Piaget, but all contribute to the same end of greater enlightenment gained from experience and manipulation.

Teaching the beginnings of science in primary schools illustrates well how much we can learn from experiments on thinking. Nature study and weather study can be made the experiential basis for promoting the child's power to classify and cross-classify. Both aspects of the child's experiences mentioned earlier by Piaget, namely physical action on the material (collection

• • • • • • • •

SOURCE: Adapted and abridged from the *Journal of Research in Science Teaching*, 2 (1964), 227–229. (With permission of the author and the *Journal*.)

and examining) and logical-mathematical action in the formation of classes (inclusions, exclusions, orderings, etc.), are developed.

But this is not enough. Most of the basic concepts of science do not mature in their invariant conserved form until the child is well beyond nine years of age. Thus, weight is not conceived as something independent of shape and substance until nine or ten years, and volume as cubic capacity until eleven or twelve years.

Hence, science education in primary schools should be based on experience leading to the formation of concepts. As this experience becomes more systematized, the basic concepts of weight, volume, time, speed, etc. are established. Then within the framework of the "invariants" the child groups, systematizes, and selects his observations to lead to the induction of concepts and laws. The stage of taking the invariants for granted and seeing nature in their terms is concrete thinking. I would call it describer-thinking.

The last stage of the induction of laws and formation of further concepts constitutes a bridge in thought between description and explanation. This bridge is important in the development of science thinking in the junior and high school pupil. We may not have made our study of this bridge explicit enough, although it is implicit in Piaget's developmental system. Ideas of concept formation and attainment and generalization and abstraction are all involved.

Extension of a concept was brought out in Piaget's example of the observer of a moving object. Once we consider the situation where the observer is also moving, the concept of absolute motion becomes that of relative motion. We see that the concept has become more general and to that extent has the potentiality of a more powerful explanatory tool. As I see it, physics is primarily concerned with the general and not with the abstract. This is a major distinction between it and mathematics which is primarily concerned with abstraction. We see the increased generalization of physical concepts in the study of motion. The normal sequence of study is speed, velocity (compounding speed and direction), relative velocity (direction and magnitude), and the special theory of relativity, all of which are at the same level of abstraction but show a progression in generalization. We have not examined this problem of concept generalization sufficiently. The bridging operation by concepts seems very important everywhere, but particularly so in England where transition from primary to secondary education takes place at eleven years of age, just when concept formation is beginning to be most significant.

The formation of concepts as opposed to their attainment poses yet another problem at this stage of transition between describer and explainer thinking. Most of our sensitive tests of concept formation are given to younger children. Where they are given to older groups they are bound to test a growing element of concept attainment, since by now the student has available the logical machinery of classifying and relation-finding and most of the basic first-order concepts required for action and perception. But we should find out a little more about concept formation in adolescence, particularly with material which does not lend itself easily to first-order conceptualizations. The use of verbal data can provide such conditions.

In mature scientific thinking, what goes on is a mixture of concept formation and concept attainment. Superficially, Mendel's discovery of the hereditary laws looks like concept formation, but in fact, Mendel was an experienced horticulturist and gardener and had already half-formed notions about parent–offspring relations. Another instance can be seen in the deciphering of the Mycenaen script of Linear B. We can be sure that mature scientific thinking involves both attainment and formation of concepts. An important question still remains unanswered. Is the concept formation of the adolescent different in quality from that of the child? It would seem that by the end of childhood, he already has available the operations of adding and multiplying classes and the repertoire of many of the concepts required for ordinary action and perception. In order to achieve this command of concepts he has in early childhood had to discover both the experiential criteria which form the basis of the concept and the laws of class addition and multiplication.

In adolescence, he will have the latter, but in any wholly novel situation he will have to find criteria anew. So it looks as if concept formation in adolescence and adult life differs from concept formation in childhood only in that the hierarchical and multiplicative structures of the logic of classes and relations are available. But new criteria of action (mental and physical) and perception may still have to be constructed at all ages.

It is interesting to speculate how the ideas put forward by Inhelder and Piaget in their *The Growth of Logical Thinking From Childhood to Adolescence* in connection with science and material situations may apply to the learning of history and geography. The data of history are not like those of science, consisting essentially of the intentions behind the actions of people in the past. Therefore, the first bridge the teacher of history has to cross is that between present and past. He accounts for the past by whatever knowledge he can use from the child's present experience and by whatever concrete historical material he has available. In this way he builds up the right historical data. This stage would correspond with what I have called describer-thinking. But there is more to history than this. Its course can be viewed as a series of equilibria and disequilibria between the acts and intentions of men. The mature student of history is sensitive to the fine interplays and balance in such situations as the events in 1939 leading up to the Second World War or in the events of England among the working classes before and after the Reform Act of 1832. A more recent interplay of forces between men was seen in the recent situation in Cuba.

The balance of powers, physical or human, involves the two important principles of cancellation and compensation which form an essential part of Piaget's account of adolescent thinking. Some investigations carried out recently using short passages of history demonstrated that this sensitivity is, under present educational circumstances, a characteristic of mid-adolescence.

Geography also reveals the same balance between environmental and behavioral forces. Thus, wherever mankind has upset the balance of nature in his attempts to produce more food, etc., the same interplay of canceling and compensating can be revealed. When pupils are confronted with such situations as tests of thinking in geography, as we are doing at Birmingham, we have found again that coordinated judgments do not appear to be widespread until mid-adolescence.

It seems, in conclusion, that whatever school subject we are concerned with — science, mathematics, history, or geography — and whatever level we are concerned with it, something very near to the basic ideas put forward by Piaget, Inhelder, and their coworkers, or ideas developing from them, seems essential for a helpful account of the pupil's growth of learning and thinking.

Training Techniques for the Concept of Conservation

■■■ E. MERMELSTEIN / E. CARR / D. MILLS / J. SCHWARTZ

Science educators will be particularly interested in the results of a study of the efficacy of four training techniques for inducing the concept of conservation of substance. The negative findings for all four techniques tend to confirm Piaget's view and lead the investigators to speculate on the basic differences between cumulative life experiences and contrived experiences of the kind described.

Increased emphasis on revision of the mathematics curriculum and the introduction of modern mathematics as early as kindergarten has led to controversy over the most appropriate time to teach the concept of number. As a result, a renewed interest in Piaget's experiments on the child's conception of number has become evident.

According to Piaget, the concept of number is predicated on the concept
• • • • • • • •
SOURCE: Adapted and abridged from the *Alberta Journal of Educational Research*, 13 (1967), 185–200. (With permission of the authors and the *Journal*.)

of conservation of substance. The attainment of the concept of conservation of substance enables the child to recognize that the "amount" or "number" remains the same in spite of spatial rearrangements.

Piaget maintains that specific training or teaching plays little or no role in the acquisition of this concept. He suggests that the child attains the concept of conservation of substance by interaction with his "total" environment. In contrast, Bruner (1964), Sigel and Roeper, (unpub.), Beilin (1965), and Smedslund (1961c) suggest that one can teach or induce the concept of conservation of substance in the child.

Because there are theoretical reasons for believing that the concept of conservation of substance is relevant to a child's number development, the question arises whether or not children can be taught the concept of conservation of substance.

Theory

Acquisition of the concept of conservation of substance implies a modification of the child's intellectual structure. According to Piaget, this modification occurs as a consequence of all the child's activity in contrast to specific short-term training.

"All" of the child's activity refers to two kinds of experiences: physical and logical–mathematical. Whereas physical experiences refer to knowledge acquired by the child's manipulation of objects (i.e., playing with chips), logical–mathematical experiences refer to knowledge acquired as a consequence of manipulation (i.e., awareness that two rows of six chips each have the same number despite rearrangement). Although it is apparent that physical experiences are a necessary condition for the acquisition of concepts and indeed short term exposure may be adequate, logical–mathematical experiences require a longer period of time because properties or concepts refer not to objects but rather to relationships to objects. Knowledge acquired as a consequence of manipulation implies an awareness of the spatial relationships between objects. These spatial relationships cannot be acquired or induced in short-term training.

Obviously if these relationships are acquired over a period of time, the contention that short-term training on a few specific tasks would induce conservation is as specious as the contention that specific training on a limited number of tasks from IQ tests would improve intelligence. Increased performance on these IQ tests as a consequence of training does not necessarily imply increased intelligence. So too, specific training on conservation tasks does not guarantee the acquisition of the concept of conservation.

Although Piagetian theory and specific training are incompatible, some of the literature reported below suggests that intellectual structures can be modified over a relatively short period of time. The problem of this study, then, is to provide more evidence on the question of whether or not mental structures can be modified over a relatively short period of time.

Related Literature

The literature appears equivocal as to the feasibility of inducing the concept of conservation. Consistent with Piagetian theory, Wohlwill (1960b) has been unsuccessful in inducing conservation of number. Similarly, Beilin and Franklin (1962) have been unsuccessful in inducing conservation of area. Prager (1962), using her own class, was also unable to induce conservation of substance. These studies seem to suggest that regardless of the kind of conservation that one tries to induce, in general such training is not successful.

In testing for the presence of conservation, rather than attempting to induce it, Mermelstein and Shulman (1967) found no difference in performance on conservation of substance tasks between those children who had formal schooling and those who did not. Similarly, Goodnow's study (1966) with Hong Kong children and Price–Williams's study (1962) with African bush children indicate no difference in performance on conservation of substance tasks between children who had and those who did not have formal schooling. These studies suggest that even more generalized training such as formal schooling does not necessarily modify intellectual structures.

On the other hand, although Smedslund (1961c) reports negative results in attempting to induce conservation of weight, in another study in which he introduces the idea of cognitive conflict, he appears to have had some success in inducing the concept of conservation of substance. Similarly, Gruen (1966), Bruner (1964), Wallach and Sprott (1964), Sigel and Roeper (unpub.), utilizing various training techniques, induced various kinds of conservation.

If specific training does make a difference in acquiring the concept of conservation, the present investigators feel that Smedslund's cognitive conflict theory provides the greatest promise for success because of its similarity to Piaget's theory of adaptation. Briefly, cognitive conflict theory involves a set of competing responses in a given situation. This set of competing responses induces a conflict which reorganizes the intellectual structures and insures conservation. Piaget's discussion on strategies to decrease egocentric thought in the child provides a good illustration of the similarity of the cognitive conflict position and the adaptation position.

Furthermore, both the adaptation and the cognitive conflict processes employ the disequilibrium–equilibrium model. In each instance, the child moves toward a state of temporary equilibrium from a state of disequilibrium. Thus, similarities in the two processes would suggest that training procedures based on a cognitive conflict position may be in part successful.

A translation of Smedslund's theoretical position into practice as well as a translation of Bruner's, Beilin's, and Sigel's theoretical position are described in the procedure section.

These studies constitute a representative sample of the various theoretical positions described in the literature which claim success in training on conservation.

Whereas Smedslund's theoretical position is consistent with Piaget, Sigel, Beilin, and Bruner present arguments for inducing conservation which are either wholly inconsistent or only partially consistent with Piagetian theory.

Sigel's argument is predicated on the assumption that one must base the learning of complex structures on simpler structures. He claims that acquisition of conservation of substance follows the acquisition of simpler structures such as multiple labeling, multiple classification, multiple relations, and reversibility. More specifically, he maintains that training in multiple labeling, multiple classification, multiple relations, and reversibility, in that order, should facilitate the acquisition of conservation.

Although Sigel's procedures indeed are necessary conditions for conservation of substance, they are not, however, sufficient conditions. Sigel's training assumes that, once the prerequisites for conservation have been met, the concept of conservation necessarily has been attained. Sigel assumes further that because the material is presented in a prescribed manner, the child will assimilate the material in the corresponding order. Such a claim is not consistent with Piagetian theory for, if the child constructs his reality, it does not necessarily follow that he will assimilate the material in the same manner presented.

Whereas Sigel's training originated in part from Piagetian theory, Beilin's training procedure appears to violate Piagetian theory. Beilin's training procedure, verbal rule instruction, provides the child with a statement of a rule to be applied to the problem in each instance of an unsuccessful trial response on a conservation task.

The use of a rule in a training technique appears inconsistent with Piagetian theory. To begin with, the egocentric nature of the child's thought seriously hampers his ability to adopt another point of view. Secondly, the syncretic nature of the child's mental structure with its behavioral manifestations of juxtaposition prevents him from accurately perceiving the rule. Further, Mermelstein and Shulman's research (1967) indicated that children under nine years of age perceive only the gist of questions or the events of the questions. It follows from this that two sentences which stress "amount," for example, but in very different ways, will be perceived as similar by the child. This casts doubt on the child's ability to understand a "specific" rule.

Similarly, Bruner's contentions on language training also appear to be inconsistent with Piagetian theory. Bruner's training position is predicated on the assumption that focusing on the linguistic aspect of a situation will decrease the strength of the perceptual cues resulting in a mental structure which is a function of the language activated. This differs markedly from Piagetian theory in that Piaget believes that mental structure precedes language development.

To recapitulate, because the concept of conservation derives from Piagetian theory and further because the rationale for the Sigel, the Beilin, and the Bruner training are judged to be inconsistent with Piagetian theory it was hypothesized that these training procedures would not be effective. On the other hand, because of the greater congruence of Smedslund's position to Piagetian theory, it was hypothesized that such training would be more successful than the other three training procedures.

Objectives

Accordingly, the objectives of this study were to ascertain whether various training procedures can influence the acquisition of the concept of conservation of substance. In view of these objectives the following hypotheses were forwarded:

1. A significant difference exists in the performance in conservation tasks between children who had cognitive conflict training and those who had no training.
2. No significant difference exists in the performance on conservation tasks between children who had multiple classification training and those who had no training.
3. No significant difference exists in the performance on conservation tasks between children who had verbal rule training and those who had no training.
4. No significant difference exists in the performance on conservation tasks between children who had language activation training and those who had no training.

Method

Subjects

In order to assess the effects of various training procedures on the attainment of the concept of conservation of substance a sample of 120 kindergarten children from the Long Island area was selected for study. Five-year-olds were chosen because the writings of Piaget indicate that children of this age generally have not attained the concept of conservation of substance. These primary school children were between 5.0 and 6.2 years of age. The subjects were randomly assigned to four training conditions; cognitive conflict, language activation, multiple classification, and verbal rule instruction. This random assignment was made with two restrictions. First, equal numbers of males and females were assigned to each condition. Second, nonwhite children were excluded from the population. The purpose of these restrictions was to control the possible sex and ethnic effects. Twenty subjects were drawn for each of the four training groups and for the two control groups.

The apparatus for all the training techniques conformed in principle to the requirements of each training procedure. Although the present study may not be regarded as an explicit replication of the Smedslund, Bruner, Sigel or Beilin training techniques, it is felt to be a fair test of the principles which underlie these techniques. In other words, while there were some slight variations in procedure to make the experimental tasks comparable, the basic assumptions stated by these investigations were not violated.

Procedure

Description of the Pretest and Scoring of Responses

In order to ascertain the effects of pretesting one control group was given a pretest whereas the other control group and the four training groups were not. The possibility of the pretest serving as an additional training session or differentially affecting the various training techniques necessitated its elimination from the training conditions.

The pretest task employed the collapsible box and twenty poker chips. As the experimenter set up ten chips down one side of the top of the box the subject simultaneously set up ten chips in one-to-one correspondence with those of the experimenter. After the experimenter verbally established that he and the child had equal numbers of chips, one row of chips was collapsed by the experimenter, and hence, perceptually distorted. The subject was then asked whether the chips on the collapsed side were still the same amount as those on the stationary side. If the subject's response was positive and his explanation indicated understanding, that is, if he realized the chips merely changed position, he was scored as a conserver. A subject who answered affirmatively without an adequate explanation, or a subject who answered negatively was scored as a nonconserver.

Training Procedures

The four training conditions, cognitive conflict (Smedslund), multiple classification (Sigel), verbal rule instruction (Beilin), and language activation (Bruner), each began with free play and were followed by eight training sessions, two per week, for approximately ten minutes each. The first training session was devoted entirely to introducing the subjects to the red, white, and blue poker chips and allowing them to manipulate them in any way they chose. In each of the successive eight training sessions for the first two minutes, the subjects were permitted to play with the chips. The remainder of each session was devoted to formal training.

Smedslund: Cognitive Conflict. The cognitive conflict training involved the collapsible box and twenty poker chips. Following the free play, where the subjects were allowed to manipulate the chips, the group of subjects received ten chips of one color and the experimenter received ten chips of the same color. In the first session, red chips were employed, in the second session blue, and in the third white, with this color order being maintained throughout the remaining sessions. As the experimenter placed a chip on one side of the top of the box, the subjects simultaneously placed another chip next to it until all twenty chips were in one-to-one correspondence. Following the placement of each pair of chips, the experimenter asked the subjects questions such as, "Are there the same amount of chips on both sides of the box? Do the children have the same amount as the teacher? How do you know?" If the subjects did not realize the equality of the two rows of chips, they were encouraged to count the chips. After five sessions of setting up the chips in one-to-one correspondence, the task was altered. In the next three sessions, after the chips were similarly set up in one-to-one correspondence and the sameness of the two rows of chips was established, the experimenter moved the switch hinged on the side of the box and one of the rows of chips fell to the center of the collapsed side. The subjects were asked, "Are there still the same amount of chips on both sides?"

Sigel: Multiple Classification. The multiple classification training also involved twenty poker chips and a collapsible box. Free play with the chips preceded the formal training. The training was divided into four phases:

1. multiple labeling,
2. multiple classification,
3. multiple relations,
4. reversibility.

For the first four training sessions, one training session was devoted to each phase while each of the remaining four sessions encompassed all four phases.

In multiple labeling training, the experimenter initiated discussion which elicited the naming of the poker chips in a variety of ways; viz., a poker chip can also be a checker or toy money. This "naming" was clarified for the subjects by the experimenter suggesting that a person could have many names; viz., mother, teacher, woman, wife, and others.

In the multiple classification training, the experimenter initiated discussion which elicited from the subjects the common properties of the chips; i.e., all the chips have color, shape, purpose, texture, and size.

In the multiple relations training, the experimenter initiated discussion which led the subjects to understand that a chip can be two things at the same time. That is, a chip can have a color and shape at the same time. The question that was posed is, "Can you think of two things this poker chip can be at the same time?" Since a different colored poker chip was used at each session, three relationships were established: (1) round and red, (2) round and blue, and (3) round and white.

In the reversibility training, the collapsible box and twenty chips were employed. The experimenter and the subjects set up the chips in one-to-one correspondence so that the subjects could see the sameness of the two rows of chips. After the subjects responded positively to the question, "Are there the same amount of chips on both sides?", the experimenter collapsed one side of the box. Again, the subjects were asked whether there was the same amount of chips on both sides of the box and why. An informal explanation to establish the equivalence of both sides was then provided by the experimenter.

It should be pointed out that although superficial similarities exist between Smedslund's cognitive conflict training and the reversibility training of Sigel, they differ in that in the Sigel reversibility training, the equality of the rows of chips and the subsequent collapse of one row was accomplished in one training session whereas Smedslund's training procedure had four training sessions on the equality of chips prior to collapse of one row of chips. In addition, the Sigel technique provided explanations for the equivalence of both rows after the deformation, whereas the Smedslund technique did not.

Beilin: Verbal Rule Instruction.   The verbal rule instruction, as well as multiple classification, employed the collapsible box and twenty chips. Following the free play, the group of subjects and the experimenter each received five chips of one color. As in the cognitive conflict training, the chips were set up in one-to-one correspondence and their equivalence was established. But in contrast to the cognitive conflict training, the experimenter immediately collapsed one side of the box and asked whether there were the same amount of chips on both sides. Regardless of the positive or negative responses of the subjects, the experimenter said the following rule while manipulating the box accordingly: "Now I am moving them. See, they are standing in a different place, but there are as many chips as before. They only look different. See, I can put them back just the way they were, so you see, there are still the same number as before because I did not add any chips or take away any chips. I only moved them." In the next session, twenty chips of the same color used in the preceding session were used, and in subsequent sessions, for each color, first ten and then twenty chips were used.

Bruner: Language Activation. The language activation training involved three wooden boxes, each with two transparent parallel sides, two of which were identical, while the third was the same height but wider than the others, a screen, and twenty chips. Following the free play, using a one-to-one correspondence technique, the subjects filled one box with ten poker chips while the experimenter simultaneously filled the other identical box. The third box was placed with the two filled boxes behind the screen so that only their tops could be seen. The experimenter poured the chips from one of the filled boxes into the third unfilled, wider box. The child was asked whether there was the same amount of chips in the newly filled box as in the remaining previously filled box. The screen was removed and the subject was again asked whether the boxes held the same amount. Since one box was wider, the chips in it were spread out, and were therefore perceptually different from those in the narrower box. This training procedure was repeated for each of the three color chips in subsequent sessions.

Post-Tests and Scoring of Responses

In order to test the effects of various training treatments, two nonverbal tasks in which the law of conservation of substance was violated, and one Piagetian test of conservation of substance were employed. Conservation of substance tasks were utilized because the previous investigators suggested that this concept could be induced utilizing their approach. Each subject was tested individually. The sequences in which the tasks were presented were counterbalanced to control for order effects. The criteria for the attainment of the concept of conservation of substance were Stage 3 responses on any two of the three tasks.

Tasks

1. Nonverbal Continuous Task. The first nonverbal experiment, the magic experiment for conservation of a continuous substance, consisted of first allowing each child to satisfy himself that two 150-milliliter beakers contained the same quantity of liquid. The contents of one of the beakers were then poured into a 1,000-milliliter jar which it apparently filled. The child gestures and reactions were noted. Gestures of surprise, puzzlement, smile, "wow" were scored at Stage 3, presence of conservation, whereas absence of observable changes in behavior were scored at Stage 1, absence of conservation. The illusion was created by surreptitiously opening a valve connecting the empty 1,000-milliliter jar to one which was full and hidden behind the screen. The experimenter controlled the rate at which the visible jar filled.

2. *Nonverbal Discrete Task.*   The second nonverbal magic experiment, for a discontinuous substance, again violated the law on conservation; it assumed that a child who had attained the concept would recognize the violation. Two seemingly identical wooden boxes, one with a false bottom, and twenty-six gumballs were employed. Each child was told to put eight gumballs into the wooden box with the false bottom, one by one, as the experimenter put eight gumballs into the second wooden box. Under the false bottom in the child's box were an additional ten gumballs. The child and the experimenter both poured the contents of their wooden boxes into two separate containers. When the contents of the child's box were poured, a latch released the additional ten gumballs. The child's reactions and comments to the gumballs in the containers were noted. Scoring of these responses was similar to those for the first post-test for continuous substance.

3. *Verbal Piagetian Task.*   The third task was a typical Piagetian verbal test for conservation of discrete substance. Each child was told to put eight gumballs into a 150-milliliter beaker, one by one, at the same time the experimenter put gumballs into another 150-milliliter beaker. The contents of one beaker were then poured into a 50-milliliter graduated cylinder, while the contents of the second beaker were poured into a 600-milliliter beaker. The child was then asked whether the quantities in each were the same.

The subjects in the four training conditions and two control conditions were tested one week, two months and six months after the last training session.

Results

Attempts to test hypotheses of "no difference" are replete with logical and statistical hazards. There are some who maintain that to demonstrate such a state is impossible. Others simply consider it extremely difficult. In presenting these results, it shall be understood that when the confirmation of a hypothesis of "no difference" is suggested, it is to be interpreted in the following way: The hypothesis that a large difference is demonstrable in this given situation is significantly improbable. Although this is awkward language, it remains appropriate to the objectives of this research and to the demands of statistical theory. When the research hypothesis is, in fact, one of equality, it would seem quite inaccurate to couch it in terms of an inequality only for purposes of statistical expediency.

In testing hypotheses of no difference we are primarily concerned with minimizing the likelihood of accepting this hypothesis when in fact there is a difference. In other words, we wish to minimize this probability of committing a Type II error. One way to minimize this probability is by fixing the alpha level of significance for hypotheses of no difference at 0.10. Fixing the level of significance at 0.10 rather than the normal level of 0.05 for a fixed N and for a fixed alternative reduces the probability of committing a Type II error. If, for this fixed alpha level of 0.10, we still have no reason to reject the hypothesis of no difference, the likelihood of rejecting a false hypothesis is improved. When testing hypotheses which predict differences, however, we return to the more commonly utilized 0.05 level of significance.

Since our data were clearly categorical, the chi-square statistic was utilized. The percentage of agreement between three judges on categorizing the responses on the three tasks was 90 per cent. The average number of training sessions was seven for all training conditions.

A 2 × 6 chi-square for each post-test session indicated that children who had training did not outperform children who did not have training, and further, that the pretested control group did not outperform the nonpretested control group. Accordingly, the cognitive conflict hypothesis was rejected, whereas the other three hypotheses were confirmed.

Discussion

Not only is it necessary to explain the failure of Smedslund's cognitive conflict training technique for conservation, but it is also necessary to explain why training in general for conservation appears unsuccessful. Perhaps an explanation of the criteria for demonstration of the effectiveness of training of conservation of substance is appropriate. According to Piaget (1964), for training in conservation to be effective, two criteria have to be satisfied. These are generalizability and durability. In other words, the concept which was induced not only had to transfer to other situations, but the concept should not extinguish over time. Clearly post-testing for violations of the concept of conservation over a period of six months satisfied the forementioned criteria. Whereas the criteria in these experiments satisfied Piaget's criteria, this was not the case in any of the other training studies. In Beilin's training study, the generalizability criterion for testing whether the concept was induced was extremely limited and durability criteria were not satisfied at all. Similarly, in Smedslund's and Bruner's experiments, the durability criterion was not met, whereas the generalizability criteria were limited. In Sigel's technique, although the generalizability factor was met, the durability factor was not. Because these investigators employed different criteria, it is conceivable that the success in training that Beilin, Bruner, Sigel, and Smedslund report relates not to the concept of conservation of substance as Piaget sees it, but rather to some other concept or some deformation of the concept of conservation. In support of the forementioned explanation of the consequences of not employing similar criteria, Gruen demonstrated that the different criteria and the different procedure employed by Bruner and Smedslund led to a different classification of conserving responses. Obviously then, different criteria for testing presence of the concept of conservation of substance provide explanations for the lack of success of training by any one of the training techniques.

It was mentioned earlier that the training methodology employed by Beilin, Bruner, and Sigel are generally inconsistent with the Piagetian position and that this might explain the results. This point will be elaborated on shortly. Prior to this, a further explanation is necessary to account for Smedslund's results. Although it is true that the cognitive conflict position is consistent with Piagetian theory, there is one difference which may provide an explanation of the Smedslund training results. Smedslund now suggests that the organism–object conflict which he espoused is not of sufficient moment to cause a modification of the intellectual structures. He further suggests that organism–object relation is too neutral for the child and does not or cannot create the conflict in the child. As an alternative he argues for an organism–organism conflict. In other words, a confrontation of different points of view among children is a necessary condition for modification of intellectual structures. Clearly, such a shift in position by Smedslund now makes his position identical to Piaget's rather than similar to Piaget as mentioned earlier.

Piaget's position on the syncretic nature of child thought with its behavioral manifestation of juxtaposition suggests another possible explanation of the ineffectiveness of the training. If the child's thought manifests itself by linguistic confusion such as juxtaposition, then the language dimension of the training procedure may provide an obstacle rather than facilitate acquisition of the concept. Clearly, because of the apparent ineffectiveness of the training techniques, it is likely that the language employed in the various training techniques did not facilitate acquisition of the Piagetian concept of conservation of substance. Not only is there no indication that the language provided any facilitation, but the language may have hindered acquisition of this concept. More specifically, the Sigel training technique, which required more language than the other training technique, appeared to be the least effective method for attaining the concept of conservation.

Perhaps two examples will highlight the possible interference of language in concept acquisition. A child in the first post-test on the nonverbal discrete item claimed emphatically that the marbles in both containers were the same, even though one container had thirty marbles while the other container had ten marbles (a nonconserving response). On the second post-test, this child returned to the "perceptually" more appropriate response of claiming that the marbles in both containers were not the same number (a nonconserving response). In a second example, there were several instances when children were confronted with two rows of eight chips. At first they acknowledged their equality, but when they began to count numbers of chips they lost sight of their equality and they then maintained that the rows were not equal. Consequently, it appears that the language aspect of the training may not only be inappropriately applied, but also the mere act of verbalizing may interfere with concept acquisition. Accordingly, such evidence is contrary to the position that language facilitates concept acquisition.

Because of the apparent lack of the effectiveness of various kinds of specific training, it becomes necessary to make explicit how specific training differs from cumulative life experiences which Piaget suggests are in part the determining factors for acquisition of the concept of conservation of substance.

Besides the obvious differences of time between cumulative life experiences and specific training, the ordering of experiences must be considered a relevant distinction. Clearly, the nature of any specific training involves a deliberate ordering of experiences. In other words, the sequence of presentation is paramount. The assumption here is that the child will assimilate the relevant aspects (order, etc.) of these experiences and consequently acquire the concept. But this assumption is not tenable within a Piagetian framework. For if the child constructs his reality, then it does not necessarily follow that he will assimilate the material in the order presented to him. Accordingly, it is conceivable that the child will assimilate the material in a different order and will utilize the language differently from the way it is presented (i.e., inappropriately).

Although the results lend credence to the limited utility of training and to the possible interference of language, it is clear that more research is needed to account for the reversals from one post-test to the next.

The data indicate that a number of subjects who passed the earlier post-tests, failed on later ones. These reversals need to be accounted for either by some theoretical explanation or the possible methodological difficulties described need to be answered. First, these reversals may be indicative of inherent unreliability of not only the Piagetian items, but also the Mermelstein nonverbal items. Hence the need for the construction of a reliable conservation test. Second, the reversals may be in part a function of experimenter bias over the three post-tests. Experiments controlling this factor are needed. Third, these reversals may indicate that the concept of conservation is a transitory phenomenon within a given age range; here today and gone tomorrow. The importance of longitudinal studies in this instance is obvious. Fourth, the reversals may be a function of the transitional stage, Stage II. Accordingly, there is need for a more careful examination of this period. Clearly then, not only does the choice of criteria, as Gruen and we maintain, influence the absence or presence of the concept but the items which constitute the criteria may influence the absence or presence of the concept. Thus, the problem described by Gruen may be fundamentally a theoretical and methodological one.

Conclusions

It is concluded that the "Piagetian" concept of conservation of substance, as measured by the specific criteria described, was not induced by a variety of training techniques. Further, it is suggested that language interferes with rather than facilitates acquisition of the concept of conservation of substance. Finally, it is concluded that the problems of reversals merit further exploration.

Examination of Some of Piaget's Principles in Application to Psychology of Arithmetic

■■■■ SISTER GILMARY, I.H.M.

Following a brief exposition of Piaget's theory as it applies to the area of mathematics, the author reviews the major replication studies which have been conducted in the U. S. and elsewhere. She concludes that Piaget's concept of sequential development has been validated, and examines some of the implications for teaching.

Since its publication, the *Handbook of Research on Teaching*, (Gage, 1963) has become a familiar sight tucked under the arm of almost any graduate student. There is a feature, however, or rather a failure of this book, which, in the light of modern trends in curriculum development, seems unbelievable. There is not a single study reported in it in the area of elementary-school arithmetic. Reasoning from such an omission, we might well assume that either there isn't a framework of pedagogical theory or a proper number of empirical studies in elementary arithmetic have not been done. Even a casual perusal of the "Review of Research" in the May issues of *Arithmetic Teacher*, or Brown's *Analysis of Research in the Teaching of Mathematics, 1959–1960*, or the Cooperative Research Monograph, *Research Problems in*

● ● ● ● ● ● ● ●

SOURCE: *Catholic Educational Review*, 62 (1964), 369–375. (With permission of the author and the *Review*.)

Mathematics Education (1963), would dispel the latter assumption. With respect to the first assumption, David Russell, in his book *Children's Thinking* (1956), in the ten pages concerned with mathematical concepts, lists forty different authors, who within the space of two decades, have contributed greatly to our theoretical knowledge of how children learn number and develop mathematical skills. Among such names listed are those of Buswell, Buckingham, Gunderson, Brownell, Grossnickle, and Piaget.

The work of Piaget alone, along with critiques, summaries, and replications of his experiments would justify a section in the area of elementary mathematics in the handbook. In fact, his original and ongoing experiments, combined with the findings of critical replications of his work by Elkind, Dodwell, Churchill, Wohlwill, Smedslund, Lunzer, and others, would seem to furnish an applicable psychology of arithmetic, especially in the area of the development of the concept of number in children. Indeed, as early as 1937, Piaget was demonstrating the cognitive structuring of intelligence in children through their ability to grasp the structure of mathematics. Since he was explaining the development sequence of cognition in children, his emphasis on logico–mathematic structure was not for the purpose of defining a psychology of arithmetic, but rather, to use a child's comprehension of conservation of quality, numberness, and grouping as an index of the child's own organization and process of cognition. His conclusions, however, had very practical significance for a developmentally-based psychology of learning. And, although his findings were overlooked on this continent for many years, in the present "Piagetian renaissance" we find some of his ideas of structure, stages of intellectual development in the child, mode of intuition, and process of logical operations liberally maintained by the eminent psychologist Jerome S. Bruner in his book *The Process of Education.*

Piaget's Methodology

In his early research and definitions of cognitive development in children, Piaget describes three special systems of operation which he believes are the basic thought activities: (1) composition — two separate operations may combine to produce a new unit; (2) reversibility — combined units can be separated again; (3) associativity — units may be combined in different ways to produce the same results. The child, in his various different stages of development — the sensorimotor level; concrete operations level; and formal operations level — demonstrates composition, reversibility, and associativity according to his individual stage of maturity and in that framework only. It seems inevitable that, having arrived at such conclusions as these, Piaget would find mathematics the most logical proving ground for the further development of his theories. His original experiments with number were conducted on a clinical basis with a series of individual children. The testing situation was fluid, easy, almost unstructured, and allowed for spontaneous and intuitive responses from the children. For these reasons, his experiments were somewhat of a scandal to the strict empiricists. Using, however, flasks of different heights and widths, colored liquids, beads, lollipops, sticks, and molding clay, Piaget arrived at these conclusions among others:

1. That the child learns independently and spontaneously; that when the learning is imposed it becomes entirely verbal.
2. That the child must grasp the concept of conservation of quantity before he can grasp the conservation of number and, hence, the concept of number.
3. That since number notion is a logical notion, the child needs to be able to discover relationships as a prerequisite to the formation of any concept of number.
4. That in his development of the idea of conservation, the child goes through the stages: (a) no conservation; (b) a phenomenistic, unstable sort of notion of the conservation based on the observation and manipulation of different forms and transformations; and, finally, (c) a logical, axiomatic certainty of conservation in the case of all transformations.
5. That the child attains these respective stages at the approximate ages of: (a) $4\frac{1}{2}$–5; (b) 5–6; (c) 6–$7\frac{1}{2}$.
6. That although the child can "learn to count," that is, say the number names, on a one-to-one basis for objects in a series, as early as five, he is unable to do even this if the perceptual framework is altered.
7. That mathematical concepts are built up from using concrete materials, but are independent of the actual materials used.
8. That grouping and the additive concept are developed by the child at approximately the same time as the concept of number.

But basic to the tardiness of American receptivity toward these contributions of Piaget, and yet, perhaps, giving impetus to replications of his experiments are certain shortcomings inherent in his methodology: empirical weaknesses of his designs, absence of statistics, subjectivity of data analysis and interpolation, and difficulty of style. Piaget, himself, owns that he is a difficult writer to understand, " . . . because I have written too much in the course of tackling too many problems . . . but above all, because I am not an easy writer" (Flavell, 1963). Specifically, researchers describe his reports as vague, imprecise, unstable as to definition, lacking closure as to data gathering, and overelaborate as to theory making. Nevertheless, a number of modern research specialists, reproducing his experiments under more controlled conditions, using larger numbers, and applying statistical tests of validity, have been able to identify all of the major levels Piaget describes, and this, especially with respect to his three levels of conservation, is basic to number formation.

Experimental Validation of Piaget's Theory

Dodwell (1961), working with large samplings of Canadian children from kindergarten through first grade, was able definitely to implement the Piagetian conclusion that the operation of counting is no guarantee of the concept of number or even the concept of conservation of quantity. He also concluded that Piaget is generally correct in his descriptions of operational stages, but that age levels of attainment are not so clear-cut as Piaget states; that children may also be in one Piagetian stage for one test situation and in a different one for another at one and the same time (Dodwell, 1960). As a result, likewise, of replications of Piaget's clinical methods and through standardization of a group test employing drawings, Dodwell also concludes that Piaget's tests do give insight into the cognitive processes of the child even in a relatively fluid situation, although they would, of themselves, naturally lack demonstrable consistency (Dodwell, 1961).

Feigenbaum (1963), agreeing likewise with Piaget's stages of conservation (although he qualifies the third stage as "Conservation and Quantifying Coordination"), concludes that these stages are not age-related but are merely descriptions of general trends. Furthermore, using ninety children from both Chicago and Detroit, Feigenbaum demonstrates statistically that the grasp of conservation varies directly with measurable intelligence. He makes the point further, that both the degree of intelligence and the effect of practice from one set of problems in achievement on another were factors too often disregarded by Piaget.

Elkind (1961b) testing also the factor of intelligence, by administering tests of conservation of number and of continuous and discontinuous quantity, to four-to-seven-year-old children, found that correlations between the conservation scores and the subtest scores on the Wechsler Intelligence Scale for Children, although generally positive, were not consistently significant. Moreover, in almost all of his experiments, Elkind's findings closely approximate those of Piaget.

Wohlwill (1960b), in an attempt to bridge the gap between the loosely constructed situations used by Piaget and experimental evidence, and also seeking to explain his own findings through behavioristic interpretations, did a scalogram analysis of the development of the concept of number as manifested by his own experimental subjects. He maintains: " . . . the results of our study confirm . . . the theoretical views of Piaget in demonstrating the existence of a relatively uniform developmental sequence in the area of number concept." Wohlwill is also very positive in his conclusion that his own findings contradict the negative findings of Estes (1956), who presented a brief, three-page report of entirely negative findings. Estes designed her experiment entirely upon the structure of the three tasks mentioned by Piaget in a short article published in the *Scientific American* in 1953, rather than on his original set of tasks clearly explained in his book, *The Child's Conception of Number* (1952a). Furthermore, she lists only two other references for her study, neither of them directly concerned with number, and only one of them experimental in nature. L'Abate (1962) and Flavell (1963), likewise, point out some of the shortcomings of Estes' replicatory study: restricted age samples, failure to follow faithfully the tasks proposed by Piaget, and a generally inimical attitude.

L'Abate (1962), on the other hand, using 170 children drawn on the basis of a table of random numbers from kindergarten through fifth grade, and using a picture story projective technique, reports conclusions supportive of the views of Piaget.

Thus, with the exception of Estes, the American authors listed above, along with British authors Churchill, Lunzer, and Lovell, and Smedslund of Scandanavia, are in accord with Piaget's earlier interpretations of stages of mental structuring, systems of operations, concept of conservation, and his view that mathematical concepts in children derive from an appreciation of the significance of the operations performed with sensoriperceptual materials. These same authors, of course, point out that the specific stages and levels of operation are neither rigid nor mutually exclusive, and are generally applicable to children at much earlier ages than Piaget so judged.

Piaget, in his more contemporary reports, shows a similar realization: "But progressive construction does not seem to depend on maturation, because the achievements hardly correspond to a particular age. Only the order of succession is constant" (1961).

Implication for Teaching Number

Thus, the implications of both the validated findings and the unquestioned conclusions of Piaget are of particular importance in any attempt to formulate a basic psychology of the learning of number. His first and sixth conclusions, listed above, furnish the psychological rationale for the need of the child to learn by discovery. His conclusions with respect to the stages of conservation and also with respect to the use of concrete materials are basic to the need of the child to experience number in natural situations, to manipulate and observe transformation in the use of exploratory materials. His description of the three systems of operations which he believes are basic thought activities, along with his validated conclusions that children do pass through successive stages, though not at the same time, are fairly ample warranty for the so-called "grouping on an uneven front."

By this we mean that, since children demonstrate composition, reversibility, and associativity according to their individual stage of intellectual maturity, whether it is that of the sensorimotor level, the concrete operations level or the formal operations level, all may be exploring the same number relations in the same classroom, at the same time, but each at his own depth.

For this reason, child-manipulative materials will continue to play a large part in the classroom arithmetic laboratory of the future. Such instructional materials, if used under direction and if they are themselves of a nature to foster correct mathematical ideas, have the greatest potential for the younger child, since as Piaget notes of child thought, "It is nearer to action than ours" (1928).

But in all this accent on the growth of mathematical ideas as related to the development of the child, the teacher is most significant. Children will not develop mathematical knowledge and quantitative thinking in a haphazard and totally unstructured environment. The structuring and directing of both the environment and the motives, interests, and experience of each child depends on the skill of the teacher. It is the teacher who directs discovery through furnishing the properly geared materials and through asking the leading questions. It is the teacher who arouses the interest through the initial use of real life situations. And finally, it is the teacher who assists the child to express his discovery in some action, word, or symbol, depending on that child's developmental level. And, it is probably only the skillful teacher who has the professional perceptiveness to recognize the nature of that specific level.

A Comparison of Two Techniques for Using Visual–Tactual Devices to Teach Exponents and Nondecimal Bases in Elementary School Mathematics

■■■■ CECIL R. TRUEBLOOD

The period of sensorimotor intelligence calls for the use of visual–tactual aids in teaching arithmetic. The experimenter hypothesized, in this study, that pupil (as opposed to teacher) manipulation of such aids would result in superior achievement and retention. He discusses his results in terms of Piaget's theoretical position.

The literature regarding the teaching of elementary school mathematics emphasizes the importance of teachers using visual–tactual aids to make

• • • • • • • •
SOURCE: Adapted and abridged from a paper presented at the American Educational Research Association meeting, February 10, 1968. (With permission of the author.)

learning mathematics easier for children. Some child development and learning theorists point out that children should manipulate concrete materials to develop a good stock of visual imagery before proceeding to the use of symbolic representations. Commercial sources promote the purchase of visual–tactual aids based upon the position taken by mathematics educators and child development and learning theorists. As a result, school systems spend large sums of money to equip classrooms with these devices.

Theoretical Rationale

The final decision regarding how visual–tactual aids will be employed during the learning process rests with the classroom teacher. To make such decisions, classroom teachers need a theoretical base that will help them predict what use of visual–tactual aids leads to the highest achievement, retention and transfer.

As Cronbach (1965) and Flavell (1963) point out, Piaget provides a theoretical base from which hypotheses for instruction can be deduced. They indicate that one of Piaget's fundamental tenets is that children should be engaged in direct action vis-à-vis content. Hunt (1961), in summarizing the work of Piaget, and Bruner (1960), maintain that during the concrete operations period (ages seven to eleven) children's thought processes require concrete materials and experiences for their instigation and direction. Recent replications of Piaget's studies (Dodwell, 1960; Elkind, 1961b; Hood, 1962; Wohlwill and Lowe, 1962) have supported the validity of the order as well as the characteristics of his stages of intellectual development.[1]

The Problem

The main purpose of this study was to determine whether the teacher's or pupil's manipulation of visual–tactual aids contributes most to achievement and retention during a study of exponential notation and nondecimal bases at the fourth-grade level. These subject matter areas were chosen because this content was not studied previously by any of the experimental classes. Treatment 1 (*Pupil Manipulation*) required each pupil to manipulate concrete aids to illustrate his answers to inductive question sequences posed by the teacher. Treatment 2 (*Teacher Manipulation*) required the pupil to observe the teacher manipulate the same devices to illustrate pupil answers to the same inductive question sequences. The experimenter's prediction,

• • • • • • • •

[1] Although the preceding was the basis for the prediction made by the investigator, Schopler (1966) and White (1965, 1966) provide evidence indicating that a shift from use of tactual to use of visual and auditory cues occurs during the five to seven CA period.

based upon Piaget's theory of intellectual development, was that Pupil Manipulation rather than Teacher Manipulation would result in superior achievement and retention. The study also sought to determine the relationship between post- and retention test scores and mental age.

Pilot Study

The investigator conducted a pilot study by teaching four fifth-grade classes for one semester. During this time two sets of twenty-one lesson plans for Treatment 1 (T-1) and Treatment 2 (T-2) were written and an exponential nondecimal base (EX-NDB) achievement test was designed and validated.

The post-test and retention test scores of the pilot study classes were item-analyzed. The mean item difficulty for the seventy item post achievement and retention test was .632 for the post-test and .599 for the retention test. The mean item discrimination was .615 for the post-test and .621 for the retention test. The KR-20 reliability coefficients for the post-test and retention test were .950 and .952 respectively. The item analysis computed for the fourth-grade students used in the study did not differ significantly from that of the pilot study classes.

The pilot study data were used to make these judgments: (1) the lesson plans were effective since the pupils learned, regardless of the treatments used; (2) the EX-NDB test was sensitive to the concepts contained in the lesson plans; and (3) the pupil's limited knowledge of exponents and nondecimal bases indicated that a pretest for the study would not be necessary.

Sampling and Assignment of Pupils to Treatments

The 213 pupils used in the study were from the classrooms of seven teachers who volunteered to participate in the study. These teachers (1) were from two Pennsylvania school districts which had been using the same textbook series as the pilot study classes, (2) had recently completed a modern mathematics course, and (3) had been selected to supervise student teachers.

The pupils in each class were randomly assigned to T-1 or T-2. Each teacher taught half of his class via T-1 and the other half via T-2. Possible practice effects which might result from a teacher teaching the same content in two successive periods of instruction were balanced by (1) randomly assigning the teachers to teach T-1 then T-2, or T-2 then T-1 during the first half of the experimental period and (2) reversing this order during the second half of the period.

Administration of Treatments and Tests

Prior to administering the treatments the investigator instructed the teachers concerning the proper use of the lesson plans and materials. The teachers agreed to give equal time in preparing each lesson.

After the California Test of Mental Maturity (Level 2) was administered, the teachers began the treatments. The half of the class not involved in a given treatment left the classroom and was instructed by a student teacher in other subject areas. Each teacher was visited at least five times. These unscheduled visits confirmed the belief that the teachers were using the procedures and materials as prescribed.

At the conclusion of the experimental period the investigator administered the EX-NDB test. Unannounced visits made during the four-week retention period indicated that the teachers followed the agreement not to refer in any way to the content presented during the experiment. At the end of the retention period, the investigator administered the EX-NDB test.

Analysis of the Data

The data consisted of scores made on the California Test of Mental Maturity and the EX-NDB achievement test. Analysis of the mean mental ages indicated that the T-1 and T-2 groups taught by the same teacher were equivalent in learning ability. However, the range of differences between mean mental ages of the groups within a given treatment were significantly different.

Since MA and EX-NDB post-test and retention test scores in T-1 and T-2 were high and equivalent, the decision was made to use a covariance computer program to analyze the data. This program performed on individually adjusted EX-NDB scores indicated that randomly dropping pupils did not result in findings different from the equal N covariance analysis.

The preliminary analyses indicated that the interaction between instructors and treatments was not significant at the .05 level. Therefore, the interaction sums of squares and degrees of freedom were combined with the error terms to conduct the final covariance analyses.

In the final summary for the analysis of covariance performed on the adjusted EX-NDB post-test scores, the F-ratios indicated that (1) the immediate post-test differences in favor of T-2 (Teacher Manipulation) were only marginally significant at the .10 level, and (2) the differences between instructors were significant at the .05 level.

In the final summary for the analysis of covariance performed on the EX-NDB retention test scores, the F-ratios indicated (1) the differences in favor of T-2 (Teacher Manipulation) were not significant at the .10 level, and (2) the differences between instructors were significant at the .05 level.

By comparing the gain or loss from post- to retention test for each T-1 and T-2 group, it appears that (1) both treatments resulted in higher retention than would normally be expected, (2) the variability of the gain and loss appears greater for T-2, and (3) the amount of variability among teachers in a given treatment appears greater for T-2 than T-1.

Conclusions

The conclusions that follow should be interpreted after considering these limitations: (1) the number of teachers and grade levels was small, (2) teachers were not randomly selected, (3) the pupils represented only one segment of Piaget's concrete operations stage of intellectual development, (4) the subject content included two topics taught via specified materials and inductive question sequences, and (5) the experimental period was short (four weeks). Considering these limitations the following conclusions seem warranted:

1. Exponential notation and non-decimal bases taught by inductive questioning and Teacher Manipulation of visual–tactual aids (T-2) resulted in higher post-test scores than when these topics were taught via inductive questioning and Pupil Manipulation of visual–tactual devices (T-1). The small difference, however, was only marginally significant and was opposite to prediction.
2. After a four-week retention period, there was no significant difference between the achievement scores of pupils taught by T-1 and T-2. Both treatments, however, resulted in a high degree of retention.
3. The EX-NDB scores of pupils taught by T-1 and T-2 showed a high degree of correlation with mental age.
4. Fourth-grade pupils were able to learn and retain to a high degree exponential and nondecimal base concepts presented by inductive question sequences and Teacher or Pupil Manipulation of visual–tactual devices.

Discussion

For the purpose of tying some loose ends together and to suggest some topics for future investigation, let us engage in some educated speculation.

Because Piaget's theory was used to predict whether Teacher or Pupil Manipulation of visual–tactual aids would be superior, the study provides some evidence related to the plausibility of using the theory to make such predictions. While small differences like that in favor of T-2 should certainly not be interpreted as a reversal of Piaget's developmental stages, the results would seem to be more in agreement with Schopler (1966) and White (1966). Their studies suggest that pupils aged nine to eleven have already passed the stage where incoming data from their environment are organized best from tactual sources. They maintain that pupils of this age have entered a later stage where use of visual and auditory sources are as useful as tactual sources in forming concepts. They indicate that this transition occurs during the five to seven CA period.

Since a single factor seldom explains a phenomenon, another factor may be the more varied pattern of classroom interaction provided by Treatment 2 (Teacher Manipulation). Under this treatment the pupils attended to more varied concrete illustrations supported by pupil–class and teacher–pupil interaction. In Treatment 1 (Pupil Manipulation) each pupil's attention was focused primarily upon how his manipulation of the concrete aids answered the inductive questions posed by the teacher.

A teacher's effectiveness with any procedure is also probably related to his past experience and to his attitude. The usual method of teacher exposition supported by teacher demonstration with visual–tactual devices is more closely related to Treatment 2. Therefore, when teachers were required to shift to asking inductive questions and observing pupils manipulate concrete aids, they might not have been as skillful in analyzing and providing feedback to the pupils as in T-1. A teacher's effectiveness with T-1 or T-2 could also have been related to a preference developed as he used and compared both treatments.

Finally, specific teaching techniques and strategies are usually related to special combinations of pupil and teacher characteristics. This study indicates that perhaps this is true for T-1 and T-2. Therefore, it does not provide the conclusive evidence necessary to recommend one treatment for use by all teachers. It does, however, raise some questions for future investigation.

For example, what factors explain the high retention observed in this study? Perhaps it is simply a result of the interest stimulated by the children and teachers being in an experiment. Or, does inductive questioning stimulate pupils to continue to work on the learning task after the regularly-scheduled class instruction? Or, might inductive questioning have some facilitating effect upon the chemistry associated with the long-term memory process? These and other questions might be fruitful topics for future experimentation.

Conservation, Cardination, and Counting as Factors in Mathematics Achievement

■ GRAYSON H. WHEATLEY

The research reported in this article points to the importance of Piaget's concept of conservation of number as a predictive index of arithmetic achievement. First-grade teachers, especially, will be interested in the author's findings and in the Number Concept Test which he developed as a part of this research.

Piaget (1952*a*) has developed a theory of cognitive growth and has studied, among other things, the acquisition of the concept of number. According to his theory, conservation of number, i.e., the invariance of the number of a set when the objects are rearranged, plays a significant role in developing a concept of number. He hypothesizes that all children begin life without the ability to conserve number and operate on that basis until they learn to override their immediate perceptual impressions and respond cognitively.

Although Piaget used an informal clinical method which failed to yield statistical evidence for his theory, several researchers have recently conducted extensive, statistically-controlled studies assessing the prenumber concepts of young children suggested by Piaget's work. Studies by Smedslund (1961), Elkind (1961*b*), Mannix (1960), and Beard (1963), replicated certain Piaget studies, and their findings in general substantiate Piaget's theory. One conclusion of significance is that six-year-old children do not understand conservation of number, although the age of attainment of the concept is greatly affected by such factors as general intelligence, culture, socioeconomic level, and the early experiences of the child.

Thus it follows that the first-grade nonconserver is likely to experience great difficulty in understanding the concept of addition. When the teacher pushes together a set of two objects with one of three objects and says, "See, now there are five, so $2 + 3 = 5$," the nonconserver is not going to see the "$= 5$" since the objects were moved and he believes this changes the number property. The child may learn to parrot $2 + 3 = 5$, but he will not be able to understand what it means, since the objects have been moved and to him this changes the number. The child is also likely to have great difficulty applying addition to any problem situation.

The purpose of this study was to investigate certain number concepts possessed by first-grade students and to determine their relationship to success in studying mathematics in the first grade. Specifically, the concepts of conservation, cardination, and counting were examined and their role in

• • • • • • • •

SOURCE: Adapted and abridged from a paper presented at the annual meeting of the American Educational Research Association, February 10, 1968. (With permission of the author.)

learning first-grade mathematics was explored. The primary instrument used in this investigation was a number concept test based on the ideas of Piaget and developed by the writer.

Previous Research

Hood (1962) is one of the few persons to report an investigation of the relationship between the presence of number concepts and ability in arithmetic. Hood compared the stage placement of 120 children, aged four to nine years, with teacher ratings of the children's arithmetical understanding. The children were assigned a score from 1 to 5 on understanding of arithmetic, with a score of 1 representing no number ability of any kind and a score of 5 representing the highest level of performance. He found that all students assigned a score of 1 were Stage I children on the Piagetian scale, the stage of nonconservation. Further, he reported that all children assigned a score of 5 on arithmetic ability were at Stage III. He concluded that conservation of number is the key factor in number readiness. The results are colored by the fact that teacher judgments were used to measure ability in arithmetic. The teachers were asked to make global judgments and they may have been using different standards. Furthermore, the teachers may have consciously or unconsciously used skill in rote procedures rather than understanding as a basis for rating the students. This procedure is slightly better than using teachers' term marks of students which Dodwell (1961) found to be completely useless. It is possible that with a more reliable and valid measure of children's arithmetic ability, the relationship between number concepts and ability in arithmetic would have been more pronounced than in Hood's study.

Williams (1958), in analyzing the results of administering a number concept test to twenty children aged four years and six months to six years, concluded that there appeared to be a high positive correlation between scores on a conservation test and students' understanding of addition and subtraction. However, the exact correlation was not reported and sample size was small.

Dodwell (1961) administered a number concept test to forty entering first-grade students and compared the results with scores obtained on a teacher-made achievement test seven months later. He found a correlation between these two measures of .59, which he considered promising. The reliability and validity of the teacher-made test is questionable.

Steffe (1966) classified 132 first-grade students into four levels of conservation of number. Subjects scoring low on conservation (level four) scored significantly lower on a problem solving test than Ss in the upper three levels of conservation, showing a definite relation between failure in conservation and failure in problem solving in arithmetic.

Almy (1966) conducted a longitudinal study of the relation between conservation of quantity and school achievement. Sixty-five Ss were tested twice in kindergarten, twice in the first grade, and once in the second grade. The scores were pooled to obtain a single measure of conservation of quantity. The correlations of these scores with the two parts of a second-grade mathematics achievement test were calculated. Two schools were used; a middle-class urban school and a lower-class urban school. For the middle-class school the correlations were .26 and .53, and for the lower-class school they were .41 and .38. The results were affected by two factors: the students in the middle-class school scored at the top of the achievement test due to the low difficulty of the test for the group, and language was a problem for the students of the lower-class school. It is likely that the correlations would have been more valid if these factors had not been present.

Method

Subjects

A sample of forty-one first-grade children, twenty-one boys and twenty girls, was selected from the Newark Special School District of Newark, Delaware. The district draws from a predominantly middle-class suburban area of the upper part of the state. From the ten elementary schools in the Newark District, two were selected as being representative of the various ethnic and socioeconomic groups in the district, but including neither a high proportion of children from upper- or lower-class homes. From these two schools, having 286 first-grade children in ten classes, the sample of forty-one subjects was randomly selected and, as it happened, included children from all of the classes.

The Curriculum

The course of study for all subjects was the first-year text of the Greater Cleveland Mathematics Program published by Science Research Associates, Inc. The main objective of this program, as stated in the teacher's manual, is to develop understanding as well as computational skill. This text is one of the newer ones which has been prepared in the recent national revision of the mathematics curriculum.

The Number Concept Test

A review of the instruments which have been used to investigate children's understanding of number concepts resulted in the conclusion that none of the existing tests was suitable for the present investigation. Thus a Number Concept Test was developed.[1] It was developed over a three-year period with two forms preceding the final one. Each of the previous forms was tested on small groups of children at the kindergarten and first grade level. Changes were made as a result of the pilot work, and the final form contained 31 items, 27 of which were scored, the other 4 being used to establish prior conditions for questioning. The test contained 6 items on conservation of number, 6 on counting, 12 on cardination, 2 on one-to-one correspondence, and 1 on conservation of length. The first three categories mentioned above were considered as subtests and their relation to achievement was examined separately.

The reliability of the test was determined using Hoyt's method of analysis of variance to compare variance due to student, item, and error. The hypotheses were tested that there was no significant difference between individuals and between items. Each of these hypotheses was rejected at the .01 level. The reliability coefficient obtained by this procedure was .92 and the standard error of measurement was 1.94.

The NCT was administered individually to the 41 subjects in one sitting, requiring approximately twenty minutes per subject. The subjects and the experimenter were in a private room, free from distractions, with the subject seated at a low table and the materials displayed in front of him on the table as each question was asked. The experimenter sat to one side, recording scores and pertinent comments made by the subject. The same order of questioning was followed for all subjects and all other testing procedures were standardized.

The test was administered first in late September 1965, and again in May 1966. The testing was conducted over a period of four days, two days being spent in each school.

The Achievement Test

The 1965 edition of the Stanford Achievement Test, Arithmetic Section (SAT) was chosen as the test most appropriate for the curriculum in the school district being used for this study. Independently, the district administrators selected this test for administration to all first-grade students in the district. The Arithmetic Section consisted of four parts: Measurement, Problem Solving, Number Concepts, and Computation. The first three of these sections were considered as measures of understanding and, for some analyses, were considered as a unit.

• • • • • • • •
[1] Included at the end of this article.

The SAT was administered to the subjects in a group setting in May 1966.

The reliability of the SAT used was reported in the test manual to be .95 and the standard error of measurement was 1.0.

Results

One of the major considerations of this study was the degree to which the Number Concept Test, developed for this study, would serve to predict achievement at the first-grade level. The correlations between the NCT and the SAT, Arithmetic Section, was .75. This correlation was significant at the .001 level and the 95% confidence interval was .57 to .86. When the effects of intelligence were partialed out, the correlation was .65, significantly different from zero at the .001 level. This was taken as evidence that the NCT was measuring, at least in part, factors different from those measured by the intelligence test used in this study.

When the correlations of the NCT with the four subsections of the SAT were examined, it was noted that all of the correlations were approximately the same (.59) except for NCT with Measurement, which was .76. This can be explained by the important role conservation plays in measurement.

Looking at the correlations in another way, of the three factors of the NCT (conservation, counting, and cardination), conservation appears to be the best single predictor of achievement. Although the differences between the correlations are not significant, they approach significance at the .05 level in some instances.

Counting by ones was used as a dichotomizing criterion and the SAT scores of the subjects that could count rationally to 23 and those that could not, were compared.

Using a t test of difference of means, a t of 1.69 was obtained, a value falling short of significance at the .05 level, thus indicating that the ability to count rationally is not an adequate basis for judging achievement.

As a further check on the importance of conservation of number for learning arithmetic, the subjects were classified as conservers or nonconservers on the basis of having five or more correct responses on the six-item conservation of number subtest. The difference between the mean scores of the two groups on the achievement test was tested for significance using Student's t test. Since there was no homogeneity of variance for the two groups, a form of the test was chosen which did not make this assumption. The t value of 5.63 was significant at the .01 level.

The percentage of correct responses to the conservation of number questions ranged from 24 to 51 per cent; 26.7 per cent of the subjects in the sample were judged to be conservers of number. Only 9 per cent of the subjects answered correctly on conservation of length, a very stable result confirmed in testing two other samples of 30 each at the same level.

Discussion

Although the English translation of Piaget's *The Child's Conception of Number* appeared in 1952, textbook writers have made little use of the ideas of conservation of number. It is clear from this study that the majority of first-grade-entering students do not understand conservation of number and although a causal relationship between conservation ability and arithmetic achievement is not implied by the high positive correlation of the two tests, the fact that conservers as a group scored significantly higher on the achievement test warrants attention. This would seem to indicate that conservation is an important factor in learning arithmetic at the first-grade level.

Since there is a high correlation between intelligence and arithmetic achievement the question might be raised whether a conservation test yields different information from intelligence tests. The fact that a partial correlation coefficient of .65 was found between conservation and arithmetic achievement when intelligence was held constant would seem to warrant an affirmative response to this question. Actually, knowledge of conservation could readily be obtained by teachers and used for planning first-grade curricula. Readiness activities could be developed for those scoring low on conservation. Other research such as Wallach and Sprott's (1964) indicates that such attempts would be profitable. This is a topic for further investigation. It would also appear fruitful to determine whether students who had been taught conservation would be as successful in studying arithmetic as a comparable sample of natural conservers.

Certainly there are broad implications in these findings for curriculum development. Just what aspects of the first-grade arithmetic are conservation-dependent? Does it bother nonconservers to move objects about?

The inherent difficulty of the counting procedure should be recognized. While it is rather easy for students to memorize the number names, it is quite another thing for them to use rational counting to draw conclusions, such as the equality of sets. When a child points to the last object in a set and says, "five," he is thinking of a correspondence such that "five" and the last object are put into one-to-one correspondence. But then it is necessary for the child to infer that since the last one is "five," the cardinal number of the set is five also. This is a subtle interplay between the ordinal and cardinal use of number. It is not unusual for a child to count two sets and say they are both "five" and still not realize that the two sets have the same number.

Parents and teachers alike tend to place undue importance on a child's ability to count. The results of this study indicate that counting is a poor basis for judging potential in arithmetic; counting often is a meaningless set of responses. On the other hand, the unrecognized ability to conserve is a prerequisite for understanding number and a very useful concept for predicting success in arithmetic.

Number Concept Test

1. a. Here are some colored discs. See how many you can count.
   b. Here are several bundles of sticks. There are two sticks in each bundle. Count the sticks two at a time.
   c. Here are several bundles of sticks. There are 5 sticks in each bundle. Count the sticks 5 at a time.
   d. Here are several bundles of sticks. There are 10 sticks in each bundle. Count the sticks 10 at a time.
2. Show subject a pile of red discs and tell him, "Give me seven of them."
3. Lay six red discs on a table. Ask subject to take from a box as many blue discs as there are red discs on the table. Make a row which has as many.
4. Show subject a display of ten different sets of colored buttons arranged in the following way:

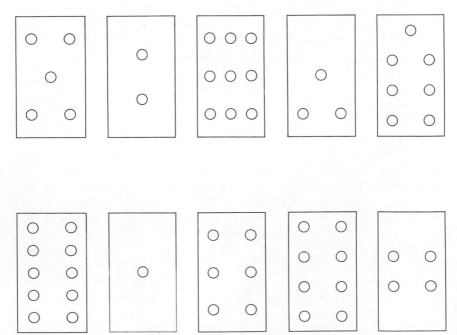

Ask subject to point to the one which shows:

a. three buttons   g. four buttons
b. eight buttons   h. ten buttons
c. five buttons   i. seven buttons
d. one button   j. five buttons
e. seven buttons   k. nine buttons
f. two buttons   l. six buttons

5. Place two piles of discs on the table, one pile containing five blue discs and the other pile containing six red discs.
   a. Ask subject, "Which pile has more or do both piles have the same?"
   b. Ask subject, "Is there a blue disc for every red disc?"
   c. Ask subject, "How do you know?"

6. Lay ten red discs on the table.
   a. Ask subject to count them. Then rearrange the discs in a more complex pattern or in piles.
   b. Ask subject to count them in this arrangement.

7. Make two rows of nine discs on the table so that the discs match one-to-one. (Examiner make sure the subject understands one-to-one before proceeding further.)
   a. Ask subject, "Do both rows have the same number of discs?" Rearrange one row of discs in a pile.
   b. Ask subject, "Do they still have the same number of discs?" Rearrange the two rows of nine discs in a one-to-one pattern. Spread one row beyond the limits of the other row. (One row of discs will be approximately twice as long as the other row.)
   c. Ask subject, "Which row has more, or do they both have the same?"

8. a. Ask subject to put twelve balls, one at a time in two receptacles of identical shape and size with both hands simultaneously. Ask subject, "Which has more, or do they have the same?" (Examiner should make effort to determine what subject is thinking at this step.) Examiner puts the balls in a receptacle of different size and shape.
   b. Ask subject, "Which has more, or are they the same?"

9. Ask subject to put eight balls, one at a time, in two receptacles of different size and shape with both hands simultaneously. Ask subject, "Which has more, or are they the same?"

10. a. Place two blocks side by side so that the ends are aligned. Ask subject, "Are the two blocks the same length?"
    b. Then push one block so that its end projects beyond the other. Ask subject, "Are the blocks still the same length?"

Conservation of Length and the Teaching of Linear Measurement: A Methodological Critique

■ DAIYO SAWADA / L. DOYAL NELSON

Educators have long been aware that correct verbal responses do not necessarily reflect understanding on the part of the student. Conversely, understanding may outstrip the ability to respond to verbal questioning. Piaget's methodology has been criticized by several authors as being too dependent on verbal techniques. Holt (1966), for example, has argued that a young child's inability to solve conservation problems may be less a function of stage dependence than of misunderstanding the questions posed by the experimenter. The authors of this article developed a non-verbal method for assessing conservation of length, and found that five- and six-year-old children could understand the concept under these conditions. Consideration of these results in conjunction with Piaget's finding of seven or eight as the age for conservation suggested to the authors that the teaching of any scientific or mathematical concepts by nonverbal methods might ensure superior understanding of later verbal and symbolic meanings.

Important insights into the young child's conception of basic mathematical and scientific concepts have arisen out of the experimental work conducted by Piaget (1952a, 1964). In assessing the degree to which a child has acquired a concept, Piaget often uses the criterion of conservation. He has shown that children of four to six do not in general conserve certain basic properties of objects or sets of objects. For example, a young child may think that the number of blocks in a row is increased if the row is elongated, or that a wooden rod becomes shorter when it is rotated through 90 degrees. Such a child is said to be a "nonconserver" of number in the first case, and a "nonconserver" of length in the second case.

It would be unwise to use sets of objects to teach the child the addition of numbers if the rearrangement of the objects within the set caused the child to believe that the number of objects in the set had changed. Similarly, it would not be wise to teach linear measurement using rods of various lengths if the child thought that the length of a rod changed whenever the position of the rod changed. The implication is that formal instruction in the process of linear measurement should not be initiated until the child realizes that (1) the length of a rigid body remains invariant under changes of position and (2) the length of a whole remains invariant whenever each of its parts remains the same length. In short, we must be sure that the child is a conserver of length before we provide him with formal instruction in linear measurement. Otherwise we risk the probability of turning our instruction into a rote and mechanical manipulation of sticks.

• • • • • • • •

SOURCE: Adapted and abridged from *Arithmetic Teacher, 14* (1967), 345–348. (With permission of the authors and the National Council of Teachers of Mathematics.)

Assessing the Child's Acquisition of the Conservation of Length

Piaget (Ripple and Rockcastle, 1964) has been the pioneer in devising ways of assessing the child's acquisition of the conservation of length. For example, Piaget would place two sticks of equal length side by side on a table in front of the child. Having asked the child if the sticks were the same "length" and having received a positive response, Piaget would move one of the sticks a short distance to the right or the left. The child would again be asked which stick was "longer" or whether they were the same "length." Many subjects thought that one stick was now "longer" than the other.

Some other test items of Piaget's are of a similar nature, all requiring the child to respond to questions involving the word "length." Piaget's methodology has been severely criticized by Braine (1959, 1962, 1964) as being too highly dependent on verbal means of expressing the property (length in this case) about which the child was to make decisions. If the child interprets the word "length" to mean the "alignment of the end points of the rods" (and this is quite possible since the word is first used with reference to the rods as aligned), then when one rod is moved to the right or to the left the end points are no longer aligned and therefore the "length" has changed. Thus the child can give nonconservation responses simply because the word "length" does not mean the same to him as it does to adults. However, this does not necessarily mean that he does not have the concept of length. It may simply mean that he has not attached the concept to its commonly accepted symbol, the word "length."

The use of verbal stimuli (in this case the word "length") to communicate that property whose magnitude the child is to make decisions about, makes it difficult to interpret whether the child is a conserver or a nonconserver. The child may think that the experimenter wants him to judge whether one stick looks longer than the other, and indeed one stick may look longer.

On the basis of verbally-dependent methods of communicating "length," Piaget and others, such as Murray (1965), have shown that the age for the acquisition of conservation of length is between seven and eight. This would indicate that many first-grade children would be nonconservers of length. However, Braine (1959) has shown that by using nonverbal techniques it is possible to lower some of Piaget's age norms by more than two years. If Braine's conclusions are valid (see Smedslund, 1963, for a penetrating and sometimes not too favorable critique), it might be reasonable to hypothesize that the use of essentially nonverbal techniques would allow the child to reveal his acquisition of the conservation of length at an age somewhat younger than seven or eight. The implications of such a hypothesis, if found to be true, are clear. An obvious implication is that most first-grade children would be conservers of length. However, more importantly from the pedagogical viewpoint, the cruciality of the role of verbal as against essentially nonverbal modes of communication in diagnostic testing, and indeed in the presentation of concepts in the daily teaching lesson, is indicated. For if an essentially nonverbal technique of presenting the property of length allows the child to conserve that property, whereas, verbal techniques mask this attainment until seven or eight, then to take advantage of the increased sensitivity and justification for teaching linear measurement in first grade that nonverbal techniques grant us, we as teachers must couch our instruction in linear measurement in as concrete terms as our imagination can furnish so as to minimize the cruciality of verbal symbols which could turn our conserver (conserver as indicated by a nonverbal test) into a nonconserver.

There are other implications; but, first, is the hypothesis a valid one?

The Experiment

The hypothesis was tested by conducting an experiment in Edmonton, Alberta, using sixty-two children between the ages of five and seven. The children were randomly selected from two schools at the Canadian Forces Base in Edmonton.

A concerted attempt was made to eliminate the dependence on verbal symbols for communicating the property of length to the child. It was essential that the property be communicated to the child, since the experimenter wished to test only whether the child could conserve this property, not whether the child possessed the concept of length or not.

To remove the dependence on the word "length," calipers were used to define to the child that property about which he was to make decisions. A thorough training session lasting about twelve minutes per child was given to teach the child how to apply the calipers to the various kinds of rods used to exhibit the property of length. The child was taught to arrange the rods in a straight, compact line before attempting to apply the calipers. The calipers, of which there were three sizes — 9 cm, 9.5 cm, and 10 cm — always fitted the rods (which ranged in length from 8.5 cm to 10.5 cm) in only three ways:

1. The calipers were .5 cm too long for the rods.
2. The calipers were just right for the rods.
3. The calipers were .5 cm too short for the rods.

The three different "fits" were each associated with one of three "doors" on a specially constructed response apparatus by placing a "model fit" above each of the doors. The child was trained to apply the calipers to a set of rods placed in front of him, note how the calipers fit, locate the equivalent model fit, and open the corresponding "door" which led to a candy reward. Every child had to and could make four consecutive correct responses (i.e., find the candy) before going on to the test proper.

For each test item:

1. A rod or set of rods was placed in front of the child.
2. The child applied the calipers to the rod(s).
3. The experimenter removed the calipers and transformed the rods in some way, e.g., the rod was moved to left or right, or the rod was rotated horizontally or vertically, or .5 cm was added to the rod or taken from the rod, or the rods in the set were arranged in the form of an N, or the Plasticine rod was rolled between the tabletop and the palm, and so on. (Some rods were of Plasticine and others were of wood. In most cases the Plasticine rods were changed in length.)
4. The child was asked how the calipers would fit if he were allowed to apply the calipers again. "How would they fit if you tried to put them on again? Like this, or this, or this?" the experimenter asked, pointing at the model fits. "Find the candy."

A child was classified as a conserver of length if he gave at least eleven correct responses out of sixteen (better than chance at the .01 level).

The Findings

Results on the threshold age of the acquisition of conservation (or other logical operation) are usually reported as the age at which 50 per cent of the children of that age give evidence of conserving (Braine, 1964; Smedslund, 1963).

The data collected in this study showed that nearly 100 per cent of the children between the ages of 7 years, 2 months and 8 years, 0 months were conservers of length. Nearly 70 per cent of the children between 6 years, 3 months and 7 years, 1 month were conservers; and about 60 per cent of the children between 5 years, 4 months and 6 years, 2 months could conserve. It appears safe, therefore, to conclude that the threshold age for the acquisition of conservation of length is between five and six. The hypothesis about the efficacy of nonverbal techniques is therefore accepted.

Implications

In addition to implications cited above, the validity of the hypothesis indicates that using concrete operational techniques is preferable to using highly verbal ones when working with young children. Highly verbal techniques appear to interfere with a child's ability to express his understanding of conservation of length to such an extent that a verbal conservation test can turn a conserver into a "nonconserver." Since verbal techniques place the age of acquisition of the conservation of length between seven and eight, an implication is that a five- to six-year-old child will behave as a conserver only if essentially nonverbal techniques are used to facilitate communication about the property called "length." Accordingly, predominantly verbal methods of teaching linear measurement to a five- or six-year-old child may make the child behave as a nonconserver. This undesirable transformation is preventable if the teaching of linear measurement proceeds (at least in the beginning) along highly concrete lines involving a minimum of dependence on the word "length" to invoke the concept we wish the child to think about. Only after we are sure that the word "length" has been assigned a concrete operational meaning can we safely use the word "length" with validity.

A generalization to other concepts would suggest that any basic concept when it is first introduced should be approached in concrete operational ways so that the word assigned to the concept can be given concrete operational meaning before it is used to invoke the concept.

Test Development

VI

Much dissatisfaction with traditional intelligence tests has been expressed in recent years, especially with respect to their inadequacy for assessing the potential of inner-city children. Scales based on Piaget's tasks would appear to offer a viable alternative, which may be of greater diagnostic value to the teacher than an IQ score. In the first place, the scales are based on a theoretical conception of cognitive growth, rather than being empirically derived from a large number of tasks which differentiate at particular age levels. Second, the reliance on verbal facility is considerably reduced, emphasis being placed on intellectual behavior. Finally, the test materials, being diagnostic, may also be used for teaching purposes, and in some cases may be autoinstructional; thus, creating a bridge between the assessment of intellectual achievement and classroom teaching.

A Scale of Mental Development Based on the Theory of Piaget: Description of a Project

■■■ ADRIEN PINARD / MONIQUE LAURENDEAU

Pinard and Laurendeau have been working for the past seven years on a longitudinal study to validate Piaget's stages in a French Canadian context. In the course of this endeavor they have produced an ordinal scale of mental development which combines some of the merits of traditional intelligence tests with insights gained from Piaget's clinical method. The outcome will be of interest both to educators and test specialists in the cognitive area.

Educators anxious to improve the effectiveness of teaching methods are becoming more and more interested in Piaget's theory. For this reason it may perhaps be useful to present the broad outlines of a program of research to which the efforts of the laboratory of genetic psychology of the University of Montreal have been directed for years. Actually, the "development scale"

• • • • • • • •

SOURCE: *Journal of Research in Science Teaching,* 2 (1964), 253–260. (With permission of the authors and the *Journal.*)

to which the title of this article refers is still only at the pilot stage; its development presupposes a very long theoretical study of which the first results have only recently been published. However, it may be of interest to summarize the objectives of the project as a whole, to describe briefly the structure of the proposed scale, and finally, to underline its possible pedagogical applications.

Objectives of the Project

The project as a whole has two main objectives. The first is of a theoretical or academic order. It consists in looking for the existence of Piaget's stages of mental development in a population other than that of Geneva. This study is intended to be experimental, that is, based on the systematic observation of a group of children who were given an examination that satisfied minimum conditions of objectivity and uniformity. It therefore constitutes both a resumption and an extension of Piaget's main experiments, under conditions in accord with the requirements of the experimental method. It will allow us to see to what extent the stages of mental development established by Piaget can be found in a different sociological milieu, and will therefore tend to confirm or invalidate the correctness of Piaget's stages. The study will also allow a better evaluation of the fragmentary studies that have been done in different countries on particular aspects of Piaget's theory under conditions which are not always easily comparable.

The second main objective is of a practical order, and to the authors at least, represents only a by-product. The project ought to result in the construction of an ordinal scale of mental development applicable to children from two to twelve years. There already exists, in several languages, a multitude of intelligence tests for children, but in the majority of cases these tests do not answer the proposed objective of developing an instrument which would permit the establishment of a psychological diagnosis of intelligence and not simply an evaluation of its actual functioning.

By diagnostic examination, we mean one by which not only the results but the dynamics of intellectual work can be grasped, which would reveal the character, the causes, and the degree of anomalous mental function and its possible ultimate evolution. The usual tests comprise on the one hand problems whose intellectual content is extremely limited (for instance, memory span), and on the other hand, problems whose solution requires the intervention of more truly intellectual factors (for example, "absurd" expressions). Now it is known that these problems, although very different in kind, contribute equally to the final results, and this seriously complicates their interpretation. Even supposing that they all depict the most significant dimensions of the mental function equally well, they are grouped in such a way that they can hardly serve to make known one child's intellectual growth, much less intellectual evolution in general. From one age to the other, the problems under consideration are so different that it is impossible to compare validly results obtained by the same child in successive examinations. One is limited, therefore, to a comparison of one child's performance with that of others of the same age in a pattern of intellectual tasks chosen strictly on the basis of their statistical filiation. Thus, one ends up with extremely artificial scales: the problems only very dimly reflect the dominant characters of the several stages, and the observed progressions from one age to another are far from always having equal importance.

Probably no one has pointed out the serious deficiencies of the great majority of tests for children better than Piaget (1950) and Inhelder (1963). This is not the place to go into their critiques in detail, but it is proper to discuss their two essential conclusions.

First, the usual tests neglect the structural and functional aspects of intelligence. They elicit an unsubtle numerical result, which is, very simply, the algebraic sum of successes and failures attained by the subject. They do not in any way illuminate the character of the intelligence they claim to measure, nor do they clarify ways by which results are obtained or conditioned by the subject's previous experiences, and they completely ignore the nature of any revealed deficiencies. Briefly, any interpretation that can result from the usual test rests purely on the phenomenological level and does not lend itself to causative analysis of mental processes, alone capable of assuring an adequate acquaintance with the unfolding of thought and its pathological manifestations.

Piaget's and Inhelder's second criticism concerns the specifically "genetic" character of intelligence. Can one say that the usual intelligence scales truly interpret a natural development, even if the problems concerned in these measurements are distributed according to chronological age? In a real evolution, the attainment of a given level generally presupposes the mastery of the preceding level. In other words, subsequent acquisitions necessarily imply integration of previous acquisitions. It is well known that in an age scale, such as Terman's, for example, this condition is not met. Thus, a six-year-old child can compensate for failures at the five-year level with successes in items localized at seven years. Such a postulate ruins even the sense of the concept of evolution: it makes mental age a simple median performance instead of a true genetic stage, and it reduces to a simple compensatory game the laws of transformation which characterize and explain the successive levels of mental development.

Now the operative theory of intelligence, as formulated by Piaget, can be nicely applied to illuminate changes of mental structure or modes of thought proper to the child's specific age, and to show the necessary sequence of mental structures which succeed each other in a precise order following a definite evolutionary principle. In studying wrong answers given by children (something that the usual tests neglect completely), Piaget has been able to show that they can be at least as instructive as the right answers, since they are always grouped in certain well-defined types, easily recognizable and apparently tied to distinct stages of mental development.

Without going into a lengthy review of Piaget's well-known theory, it would seem that an instrument capable of searching out the child's various developmental stages (so well identified by Piaget and his collaborators) would furnish an excellent index of mental development. In short, the second objective of the present research consists in constructing a scale of mental development based on a revised concept of tests for children in the light of Piaget's hypotheses. Furthermore, it is just here that the second objective rejoins and overlaps the first. The projected scale will attempt to meet the requirements of Piaget's so-called clinical method (relatively free and unstructured questionnaire) together with those of the usual psychometric method (standardized and normalized questionnaire), thus benefiting from the respective advantages of both methods.

General Description of the Experimental Test

The construction of a diagnostic test of child thought required that one deviate perceptibly from habitual technique, a technique that consists in supposing at the point of departure that each period of six to twelve months of chronological age marks a mental development large enough to be measured in some valid way. Then one tries to assemble varied and sufficiently numerous problems so that subsequent statistical analysis will allow the retention, at each age level, of a group of adequately difficult and valid items. In order to avoid the artificiality of scales built on such a technique, it was necessary, so to speak, to reverse traditional methodology, first making a thorough study of the development of thought in order to pinpoint the different stages of mental evolution and the dominant aspects of each. After this theoretical study, it became possible to construct problems calculated to uncover each of these dominant aspects, to submit them to experimentation, and finally to determine by statistical analysis the ages at which the different levels are attained. In short, instead of looking for problems which might distinguish such and such a level of chronological age, the objective was rather to find problems which might distinguish particular levels of mental development, thus leaving one free to determine later at what age, on the average, children attain each of these levels.

The experimental test constructed on this perspective comprises 57 subtests, including some 300 items or possible levels of response, capable of revealing the essential characters of one or another of the principal stages of mental development. Analysis of the content of this test allows the grouping of the subtests in three distinct categories. The first two (Tables 1 and 2) bring together 32 sub-tests, constituting an ensemble of 150 items, provided for the lower ages particularly.

Table 1.   Twenty-four Tests of Sensorimotor Coordination

Reconstruction of a divided cube	Articulation of the thumb
Nesting of boxes	Articulation of the fingers
Construction of a block tower	Bead stringing
Construction of a bridge	Manual dexterity
Construction of a door	Insertion of a small chain in a box
Construction of stairways	Insertion of cubes in a box
Pyramids of identical blocks	Carrying a glass of water
Pyramids of different blocks	Use of both hands
Classification of beads according to color	Dog puzzle
Classification of beads according to shape	Tree puzzle
Pegboard	Formboard
Paper folding	Tracing of forms

Table 2.   Eight Tests of Verbal Comprehension and Knowledge

Understanding prepositions	Usual knowledge
Use of conjunctions	Judgment
Use of the parts of speech	Numerical correspondence (homogeneous elements)
Execution of simple orders	Numerical correspondence (heterogeneous elements)

These items are all newly made, even though inspired by those already in use in conventional scales. Without being taken directly from Piaget's works, they have been chosen so as to evaluate the characteristics that Piaget assigned to the period of child development which extends from the appearance of language to intuitive intelligence. Thus, they attempt to evaluate the most complex manifestations of sensorimotor intelligence and the rudimentary forms of representative or symbolic intelligence. It is here that we find the first tests of sensorimotor coordination, as well as a certain number of tests designed to evaluate the child's mastery of language. These language tests are not vocabulary items such as one encounters in the usual tests, which seek to discover the richness or extent of language use; rather, they seek to evaluate the child's level of language comprehension or, if you please,

Table 3.   Twenty-five Tests Inspired Directly by Piaget's Work

Causality	Time, Movement, Speed
Explanation of the dream	Notion of age
Concept of life	Succession and simultaneousness of events
Origin of night	Composition of distances
Movement of clouds	Invariability of the order of linear succession
Floating objects	Speed of concentric movements

Classes, Relations, and Numbers	Space
Seriation of weights	Stereognostic representation
Seriation and ordinal correspondence	Projection of a straight line
Relativity of the notion of siblings	Localization of topographic sites
Inclusion of classes	Relativity of the notions of left and right
Centered and uniform distribution	Coordination of perspectives
Quantification of probabilities	Representation of the horizontal

Conservation
Conservation of distances
Conservation of surfaces
Conservation of quantities

the amount of his representation or symbolization of words. Even if these were conventional tests, their correction and interpretation would not necessarily be done in simple terms of success or failure. At every possible point, the analysis is qualitative rather than quantitative, and the results are classified according to stages or levels of response.

The third category (Table 3) comprises the subtests inspired directly by Piaget's operative theory. Certain of these subtests, as for example, stereognostic representation, projection of a straight line, and the localization of topographic sites, are already accessible to children of two or three years; but the greater part are designed for children at least four years old, that is, children with whom it is possible, in general, to hold a connected conversation.

Each of these problems is intended to explore one of the fundamental areas of thought. Emphasis is always placed on the qualitative value of answers given by the child, without any direct consideration of time or speed. The examiner seeks to obtain the maximum from the child, to exhaust, so to speak, his reasoning capacities through a systematic questionnaire whose standardization assures objectivity and uniformity, but which nevertheless includes sufficient flexibility and nuances to avoid rigidity and imprecision. This third category of items comprises an ensemble of twenty-five objective questionnaires giving rise to about one hundred levels of response. Five of these questionnaires analyze the first notions of causality such as are revealed by the child's beliefs concerning the representation of the world and by his explanations of a simple physical phenomenon; six aim at revealing the diverse notions intervening in the child's first spatial representations (topological space, projective space, and Euclidean space); five concern the genesis of notions of movement, time, and speed. Of the last nine questionnaires, six are concerned with the first operations relative to classification, to relations and quantification, and the last three are specifically dedicated to the fundamental problems of conservation (or of invariants), studies in the particular context of space and quantity. Except for six purely verbal tests, the manner of posing each problem consists first of doing an experiment in front of the child, then in questioning him about what he has just seen. Sometimes it happens that the child is called on to forecast the results of an experiment before it is done, and then to explain the observed results once the experiment is performed for him or by him. For example, the child is given a series of small objects (wooden ball, glass ball, metal nail, stick of wood, etc.) and is asked to predict whether each of them will float on water. Then, when the experiment is performed for him, the child should explain why each object actually floats or sinks. In order to analyze the quality of the child's reasoning better and to distinguish his true level of mental functioning, the questionnaire never stops at the first answers; the child is always led to justify or explain his answers through a byplay of subquestions, counterquestions, and even suggestions designed to test the limits of his comprehension. Most of the problems of this type, inspired by Piaget's experiments, are given to all children aged four to twelve; that is, the child of twelve undergoes nearly the same test as the child of four or five. What permits one to distinguish the several levels of success is not simply the inherent difficulty of a problem's perfect solution, but, rather, the quality of a given response; according to their mental developmental level, subjects respond to the same problem in different ways. All of the tests allow for at least three levels of response and some offer as many as six clearly differentiated levels.

Subjects and Experimental Conditions

The test was administered to a group of 700 subjects, divided equally in fourteen age levels. Between two and five years of age, the levels were arranged by six-month periods, and after five years, by twelve-month periods. At each age level, fifty subjects were chosen so as to constitute a miniature of the total French–Canadian child population of the same age in the Montreal region. Criteria in the choice of subjects were sex, age (the child was tested during the month preceding or following his birthday), the occupational status of his parents, number of children in the family, and the school grade. All children were examined individually. In the case of school-age children, the test took place during school hours in an appropriate isolated room. All preschool children were tested at home. The time devoted to administering the scale came to ten hours on the average, and was divided, according to test conditions and the children's age, into four to eight sessions. The order of administration was in no way rigorous. At the lower ages especially, the child's instability of reaction and the fluctuation of his momentary interests precluded the imposition of any rigid order and required extreme flexibility on the part of the examiner, who simply had to apply very general principles: after a verbal test, present a nonverbal one; after a boring test, a captivating one, etc.

Method of Correction

Before the first results are reported, it will be in order to outline briefly the particular correction method applied to the greater part of the tests. For items of the conventional type, correction did not pose any particular problems: the evaluation of answers conforms to the usual techniques, which take into account, according to the particular problem involved, the exactness of the solution, the time of execution, the number of errors, the quantity of elements brought together, etc. In all other cases, however, and especially in the problems borrowed from Piaget, the quest for a functional and analytical evaluation imposes the application of a special technique. In effect, it is a matter of quantifying, insofar as possible, material of an entirely qualitative nature. Correction therefore demands an all-encompassing interpretation of the subject's responses to an entire subtest, or even to several subtests. Whether good or bad, all answers must be considered. In fact, it is often the wrong answers that can best reveal the basic nature of mental operations. For every test, the establishment of a correction scale first requires a complete review of the protocols furnished by all subjects examined. Classification of different types of possible answers then furnished the necessary elements for establishing a provisional scale of levels or states, based principally on Piaget's observations. When the subject's responses are not classifiable according to Piaget's stages, any modifications brought to bear (additions, fusions, reformulations, etc.) always aim to disclose the internal structure of the child's reasoning and thus to preserve the test's diagnostic value. Such a correction method seems to satisfy well the minimum criteria of simplicity and objectivity usually looked for in psychometric instruments. Certainly it has none of their automatic or mechanical character, and it must be admitted, requires of the correctors a psychological knowledge and experience not to be expected of a simple technician.

First General Results

The testing of subjects has long since been completed and the analysis of results is in progress. It goes without saying that the inventory of this immense mass of data will involve long, exacting labor which will bring to light a number of new problems. So, for the immediate future, there is simply no question of being able to accomplish the study's second objective, that of building a scale of mental development based on these data. Before it is possible to integrate the diverse results into such a scale, it will first be necessary to carry out the study's initial objective, and to inquire whether the results obtained confirm or invalidate Piaget's positions. It is to this kind of analysis that the first reports on the project will be directed. A recently published study described the results obtained by questionnaires bearing on the development of causal thought. A second study, in preparation, will report the results of questionnaires relative to the development of notions about space.

On the whole, the results of these first analyses seem to confirm the existence of Piaget's stages. However, in certain cases it may well be necessary to eliminate certain levels which the test fails to justify, or, perhaps more frequently, to add new ones in order to take into account some totally new answers which apparently cannot be integrated with Piaget's established stages, and which seem authentically to characterize new levels of development. This phenomenon can partially be explained by the present study's greater age-spread and higher number of subjects. On the other hand, it is interesting to note that the various developmental stages are generally acquired at a slightly later age by French–Canadian children than by the children of Geneva. To take a typical but extreme example, chosen from among tests analyzed so far, let us look at a problem in which the child is asked to evaluate the respective speeds of two objects traveling simultaneously through unequal paths. Piaget (1946) placed accession to this latter stage at around seven or eight years. Now the results seem to indicate that even at twelve years this stage has been attained by only sixteen to twenty per cent of the subjects. Nevertheless, for the majority of tests observed, disparities rarely amounted to more than one or two years. To a certain extent, these variations can be accounted for by the more rigorous sampling and standardization of test methods.

Be that as it may, once these studies are finished, it will become possible to tackle problems posed by the creation of a scale composed of items most clearly indicative of the principal stages of mental development.

Pedagogical Implications

In conclusion, it is fitting to draw attention to the inherent interest for educational circles of a normative study of mental development based on Piaget's theory. Since a lengthy discussion would be out of place, suffice it to mention two principal aspects: In the first place, a study of this kind will furnish the educator with a valuable tool for analyzing the origins (*analyse génétique*) of the fundamental notions which condition all school learning. This type of analysis can be extremely useful to the specialist in education who is interested in increasing his diagnostic and prognostic precision, and can at the same time contribute to the clarification of the complex problem of the nature of aptitudes, knowledge of which is necessary to school counseling. Besides, this diagnostic instrument will provide the elements of a more rational and effective solution to the problems posed by mental deficiency and precocity. The well-known work of Inhelder (1963) on the diagnosis of mental debility, so difficult to distinguish from simple pedagogical backwardness, has already opened the way to new, broader, and still more systematic investigations in the same domain. The reciprocal problem of mental precocity itself appears in a new light if one can utilize an analytical instrument sufficiently nuanced and flexible to facilitate the development of accelerated scholastic programs without risking the upsetting of harmonious and integrated development.

In the second place, a normative study based on Piaget's theory can bring a contribution of the first order to psychological didactics. By its very nature, to begin with, it offers the principles requisite to the rational structure of study programs and to the creation of teaching methods still better adapted to the child's natural development. The researches of Johannot (1947), of Aebli (1951) and of Muller (1956) are good examples of this. Similar work is now going on at Montreal, notably in connection with the effectiveness of the Cuisenaire method of teaching mathematics, and that concerning the efficacy of traditional methods of teaching geometry. In addition, a normative study can serve directly to track down difficulties in school learning, and above all to discover their real causes and facilitate their systematic rectification. For example, problems raised by reading and writing difficulties (dyslexia, dysgraphia, etc.), are perhaps attributable at their source to perturbations bound up with the origins of particular fundamental notions. The works of Galifret–Granjon (1951) on dyslexia and of Oléron (1957) on deaf-mutism are most instructive in this regard. Studies are currently under way in Montreal on the operative representations of space in the dyslexic and the deaf-mute.

Finally, by bringing to Piaget's experiments the necessary normative complement, the proposed new scale will offer inexhaustible opportunities for research.

Psychometricizing Piaget's *Méthode Clinique*

■■■■ READ D. TUDDENHAM

One of the very interesting aspects of all the researches generated by Piaget's theory is the possibility of developing new and perhaps more exacting methods of assessing the cognitive status of children. Professor Tuddenham and his students have been working toward this end for the past four to five years. This article relates the logic, direction, and progress that they have made in the development of a new scale of intelligence.

Before reporting our explorations in psychometricizing Piaget's *méthode clinique*, apologies are due to any true Piagetians who may have been scandalized by the title. It was chosen to indicate the direction of our recent work, but I acknowledge that my title is almost a contradiction in terms, since the American mental test method has little in common with the probing, highly individualized interrogation which Piaget has used so fruitfully to elicit the patterns of children's thought. But different problems require different methods. Where Piaget has been centrally concerned with establishing the regularities of cognitive development among children, my students and I have been concerned with the extent and range of differences among them, and with the implications of these differences. Bearing in mind the focus of this study, one may readily appreciate why psychometric considerations have taken precedence over the qualitative subtleties of the *méthode clinique*. Indeed, the research reported here is so different in purpose and method from Piaget, that having acknowledged my general indebtedness to him, I hereby absolve him from all further responsibility!

Our central purpose over the last four or five years has been to develop a scale of intelligence founded upon Piaget's theory of cognitive development, yet aspiring to the rigor of the Stanford–Binet or WISC with respect to administration and scoring. These latter tests, although widely used for many purposes, have lacked a really firm anchoring in developmental theory. They have aimed at sampling broadly among the cognitive abilities, but their choice of content owes more to experience than to theory, and the scaling of specific items is determined by statistical rather than develop-

• • • • • • • •

SOURCE: Revised by the author from a paper presented as a part of the colloquium, "New Ways of Measuring Intelligence," at the American Educational Research Association meeting, February 10, 1968. (With permission of the author.)

mental considerations. Valuable as they are for assessing a child's general intellectual level, such tests, especially the Binet, have not been particularly well adapted to discovering specific cognitive deficits in the individual, nor to indicating the remedies. Piaget's reduction of problem solving of many sorts to its basic logical forms, and the assignment of these forms to sequential stages of development, suggested that a test based upon this fundamental theory might diagnose more precisely than MA or IQ both a child's cognitive status and the instructional approaches best suited to his needs. We shall require tests of this general sort not only to evaluate particular children, but also to evaluate innovations in teaching curricula, especially those shaped by Piagetian theory. Apart from such practical concerns, a Piaget-based test might contribute to the theory itself by establishing more accurately the relationship between stage and age, for different types of content.

If one grants the potential value of a Piagetian scale, one might still ask, "Why abandon the *méthode clinique?*" The reason is that the flexibility which enables one to shape the dialogue to the responses of the particular child is no advantage when one's purpose is not to substantiate a theory, but rather to compare children under identical conditions. Moreover, the interrogation designed to reveal the process of a child's thinking takes too long for the examiner to cover any substantial number of problems. Yet the greatest practical and theoretical interest attaches to determining whether the cognitive stage which a child has achieved is or is not invariant across different sorts of content.

My students and I are by no means the first ones to work toward developing a cognitive scale based on Piaget's theoretical formulations and utilizing adaptations of his experiments. In Piaget's own laboratory, Vinh–Bang, in collaboration with Inhelder, has arranged a sequence of experiments and determined provisional per cents passing for various ages. So far as I am informed, this scale is not finished; for as M. Vinh–Bang told me, he had trouble finding time to work on it, because Piaget set higher priority upon the regular program of experimentation. Perhaps the broadest attack has been the collaborative program of the New York Schools with Dr. Helmick and his colleagues at Educational Testing Service, though here the emphasis on testing is secondary to that on developing curricular materials. Laurendeau and Pinard, Almy, and Nassefat have published important investigations of parts of the developmental sequence. Additionally, a great deal of excellent work has been done elaborating one or more of Piaget's experiments in order to test his conclusions. Names such as Dodwell, Elkind, Lovell, Smedslund, and Wohlwill come to mind. The list of contributors is already long and growing rapidly.

The work my students are doing in Berkeley is by no means a completed project. To date, we have made rather extensive explorations of fifteen items on a sample of 350 children in the first four grades. Our items cover a considerable range of content, but have mostly been aimed at the transition from the preoperational stage to the stage of concrete operations. The conservation of quantity is measured by adaptations of the experiments on lumps of clay deformed in shape and water poured into shallow versus deep containers. Conservation of area is tested with grouped versus dispersed barns in fields of equal size; conservation of volume by apartments built on islands of various shapes and sizes. Two items involve spatial reversals. In one, a child must correctly place a small car painted red on one side, blue on the other, at various places on a spiral track. In the other, he must select from among several small photographs the one which shows how a small farm would look from various vantage points. Also presented in multiple choice format is the well-known problem on the horizontality of water levels. The task of placing small sticks in serial order is presented at various levels of difficulty, as are some of the geometric problems formulated by Piaget. We have collected data on the transitivity-of-length problem studied by Smedslund, and are developing items on classification and on conservation of length and of number. For work with fourth-graders, we have developed items dealing with probability, with the conservation of weight, and with the relationships of weight and volume to displacement of a liquid. We think that some of our items now embody the essential idea of the corresponding Piagetian experiments in a much more objective and quantifiable format. Other items, despite numerous revisions, are not as satisfactory. One of the problems is deciding upon the most promising format from among so many inviting possibilities.

In what respects has our work differed from that of others? Most investigators have stayed a good deal closer to Piaget than we have, in that they have relied upon verbal interrogations, even though the questions were sometimes read from a standard list. We are trying, not always successfully, to set up situations in which the child's reasoning may be inferred from what he does rather than from what he says. An example of what we are seeking is Smedslund's transitivity problem, where the child's choice between sticks reveals either the perceptual or the logical basis of his thought.

A second goal, and one where we have had some success, is to develop methods of test administration and scoring which approach the Stanford–Binet or WISC in explicitness and reproducibility. Inasmuch as our items are intended to be constituents of a scale, they have been developed with the practical constraints of brevity, portability, and interest to children in mind.

A third goal has been to build into our items checks upon the child's understanding of the directions, especially his knowledge of relational terms — "more," "less," "the same," "longer," "shorter," etc. Such precautions are necessary to avoid imputing to reasoning level what may be only a question of vocabulary.

A fourth goal, and incidentally a sharp departure from ordinary mental tests, has been to provide measured amounts of practice or assistance, to see whether or not the child's performance can be improved in the course of the testing itself. Generally speaking, this has not significantly improved performance, though it sometimes enables one to distinguish the children who are transitional and beginning to grasp the concept from those who are not.

Lastly, we have been experimenting with weighting schemes such that the assigned score on an item conveys not only the general merit of the performance but also the precise pattern of the subject's performance across the several parts of the item. A record of such patterns is essential to testing empirically the sequential consistency of subjects as demanded by theory. Other workers have "classified" patterns but have not attempted to reduce such classifications to a linear scale. It can be done by using binary numbers and assigning each part to a different column of the item score, but the results are cumbersome when the items are to be combined in a scale like Binet items. We fear this attempt will have to be written off as a good idea that didn't always work! Some items embody weighting schemes such as I have just described. Others have simple summation scores over equally weighted parts. These raw scores, weighted or summative, were used to calculate sex, race, and grade differences to be reported below. For reporting results back to the schools, the raw scores were converted to normalized standard scores. It was also possible to trichotomize the raw scores on each item into the categories "Has concept," "Transitional" (i.e., grasps concept only after demonstration or practice), or "Lacks concept."

What, if anything, has been found out to date? At this stage, results are provisional and some analyses are incomplete. Here are a few highlights, but first a word about our sample and our testing procedure.

Our subjects to date have been 350 children in the first four grades drawn from schools in three school districts of the Bay Area in California. The schools were deliberately selected to cover a wide range of socioeconomic levels. Approximately 20 per cent were Negro, somewhat over 10 per cent were Oriental. Data were collected in a school by a team of examiners, usually five, who set up five tables in a lunchroom or auditorium, each table equipped with materials for two of the items under development. Children were brought in in groups of five, one for each table. Every ten minutes each child moved to the next table in the circle, completing our quasi-musical-chairs game in the fifty-minute period between recesses. This procedure imposed stringent constraints on the length of each item — probably good discipline for experimenters confronted with an almost infinite array of attractive possibilities. On the whole, it worked very well — systematically eliminating order effects as between items and providing a good deal of social facilitation to the children being tested.

Now some data on our ten easier items:

Item 1 (Clay) is an adaptation of Piaget's famous experiment on the invariance of a mass of Plasticine under shape transformations. Our procedure provides several demonstrations for the child who initially lacks the conservation. However, as others have noted, there are few instances where demonstration is helpful to the child who doesn't have the concept. Although few fall into the transitional category, there are highly significant differences in mean score from one grade level to the next. The difference between whites and Negroes (grades combined) is also significant at the .01 level, with a larger percentage of whites having attained the concept.

Item 2 (Water Pouring) concerns the invariance of a quantity of water in containers of different shapes. The results are quite similar to those for *Clay*, and the correlation between the two tasks proved to be .65 for this sample.

Item 3 (Conservation of Area) is somewhat easier and does not show as marked an age progression. Neither grade, sex, nor race differences are significant.

Item 4 (Islands). Here the child must build "apartment houses" from blocks, while maintaining the constant volume of his buildings by adjusting their heights to compensate for differences in the size of the base. This item is discriminating among fourth-graders but is too hard for younger children. Unusual is the fact that a sizable proportion of children at all grade levels seem to be helped by a demonstration, and earn transitional scores. *Islands* is also one of the several items on which Oriental children did better than whites. Unfortunately, our Oriental sample was too small to establish the significance of the result.

Item 5 (Reversal of Perspective) is also an excellent item for grades three and four and, like *Islands*, shows a slight superiority for Oriental children. For some reason, it appears to be unusually difficult for Negroes, although once the principle is demonstrated to them, they do very well.

Item 6 (Lateral Reversal) requires a child to place a car correctly on a spiral track. It is a poor item in that momentary confusion can lower one's score. Since the level of chance success on each part is 50 per cent, a good many determinations are required. The score is a simple sum of parts. "Transitional" scores in this instance reveal not partial grasp of a complex idea but partial success in handling a very simple idea. This item might be expected to correlate with such things as digit span. It does not correlate well with other Piagetian items.

Item 7 (Seriation) is perhaps the best item from a purely psychometric point of view, inasmuch as the age progression is very marked. Here, as in so many things, we have been anticipated by Binet himself. A seriation item occurs on the 1908 and 1911 scales, as well as on the 1916 Stanford–Binet. However, the Binet item involves seriation of five weights identical in appearance, and is rather more difficult than Piaget's seriation of sticks of various lengths.

Item 8 (Transitivity), as adapted from Smedslund, is also quite good. This item and the preceding one seem to depend more upon conceptual reasoning and less upon possession of specific information.

Item 9 (Geometric Forms) assesses children's success in identifying the plane figures which can be folded into simple geometric figures — a cube, a tetrahedron, a cone, and a cylinder. The cube is inordinately difficult for children age ten or less. Failure on this item reduced the number of perfect scores and inflated the number in the transitional category.

Item 10 (Water Level). Here children must identify from several drawings the one which shows how a wrapped bottle half filled with water and held in various positions would look if it were unwrapped. Sex differences do not appear until grade three when 60 per cent of the boys but only 30 per cent of the girls attain the concept. There is a further significant difference favoring the whites when all grades are combined.

To summarize the results: Avoiding much verbal interrogation, it is nevertheless possible to categorize children into the stages Piaget and others have reported. On any given item, some can do it, some can't, and some are in the middle. This, of course, means only that most of our tests are discriminating at the age levels where we have tried them. It is interesting, however, that many of the distributions, especially those concerned with conservation, are bimodal, with relatively few children in the transitional stage. These are the children who do not succeed initially, but who can utilize the experience of the test itself to learn. Our data agree with Piaget and with many others that demonstrating a phenomenon is often useless, because the prerequisite structures of thought are absent. Once these are acquired, the child moves rapidly to the point where he *knows* the answer, and the experimenter's demonstration is not needed.

Our data show some superiority of boys over girls, especially on transitivity, perspectives, and most of the conservation problems, although all children ultimately acquire the same logical structures for problem solving. This result is in contrast to the well-known tendency of girls to excel boys on verbal measures during these years.

Grade differences are marked on certain items, especially the most complicated ones like *Seriation* and *Islands,* but are slight on some of the others presumably measuring the same stage of cognitive development. This was not anticipated.

Although we had no direct measures of socioeconomic status, it was possible to analyze the data by race, and in this sample, race and socioeconomic status were strongly correlated. Race differences tend to be larger than sex differences. Negroes do less well than whites on every test, and on *Clay, Seriation, Perspectives,* and *Water Level,* the difference is significant at the .01 level. What may be more surprising is that the Oriental children are superior to the whites on at least half of the items, though the number of Orientals is too few to establish the significance of the result.

Perhaps the most interesting results are the intercorrelations between items which are available for the sample of 200 children in primary grades mentioned before. Although occasional values are as high as .4 and at least the *Clay* and *Water Pouring* conservation items intercorrelate .65, the values are typically around .25. Unreliability has attenuated all our correlations in unknown degree, but our data strongly suggest that the attainment of concrete operations on one problem is no guarantee that the child will achieve a comparable level when another problem is posed. Our results agree in this respect with Dodwell, Lovell and Ogilvie, and others who have published data showing noncorrespondence of cognitive stage across different content areas. As Almy and as Lunzer have implied, the pervasiveness and clear demarcation of the stages of development are much clearer in Piaget's theoretical formulation than they are in individual children.

It is not surprising in the light of the grade comparisons that correlations with age are virtually all positive. Nevertheless, the correlations were lower than expected, even allowing for the relative unreliability of items as brief as these. We are now working to obtain correlations with mental ages, which we expect to be appreciably higher.

Correlations with father's occupation are also all positive and higher than the correlations with age, although these items tend to involve reasoning about matters universally available to observation, e.g., the horizontality of water levels. It is hard to see how social advantage could be a very large factor in success on some of these items. The genetic selection implicit in occupational level may well have more to do with it, but on this point we have no data.

Conclusions from our work are not final, but the relative specificity and independence of the various items have extinguished whatever hope we might once have entertained that we could place each child on a single developmental continuum equivalent to mental age, and from his score predict his performance on content of whatever kind. It is doubtful whether a global developmental score would be more useful than an MA or IQ of the conventional sort. On the other hand, a more diagnostic approach, already foreshadowed by the ETS studies, might be a very helpful guide to specific remedial efforts. Obviously, understanding of number, time, and space does not exhaust what a child needs to know. Diagnostic evaluation will, therefore, need to cover as well the perceptual and motor skills and, of course, the verbal abilities assessed by tests of the traditional sort.

Our concern with remediation should not blind us to the fact that the substrate of experience which most directly underlies the cognitive structures sampled here is available to almost every child. Fluid levels are as horizontal in a beer bottle as in a vase. Reversals of perspective are as readily observed in an alley as in a boulevard. Like the man who belatedly discovered he had been speaking prose all his life, we have all been conserving since we were six or seven, and no one taught us how. Piaget has himself properly cautioned us against overemphasis upon trying to instill by direct tutelage what must in the last analysis depend upon the child's own intellectual activity. It would be unfortunate if we should base upon Piaget's formulations an uncritical environmentalism which is quite foreign to Piaget's own views.

Another danger, exacerbated by the sweep and symmetry of Piaget's theory, is to lose sight of the intractable individuality of the particular child, which contrasts with the smooth regularity of the group average.

Almy (1966) has put the problem clearly: "It is considerably easier to organize instruction around what are presumed to be the cognitive capabilities of an average or typical four-, five-, or six-year-old than it is to match that instruction to the conceptual repertoire of a specified child." Hopefully, given time, money, and inventiveness enough we can improve both our tests and our teaching methods to achieve that match. Here is the real challenge!

Piaget for First-Grade Teachers: Written Exercises for Assessing Intellectual Development

■■■ MASAKO TANAKA / JOEL T. CAMPBELL / JOHN S. HELMICK

The present study describes the development of a series of paper-and-pencil tasks centered around Piaget's logical reasoning and designed to give first-grade teachers an estimate of a child's cognitive ability at the time of school entrance.

One objective of a project for first-graders for the New York City Board of Education was to develop a set of paper-and-pencil tasks which would give the teacher an objective assessment of the entering pupil's developed ability early in the school year. The rationale for the project is presented

• • • • • • • •

SOURCE: Educational Testing Service Research Memorandum, July 1966. (Reprinted by permission of the Educational Testing Service.)

in the Teacher's Guide discussed in ETS Research Memorandum 66-9, en-titled *Piaget for First-Grade Teachers: A Guide for Understanding Intellectual Devel-opment*. The purpose of the present paper is to report on the development of the paper-and-pencil tasks called written exercises, and to describe the performance of first-grade children on these materials.

Six areas were chosen which would offer the first-grade teacher useful information regarding the abilities of children at this age level, and a set of written exercises was constructed for each of them. This resulted in six sets of materials, each including five exercises (one for each day of the week), with one set on each of the following areas: Shapes and Forms, Spatial Relations, Time Concepts, Communication Skills, Mathematical Under-standing, and Logical Reasoning. It must be evident that the titles of these sets are not mutually exclusive — in a sense, all of them could be included under the title "Logical Reasoning." The explanation is that the titles were chosen in order to relate the material to similar areas in the teacher's guide referred to above.

The task then was to prepare two forms of experimental materials which would not require reading ability, would be city culture oriented, could be group administered, and which would provide some information on tasks which could be related to the Piagetian principles in the guide.

The use of a pictorial presentation (including pictures for page numbers) of items which were familiar to the urban child filled some of the require-ments listed. For a group of children with limited knowledge of such pro-cedures, the problem of group-administered paper-and-pencil tasks presented something of a challenge. The solution which was developed provided three days of practice work in each area followed by two days of assessment. By this procedure, it was hoped that not only would the children have an opportunity to become familiar with the mechanics of "test-taking," but they would also learn something about those concepts which were considered important enough to assess. Thus the written exercise materials were designed for both instruction and evaluation.

The experimental forms of the materials were ready for administration in the middle of the school year 1964–1965, and the tryout results in the twenty-five experimental schools (one in each school district of New York City) were most encouraging. Each set of exercises was administered to groups of 100 to 200 children, and the mean scores on the sets ranged from sixty-one per cent to ninety-three per cent, indicating that they were well within the understanding and abilities of the children at that time of the school year, and that they would probably not be too difficult for the begin-ning of the school year. As these exercises were the first testlike experience for many of these children, it was felt that it was important for them to be rewarding and enjoyable. The teachers reported that the children enjoyed doing the exercises, and they quoted such comments from the children as: "That was fun!" and "Can we do more?"

The following is a brief description of the types of items used in these sets of exercises. Reference is made to the sample items appended. In keeping with the interest in the development of certain cognitive skills and behaviors as investigated by Piaget, some of the items represent attempts to translate a few of his tasks into paper-and-pencil form.

Set I. Shapes and Forms involves the direct matching of whole objects, partial rotation of objects on the same plane, addition of details, and the rotation or reversal of the stimulus pattern. Since this was likely to be the child's first experience with exercises of this type, a deliberate attempt was made to make this set relatively easy.

Set II. Spatial Relations explores the child's understanding of the three-dimensional world. These exercises include items of perspective or distance, spatial fit, missing blocks, size similarity, and right and left orientation. This set also includes some items which explore the ability of a child to see things from a different point of view or, in more Piagetian language, to explore the egocentric behavior of the child. Item 1 was a practice item with the instructions: "Here is a picture of Mary and her little brother. How does her little brother look to Mary?" As in all the practice items used in the exercises, the children did this one together. In Item 2, a test item, the question was reversed and the class was asked, "How does *Mary* look to her little brother?" Only twenty-three per cent of 120 children answered this item correctly, because this time one of the answer choices showed the *same* view of Mary's face as was in the stem drawing. In other words, most of the children could not visualize what Mary would look like from a point of view other than their own.

A similar item was used with another group of 115 children, and thirty-seven per cent of them were able to choose the correct response. It is interesting to note that when the answer choices did *not* include the viewer's point of view, fifty-one per cent of the group were able to find the correct response.

Set III. Time Concepts considers the idea of time in several different ways. The understanding of *age* is explored by asking not only, "Which one is the youngest?" but also "Which object *belongs* to the youngest?" This set also includes items on the amount of time required to cover vertical and horizontal distances as well as single and dual time sequences.

Items 4 and 5 are both time series problems in which the child is told that the drawings on the left tell a story and is then asked: "Can you find the picture which is missing in the story?" The percentage of correct responses in a group of 115 children was seventy-seven per cent on Item 4 and seventy per cent on Item 5. This last item is interesting because, although there is only one "hand" and the face is empty, the children of this age presume that it is a clock and are familiar with the direction of hand rotation. We were also interested in finding out whether children of this age could *compare* two sequences and find the sequence which takes a shorter time. In Item 6, which is representative of this item type, eighty-one per cent of the children chose the correct response.

Set IV. Understanding Mathematics includes some items which are related to Piaget's concept of conservation and the concept of one-to-one correspondence. Some of the items explore the conservation of quantity, showing pieces of paper which undergo perceptual changes such as folding or being cut into pieces. Other items are based on an understanding of problems involving "greater and less than," addition, subtraction, and ordinal position.

Set V. Communication Skills is perhaps the most closely related to the curricular emphasis on language skills in first grade. The items include listening discrimination of beginning sounds, whole-word sounds, and two-line rhymes, as well as comprehension based on single sentence recall and longer story sequences.

Set VI. Logical Reasoning involves the use of different methods of categorization and classification. The children were asked to group by various dimensions such as color, physical characteristic (i.e., "feathers"), and utility.

Item 8, which belongs to this set, is referred to as an "inclusion" problem, in which the student is asked to decide for himself why the drawings in the stem are grouped together, and "to find something else that *belongs* with the group." On this item, eighty-two per cent of the children chose the correct response. To compare "inclusion" items with "exclusion" items, in which a child is asked to mark the one that *doesn't* belong, one group of children were presented with inclusion items which were repeated in exclusion form later in the week. This procedure was reversed for another group of children. Very small differences in score were found, and the differences were not consistently in favor of either the "inclusion" or "exclusion" method of problem presentation.

As mentioned earlier, two forms of the exercises were tried out during the experimental year. Reliabilities of the twenty item measurements (the sums of Thursday and Friday exercises) for the different areas were projected from item-test coefficients for *unselected* items. These were in the high 80s and low 90s. The formal reliability estimates will, of course, be secured on the revised exercises which are being administered this year.

After item analysis, items were selected for a single form on the basis of item difficulty and item-test correlation. There are, of course, many questions still to be answered, such as: How do these measures relate to other measures and to later performance? How do the items which attempt to translate some of the Piagetian concepts compare with an individualized interview approach? Can teachers use the information shown by these measures to provide better instruction? What effect will using these materials have on the cognitive development of the child? These are the kinds of questions now being explored. This is only the beginning of what is hoped will be part of a new approach to the instruction and assessment of the child in first grade.

From Theory to Classroom

■ ANNE M. BUSSIS

Traditional intelligence tests have been based on a number of assumptions which are now being seriously questioned. Moreover, the approach to test construction has been empirical rather than theoretical. In this article, the author provides background information on the First Grade Project in New York City Schools. Materials based on a new set of assumptions, and adhering closely to Piaget's theory, have been developed for both teaching and testing purposes.

Why a Fresh Approach Is Needed

Teachers have for centuries used some form of testing. The earliest recorded use of formal testing was in the year 1115 B.C., at the beginning of the Chan dynasty in China, when examinations were established for candidates for public office. The examining procedures consisted of job-sample tests requiring proficiency in the five basic arts of music, archery, horsemanship, writing, and arithmetic, and a test of knowledge in the rites and ceremonies of public office. From these ancient Chinese practices to the standardized multiple-choice examinations of present-day America, testing has always been a method for estimating the extent to which a person has developed a specific type of knowledge or skill. In the mass testing practices of today, however, there is a tendency to lose sight of this one essential function of the test.

With great refinements in our measurement techniques over the last forty years and increasing numbers of students to be assessed by our schools, there has been a growing reliance on standardized tests prepared by test experts outside of the school. Today standardized tests are used extensively throughout the country for a variety of educational purposes. There is little doubt that the specialized science and technology of measurement have provided the schools with better and more useful tests. But like all earmarks of progress, this particular specialization has its drawback — it has meant the separation of test maker and test user. In the case of tests used to assess learning ability this separation of test and teacher has often resulted in a

• • • • • • • •

SOURCE: *From Theory to the Classroom*. New York: Board of Education for the City of New York, 1965. (With permission of the author and the Board of Education for the City of New York.)

confusion of the underlying test assumptions with assumptions about the nature of intelligence. Specifically, there is a rather widely accepted idea that intelligence means a person's inherited potential and that an ability test or intelligence test measures this potential. While the idea of intelligence as inherited potential will be dealt with specifically in the next section, suffice it to say here that the confusion of this idea with the underlying assumptions of standardized tests constitutes, in and of itself, one limitation to the continued use of these tests.

On the other hand, standardized ability tests have been used effectively by many educators for a variety of purposes. A further examination of the actual underlying characteristics of current standardized tests may clarify the difficulties involved in depending solely on them as the most suitable approach to assessing the intellectual development of New York City's young schoolchildren.

Basic Characteristics of Standardized Tests

Essentially, standardized testing compares the performance of one student with the performance of some specified group of students on a particular task. A student's score is then expressed in terms of how he compares with the group. That is, the score — be it a percentile, standard score, grade placement score, or IQ — is a measure of relative achievement.

A second basic characteristic of standardized tests is that they measure past learning of one kind or another. While it is usually obvious that the questions on achievement tests relate directly to past learning in a specific subject matter, most ability tests measure previous school learning of a general nature. Such tests are quite appropriately called "school ability" or "scholastic aptitude" tests, and what they measure is the general development of a child's verbal and numerical skills — the kind of skills normally emphasized in school. The assumption of the test, the interpretation of the child's test performance, and the logical inference drawn from it are really quite simple:

Assumption: Assuming equal exposure to a school environment and school-type learning,

Score
Interpretation: the children who have benefited most from this exposure — i.e., those who have developed their verbal and numerical skills most highly,

Inference: are the children who will continue to benefit most from exposure to school.

This inference is straightforward and based simply on the observation of what has happened in the past. And for a number of purposes, this inference has proved reasonably valid, provided the test user has exercised proper precautions in score interpretation. Overriding all other precautions set forth by test publishers is the obvious warning that: The assumption of equal exposure to a school environment must hold reasonably well, or the score will not accurately reflect the student's demonstrated ability to benefit from past school experience.

It is evident, however, that aptitude tests which assume the development of certain skills based on past school learning are inappropriate for use in the early elementary grades. Such tests are more appropriately administered only after the child has had a sufficient exposure to the school's instruction. In practice, this has usually meant that scholastic aptitude tests are not administered below grade four.

Limitations for the Early Grades

Certain ability tests are commonly administered below grade four, however, and these make a slightly different assumption. This assumption — inherent in most general IQ tests — is simply that, on the whole, children have had very similar environmental experiences. If this is true, one might test for certain skills children presumably should have learned from their general exposure to life, compare them on the basis of test results, and make the same kind of inference as the aptitude test. Needless to say, this assumption of similar environmental experience is clearly inappropriate when applied to children in large urban areas who come from a wide diversity of backgrounds. In this way, then, modern urban society poses some problems for current ability tests used at the early grade levels.

An even greater limitation to the practical utility of such tests is posed by our growing knowledge of intellectual development in the early years. Standardized tests are empirical instruments — their inference is based strictly on what has happened in the past under the conditions of the past. A test score tells the teacher how child "X" stands in comparison to other children with respect to some scale of development, or what the teacher may do to foster development one notch further along the scale. To do this, tests would have to be based more on a theoretical understanding of how abilities develop than they are at present.

The fact that ability tests are not now rooted in theory is inconsequential in many situations, since test information may still be valuable for a variety of purposes. However, it does constitute a limitation for the teacher of the early grades whose responsibility it is to develop the broad intellectual foundation for all future learning. And as the full importance of these early years becomes increasingly evident, it will become increasingly important for every first-grade teacher to understand how intellect develops . . . and to help develop it.

Thus, for the job of assessing the intellectual development of young children in the New York City schools, sole reliance on current ability tests seems an inadequate approach. What should be sought is the compilation of the best available theory and evidence we now have and the translation of that information into practical, helpful tools for the teacher. As we come nearer to achieving this goal, it will become increasingly difficult to distinguish between the functions of teaching and testing. They will blend imperceptibly into each other.

Outline of a Working Theory

Ask about the "development" of young children in almost any circle of teachers today, and most of the ensuing discussion will center around various aspects of emotional, social and motor development. It is not that teachers are unconcerned about intellectual development, but rather that psychology and education have given them few resources to draw upon. There are already substantial signs of change in this picture, and it is almost certain to change dramatically within the next few years.

Since World War II, and more notably within the last decade, various avenues of research have provided us with important insights about the nature of intellectual processes — insights which carry significant implications for educational practice. There will, however, be no systematic attempt to review and integrate these various lines of research in this article. The following is simply an attempt to set forth and explain some of the major theoretical ideas upon which the New York City project rests. These are presented below in the form of four basic assumptions:

1. Intelligence is essentially a set of developed skills rather than an inherited characteristic.
2. Intellectual skills develop as a result of the child's continuous interaction with his environment.
3. Children are inherently motivated to explore and master their environment.
4. Intellect develops through a sequence of related stages that produce qualitative change in the way children think and are able to deal with the world.

Assumption 1. Intelligence is essentially a set of developed skills rather than an inherited characteristic.

The idea that intelligence is man's overall potential "to understand," or "to acquire knowledge," or "to profit from experience," or simply "to act intelligently" — and that this potential is fixed by heredity — has permeated our thinking to the extent that it is now commonly accepted as "fact." It is so central to everyday thinking about man that to challenge it may arouse nothing short of an emotional response. Nonetheless, it is the educator's responsibility to set this idea in perspective and attempt to analyze it objectively.

The question of how man acquires knowledge is certainly not new. It intrigued the ancient Greek philosophers and is the subject of one of Plato's finest dialogues. The beginning of modern concern with the problem, however, is usually dated with the seventeenth century philosopher John Locke's writing of *An Essay Concerning Human Understanding.* In this work, Locke set down his now famous "appeal to experience" argument — the belief that the mind at birth is a blank upon which human experience inscribes all knowledge.

The roots of a scientific belief in fixed, inherited intelligence may be traced to Darwin's theory of evolution in the mid-nineteenth century. Although not stated outright, implicit in this theory is the assumption that the characteristics of any living thing are predetermined by genetic heredity. It is probable, however, that this implicit assumption would never have caught on with the force it did had it not been for two outstanding figures in the history of psychological testing. The first of these figures, Sir Francis Galton, is generally conceded to be the father of modern psychological measurement. Although Galton's measures were a far cry from modern tests, he nevertheless founded the first laboratory for the systematic measurement of human characteristics. And it was Galton who made explicit the notion that adult characteristics are determined by heredity. Both Galton's ideas and measures were brought to America in the late 1800s. The other outstanding figure was G. Stanley Hall, a psychologist and cofounder of Clark University, who helped spread Galton's ideas in this country. Hall was profoundly influenced by the theory of evolution, and transmitted his belief in the notion of "fixed intelligence" to his students at Clark. Among his students were three of the most important leaders of the "new psychology" in America — a psychology of individual differences that perfected measurement techniques and introduced tests that were the forerunners of those used today.

In a monumental analysis, J. McV. Hunt (1961) traces not only the history of the idea of fixed intelligence, but also the history of research investigations that seemed to support this idea. He then goes on to tie together the various strains of more recent research concerning the effects of early experience on intellectual development — from studies on human and animal learning to recent investigations of brain functioning, to the prolific research of the Swiss biologist, Jean Piaget, on the development of thought processes in young children. A significant aspect of many of these studies is that they have freed themselves from the idea of intelligence as an overall potential and have concentrated on the various skills and elements of thinking *per se.* For the first time, modern science is looking at intelligence as a set of skills and techniques by which a person represents information from the environment and then acts upon that information in such a way as to produce more and more abstract ideas. Hunt's conclusion from this analysis — and one shared by a number of psychologists and educators today — is simply that the belief in fixed intelligence is no longer tenable. Intelligence may be more profitably thought of and studied as a set of skills which emerge only as they are nurtured by the environment. To the extent that this assumption continues to produce insightful research, education will become increasingly concerned with the development of those skills by which we form and effectively use abstract ideas.

Assumption 2. Intellectual skills develop as a result of the child's continuous interaction with his environment.

The idea of fixed intelligence carried with it the twin notion of a fixed rate of development (maturation rate) that was also determined by genetic makeup. In other words, both the extent and rate of intellectual development were thought to be predetermined by heredity and relatively immune to environmental influence. The term "maturation" thus became commonly used to refer to a biological process that went on inside the child.

Among other things, this position implied that education could present the child with knowledge and skills once his intelligence had matured sufficiently to grasp them, but that there was little education could or should do to influence the basic course of his development and the resulting amount of intelligence he possessed. Like the metamorphosis of the tadpole to the frog, the development of the child's intelligence was thought to have a course prescribed by nature. In fact, if training or "tampering" with the course of development had any effect at all, it was thought that it would have a harmful effect. Such a view is hardly inspiring for any educator, past or present, but it is a view still adhered to by many today.

An interaction viewpoint, on the other hand, places great stress on the child's environmental experiences as the vital factor influencing development, especially during the early years of life. It also stresses the importance of continuity of experiences within the environment. A detailed presentation of the diverse body of research evidence supporting this theory may also be found in Hunt's book. Essentially the theory holds that intellectual skills develop as a result of the child's interaction with his environment, especially his encounter with a wide variety of sensory experiences, and that these skills develop in a series of related stages. That is, the skills acquired at one stage become in turn the building blocks for the acquisition of new skills at the next stage. If there is a dearth of "appropriate experiences" at any point along the way and the skills of a given stage are not sufficiently nurtured, they can add little to the next stage. To the extent that this occurs, the child's entire complex of thought processes will be correspondingly weakened.

Such a viewpoint suggests at least two significant implications for the teacher of young children. In the first place, it suggests the vital importance of programming "appropriate experiences" for the child — of providing him with a situation in which he can apply acquired skills to master new learnings. It also suggests that those involved in early education must explore the possibility of compensating for inadequate or inappropriate experience of the past.

Assumption 3. Children are inherently motivated to explore and master their environment.

A baby does not have to be threatened, cajoled, or enticed to turn his head toward a sound, explore his toes, attempt to crawl, or bang the pot lids together. Perhaps this statement sounds like obvious trivia to anyone who has ever watched a baby, but it is in just such activities as "toe exploration" that learning — and intellectual development — begin. Throughout the first few years of life, children generally engage in such learning activities with natural enthusiasm and delight.

Yet our psychological theories of learning have long tended to ignore this basic observation of human life. While these theories have given us great insight into principles that influence certain types of learning, they have tended to lead us astray with respect to the ways in which children learn and develop their basic thinking skills. For the most part, these theories have been founded on what might be called "push–pull" assumptions, in which the human is viewed as an essentially inert creature who must be activated. In the case of the "push" theories, learning is instigated by internal drives and impulses; while in the case of the "pull" theories, it is motivated by external incentives and reinforcements. Although this type of assumption began to be repudiated in the 1930s by certain personality theorists, it was not until after World War II that learning psychology started giving serious consideration to the idea that curious exploration and constructive learning behavior might be inherently satisfying and "natural" to man.

There is an important qualification to this position that must be kept in mind. The child's natural tendency to explore, manipulate, and master the environment — his "motivation for competency" as White (1959) has called it — does not continue to operate automatically for an indefinite period of time. This built-in mechanism for learning may either be sustained, encouraged and directed by the responsive environment, or dulled by an unresponsive one. The school may have a crucial influence in determining what happens on this score, for the implication seems quite clear that an environment which fosters learning motivated by "fear of failure" or the desire for "external rewards" is an environment that will soon stifle the child's natural motivation for learning.

Assumption 4. Intellect develops through a sequence of related stages that produce qualitative change in the way children think and are able to deal with the world.

Human intelligence does not grow like an oak tree, simply getting bigger and bigger. Although development is characterized by gradualness and continuity, it also involves striking qualitative changes in the way children think. These changes occur as the child progressively develops more effective ways of representing information from his environment and then acting upon that information; and this developmental process follows a sequence of related stages. While "representing information" and "acting upon information" may sound like strange terms for talking about intelligence, recent studies of intellectual development have made headway because they have focused largely on these two issues. (1) the ways a person learns to select and represent information from the environment; and (2) the ways he then acts upon these representations in order to make inferences, reach conclusions, or form more abstract ideas.

Of central importance to the New York City project are the two broad and overlapping stages of prelogical and logical concrete thinking.[1] To oversimplify the case, prelogical thought is characterized by concrete images or "picturelike" representations of the environment, while logical concrete thought is characterized by more abstract and symbolic representations. Until a child has developed to the stage of more symbolic thought structures, he has great difficulty understanding and dealing with his world logically.

The child's learning of language during the prelogical stage is a vital acquisition, but it is one that can often throw confusion into the picture of his true developmental stage. The confusion occurs because children can use words in such a way as to indicate greater understanding than they actually possess. Their ability to verbalize may be way ahead of their level of logical thinking skills. For example, a child may fluently use class labels he has heard — "dogs and cats are animals" — without really grasping the

• • • • • • • •

[1] These stages are based primarily on the work and theory of Piaget, but we have chosen to use slightly different terminology than his.

idea of classification. On the other hand, the ability to manipulate language is an important tool for the development of more abstract and symbolic thinking skills. Appropriate experience in the language environment is therefore crucial to optimum intellectual growth.

While any detailed discussion of the "stage concept" of development is beyond the scope of this article, a few of the points which form an important part of the project theory are discussed below:

— Logical concrete thinking, as the name implies, enables the child to deal logically with concrete ideas, objects, and events. Prelogical thinking, on the other hand, does not operate by the rules of adult logic. Thus, the simplest kind of logical inference ($A = B$; $B = C$; therefore: $A = C$) is not mastered by the prelogical child. If block A is exactly the same size as block B; and block B is exactly the same size as block C; the younger, prelogical child cannot infer that blocks A and C must also be of equal size. Rather, he must rely on a direct visual comparison of A and C in order to reach the conclusion that they are equal.

— The prelogical and logical concrete stages are broad and overlapping, so age boundaries are likely to be misleading when applied to any one child. Generally speaking, however, the prelogical stage extends roughly from eighteen months to about age six or seven. The logical concrete stage extends roughly from age six or seven to about age eleven or twelve. The overlapping nature of the stages also implies that there are periods of transition in which children may show characteristics of both stages.

— Transition periods are periods of some normal disruption in intellectual life. As the child learns new ways to structure his world and develops new concepts, the world may become somewhat confusing because his understanding of it has changed. As the older, familiar and more stable concepts begin to break down, the child starts to bring more adequate but less stable concepts to bear on his environment. The result is that his behavior may appear less predictable or even confusing. For example, he may not function at the same level or stage across all areas of his intellectual life. At certain times his level of functioning may even vacillate within a given area. In handling quantitative relationships, for instance, the child may show logical understanding at one time and fail to demonstrate it the next.

— There are specific characteristics of thinking that identify each stage of development. While it is not important to discuss them from a theoretical standpoint, it is important to note that these characteristics of the child's thought are inferred from his behavior. In other words, signs of developmental level may be observed in the child's behavior — presumably by anyone who knows what to look for.

— A variety of concrete sensory experiences, the opportunity for active manipulation of things, and certain kinds of language experience are all vital factors that foster the child's development from prelogical to logical concrete thinking. In other words, the prelogical child does not develop the skills necessary for logical thinking simply by hearing logical principles repeated to him. While this type of purely verbal instruction may be appropriate for an adult, the prelogical child has not yet developed the intellectual equipment to handle such experience in a meaningful way. He may learn to repeat verbal instruction by rote memory, but it will add little to the development of his abilities to think.

These, then, are some of the major theoretical ideas upon which the New York City project is based. While everyone would not subscribe to this particular set of assumptions, it is safe to say that there is no theory to which all would subscribe. Much more important than unanimous agreement, however, is the fact that this position is supported by a large body of evidence and that it has obvious educational significance and utility.

Putting the Theory to Work

From the practitioner's viewpoint, theories must be put to work to be worth the words it takes to describe them. This calls for some explicit extensions of the theory to the school setting. We are still in the process of formulating some extensions and reformulating others, but three initial assumptions were made in order to bridge the gap from theory to classroom.

First, we assumed that teachers can detect important clues of intellectual development by observing the child's behavior, provided they know what to look for.

A second assumption was that certain "unnatural" disruptions of intellectual life occur when the child's environment changes drastically and his experiences are discontinuous. The transition from home to school is just such a disruption for most children. But for most children it is only short-lived because the two environments contain many important similarities. The kinds of things to which the child is exposed and the kinds of behaviors that are expected of him at home are generally the kinds of things to which he is exposed and the kinds of behaviors that are expected of him at school. Thus, the transition poses few major or lasting problems.

But this is not always the case. For some children, the school situation may be so radically different from their previous home environment that they are totally unable to apply their past learning to it. They may appear confused, dull, or even "unteachable."

Finally, it was assumed that if the school can provide "appropriate experiences" for the child — situations in which he can apply past learning to master new concepts which stimulate further modifications and refinements of his thinking skills — then intellectual development and a "natural" motivation for learning will be fostered. To help teachers discover what constitutes an "appropriate experience" is, of course, a primary objective of this project. Whatever else may be involved, however, the right match between the child and his immediate learning environment will depend in large part both upon the child's stage of development and upon the content of his past learning environment.

With these additional assumptions as an educational base, the project strategy was to proceed along three related lines of work: (1) the development of a guide for teachers; (2) the development of assessment and instructional materials for the classroom; and (3) the development of a series of written exercises.

The Guide — Let's Look at First-Graders

An essential step in putting any theory to work is translating it into terms that can be used. Since astute teaching in the primary grades has always centered around careful observation of the child, and since signs of a child's developmental stage may be observed in his behavior, the most useful translation seemed to be a behavioral one.

Upon closer inspection, this translation step actually becomes a twofold job: (1) translating our theoretical concepts about intellectual development into nontechnical, commonsense English; and (2) illustrating these concepts with concrete examples of behavior that are likely to be visible to the teacher. We have attempted to accomplish both of these objectives in a guide for teachers entitled *Let's Look at First-graders*. In chronological order, however, it was the second job we tackled first.

Research literature naturally provided one source of behavioral illustrations of developmental concepts. But illustrations taken from a research setting may appear unrealistic or even pallid to the classroom teacher. Thus, for a second source of behavioral clues we turned to another group of professionals — teachers in the primary grades who see six-year-olds daily. In the spring of 1964 the project staff visited some one hundred teachers in New York City elementary schools (including at least one school in each borough) to ask them about the behavioral signs of intellect they saw in the classroom. No mention was made of any theory — teachers were simply encouraged to talk about specific occasions when particular children, by their behavior, gave the teacher deeper insight into their intellectual development.

Specifically, teachers were asked: "What kinds of things have you seen a child do that made you think . . . 'that child is smart'?" The teachers were most cooperative in their response and proved to be a rich source of behavioral illustrations. Some behaviors, repeated at practically every school we visited, were the more familiar and common signs that teachers are used to looking for — behavior such as "following directions" or "organizing work well." In other words, they were the behaviors of a child who has had the advantage of a home environment that is much like the school environment — a child whose transition from home to school has caused little disruption in his intellectual life. Other behaviors were not mentioned so often, but came from extremely perceptive teachers. These rarer illustrations focused on behaviors of the shy child, behaviors of the child from a disadvantaged learning environment, and behaviors that might be considered annoying or impertinent by a teacher.

Naturally, we could not and did not use every behavior that every teacher mentioned. Some behavioral examples stirred a great deal of controversy among the teachers themselves, and others simply did not illustrate the particular kinds of development in which we were interested. For example, behaviors concerning motor coordination and emotional stability were ruled out by the decision to concentrate on intellectual skills. In the final analysis, however, the perceptions of New York City classroom teachers provided a great many of the concrete examples we needed to illustrate important developmental concepts.

The next job was to translate the theoretical concepts into commonsense English for inclusion in the guide, *Let's Look at First-graders*. The guide is divided into six broad areas, with various major subheadings within each area. Each major subheading is devoted to a brief discussion of some important aspect of intellectual development. Where possible, we have tried to trace each intellectual skill in a truly developmental way, indicating the nature of growth through the prelogical stage to its manifestation in logical concrete thought. Our primary concern, however, has been to describe and illustrate important characteristics of logical concrete thinking. Thus, every behavioral illustration used in the guide is, in our best judgment, an illustration of logical concrete behavior.

By discussing various aspects of intellectual development in nontechnical language, the guide serves as a simple instructional handbook for teachers. By illustrating each aspect of development with concrete examples of behavior, it also serves as a practical assessment tool for the teacher. Although the examples in the guide are simply illustrative and not exhaustive of all behaviors that might indicate logical concrete thinking, an informal but systematic record of the clues a teacher has observed should help her to estimate the approximate stage of each child's intellectual development.

The six broad areas and the concepts discussed within each area in the guide are:

Major Area	Developmental Concept
Basic language skills	Auditory discrimination and attention Listening comprehension Learning to communicate Language for thinking
Concepts of space and time	Learning shapes and forms Spatial perspective The notion of time
Beginning logical concepts	Logical classification Concepts of relationship
Beginning mathematical concepts	The conservation of quantity One-to-one correspondence Number relations
The growth of reasoning skills	Understanding cause and effect Reasoning by association Reasoning by inference
General signs of development	Growing awareness and responsive- ness Directed activity General knowledge Developing imagination

In summary, then, the first phase of the project is aimed at providing materials and a method by which first-grade teachers can become familiar with important aspects of intellectual development in six-year-olds and can keep a systematic record of those signs of development that will be useful.

Assessment and Instructional Materials for the Classroom

From the very beginning of the project, when the staff was combing research literature for specific examples of concrete logical thinking, it was apparent that not all of the behavioral signs could be seen by just waiting for them to happen. Some of them — often important ones — have little chance of happening in the ordinary course of events in the first-grade classroom or on the playground.

It was also apparent from the beginning of the project that there are children for whom the classroom situation is so strange or so threatening that they simply withdraw and reveal little behavior of any kind. These are the "hard-to-see" children who rarely engage in any classroom activities in which their developed intellectual skills can be observed.

For these reasons, the project was planned to consist of a second phase, or element, which concentrated on the development of various materials and tasks for eliciting intellectual behavior. If, for any one of several reasons, the teacher is unable to see important signs of intellect in the spontaneous behavior of children, she may use these tasks and materials to make sure they have an opportunity to demonstrate certain skills and understandings. Some of the tasks are amenable to class administration and some to small groups or to individual children. Some require no special equipment beyond what is normally found in the classroom or is easily obtainable by the teacher; others have been designed and constructed by the project staff. All of these materials are described in detail in a supplementary manual for teachers, *Instructional and Assessment Materials for First-graders.*

Many of the materials have some "built-in" provision for obtaining a permanent record of the child's performance. That is, the child indicates his performance in some simple way on paper. He may copy the numbers that make a balance beam "balance," cross out a picture that completes a matrix puzzle, or draw something to complete the task. In other cases, the teacher must make notes directly from her observation of the situation. To summarize, all of the tasks are designed to give children an opportunity to demonstrate some kind of logical concrete intellectual behavior and to provide teachers with a relatively standard opportunity to observe this behavior.

In addition to allowing a child to demonstrate his understanding and the teacher to observe it, many of these tasks also have instructional value in that they provide children with the kind of experience needed to develop their understanding. It is at this point that what is often called "assessment" or "measurement" blends wholly into what is really teaching.

Since the functions of observation and instruction frequently overlap, the purpose in presenting a particular task really becomes a matter of emphasis. A teacher may be primarily interested in observing a particular child or the entire class (perhaps in order to decide upon appropriate instruction), or primarily concerned with providing an instructional situation. The line between these two functions is often thin and blurred. In general, however, whenever the developmental tasks are used as instructional situations, they should not be thought of as "one-shot" affairs in which the child is told he is either "right" or "wrong." Nor are the tasks even to be thought of as situations in which the teacher teaches, in the sense that she provides the child directly with certain knowledge or principles. Rather, they are gamelike situations designed to provide an opportunity for the child to discover new concepts and develop new skills of thinking. Thus, the major instructional value of many of these tasks lies in the fact that:

1. They have a self-corrective "feedback" feature that enables the child to see for himself whether he is right or wrong in a particular response. He does not have to be told by the teacher.
2. They involve materials that children can manipulate over and over again on their own.

Together, these two features mean that if interest is maintained (if the game or task situation is not too unfamiliar and threatening), children may "play" with the materials for however long it takes them to master the problem. The length of time involved may range from minutes to repeated play sessions with the materials over a period of days, weeks, or even months. But failure experience, at least in the usual absolute sense of that term, rarely occurs.

The Written Exercises

The third of the related elements of developmental work in the project is the written exercises. This final element is the most "testlike" of any. Although the written exercises are similar in some ways to existing tests, they do contain at least two important features that make them quite distinct.

First, the exercises are related to various theoretical concepts in the guide. Specifically, they have been designed to tap the child's understanding and developed ability in the areas of:

> Shapes and forms
> Spatial relations
> Time concepts
> Mathematics
> Communication skills
> Logical reasoning

Secondly, they are designed to give the child extensive practice before any "measure for the record" is made. In each of the areas listed above, there are actually five exercises, one to be given on each day of the week. The first three are for practice and instructional purposes; only the results of the last two exercises will be recorded by the teacher as a measure of the child's developed skill in that area. By this procedure we hope not only to give the child an opportunity to become familiar with the mechanics of "test taking" but also to instruct him in those concepts which we consider important enough to test. In effect, we are attempting to make instructional materials and "test" materials one and the same thing.

In final form, the written exercises will be designed to give the teacher, early in the school year, information on a number of aspects of the child's developed intellectual skills. Tentatively it is planned that this information will include both a learning rate score (an index of the child's improvement with instruction) and an achievement score (the result of his performance on the last two exercises).

Progress and Future Plans

Initial forms of all project materials were used in twenty-five of New York City's elementary schools during the 1964–1965 school year. Special workshop sessions and visits of the project staff to individual schools served as a means for instructing the teachers in the project philosophy and methods. The materials were introduced in stages, with the guide being presented in the fall and the balance of the materials introduced at various intervals after December.

In no sense has the past year been a year of "experimental research." It has been a year of developmental work and initial tryout. To those principals and teachers who have participated in this tryout, it would be difficult to express adequate appreciation. They have gently but firmly pointed out any impracticable techniques or downright mistakes all along the way, and have supplied us with better ideas in their place. Their enthusiasm about the project as a whole has been our greatest sign of success. All the project materials are currently undergoing revision based on the data we obtained and on the constructive criticism of the principals and teachers.

During the 1965–1966 academic year, the revised project materials will be introduced into a larger number of schools for further tryout. At the same time, however, research investigations will be carried out in a selected sample of schools in an attempt to get some more definitive answers about the effects of the project and the course of intellectual development in New York City's schoolchildren.

Materials of the kind being developed in this project are never completely final or finished — they cannot be. Not only is knowledge extending but the patterns of society are changing all the time. What we do hope, however, is that our general theoretical approach and the classroom tools we have derived from it will prove more suitable to our times and amenable to modification in the light of future knowledge and changing demands. We are encouraged to think that they will.

At present, special recognition has been given to the fact that children enrolling in the schools of New York City come from widely differing cultural, ethnic, and social backgrounds and to the fact that the schools have a responsibility to reach and teach all of these children. Crystal ball gazing is always a dangerous pastime. But if this project produces some improved materials and methods for use in the first grade, it would be expected that similar efforts will be undertaken in the future at other grade levels.

Concept Assessment Kit–Conservation

■■■ MARCEL L. GOLDSCHMID / PETER M. BENTLER

The preceding articles in this section were concerned with the development of instruments based on Piagetian concepts. In this article, the authors describe their Concept Assessment Kit–Conservation which is already available. The kit is designed primarily for assessment of concept development in preschool and early-school children to aid in placement. The items were constructed to assess the child's conservation as well as assessing his comprehension of the principle involved.

The Concept Assessment Kit–Conservation was developed for use in assessing cognitive development among preschool- and early-school-age children. The Kit is among the few theory-based measurement techniques available for use with children. This is in contrast to most traditional intelligence tests which are merely an agglomeration of tasks empirically related to school achievement.

Development of the Kit was based on Jean Piaget's systematic developmental theory of cognitive structure depicting a stage-by-stage progress of a child's thinking. The Kit measures the concept of conservation which is seen to represent a pivotal construct in the child's cognitive transition from the "preoperational" stage to "concrete operations." This reflects Piaget's observation that with increasing age the child tends to rely relatively more on such abstract concepts as quantity, volume, and weight, and relatively less on such specific attributes of the stimulus object as form and shape. The comprehension of this principle of constancy signals the transition from a prelogical to a logical phase of development. When a child is able to conserve, he realizes that certain properties, such as substance, weight, volume, or number, remain unchanged in the face of certain transformations, such as changing an object's form, shape, color, or position. Items in the Kit assess such conservation behavior; i.e., can the child indicate whether a transformation leaves a characteristic of an object the same, as well as assessing his comprehension of the principle involved. While some investigators who have used test materials similar to those of Piaget have suc-

● ● ● ● ● ● ● ●

SOURCE: With permission of the authors and publishers of the KIT, the Educational and Industrial Testing Service, Box 7234, San Diego, California, 92107.

cessfully validated many of his observations, few attempts have been made to construct standardized procedures to assess these concepts. The Concept Assessment Kit provides such procedures and introduces a psychometrically sound method of measuring conservation.

Thus, the purpose of the Concept Assessment Kit is to provide a brief and practical assessment of a child's comprehension of the principle of conservation. The child's level of conservation will serve as an indication of his general development of concept formation, of his readiness to fully comprehend school-related academic subjects, and of his verbal ability. Several studies have indicated that conservation is correlated with other cognitive concepts (especially transitivity, probability, and perspective), achievement in school (especially in arithmetic and science), mental age, vocabulary, and personality characteristics typically thought of as enhancing cognitive functioning and interpersonal relationships.

The Concept Assessment Kit–Conservation consists of three Forms: A, B, and C. Forms A and B are parallel forms including tasks measuring conservation of two-dimensional space, number, substance, quantity, weight, and discontinuous quantity. Form C measures a slightly different dimension of conservation including conservation of area and length. Since parallel forms are available, repeated assessments of the same child can be carried out independently of substantial increases due to practice effects. These assessments could be undertaken in the regular classroom and kindergarten to third or fourth grade, in special education classes, rehabilitation programs, or in children's hospitals and clinics. The parallel forms may also serve to measure gains after a training program for concept development has been initiated. Transfer to untrained tasks can be evaluated by means of either one of the parallel Forms A or B or Form C. In a research study, Form A may well serve as a pretest, Form B as a post-test after some intervening experimental treatment, and Form C for transfer effects.

Bibliography

Adler, M. J. "Some Implications of the Theories of Jean Piaget and J. S. Bruner for Education." *Canadian Education and Research Digest*, 4 (1964), 291–305.

Aebli, H. *Didactique Psychologique: Application à la Didactique de la Psychologie de Jean Piaget.* Neuchâtel: Delachaux et Niestlé, 1951.

Aebli, H. *Über die Geistige Entwicklung des Kindes.* Stuttgart: Ernst Klett Verlag, 1963.

Aldrich, V. *Philosophy of Art.* Englewood Cliffs, New Jersey: Prentice-Hall, 1963.

Allport, F. *Theories of Perception and the Concept of Structure.* New York: Wiley, 1955.

Almy, M. "Wishful Thinking About Children's Thinking." *Teachers College Record*, 5 (1961), 396–408.

Almy, M., E. Chittenden, and P. Miller. *Young Children's Thinking.* New York: Teachers College Press, 1966.

Anthony, E. J. "The Significance of Jean Piaget for Child Psychiatry." *British Journal of Medical Psychology*, 29 (1956), 20–34.

Anthony, E. J. "The System Makers: Piaget and Freud." *British Journal of Medical Psychology*, 30 (1957), 255–269.

Archer, J. E. "Concept Identification as a Function of Obviousness of Relevant and Irrelevant Information." *Journal of Experimental Psychology*, 63 (1962), 616–620.

Archer, J. E., L. Bourne, and F. Brown. "Concept Identification as a Function of Irrelevant Information and Instruction." *Journal of Experimental Psychology*, 49 (1955), 153–164.

Atkin, J. and R. Karplus. "Discovery or Invention?" *Science Teacher*, 19 (1963), 45–51.

Ausubel, D. P. and H. M. Schiff. "The Effect of Incidental and Experimentally Induced Experience in the Learning of Relevant and Irrelevant Causal Relationships by Children." *Journal of Genetic Psychology*, 84 (1954), 109–123.

Baldwin, A. L. *Theories of Child Development.* New York: Wiley, 1965.

Banks, S. H. "How Students in a Secondary Modern School Induce Scientific Principles from Scientific Experiments." Unpublished doctoral dissertation, Birmingham University, Birmingham, England, 1958.

Bardecke, A. "The Child's Appreciation of the Relation of Part and Whole." *Psychologie Wychowaucza, 2* (1959), 385–399.

Bartley, S. H. *Principles of Perception.* New York: Harper, 1958.

Beard, M. "The Order of Concept Development Studies in the Two Fields, Section I, Number Concept in the Infant School." *Educational Review, 15* (1963), 105–117.

Beilin, H. "Learning and Operational Convergence in Logical Thought Development." *Journal of Experimental Child Psychology, 2* (1965), 317–339.

Beilin, H. and I. Franklin. "Logical Operations in Length and Area Measurement: Age and Training Effects." Paper read at the Society for Research in Child Development, Pennsylvania State University, 1961.

Beilin, H. and I. Franklin. "Logical Operations in Area and Length Measurement: Age and Training Effects." *Child Development, 33* (1962), 607–616.

Bereiter, C. and S. Engelmann. *Teaching Disadvantaged Children in the Preschool.* Englewood Cliffs, New Jersey: Prentice-Hall, 1966.

Berlyne, D. "Recent Developments in Piaget's Work." *British Journal of Educational Psychology, 27* (1957), 1–13.

Berlyne, D. *Structure and Direction in Thinking.* New York: Wiley, 1965.

Biggs, F. "An Experimental Comparison of Three Methods of Teaching Addition and Subtraction of Fractions in Grade Five." *Dissertation Abstracts, 25* (1964), 185.

Binet, A. and T. Simon. *A Method of Measuring the Intelligence of Young Children.* Chicago: Chicago Medical Books, 1915.

Binnie, C., D. Elkind, and J. Stewart. "A Comparison of the Visual-Perceptual Abilities of Acoustically Impaired and Hearing Children." *International Audiology, 5* (1966), 233–241.

Birch, H. "Health and the Education of Socially Disadvantaged Children." Mimeographed, 1969.

Bobroff, A. "The Stages of Maturation in Socialized Thinking and the Ego Development of Two Groups of Children." *Child Development, 31* (1960), 321–338.

Braine, M. D. S. "The Ontogeny of Certain Logical Operations: Piaget's Formulation Examined by Nonverbal Methods." *Psychological Monographs, 73* (1959), 43.

Braine, M. D. S. "Piaget on Reasoning: A Methodological Critique and

Alternative Proposals." *Monographs of the Society for Research in Child Development, 27* (1962), 41–61.

Braine, M. D. S. "Development of a Grasp of Transitivity of Length: A Reply to Smedslund." *Child Development, 35* (1964), 799–810.

Brison, D. W. "Acceleration of Conservation of Substance." *Journal of Genetic Psychology, 109* (1966), 311–322.

Brown, K. E. and T. L. Abell. *Analysis of Research in the Teaching of Mathematics.* U.S. Office of Education, Bulletin No. 28, 1965.

Brownell, W. A. "Arithmetical Abstractions — Progress Toward Maturity of Concepts under Differing Programs of Instruction." *Arithmetic Teacher, 10* (1963), 322–329.

Bruner, J. S. "The Viewpoint of a Psychologist." Review of B. Inhelder and J. Piaget, *The Growth of Logical Thinking. British Journal of Psychology, 50* (1959), 363–370.

Bruner, J. S. *The Process of Education.* Cambridge, Massachusetts: Harvard University Press, 1960.

Bruner, J. S. "The Course of Cognitive Growth." *American Psychologist, 19* (1964), 1–15.

Bruner, J. S. *Toward a Theory of Instruction.* Cambridge, Massachusetts: Harvard University Press, 1966.

Bruner, J. S., J. J. Goodenough, and G. A. Austin. *A Study of Thinking.* New York: Wiley, 1956.

Bruner, J. S. and H. J. Kenney. "Representation and Mathematics Learning." *Monographs of the Society for Research in Child Development, 30,* 1 (1965), 50–59.

Bruner, J. S., R. R. Olver, and P. M. Greenfield. *Studies in Cognitive Growth.* New York: Wiley, 1966.

Bulgarella, R. G. and J. E. Archer. "Concept Identification of Auditory Stimuli as a Function of Amount of Relevant and Irrelevant Information." *Journal of Experimental Psychology, 63* (1962), 254–257.

Burt, C. "Review of the California Test of Mental Maturity." In O. K. Buros (ed.), *The Fifth Mental Measurements Yearbook.* Highland Park, New Jersey: Gryphon, 1959, 313.

Burton, D. "Teaching Students to Read Imaginative Literature." In D. Burton and J. Simmons (eds.), *Teaching English in Today's High Schools.* New York: Holt, Rinehart and Winston, 1965.

Buss, A. H. "Rigidity as a Function of Reversal and Nonreversal Shifts in the Learning of Successive Discriminations." *Journal of Experimental Psychology, 45* (1953), 75–81.

Carlson, J. S. "Effects of Instruction on the Concept of Conservation of Substance." *Science Education,* 4 (1967), 285–291.

Carpenter, T. E. "A Pilot Study for a Quantitative Investigation of Jean Piaget's Original Work on Concept Formation." *Educational Review,* 7 (1955), 142–149.

Cassirer, E. *The Philosophy of Symbolic Forms* (3 vols.: *I — Language; II — Mythical Thought; III — Phenomenology of Knowledge*). New Haven: Yale University Press, 1953–55, 1957.

Castaneda, A., B. R. McCandless, and D. Palermo. "The Children's Form of the Manifest Anxiety Scale." *Child Development,* 27 (1956), 317–326.

Charlesworth, W. R. "Development and Assessment of Cognitive Structures." *Journal of Research in Science Teaching,* 2 (1964), 214–219.

Churchill, E. M. "The Number Concepts of the Young Child." *Researches and Studies,* 17, 18 (1958), 34–49, 28–46.

Ciardi, J. "The Act of Language." In *Dialogue with an Audience.* Philadelphia: Lippincott, 1963.

Crawford, D. H. "The Work of Piaget as It Relates to School Mathematics." *Alberta Journal of Educational Research,* 6 (1960), 125–136.

Cronbach, L. J. *Essentials of Psychological Testing.* New York: Harper, 1954.

Cronbach, L. J. "Issues Current in Educational Psychology." *Monographs of the Society for Research in Child Development,* 30, 1 (1965), 109–126.

Cronbach, L. J., N. Rajaratnam, and G. C. Glesser. "Theory of Generalizability: A Liberalization of Reliability Theory." *British Journal of Statistical Psychology,* 16 (1963), 137–163.

Crossland, H., H. Taylor, and S. Newson. "Intelligence and Susceptibility to the Müller-Lyer Illusion." *Journal of Experimental Psychology,* 9 (1926), 271–298.

Crossland, H., H. Taylor, and S. Newson. "Practice and Improvability in the Müller-Lyer Illusion in Relation to Intelligence." *Journal of Genetic Psychology,* 21 (1929), 290–304.

Dailey, J. T. In O. K. Buros (ed.). *The Sixth Mental Measurements Yearbook.* Highland Park, New Jersey: Gryphon, 1965.

Dennis, W. and M. G. Dennis. "Cradles and Cradling Practices of the Pueblo Indians." *American Anthropologist,* 42 (1940), 107–115.

Deutsche, J. M. *The Development of Children's Concepts of Causal Relations.* Minneapolis: University of Minnesota Press, 1937.

Deutsche, J. M. "Facilitating Development in the Preschool Child: Social and Psychological Perspectives." *Merrill–Palmer Quarterly, 10,* 3 (1964), 149–163.

Dienes, Z. P. "The Growth of Mathematical Concepts in Children Through Experience." *Educational Research, 2* (1959), 9–28.

Dodwell, P. "Children's Understanding of Number and Related Concepts." *Canadian Journal of Psychology, 13* (1960), 191–203.

Dodwell, P. "Children's Understanding of Number Concepts: Characteristics of an Individual and Group Test." *Canadian Journal of Psychology, 15* (1961), 152–160.

Domino, G., M. L. Goldschmid, and M. Kaplan. "Personality Traits of Institutionalized Mongoloid Girls." *American Journal of Mental Deficiency, 68* (1964), 498–502.

Dorn, M. S., K. Wann, and E. Liddle. *Intellectual Development of the Young Child.* New York: Teachers College, Columbia University Press, 1963.

Drever, J. "Perceptual Learning." *Annual Review of Psychology, 11* (1960), 131–160.

Durkin, D. "Children's Concepts of Justice: A Comparison with the Piaget Data." *Child Development, 30* (1959), 59–60. (*a*)

Durkin, D. "Children's Concepts of Justice: A Further Comparison with the Piaget Data." *Journal of Educational Research, 52* (1959), 252–257. (*b*)

Dymond, R. F., A. S. Hughes, and V. L. Raabe. "Measurable Changes in Empathy with Age." *Journal of Consulting Psychology, 16* (1952), 202–206.

Educational Testing Service. *Let's Look at First-Graders.* New York: Board of Education of the City of New York, 1965.

Elkind, D. "Quantity Conceptions in Junior and Senior High Students." *Child Development, 32* (1961), 551–560. (*a*)

Elkind, D. "The Development of Quantitative Thinking: A Systematic Replication of Piaget's Studies." *Journal of Genetic Psychology, 98* (1961), 37–46. (*b*)

Elkind, D. "Children's Discovery of the Conservation of Mass, Weight, and Volume: Piaget Replication Study II." *Journal of Genetic Psychology, 98* (1961), 219–227. (*c*)

Elkind, D. "The Child's Conception of His Religious Denomination: III. The Protestant Child." *Journal of Genetic Psychology, 103* (1963), 291–304.

Elkind, D. "Ambiguous Pictures for Study of Perceptual Development and Learning." *Child Development, 35* (1964), 1391–1396.

Elkind, D. "Nonverbal Exercises for Remedial Reading Instruction." *Journal of the Colorado Education Association, 81,* 12 (1966), 37.

Elkind, D. "Piaget's Theory of Intellectual Development: Its Application to Reading and Special Education." *Journal of Special Education, 4* (1967), 357–361.

Elkind, D. "Piagetian and Psychometric Conceptions of Intelligence." *Harvard Educational Review, 39,* 2 (1969), 319–337.

Elkind, D., R. B. Barocas, and E. P. Johnsen. "Concept Production in Children and Adolescents." *Journal of Experimental Child Psychology* (forthcoming).

Elkind, D., R. B. Barocas, and R. Rosenthal. "Concept Production in Slow and Average Readers." *Journal of Educational Psychology* (forthcoming).

Elkind, D. and J. Deblinger. "Reading Achievement in Disadvantaged Children as a Result of Nonverbal Perceptual Training" (forthcoming).

Elkind, D., R. R. Koegler, and E. Go. "Effects of Perceptual Training at Three Age Levels." *Science, 137* (1962), 744–756.

Elkind, D., R. R. Koegler, and E. Go. "Studies in Perceptual Development: II. Part–Whole Perception." *Child Development, 35* (1964), 81–90.

Elkind, D., R. R. Koegler, E. Go, and W. VanDoorninck. "Effects of Perceptual Training on Unmatched Samples of Brain-Injured and Familial Retardates." *Journal of Abnormal Psychology, 70,* 2 (1965), 107–110.

Elkind, D., M. Larson, and W. VanDoorninck. "Perceptual Decentration, Learning, and Performance in Slow and Average Readers." *Journal of Educational Psychology, 56* (1965), 50–56.

Elkind, D. and L. Scott. "Studies in Perceptual Development: I. The Decentering of Perception." *Child Development, 33* (1962), 619–630.

Elkind, D. and J. Weiss. "Studies in Perceptual Development: III. Perceptual Organization." *Child Development, 38* (1967), 553–561.

English, H. *Objective Test Analysis.* Buffalo, New York: Student Testing Center, State University of New York at Buffalo, 1966.

Erikson, E. H. *Childhood and Society.* New York: Norton, 1950.

Erikson, E. H. "Identity and the Life Cycle." *Psychological Issues, 1* (1959), 1–171.

Estes, B. W. "Some Mathematical and Logical Concepts in Children." *Journal of Genetic Psychology, 88* (1956), 219–222.

Fahey, G. L. "The Questioning Activity of Children." *Journal of Genetic Psychology, 60* (1942), 337–357.

Fantz, R. L. "Pattern Vision in Newborn Infants." *Science, 140* (1963), 296–297.

Feffer, M. H. "The Cognitive Implications of Role-taking Behavior." *Journal of Personality, 27* (1959), 152–168.

Feffer, M. H. and V. Gourevitch. "Cognitive Aspects of Role-taking in Children." *Journal of Personality, 28* (1960), 383–396.

Feffer, M. H. and L. Suchotliff. "Decentering Implications of Social Interactions." *Journal of Personality and Social Psychology, 4* (1966), 415–422.

Feifel, A. and I. Lorge. "Qualitative Differences in the Vocabulary Responses of Children." *Journal of Educational Psychology, 41* (1950), 1–18.

Feigenbaum, K. D. "An Evaluation of Piaget's Study of the Child's Development of the Concept of Conservation of Discontinuous Quantities." *American Psychologist, 16*, 7 (1961), 364.

Feigenbaum, K. D. "Task Complexity and IQ as Variables in Piaget's Problems of Conservation." *Child Development, 34* (1963), 423–432.

Fernald, G. M. *Remedial Techniques in Basic School Subjects.* New York: McGraw-Hill, 1943.

Finn, J. D. *Multivariance: Fortran Program for Univariate and Multivariate Analysis of Variance and Covariance.* Buffalo, New York: Department of Educational Psychology, School of Education, State University of New York at Buffalo, 1967.

Fitts, P. M. and M. I. Posner. *Human Performance.* Belmont, California: Brooks–Cole, 1967.

Flavell, J. H. *The Developmental Psychology of Jean Piaget.* Princeton, New Jersey: D. Van Nostrand, 1963.

Flavell, J. H., P. T. Botkin, C. L. Fry, J. W. Wright, and P. E. Jarvis. *The Development of Role-taking and Communication Skills in Children.* New York: Wiley, 1968.

Fournier, E. "Un Apprentissage de la Conservation des Quantités Continués par une Technique d'Exercices Opératoires." Unpublished doctoral dissertation, Université de Montréal, Montréal, P. Q., 1967.

Fowler, W. "Cognitive Stimulation, IQ Changes, and Cognitive Learning in Three-year-old Identical Twins and Triplets." *American Psychologist, 16* (1961), 373 (Abstract).

Fowler, W. "Cognitive Learning in Infancy and Early Childhood." *Psychological Bulletin, 59*, 2 (1962), 116–152.

Fowler, W. "A Study of Process and Learning in Three-year-old Twins Learning to Read." *Genetic Psychology Monographs, 72* (1965), 3–89.

French, J. W. "The Relationship of Problem-Solving Styles to the Factor Composition of Tests." *Educational and Psychological Measurement, 25* (1965), 9–28.

Freud, A. *The Ego and the Mechanisms of Defense.* New York: International Universities Press, 1946.

Fry, C. L. "The Effects of Training in Communication and Role Perception on the Communicative Abilities of Children." Unpublished doctoral dissertation, University of Rochester, 1961.

Gabel, O. J. "The Effect of Definite Versus Indefinite Quantitative Terms upon the Comprehension and Retention of Social Studies Material." *Journal of Experimental Education, 9* (1940), 177–186.

Gage, N. L. *Handbook of Research on Teaching.* Chicago: Rand-McNally, 1963.

Gagne, R. M. *The Conditions of Learning.* New York: Holt, Rinehart and Winston, 1965.

Gagne, R. M. "The Learning of Principles." In H. J. Klausmeier and C. W. Harris (eds.), *Analyses of Concept Learning.* New York: Academic Press, 1966, 81–95.

Gagne, R. M. and E. C. Smith. "A Study of the Effects of Verbalism on Problem Solving." *Journal of Experimental Psychology, 63* (1962), 12–18.

Galifret–Granjon, N. "Le Problème de L'Organisation Spatiale dans les Dyslexies d'Évolution." *Enfance, 4* (1951), 445–479.

Gardner, D. E. M. *Testing Results in the Infant School.* London: Methuen, 1930.

Gardner, D. E. M. *Experiment and Tradition in Primary School.* New York: Barnes and Noble, 1966.

Garner, W. R. *Uncertainty and Structure as Psychological Concepts.* New York: Wiley, 1962.

Garner, W. R. "To Perceive Is to Know." *American Psychologist, 21* (1966), 11–19.

Gaudreau, J., G. Lavoie, and A. Delorme. "La Perception des Illusions de Müller–Lyer et D'Oppel–Kundt chez les Déficients Mentaux." *Canadian Journal of Psychology, 17,* 3 (1963), 259–263.

Gellman, R. "Conservation, Attention, and Discrimination." Unpublished doctoral dissertation, University of California at Los Angeles, 1967.

Gibson, E. J. and V. Olum. "Experimental Methods of Studying Perception in Children." In P. H. Mussen (ed.), *Handbook of Research Methods in Child Psychology,* New York: Wiley, 1960, 311–373.

Gibson, J. J. and E. J. Gibson. "Perceptual Learning: Differentiation or Enrichment?" *Psychological Review, 62* (1955), 32–41.

Goldschmid, M. L. "Different Types of Conservation and Nonconservation and Their Relation to Age, Sex, IQ, MA, and Vocabulary." *Child Development, 38* (1967), 1229–1246.

Goldschmid, M. L. and P. M. Bentler. "Dimensions and Measurement of Conservation." *Child Development, 39* (1968), 579–589.

Goldschmid, M. L. and G. Domino. "Some Paradiagnostic Implications of the IQ Among Mentally Retarded Patients." *Training School Bulletin, 61* (1965), 178–183.

Goldstein, H. and C. Kass. "Incidental Learning of Mentally Retarded Children." *American Journal of Mental Deficiency, 66* (1961), 245–249.

Gollin, E. S. "Forming Impressions of Personality." *Journal of Personality, 23* (1954), 65–76.

Gollin, E. S. "Organizational Characteristics of Social Judgment: A Developmental Investigation." *Journal of Personality, 26* (1958), 139–154.

Goodlad, J. I. "Can Individualization Work in Your School System?" Part I of five films, *How to Provide a Personalized Education in a Public School.* Malibu, California; Special Purpose Films, 1966.

Goodnow, J. J. "A Test of Milieu Effects with Some of Piaget's Tasks." *Psychological Monographs, 76* (1962), 1–22.

Goodnow, J. J. "Piaget's Tasks: The Effect of Schooling and Intelligence." *Child Development, 37* (1966), 431–437.

Gotkin, L. G. *Language Lotto.* New York: Appleton-Century-Crofts, 1966.

Gotkin, L. G. *Matrix Games.* New York: Appleton-Century-Crofts, 1967.

Gough, H. G. "A Sociological Theory of Psychopathy." *American Journal of Sociology, 53* (1948), 359–365.

Gough, H. G. "The Adjective Checklist as a Personality Assessment Research Technique." *Psychological Reports, 6* (1960), 107–122.

Greco, P. "L'Apprentissage dans une Situation à Structure Opératoire Concrèt: Les Inversions Successives de l'Ordre Lineaire par des Rotations de 180°." In J. Piaget (ed.), *Études d'Épistémologie Génétique.* Paris: Presses Universitaires de France, *8* (1959), 68–182.

Gruen, G. E. "Experiences Affecting the Development of Number Conservation in Children." *Child Development, 36* (1965), 963–980.

Gruen, G. E. "Note on Conservation: Methodological and Definitional Considerations." *Child Development, 37* (1966), 977–983.

Guenther, W. C. *Analysis of Variance.* Englewood Cliffs, New Jersey: Prentice-Hall, 1964.

Gulliksen, H. *Theory of Mental Tests.* New York: Wiley, 1950.

Hanfmann, E. and J. Kasanin. "A Method for the Study of Concept Formation." *Journal of Psychology*, 3 (1963), 521–540.

Harlow, H. F. and R. R. Zimmerman. "Affection in the Infant Monkey." *Science, 130* (1959), 421–432.

Harshman, H., D. Wells, and J. Payne. "Manipulative Materials and Arithmetic Achievement in Grade One." *Arithmetic Teacher, 9* (1962), 188–192.

Hayakawa, S. I. *Language in Thought and Action.* New York: Harcourt, Brace and World, 1964.

Haygood, R. C. and L. E. Bourne, Jr. "Attribute and Rule Learning Aspects of Conceptual Behavior." *Psychological Review, 72* (1965), 175–195.

Hays, W. L. *Statistics for Psychologists.* New York: Holt, Rinehart and Winston, 1965.

Hess, R. D. and V. C. Shipman. "Cognitive Environments of Urban Preschool Children." *Progress Report, Urban Child Center.* Chicago: University of Chicago Press, 1963.

Hilgard, E. R. "Learning and Maturation in Preschool Children." *Journal of Genetic Psychology, 41* (1932), 31–56.

Hilgard, E. R. "Human Motives and the Concept of the Self." *American Psychologist, 4* (1949), 374–382.

Hilgard, E. R. *Theories of Learning* (second ed.). New York: Appleton-Century-Crofts, 1956.

Hochberg, J. "Nativism and Empiricism in Perception." In L. Postman (ed.), *Psychology in the Making.* New York: Knopf, 1962, 255–330.

Hollis, L. "A Study to Compare the Effect of Teaching First- and Second-grade Math by Cuisenaire-Gattegno Method with a Traditional Method." *School Science and Mathematics, 65* (1965), 683–687.

Holmes, J. A. "Speed, Comprehension, and Power in Reading." In J. A. Figurel (ed.), *Challenge and Experiment in Reading. International Reading Association Conference Proceedings.* New York: *Scholastic Magazines,* 7 (1962), 143–149.

Holt, J. "A Little Learning." *New York Review of Books* (May, 1966).

Hood, H. B. "An Experimental Study of Piaget's Theory of the Development of Number in Children." *British Journal of Psychology, 53* (1962), 273–286.

Hovland, C. I. "A Communication Analysis of Concept Learning." *Psychological Review, 59* (1952), 461–472.

Hovland, C. I. and W. Weiss. "Transmission of Information Concerning Concepts Through Positive and Negative Instances." *Journal of Experimental Psychology, 45* (1953), 82–96.

Howard, C. "Three Methods of Teaching Arithmetic." *California Journal of Educational Research, 1* (1950), 25–29.

Huizinga, J. *Homo Ludens: The Play Element in Culture.* London: Routledge and Kegan Paul, 1949.

Hunt, J. McV. *Intelligence and Experience.* New York: Ronald Press, 1961.

Hunt, J. McV. "Has Compensatory Education Failed?" *Harvard Educational Review, 39,* 2 (1969), 278–300.

Huttenlocher, J. "Effects of Manipulation of Attributes on Efficiency of Concept Formation." *Psychological Reports, 10* (1962), 503–509.

Hyde, D. M. "An Investigation of Piaget's Theories of the Development of the Concept of Number." Unpublished doctoral dissertation, University of London, 1959.

Inhelder, B. *"Le Diagnostic du Raisonnement chez les Débiles Mentaux."* Neuchâtel: Delachaux et Niestlé, 1943. Deuxième Édition Augmenté, 1963.

Inhelder, B. "Operational Thought and Symbolic Imagery." *Monographs of the Society for Research in Child Development, 30,* 2 (1965), 4–18.

Inhelder, B. "Cognitive Development and Its Contributions to the Diagnosis of Some Phenomena of Mental Deficiency." *Merrill–Palmer Quarterly, 12* (1966), 299–319.

Inhelder, B., M. Bovet, H. Sinclair, and C. D. Smock. "On Cognitive Development." *American Psychologist, 27* (1966), 160–163.

Inhelder, B. and J. Piaget. *The Growth of Logical Thinking from Childhood to Adolescence.* New York: Basic Books, 1958. (French edition, 1955).

Inhelder, B. and J. Piaget. "The Growth of Logical Thinking." *British Journal of Psychology, 50* (1959), 363–370.

Inhelder, B. and J. Piaget. *The Early Growth of Logic in the Child.* New York: Harper and Row, 1964.

Isaacs, N. *Piaget's Work and Progressive Education.* London: National Froebel Foundation, 1965.

Jamison, K. W. "An Experiment with a Variable Base Abacus." *Arithmetic Teacher, II* (1964), 81–84.

Jenkin, N., and S. M. Feallock. "Developmental and Intellectual Processes in Size-Distance Judgment." *American Journal of Psychology, 73* (1960), 268–273.

Jennings, F. G. "Jean Piaget: Notes on Learning." *Saturday Review* (May 29, 1967), 82.

Jensen, A. R. "How Much Can We Boost IQ and Scholastic Achievement?" *Harvard Educational Review, 39,* 1 (1969), 1–123.

Johannot, L. *Le Raisonnement Mathématique de l'Adolescent.* Neuchâtel: Delachaux et Niestlé, 1947.

Kagan, J. "Inadequate Evidence and Illogical Conclusions." *Harvard Educational Review, 39,* 2 (1969), 274–277.

Kagan, J., H. A. Moss, and I. E. Sigel. "Psychological Significance of Styles of Conceptualization." In J. C. Wright and J. Kagan (eds.), *Basic Cognitive Processes in Children. Monographs of the Society for Research in Child Development, 28,* 2 (1963).

Kamii, C. K. and N. Radin. "A Framework for a Preschool Curriculum Based on Some Piagetian Concepts." *Journal of Creative Behavior, 1* (1967), 314–324.

Kamii, C. K., N. Radin, and D. Weikart. "A Two-year Preschool Program for Culturally Disadvantaged Children: Findings from the First Three Years." Paper read at the American Psychological Association Meeting, New York, September 1966.

Kamii, C. K., N. Radin, *et al.* "The Ypsilanti Early Education Program." Paper mimeographed at the Ypsilanti, Michigan, Public Schools, 1967.

Karplus, R. "Meet Mr. O." *Science and Children, 1* (1963), 19–24. (*a*)

Karplus, R. "Relativity and Motion." Science Curriculum Improvement Study, University of California (mimeographed), 1963. (*b*)

Katona, G. *Organizing and Memorizing.* New York: Teachers College, Columbia University Press, 1940.

Kaya, E. "A Curricular Sequence Based on Psychological Processes Rather Than Subject Content." *Exceptional Children, 29* (1961), 425–428.

Kelleher, R. T. "Discrimination Learning as a Function of Reversal and Nonreversal Shifts." *Journal of Experimental Psychology, 51* (1956), 379–384.

Kendler, H. H. and M. F. D'Amato. "A Comparison of Reversal Shifts and Nonreversal Shifts in Human Concept Formation Behavior." *Journal of Experimental Psychology, 49* (1955), 165–174.

Kendler, T. S. "Development of Mediating Responses in Children." *Monographs of the Society for Research in Child Development, 86* (1963), 33–48.

Kendler, T. S. and H. H. Kendler. "Reversal and Nonreversal Shifts in Kindergarten Children." *Journal of Experimental Psychology, 58* (1959), 56–60.

Kendler, T. S., H. H. Kendler, and D. Wells. "Reversal and Nonreversal Shifts in Nursery-School Children." *Journal of Comparative and Physiological Psychology, 53* (1959), 83–87.

Kephart, N. C. *The Slow Learner in the Classroom.* Columbus, Ohio: Merrill, 1960.

Kessen, W. "Intellective Development in Children: A Conference on Piaget's Contributions in Relation to Other Theories of Children's Thinking." *Items, 14* (1959), 25–30.

Kessen, W. and C. Kuhlman (eds.). *Thought in the Young Child. Monographs of the Society for Research in Child Development, 27,* 2 (1962).

Kohler, W., and H. Wallach. "Figural Aftereffects: An Investigation of Visual Processes." *Proceedings of the American Philosophical Society, 88* (1944), 269-357.

Kooistra, W. "Developmental Trends in the Attainment of Conservation, Transitivity, and Relativism in the Thinking of Children: A Replication and Extension of Piaget's Ontogenetic Formulations." Unpublished doctoral dissertation, Wayne State University, 1963.

Kuenne, R. "Experimental Investigation of the Relation of Language to Transposition Behavior in Young Children." *Journal of Experimental Psychology, 36* (1946), 471–490.

L'Abate, L. "Consensus of Choice Among Children: A Test of Piaget's Theory of Cognitive Development." *Journal of Genetic Psychology, 100* (1962), 143–149.

Lambercier, M. "Recherches sur le Développement des Perceptions. VI. La Constance des Grandeurs en Comparaison Sériales." Geneva: *Archives de Psychologie, 31* (1946), 1–204.

Lambert, W. E. and O. Klineberg. *Children's View of Foreign Peoples.* New York: Appleton-Century-Crofts, 1967.

Laurendeau, M. and A. Pinard. *Causal Thinking in the Child.* New York: International Universities Press, 1962.

Laycock, F. "Significant Characteristics of College Students with Varying Flexibility in Reading Rate." *Journal of Experimental Education, 23* (1955), 311–330.

Laycock, F. "Flexibility in Reading Rate and Einstellung," *Perceptual and Motor Skills, 8* (1958), 123–129.

Lovell, K. "A Follow-Up Study of Some Aspects of the Work of Piaget and Inhelder on the Child's Conception of Space." *British Journal of Educational Psychology, 29* (1959), 104–117.

Lovell, K. "A Follow-Up Study of Inhelder and Piaget's 'The Growth of Logical Thinking.'" *British Journal of Psychology, 52* (1961), 143–153. (*a*)

Lovell, K. *The Growth of Basic Mathematical and Scientific Concepts in Children.* New York: Philosophical Library, 1961. (*b*)

Lovell, K., D. Healey, and A. Rowland. "Growth of Some Geometrical Concepts." *Child Development, 33* (1962), 751–767. (*a*)

Lovell, K., B. Mitchell, and I. Everett. "An Experimental Study of the Growth of Some Logical Structures." *British Journal of Psychology, 53* (1962), 175–188. (*b*)

Lovell, K. and E. Ogilvie. "A Study of the Conservation of Substance in the Junior School Child." *British Journal of Educational Psychology, 30* (1960), 109–118.

Lovell, K. and A. Slater. "The Growth of the Concept of Time: A Comparative Study." *Journal of Child Psychology and Psychiatry, 1* (1960), 179–190.

Lubker, B. J. and C. C. Spiker. "The Effects of Irrelevant Stimulus Dimensions on Children's Oddity-Problem Learning." *Journal of Experimental Child Psychology, 3* (1966), 207–215.

Lucow, W. H. "Testing the Cuisenaire Method." *Arithmetic Teacher, 10* (1963), 435–438.

Lunzer, E. A. "A Pilot Study for a Quantitative Investigation of Jean Piaget's Original Work on Concept Formation: A Footnote." *Educational Review, 1* (1956), 193–200.

Lunzer, E. A. "Some Points of Piagetian Theory in Light of Experimental Criticism." *Journal of Child Psychology and Psychiatry, 1* (1960), 191–200.

Luria, A. R. "The Role of Language in the Formation of Temporary Connections." In B. Simon (ed.), *Psychology in the Soviet Union.* Stanford, California: Stanford University Press, 1957.

Lyda, W. J. and M. D. Taylor. "Facilitating an Understanding of the Decimal Numeration System Through Modular Arithmetic." *Arithmetic Teacher, 11* (1964), 101–103.

McCandless, B. R. and H. Marshall. "A Picture Sociometric Technique for Preschool Children and Its Relation to Teacher Judgments of Friendship." *Child Development, 28* (1957), 139–147.

McGraw, M. B. "Behavior of the Newborn Infant and Early Neuromuscular Development." *Research Publications Association on Nervous and Mental Disorders, 19* (1939), 244–246.

McNemar, Q. "Note on Wellman's Reanalysis of IQ Changes of Orphanage Preschool Children." *Journal of Genetic Psychology, 67* (1945), 215–219.

Maccoby, E. E., E. M. Dawley, J. Kagan, and R. Degerman. "Activity Level and Intellectual Functioning in Normal Preschool Children." *Child Development, 36,* (1965), 761–770.

Maier, H. W. *Three Theories of Child Development.* New York: Harper, 1965.

Mannix, J. "The Number Concepts of ESN Children." *British Journal of Educational Psychology, 30* (1960), 180–186.

Matalon, B. "Apprentissages en Situations Aléatoires et Systématiques." In M. Goustard, P. Greco, B. Matalon, and J. Piaget. "La Logique des Apprentissages." In J. Piaget (ed.) *Études d'Épistémologie Génétique.* Paris: Presses Universitaires de France, *10,* (1959), 61–91.

Mead, G. H. *Mind, Self, and Society.* Chicago: University of Chicago Press, 1934.

Mermelstein, E., E. Carr, D. Mills, and J. Schwartz. "The Effects of Various Training Techniques on the Acquisition of the Concept of Conservation of Substance." U. S. Office of Education Cooperative Research Project No. 6–8300, 1967.

Mermelstein, E. and L. Shulman. "Lack of Formal Schooling and Acquisition of Conservation." *Child Development, 38* (1967), 39–52.

Meyer, E. "Comprehension of Spatial Relations in Preschool Children." *Journal of Genetic Psychology, 57* (1940), 119–151.

Meyer, W. J. *Developmental Psychology.* New York: Center for Applied Research in Education, 1964.

Meyer, W. J. and S. Offenbach. "Effectiveness of Reward and Punishment as a Function of Task Complexity." *Journal of Comparative and Physiological Psychology, 55,* 4 (1962), 532–534.

Milgram, N. and H. Goodglass. "Role Style Versus Cognitive Maturation in Word Associations of Adults and Children." *Journal of Personality, 29* (1961), 81–93.

Miller, G. A. "What is Information Measurement?" *American Psychologist, 8* (1953), 3–11.

Miller, G. A. "The Magical Number Seven, Plus or Minus Two: Some Limits on Our Capacity for Processing Information." *Psychological Review, 63* (1956), 81–97.

Miller, M. B. and H. H. Spitz. "Differences in Reversal Rate of Ambiguous Figures as a Function of Stimulus 'Meaningfulness' in a Retarded Group: An Exploratory Study." *Abstract of the Peabody Studies of the Mentally Retarded, 1* (1955–1960), 63.

Mogar, M. "Children's Causal Reasoning about Natural Phenomena." *Child Development, 31* (1960), 59–60.

Moltz, H. "Contemporary Instinct Theory and the Fixed Action Pattern." *Psychological Review, 72* (1965), 27–47.

Montessori, M. *The Montessori Method.* New York: Schocken Books, 1964. (*a*)

Montessori, M. *Spontaneous Activity in Education.* Cambridge, Massachusetts: Robert Bentley, 1964. (*b*)

Moore, O. K. "Problem Solving and the Perception of Persons." In R. Tagiuri and L. Petrullo (eds.), *Person Perception and Interpersonal Behavior.* Stanford, California: Stanford University Press, 1958, 131–150.

Moore, S. and R. Updegraff. "Sociometric Status of Preschool Children Related to Age, Sex, Nurturance-giving, and Dependency." *Child Development, 35* (1964), 519–524.

Moore, W. J. "The Skimming Process in Silent Reading." In J. A. Figurel (ed.), *Challenge and Experiment in Reading. International Reading Association Conference Proceedings.* New York: *Scholastic Magazines, 7* (1962), 203–206.

Morf, A. "Les Relations Entre la Langue Lors du Passage Raisonnement Concrèt au Raisonnement Formal." In J. Piaget (ed.), *Études d'Épistémologie Génétique.* Paris: Presses Universitaires de France, 1 (1956).

Morf, A. "Apprentissage d'une Structure Logique Concrèt (inclusion): Effets et Limites." A. Morf, J. Smedslund, Vinh-Bang, and J. F. Wohlwill. "L'Apprentissage des Structures Logiques." In J. Piaget (ed.), *Études d'Épistémologie Génétique.* Paris: Presses Universitaires de France, 9 (1959), 15–83.

Muller, L. *Recherches sur la Compréhension de Règles Algébriques chez l'Enfant.* Neuchâtel: Delachaux et Niestlé, 1956.

Murphy, G. *Freeing Intelligence Through Teaching.* New York: Harper, 1961.

Murray, F. B. "Conservation of Illusion, Distorted Lengths, and Areas by Primary School Children." *Journal of Educational Psychology, 56* (1965), 62–66.

Nasca, D. "Comparative Merits of a Manipulative Approach to Second-Grade Arithmetic." *Arithmetic Teacher, 13* (1966), 221–226.

Nassefat, M. *Etude Quantitative sur l'Evolution des Opérations Intellectualles: Le Passage des Opérations Concrètes aux Opérations Formelles.* Neuchâtel: Delachaux et Niestlé, 1963.

Neal, G. "The Age-placement of Science in a Junior School." Unpublished doctoral dissertation, Birmingham University, Birmingham, England, 1959.

Odier, C. *Anxiety and Magical Thinking.* New York: International Universities Press, 1956.

Odom, R. D. and R. C. Coon. "The Development of Hypothesis Testing." *Journal of Experimental Child Psychology, 4* (1966), 285–291.

Ojemann, R. H. and K. Pritchett. "Piaget and the Role of Guided Experiences in Human Development." *Perceptual and Motor Skills, 17* (1963), 927–940.

Oléron, P. *Recherches sur le Développement Mental des Sourds-muets: Contribution* à l'Étude de Problème "Langage et Pensée." Paris: Centre National de la Recherche Scientifique, 1957.

Olson, W. and B. Hughes. "Growth of the Child as a Whole." In J. Barker (ed.), Child Behavior and Development. New York: McGraw-Hill, 1943, 199–208.

Osler, S. F. and M. F. Fivel. "Concept Attainment: I. The Role of Age and Intelligence in Concept Attainment by Induction." Journal of Experimental Psychology, 62 (1961), 1–8.

Osler, S. F. and E. Kofsky. "Stimulus Uncertainty as a Variable in the Development of Conceptual Ability." Journal of Experimental Child Psychology, 2 (1965), 264–279.

Osler, S. F. and E. Kofsky. "Structure and Strategy in Concept Learning." Journal of Experimental Child Psychology, 4 (1966), 198–209.

Osler, S. F. and G. E. Trautman. "Concept Attainment: II. Effects of Stimulus Complexity upon Concept Attainment at Two Levels of Intelligence." Journal of Experimental Psychology, 62 (1961), 9–13.

Page, E. "Haptic Perception: A Consideration of One of the Investigations of Piaget and Inhelder." Educational Review, 11 (1959), 115–125.

Palermo, D. "Racial Comparisons and Additional Normative Data on the Children's Manifest Anxiety Scale." Child Development, 30 (1959), 53–57.

Palmer, E. L. "How Elementary Schoolchildren Resolve Experimentally Produced Conflicts in Thinking." U. S. Office of Education Cooperative Project No. 3216, August, 1966.

Palmer, E. L. "Factors Related to Persistence in Inquiry." Alberta Journal of Educational Research, 13 (1967), 15–25.

Passow, A. H. "Intellectual Development: Another Look." Papers from the American Society for Child Development, Eighth Current Institute, 1966.

Passy, R. A. "The Effect of Cuisenaire Materials on Reasoning and Computation." Arithmetic Teacher, 10 (1963), 439–440.

Peel, E. "Experimental Examination of Some of Piaget's Schemata Concerning Children's Perceptions and Thinking, and a Discussion of Their Educational Significance." British Journal of Educational Psychology, 29 (1959), 89–103.

Peel, E. The Pupil's Thinking. London: Oldbourne Press, 1960.

Peters, R. S. The Concept of Motivation. New York: Humanities Press, 1958.

Peterson, G. M. "An Empirical Study of the Ability to Generalize." Journal of Genetic Psychology, 6 (1932), 90–114.

Piaget, J. La Représentation du Monde chez l'Enfant. Paris: Presses Universitaires de France, 1926. (Troisième édition, 1947). *The Child's Conception of the World*. New York: Harcourt and Brace, 1929.

Piaget, J. *Judgment and Reasoning in the Child*. New York: Harcourt and Brace, 1928.

Piaget, J. *The Child's Conception of Physical Causality*. New York: Harcourt and Brace, 1930.

Piaget, J. *The Moral Judgment of the Child*. London: Kegan Paul, 1932.

Piaget, J. *Les Notions de Mouvement et de Vitesse chez l'Enfant*. Paris: Presses Universitaires de France, 1946, 131 ff.

Piaget, J. "Les Illusions Relatives aux Angles et à Longue de Leurs Côtés." *Archives de Psychologie, 32* (1949), 281–307.

Piaget, J. *The Psychology of Intelligence*. New York: Harcourt and Brace, 1950.

Piaget, J. *Play, Dreams, and Imitation in Childhood*. New York: Norton, 1951, 1962.

Piaget, J. *The Child's Conception of Number*. New York: Humanities Press, 1952. (*a*)

Piaget, J. *The Origins of Intelligence in Children*. New York: Norton, 1952. (*b*)

Piaget, J. "How Children Form Mathematical Concepts." *Scientific American, 189* (1953), 74–78.

Piaget, J. "Les Relations entre l'Intelligence et l'Affectivité dans le Développement de l'Enfant." *Bulletin Psychologique, 7* (1953–1954), 143–150, 346–361, 522–535, 699–701.

Piaget, J. *The Construction of Reality in the Child*. New York: Basic Books, 1954.

Piaget, J. "Essai d'une Nouvelle Interprétation Probabiliste des Effets de Centrations de la Loi Weber et Celles des Centrations Relatives." *Archives de Psychologie, 35* (1955), 1–24. (*a*)

Piaget, J. "Perceptual and Cognitive (or Operational) Structures in the Development of the Concept of Space in the Child." *Acta Psychologica, 11* (1955), 41–46. (*b*)

Piaget, J. "The Child and Modern Physics." *Scientific American, 196* (1957), 46–51. (*a*)

Piaget, J. *The Language and Thought of the Child*. Translated by M. Gabian. New York: Meridian Books, 1957. (*b*)

Piaget, J. *Logic and Psychology*. New York: Basic Books, 1957. (*c*)

Piaget, J. "Le Développement des Mécanismes de la Perception." *Bulletin de Psychologie*, (1960), Cours des 17 octobre et 17 novembre 1960.

Piaget, J. *Les Mécanismes Perceptifs: Modèles Probabilistes, Analyse Génétique, Relations avec l'Intelligence*. Paris: Presses Universitaires de France, 1961. (*a*)

Piaget, J. "The Genetic Approach to the Psychology of Thought." *Journal of Educational Psychology,* 52 (December 1961), 277. (*b*)

Piaget, J. "Three Lectures." *Bulletin of the Menninger Clinic,* 26 (1962), 120–145.

Piaget, J. "The Attainment of Invariance and Reversible Operations in Developmental Thinking." *Social Research,* 30 (1963), 283–299.

Piaget, J. "Development and Learning." *Journal of Research in Science Teaching,* 2 (1964), 176–186.

Piaget, J. "The Role of the Concept of Equilibrium in Psychological Explication." In David Elkind (ed.), *Six Psychological Studies by Jean Piaget.* New York: Random House, 1967.

Piaget, J. and D. E. Berlyne. "Théorie du Comportement et Opérations." *Etudes d'Épistémologie Génétique.* Paris: Presses Universitaires de France, 12 (1960), 1–70.

Piaget, J. and B. Inhelder. *The Child's Conception of Space.* London: Routledge, 1956; New York: Norton, 1967.

Piaget, J., B. Inhelder, and A. Szeminska. *The Child's Conception of Geometry.* New York: Harper and Row, 1964.

Piaget, J. and M. Lambercier. "Recherches sur le Développement des Perceptions: XII. Le Comparaison des Grandeurs Projectives chez l'Enfant et chez l'Adulte." *Archives de Psychologie,* 33 (1951), 31–130.

Piaget, J. and M. Lambercier. "Recherches sur le Développement des Perceptions: XXIX. Grandeurs Réeles avec Étalon Éloigné." *Archives de Psychologie,* 35 (1956), 247–280.

Piaget, J., M. Lambercier, E. Bosch, and B. von Albertini. "Recherches sur le Développement des Perceptions: I. Introduction à l'Étude des Perceptions chez l'Enfant et Analyse d'une Illusion Relative à la Perception Visuelle des Cercles Concentriques (Delboeuf)." *Archives de Psychologie,* 29 (1942), 1–107.

Piaget, J., F. Maire, and F. Privat. "Recherches sur le Développement des Perceptions: XVIII. La Résistance des Bonnes Formes à l'Illusion de Müller–Lyer." *Archives de Psychologie,* 34 (1953–1954), 155–201.

Piaget, J. and A. Morf. "Les Isomorphismes Partiels entre les Structures Logiques et les Structures Perceptives." J. S. Bruner, F. Brasson, A. Morf, and J. Piaget. *Logique et Perception,* J. Piaget (ed.), *Études d'Épistémologies Génétique.* Paris: Presses Universitaires de France, 6 (1958), 49–116.

Piaget, J., Vinh-Bang, and B. Matalon. "Note on the Law of the Temporal Maximum of Some Optico-Geometric Illusions." *American Journal of Psychology,* 71 (1958), 277–282.

Piaget, J. and B. von Albertini. "Recherches sur le Développement des Perceptions: XI. L'Illusion de Müller–Lyer." *Archives de Psychologie, 31* (1950), 331–348.

Piaget, J. and B. von Albertini. "Recherches sur le Développement des Perceptions: XIX. Observations sur la Perception des Bonnes Formes chez l'Enfant par Actualization des Lignes Virtuelles." *Archives de Psychologie, 34* (1954), 203–243.

Pinter, R. and M. M. Anderson. "The Müller–Lyer Illusion with Children and Adults." *Journal of Experimental Psychology, 1* (1916), 200–210.

Posner, M. I. "Information Reduction in the Analysis of Sequential Tasks." *Psychological Review, 71* (1964), 491–504.

Postman, L. "Association Theory and Perceptual Learning." *Psychological Review, 62* (1955), 438–446.

Prager, B. "The Effects of Cognitive Conflict on the Acquisition of the Concept of Conservation." Unpublished study, 1962.

Price-Williams, D. R. "A Study Concerning Concepts of Conservation of Quantities among Primitive Children." *Acta Psychologica, 18* (1961), 297–305.

Price-Williams, D. R. "Abstract and Concrete Modes of Classification in a Primitive Society." *British Journal of Educational Psychology, 32* (1962), 50–61.

Prior, F. M. "The Place of Maps in the Junior School." Unpublished doctoral dissertation, Birmingham University, Birmingham, England, 1959.

Radin, N. and H. Sonquist. "The Gale Preschool Program Final Report." Mimeographed at the Ypsilanti, Michigan, Public Schools, 1968.

Reese, H. W. "Verbal Mediation as a Function of Age Level." *Psychological Bulletin, 59* (1962), 502–509.

Rignano, E. *The Psychology of Reasoning.* New York: Harcourt, 1923.

Ripple, R. E. and V. N. Rockcastle (eds.). "Piaget Rediscovered: Report of the Conference on Cognitive Studies and Curriculum Development." *Journal of Research in Science Teaching, 2,* 3 (1964), 167–266.

Roberts, J. M., M. J. Arth, and R. R. Bush. "Games in Culture." *American Anthropologist, 61* (1959), 597–605.

Roberts, J. M. and B. Sutton-Smith. "Child Training and Game Involvement. *Ethnology, 1* (1962), 166–185.

Robinson, H. B. "An Experimental Examination of the Size-Weight Illusion in Young Children." *Child Development, 35,* 1 (1964), 91–107.

Robinson, H. B., K. Katsushege, and E. McDowell. "The Size-Weight Illusion in Young Children." *American Psychologist, 16* (1961), 364.

Ross, J. E. "An Enquiry into the Ability of Junior and First-year Secondary Modern Children to Reason about Sound." Unpublished doctoral dissertation, Birmingham University, Birmingham, England, 1959.

Rowe, M. "Influence of Content-learning on Solution of Task-oriented Science Problems." *Journal of Research in Science Teaching, 3* (1965), 12–18.

Russell, D. H. *Children's Thinking.* Boston: Ginn, 1956.

Schopler, E. "Visual Versus Tactual Receptor Preferences in Normal and Schizophrenic Children." *Journal of Abnormal Psychology, 71* (1966), 108–114.

Science Curriculum Improvement Study, "Material Objects," University of California, Berkeley, California, April 1963.

Science Curriculum Improvement Study, "Variation and Measurement," University of California, Berkeley, California, April 1964.

Sears, R. R., E. E. Maccoby, and H. Levin. *Patterns of Child Rearing.* Evanston, Illinois: Row, Peterson, 1957.

Shipp, D. and G. Deer. "The Use of Class Time in Arithmetic." *Arithmetic Teacher, 7* (1960), 117–121.

Shoben, E. J., Jr. "The Assessment of Parental Attitudes in Relation to Child Adjustment." *Genetic Psychology Monographs, 39* (1949), 102–148.

Shuford, E. H., A. Albert, and H. E. Massengill. "Admissible Probability Measurement Procedures." *Psychometrika, 31* (1966), 125–145.

Sigel, I. E. "The Attainment of Concepts." In M. L. Hoffman and L. W. Hoffman (eds.), *Review of Child Development Research (SRCD).* New York: Russell Sage Foundation, 1964.

Sigel, I. E. and L. M. Anderson. "Categorization Behavior of Lower and Middle Class Negro Preschool Children: Differences in Dealing with Representation of Familiar Objects." Paper read at Society for Research in Child Development meeting, Minneapolis, March 1965.

Sigel, I. E. and A. Roeper. "The Acquisition of Conservation: A Theoretical Analysis." (Unpublished study.)

Sigel, I. E., A. Roeper, and F. H. Hooper. "A Training Procedure for Acquisition of Piaget's Conservation of Quantity: A Pilot Study and Its Replication." *British Journal of Educational Psychology, 36* (1966), 301–311.

Silverman, I. W. "Effect of Verbalization on Reversal Shifts in Children: Additional Data." *Journal of Experimental Child Psychology, 4* (1966), 1–8.

Singer, H. "A Theoretical Model of Reading Development in Grades Three to Six." *National Council of Teachers of English Convention Proceedings,* 1964, 1–13. (Mimeographed.)

Smedslund, J. "Apprentissage des Notion de la Conservation et de la Transitivité du Poids." In J. Piaget (ed.), *Études d'Épistemologie Génétique.* Paris: Presses Universitaires de France, 9 (1959), 85–124.

Smedslund, J. "The Acquisition of Conservation of Substance and Weight in Children: I. Introduction." *Scandinavian Journal of Psychology,* 2 (1961), 11–20. (*a*)

Smedslund, J. "The Acquisition of Conservation of Substance and Weight in Children: II. External Reinforcement of Conservation of Weight and the Operations of Addition and Subtraction." *Scandinavian Journal of Psychology,* 2 (1961), 71–84. (*b*)

Smedslund, J. "The Acquisition of Conservation of Substance and Weight in Children: III. Extinction of Conservation Acquired Normally and by Means of Empirical Controls on a Balance." *Scandinavian Journal of Psychology,* 2 (1961), 85–87. (*c*)

Smedslund, J. "The Acquisition of Conservation of Substance and Weight in Children: V. Practice in Conflict Situations Without External Reinforcement." *Scandinavian Journal of Psychology,* 2 (1961), 156–160. (*d*)

Smedslund, J. "The Acquisition of Conservation of Substance and Weight in Children: VI. Practice on Continuous Versus Noncontinuous Material in Conflict Situations Without Reinforcement." *Scandinavian Journal of Psychology,* 2 (1961), 203–210. (*e*)

Smedslund, J. "The Development of Concrete Transitivity of Length in Children." *Child Development,* 34 (1963), 309–405.

Smedslund, J. "Concrete Reasoning: A Study of Intellectual Development." *Monographs of the Society for Research in Child Development,* 29 (1964), 2.

Smedslund, J. "Performance on Measurement and Pseudomeasurement Tasks by Five- to Seven-year-old Children." *Scandinavian Journal of Psychology,* 6 (1965), 1–12.

Smedslund, J. "Les Origines Sociales de la Décentration." In F. Brasson and M. de Montmollin (eds.), *Psychologie et Épistémologie Génétiques.* Paris: Dunod, 1966. (Excerpts cited in Palmer's paper are from an English translation by Smedslund in unpublished mimeographed form.)

Smilansky, S. *An Experimental Study on the Socio-Dramatic Play of Culturally Disadvantaged Pre-School Children.* New York: Wiley, in press.

Smilansky, S. "Progress Report on a Program to Demonstrate Ways of Using a Year of Kindergarten to Promote Cognitive Abilities, Impart Basic Information, and Modify Attitudes Which Are Essential for Scholastic Success of Culturally Deprived Children in Their First Two Years of School." University of Chicago, School of Education (mimeographed), undated.

Smiley, S. S. and M. W. Weir. "The Role of Dimensional Dominance in Reversal and Nonreversal Shifts of Behavior." *Journal of Experimental Child Psychology*, 4 (1966), 296–307.

Smock, C. D. and B. G. Holt. "Children's Reactions to Novelty: An Experimental Study of 'Curiosity Motivation.'" *Child Development*, 33 (1962), 631–642.

Sonquist, H. D. and C. K. Kamii. "Applying Some Piagetian Concepts in the Classroom for the Disadvantaged." *Young Children*, 22 (1967), 231–246.

Spivack, G. "Perceptual Processes." In N. R. Ellis (ed.), *Handbook of Mental Deficiency*. New York: McGraw-Hill, 1963, 480–511.

Squire, J. R. "Form Consciousness, an Important Variable in Teaching Language, Literature, and Composition." In R. G. Stauffer (ed.), *Language and the Higher Thought Processes*. Champaign, Illinois: National Conference of Teachers of English, 1965.

Standing, E. M. *Maria Montessori*. Fresno: Academy Library Guild, 1957.

Steffe, L. "The Performance of First-Grade Children in Four Levels of Conservation of Numerousness and Three IQ Groups when Solving Arithmetic Addition Problems." Technical Report No. 14, Research and Development Center for Learning and Reeducation, University of Wisconsin, 1966.

Stein, J. "The Growth of Sensorimotor Integration and Behavior." *Mental Retardation*, 2, 5 (1964), 308.

Stevens, W. *The Necessary Angel*. New York: Knopf, 1951.

Stevens, W. *The Collected Poems of Wallace Stevens*. New York: Knopf, 1954.

Strayer, L. C. "Language and Growth: The Relative Efficiency of Early and Deferred Vocabulary Training Studied by the Method of Co-twin Control." *Genetic Psychology Monographs*, 8 (1930), 215–326.

Suchman, J. R. "The Elementary School Training Program in Scientific Inquiry." Final Report, U.S. Office of Education, Project No. 216, 1961.

Suchman, J. R. "The Illinois Studies in Inquiry Training." *Journal of Research in Science Teaching*, 2 (1964), 230–232.

Sullivan, E. T., W. Clark, and E. Tiegs. *California Test of Mental Maturity* (revised edition). Los Angeles: California Test Bureau, 1957. (Primary and Elementary Forms.)

Sullivan, E. V. "Experiments in the Acquisition of Conservation of Substance." Paper presented at the Ontario Institute for Studies in Education, Conference on Preschool Education. November 15, 1966.

Sutton-Smith, B. *The Games of New Zealand Children.* Berkeley: University of California Press, 1959.

Sutton-Smith, B. and J. M. Roberts. "Rubrics of Competitive Behavior." *Journal of Genetic Psychology, 105* (1964), 131–137.

Sutton-Smith, B., J. M. Roberts and R. M. Kozelka. "Game Involvement in Adults." *Journal of Social Psychology, 60* (1963), 15–30.

Suydam, M. "An Evaluation of Journal-published Research Reports on Elementary School Mathematics, 1900–1965." Unpublished doctoral dissertation, Pennsylvania State University, 1967.

Tanner, J. M. and B. Inhelder. *Discussions on Child Development, Volume 4.* London: Tavistock Publications, 1960.

Terman, L. and M. A. Merrill. *Measuring Intelligence.* Boston: Houghton-Mifflin, 1937.

Thomson, R. *The Psychology of Thinking.* Baltimore: Penguin Books, 1959.

Tuddenham, R. D. "Jean Piaget and the World of the Child." *American Psychologist, 21* (1966), 207–217.

Turiel, E. "An Experimental Analysis of Developmental Stages in the Child's Moral Judgment." Unpublished doctoral dissertation, Yale University, 1964.

Vernon, M. *The Psychology of Perception.* Baltimore: Penguin Books, 1962.

Vinacke, W. E. "The Investigation of Concept Formation." *Psychological Bulletin, 48* (1951), 1–31.

Vinacke, W. E. *The Psychology of Thinking.* New York: McGraw-Hill, 1952.

Vinacke, W. E. "Children's Thinking and the Principle of Relevance." *Education, 86* (1966), 1–6.

Vinh-Bang. "Elaboration d'une Échelle de Développement du Raissonement." *Proceedings of the 15th International Congress of Psychology,* 1957, 333–334.

Von Bertalanffy, L. *Modern Theories of Development.* New York: Harper and Row, 1962.

Vurpillot, E. "Piaget's Law of Relative Centration." *Acta Psychologica, 16* (1959), 403–430.

Vygotsky, L. S. *Thought and Language.* New York: M.I.T. Press and Wiley, 1962.

Wallach, M. A. "Research on Children's Thinking." *Child Psychology: Yearbook of the National Society for the Study of Education, 62* (1963).

Wallach, M. A. and R. Sprott. "Inducing Number Conservation in Children." *Child Development, 35,* 4 (1964), 1057–1071.

Walters, Sister A. "A Genetic Study of Geometrical-Optical Illusions." *Genetic Psychology Monographs, 25* (1942), 101–155.

Watson, J. B. *Psychological Care of Infant and Child.* New York: Norton, 1928.

Weir, M. W. "Developmental Changes in Problem Solving Strategies." *Psychological Review, 71* (1964), 473–490.

Welch, L. "A Preliminary Investigation of Some Aspects of the Hierarchical Development of Concepts." *Journal of Genetic Psychology, 22* (1940), 359–378.

Wellman, B. L. "Iowa Studies on the Effects of Schooling." *Yearbook of the National Society for the Study of Education, 39,* 2 (1940), 377–399.

Werner, H. *Comparative Psychology of Mental Development.* New York: Science Editions, 1965.

Werner, H. and B. Kaplan. *Symbol Formation.* New York: Wiley, 1963.

White, R. W. "Motivation Reconsidered: The Concept of Competence." *Psychological Review, 66* (1959), 297–333.

White, S. H. "Evidence for a Hierarchical Arrangement of Learning Processes." In L. P. Lipsett and C. C. Spiker (eds.), *Advances in Child Development and Behavior.* New York: Academic Press, 1965, 187–220.

White, S. H. "Age Differences in Reaction to Stimulus Variation." In O. J. Harvey (ed.), *Experience, Structure and Adaptability.* New York: Springer, 1966, 95–120.

Williams, A. "Number Readiness." *Educational Review, 10* (1958), 31–46.

Winans, J. G. *Introductory General Physics.* Buffalo: Winans, 1963.

Winer, B. J. *Statistical Principles in Experimental Design.* New York: McGraw-Hill, 1962.

Wohlwill, J. F. "The Definition and Analysis of Perceptual Learning." *Psychological Review, 65* (1958), 283–295.

Wohlwill, J. F. "Un Essai d'Apprentissage dans le Domaine de la Conservation du Nombre." In J. Piaget (ed.), *Études d'Épistémologie Génétique.* Paris: Presses Universitaires de France, *9* (1959), 125–135.

Wohlwill, J. F. "Developmental Studies of Perception." *Psychological Bulletin, 57* (1960), 249–288. (*a*)

Wohlwill, J. F. "A Study of the Development of the Number Concept by Scalogram Analysis." *Journal of Genetic Psychology, 97* (1960), 345–377. (*b*)

Wohlwill, J. F. "From Perception to Inference: A Dimension of Cognitive Development." In W. Kessen and C. Kuhlman (eds.), *Thought in the Young Child. Monographs of the Society for Research in Child Development, 27,* 2 (1962), 87–104.

Wohlwill, J. F. and R. C. Lowe. "Experimental Analysis of the Development of the Conservation of Numbers." *Child Development, 33* (1962), 153–157.

Wolfe, R. "The Role of Conceptual Systems in Cognitive Functioning at Varying Levels of Age and Intelligence." *Journal of Personality, 31* (1963), 108–123.

Wolff, P. H. "The Developmental Psychologies of Jean Piaget and Psychoanalysis." *Psychological Issues, 2,* 1 (1960), 1–181.

Woodward, M. "The Behavior of Idiots Interpreted by Piaget's Theory of Sensorimotor Development." *British Journal of Educational Psychology, 29* (1959), 60–71.

Woodward, M. "Concepts of Number in the Mentally Retarded Studied by Piaget's Method." *Journal of Child Psychology and Psychiatry, 2* (1961), 249–259.

Woodward, M. "The Application of Piaget's Theory to the Training of the Subnormal." *Journal of Mental Subnormality, viii;* 14 (1962), 17–18. (*a*)

Woodward, M. "Concepts of Space in the Mentally Subnormal: Studies by Piaget's Method." *British Journal of Social and Clinical Psychology, 1* (1962), 25–37. (*b*)

Author Index

Subject Index

377

A B C D E F G H I J 5 4 3 2 1 7 0